If Not Me, Who?

If Not Me, Who?

THE STORY OF
TONY GREIG
THE RELUCTANT REBEL

ANDREW MURTAGH

First published by Pitch Publishing, 2020

Pitch Publishing
A2 Yeoman Gate
Yeoman Way
Worthing
Sussex
BN13 3QZ
www.pitchpublishing.co.uk
info@pitchpublishing.co.uk

ISBN 978-1-78531-641-8

Typesetting and origination by Pitch Publishing
Printed and bound in the UK by TJ International Ltd.

Contents

This book is dedicated to the memory of **Squadron Leader Alexander Broom (Sandy) Greig DSO DFC (1922–1990)** and the crews of RAF Bomber Command who flew on missions during the Second World War.

'Freedom is the sure possession of those alone who have the courage to defend it.'

Pericles

'*If not now, when? If not us, then who?*'

President Kennedy announcing in 1962
his country's mission to the moon.

The story of Tony Greig, the reluctant rebel

'*I hold that a little rebellion now and then is
a good thing and as necessary in the political
world as storms in the physical.*'

Thomas Jefferson

Introduction

IT was a hot day. One of so many in that interminable summer heatwave of 1976. The young lady, only recently married, was faced with a quandary. As a working woman, she felt the need to get outside this Sunday afternoon for a spot of sunbathing, having been cooped up all day in the office during the week. But there was a mountain of ironing, mainly cricket shirts, to get through and she dare not leave it until the following weekend. And she also wanted to watch the cricket; Hampshire against Sussex in the Sunday League was on the box and she was desperate not to miss it. She looked longingly out of the open back door onto the postage stamp they called their very own garden but the pile of ironing gave her a look of such deep reproach that she sighed and went to fetch the ironing board. At least she could keep an eye on the cricket at the same time.

In fact, ironing was no chore at all, really. She actually enjoyed it and took pride in the sharp creases at the sleeves and the neat edges of the collars. The picture on the television was *not* very sharp, however. The set, admittedly on the small size, was in the sitting room where she had set out her board but the sunshine pouring through the window was so intense that the figures in white were difficult to make out. But it would do. Slowly but steadily, the pile of clothes diminished as she expertly wielded her iron. Outside, the sun blazed down from a phosphorescent sky, the air was still and heavy, there was not the faintest hint of a draught, even though all windows and back door were wide open. The only sound was the occasional thud of the iron on the padded surface of the board. She felt happy enough and it was midsummer so perhaps there would be time for an hour or so of relaxation in the garden when the sun had gone down, the heat had abated and the cricket had finished.

She paused in order to watch the bowler turn at the end of his run-up, jog forward, gathering speed as he approached the stumps to deliver the ball. What happened to the ball she couldn't make out but there was a muffled shout, the camera switched to the umpire and up went his finger. 'He's been given out!' exclaimed the disembodied voice of the commentator, 'That looked pretty plumb to me. The England captain out, lbw – for a duck!'

The ironing lady gave a squeal of elation, rushed out into the garden and excitedly lapped the postage stamp several times, her iron held aloft in jubilation, its lead snaking around in her wake, the plug having been unceremoniously ripped from its socket. Lace curtains twitched and the gossipers and busybodies in the local store told and re-told the extraordinary tale of a young woman in shorts and t-shirt cavorting in a suburban back garden as if she were a football supporter down at The Dell, home to Southampton FC. Chandlers Ford had never seen anything like it.

I remember that ball well. I was bowling down the slope at Hove and the ball was swinging. Thank God. If the ball didn't swing, at my pace I was dead in the water. The conditions, hot and sunny, were not the ones usually conducive to swing – cloud cover and a gentle breeze normally helped – but for some reason, the ball always seemed to swing at Hove. Perhaps it had something to do with the sea air. Or perhaps we were playing with one of those balls that swung. Some did. Some didn't. To be honest, the aerodynamics of a cricket ball always remained a mystery to me, and remained so throughout my career and to this day. This despite having a physics teacher for a brother who has done his best, and failed, to explain to me the mysteries of 'boundary layer', 'turbulent state', 'seam angle', 'pressure differential' and other impenetrable phrases. No matter the theory, the fact was that this ball pitched on middle and would have hit middle and if you know your angles as a ball is delivered from alongside, not in line with, the stumps, you will understand that it had got off the straight and narrow.

Tony Greig had bustled to the wicket in his usual forthright, combative manner, whirling his arms and loosening his muscles. I had seen him take a covetous glance once he had taken guard towards the shortish boundary, square on the leg side, where lay the invitingly squat contours of the pavilion and dressing rooms, weighing up in his mind whether he should have a go and try to clear its roof. Rather early on in his innings, you might think, for contemplating all-out assault on a hapless bowler but this was a Sunday League match, 40 overs per side, and Tony Greig was nothing if he wasn't a positive player, one who believed in the efficacy of attack. I knew what was coming.

Fortunately, he missed as he heaved at the ball and it hit him on the front pad, below the knee roll. Out! Plumb! Would've knocked middle stump out of the ground if only I was that quick. My bellow of appeal, supported noisily by Bob Stephenson, our wicketkeeper, and just about everybody else in the team, was delivered twisting in mid-air as I beseeched the umpire behind me. I knew it was out but I wasn't at all convinced he was going to give it. You see, Tony Greig was the captain, not only of England but also of Sussex, and in those far-off days, umpires were judged on their competence by a system of marks awarded after every match by the two captains. That is why you will find that not many captains were ever given out lbw in the county game. Furthermore, Greig was a tall, gangly fellow with long legs; a case could have been made, I suppose, that as he had a long stride, he had got far enough forward down the pitch to introduce a smidgen of doubt in the umpire's mind that the ball would definitely have gone on to hit the stumps.

Bill Alley, an Australian with sharp edges and a ready wit, was however no respecter of reputations, as you would expect of a former boxer as well as a long-serving county player. 'That's arht, Greigy!' he announced loudly in his much-imitated Aussie tones, simultaneously raising an almost accusatory finger. 'And what kinda fackin' shot was that!' he added *sotto voce*, although Bill Alley's *sotto voce* was anybody else's foghorn. I'm sure Greig must have heard him but he chose not to react; he simply shrugged, turned on his heels and quitted his crease.

'Were you watching?' I asked Lin on my return home a few days later.

'Watching what?'

'The match. On the box.'

'When you got ... er, what's his name, I've forgotten ... you know, the blond one...'

'Peter Graves?'

'No, no, not him—'

'It *was* him! I bowled him with an *unplayable* delivery!'

'No, the other blond one.'

'They're all blond at Sussex. Which one do you mean – Jerry Morley, John Spencer, Roger Knight, Alan Mansell?'

'You know who I mean. The captain, the tall one ... Tony Greig! You got him out! Well done! How exciting.'

She then described her excited lap of the back garden at Tony Greig's dismissal, a scene that I wished I had witnessed for myself.

You see, at that time in 1976, Greig was at the height of his fame – or notoriety perhaps, if you take into consideration his ill-advised comment about making the West Indies 'grovel' in advance of that summer's Test series – and it was no mean feat to have dismissed the England captain for a duck, even if it was 'only' in a Sunday League match. I was certainly determined to enjoy my 15 minutes of fame and so was my wife. I had met, and played against, Tony Greig before of course. The first time I had encountered him was three years previously, during my debut season at Hampshire. We won the Championship that year, 1973, and though my contribution towards any of the ten victories that secured the title had been minimal, I always contented myself – and bragged about it thereafter – that I had made significant contributions towards not losing a couple of matches. One of them was helping Hampshire to a draw in mid-June against Sussex, again at Hove, a happy stamping ground of mine. In a low-scoring game, I had top-scored with 47 in the first innings and when four quick wickets fell in our second innings, 'it was left to the experienced Sainsbury and his apprentice Murtagh to knuckle down and bat out the last hour and a half', as the local paper reported. Another 15 minutes of fame. Greig was the captain of Sussex and did all he could to shift the obdurate Hampshire pair, no doubt sensing if the breakthrough were made, Hampshire's tail would be exposed and John Snow would polish them off in short order. It was no fault of his that the pitch had gone dead and the notorious Hove sea fret failed to put in an appearance. He shuffled his bowling attack, shifted his points of attack, shook up his field placing and when the game was clearly dying on its feet, he accepted the inevitable with good grace. None of the snarling and sledging that blights the current game. Tony Greig was a South African, opinionated, loud, some might say brash, but he wasn't like that. He played the game hard – what South African didn't – but personal insults on the field of play was not in his lexicon.

Nor off the field either, I discovered, when I encountered him the first morning of the match I describe. He was on the stairs of the Sussex pavilion as we made our way up to our dressing room. 'Morning, Hampshire,' he announced, a wide grin splitting his face, 'no captain, heh? Taken three days off I see. Bit of a rudderless ship then!' One-nil to Sussex, and the game hadn't yet started. Greig meant no insult but he definitely meant mischief. What was wrong with a spot of banter, even if somebody on the other side didn't quite see it like that? I immediately warmed to him.

He was like a Greek god back then, all six feet seven and a half inches of him, a loose-limbed, somewhat gangly figure with a mop of blond hair and a manner that was both commanding and utterly self-assured without in any way seeming haughty. He was already an England player and had only recently taken over the captaincy of Sussex. We were all – yes, even the hard-bitten old pros in our midst – captivated by his charismatic personality and irrepressible love of a contest. Shortly, I was to be given a glimpse why. Following a bit of a knock-up and a fielding practice before play got under way, I made my way back to our dressing room. Suddenly a door was flung open. There framed in the doorway was the stooped figure of Tony Greig, stooped because his frame outdid that of the door.

'Hey, how's it, buddy? Ma name's Tiny Greig.'

I laughed. The unconscious irony of the South African pronunciation of 'Tony' tickled me.

'Do you have a captain's room all to yourself?' I asked, looking with wonder past him into what can only have been a personal changing room.

'Ah do. And quarrt raht too. Separates the men from the boys, heh.'

All the while, the wide grin never left his face. 'And whort's up with your skip?' he continued. 'Didn't fancy facing Snowy, heh?'

I mumbled something inconsequential and moved on; mention of John Snow reminded me that I would soon be facing up to England's fastest and nastiest bowler and I was nervous at the prospect.

I wish I had got to know Greig better when I had the chance. It was not that he was unapproachable or stand-offish in the members' bar at the close of play. He was buying his captain's round as animatedly and as conscientiously as any skipper I have known. I could have sidled up to him to engage him in conversation and I am sure he would not have rebuffed me. He had the easy charm and affable demeanour of many South Africans I have known and he would have bought me half a lager in the evening with the same wide smile accompanied by a bouncer the following morning. It's jaw-jaw in here, he might have said, but it's war-war out there, pal. But I did not. Whether it was shyness, trepidation, inhibition or self-restraint, I cannot say. Anyway, he looked as if he was busy, surrounded as he was by supporters, reporters, members and hangers-on. He resembled a lighthouse, casting his beam upon the multitude of little craft scurrying about beneath him. I would have enjoyed listening to his trenchant views on the game – the current one as well as the one at large – so articulately expressed in his later career as a television commentator.

For at this time he had the world at his feet, even if he might have felt a bit giddy looking so far down at it. He was a man of immense glamour, appeal, energy, authority and influence, and no little talent, let us not forget. It seems many have forgotten, judging him to be no more than a swashbuckling buccaneer with a golden touch. Of course, this is nonsense. His record as an international all-rounder stands comparison with the best; what is more difficult to determine is the effect his bravery, his flair and his self-belief had upon those around him. He was a born leader and his teams always seemed to respond to him.

And then, a year after I had snaffled him lbw at Hove, it all went wrong. Or so it seemed. The sequence of events is pretty well known but it is as well to remind ourselves how high in the public's estimation he stood at that time and how abrupt and merciless was the fall. Of course, we now know better and Tony Greig's reputation has thankfully largely been restored. Mark's Gospel reports Jesus saying, 'A prophet is not without honour save in his own country.' As we shall see in this story, he was forced to abandon the country of his birth (I'm talking about Tony Greig here, not Jesus, though to Indian fans during the MCC tour of their country in 1976/77, the tall, blond leader resembled some sort of divine figure) to come to England to seek fame and fortune. Straight from success in India – the series was won 3-1 – the team travelled to Australia for the Centenary Test. By any yardstick, the match was a resounding success. Melbourne was packed to the rafters. Many former players from both countries were in attendance. The press and TV coverage was immense. And the world of cricket was treated to a game that matched the extravagance of the occasion. Who can forget Derek Randall's heroic 174, with England chasing an impossibly high total for victory which was snatched from their grasp by an inspired Dennis Lillee, who took 11 wickets in the match, that with a painful back injury? As Australia celebrated the historic victory and England shook hands with their opponents, it was suddenly pointed out that the result, an Australian victory by 45 runs, was exactly the same as on the occasion of the first ever Test match on the same ground between the same countries one hundred years previously. It takes two to tango and by general consent it was felt that the England team, led by Tony Greig, had played an equal part in an unforgettable spectacle. The game of cricket, it seemed, was in the finest of fettles.

But it wasn't. The reasons that Kerry Packer, the Australian media magnate and owner of Channel 9, got involved in a bitter struggle for the broadcasting rights of cricket in Australia do not directly concern us here (though they will in a later chapter) but it is undeniable that his actions whipped up a perfect storm which changed the game for ever. It would not have happened of course had he not been pushing at a half-opened door. The aforesaid Dennis Lillee was not the first but probably the most prominent and vociferous cricketer to point out the almost feudal structure of remuneration for players at the time. Hang on, he ruminated aloud, I have just broken my back, almost literally, bowling for my country and I am getting paid peanuts. The MCG was sold out for this Test (250,000 fans passed through the gates over the five days) so where did all that money go? Certainly none of it into the players' pockets. It is said that Packer was appalled when Lillee told him what he was paid by the Australian Cricket Board. Looking back on it now, it seems inconceivable that some sort of revolution in the game would not have happened willy-nilly, Packer or no Packer.

The fact is that Kerry Packer was the right man in the right place at the right time. His plan was to sign up all the best cricketers in the world and organise his own 'Test' matches, with exclusive television coverage on Channel 9, of course. Central to his purpose was the recruitment of two major players, the respective captains of Australia and England, namely Greg Chappell and Tony Greig. Greg Chappell was arguably the finest batsman in international cricket at that time and as the affair was largely an Australian one, his signature was non-negotiable. Once he realised Packer was serious, he put his name to the contract with alacrity. He knew as well as anyone that the Australian Cricket Board needed a hefty boot up the backside.

In many ways, Tony Greig was equally crucial to Packer's cause. He had just led the England side to victory in India, he had charmed the Indian population, he was a natural leader and communicator, he understood the importance of good PR, his position as an assertive and positive captain was impregnable and he was popular for his combative and enthusiastic approach to the game. His importance to the venture was equally pressing.

Furthermore, Tony Greig had a cool and dispassionate notion of his own worth and that did not coincide with what the Test and County Cricket Board paid their England players. Here was an opportunity, he believed, to shake up the complacent governing bodies of the game, which had no idea how to run a large business, as cricket had now become. It was time the administrators were dragged, kicking and screaming if needs be, into the modern world and started to pay their star performers a salary commensurate with their roles as professional sportsmen. He too quickly signed on the dotted line. The die was cast.

If you wanted to sign up the top cricketers for your breakaway league, the Centenary Test was the ideal recruiting ground. The whole world and his dog were present in Melbourne and it was not long before Packer was confident that he had pretty well everyone he wanted in his pocket. Secrecy and confidentiality were paramount. Taking into account the nature of what was going on behind closed doors, it was nothing short of miraculous that the game's administrators smelt not even the faintest whiff of the gunpowder that was about to explode in their midst.

Tony Greig's role in the clandestine headhunting process was, and remains, a subject of some controversy and shall be examined later but it was typical of him and his forthright nature that once he was convinced of the efficacy and rightness of his course of action, he stuck to his guns, come hell or high water. For hell and high water was what he got. The news, when it broke, shook the very foundations of cricket in such a profound way that it had not sustained since the Bodyline crisis. The press had finally got wind of the story in, of all places, Tony's back garden. He was hosting a party for the touring Australians that summer of 1977 during their match against Sussex. A couple of Australian journalists persuaded someone to spill the beans and having quickly filed their copy in the morning papers Down Under, their scoop was promptly pinged back to the English dailies the following day. All hell broke loose. I remember the furore well. Little else was discussed in the Hampshire dressing room for weeks, though the three overseas players, Barry Richards, Andy Roberts and Gordon Greenidge – all of whom it was assumed had signed up – remained tight-lipped about it all. This was entirely understandable; the contracts drawn up by Packer would have been securely bolted and padlocked and idle chatter was necessarily *verboten*. The same conversations were going on in other dressing rooms up and down the country, we discovered. It made for an uncomfortable season for all county players, off the pitch at the very least. On the one hand, there were the Packer 'pirates' as they were soon labelled, and on the other were the rest, some who were upset they had not been invited, some who were jealous of the large sums of money being bandied about and some, probably the majority, who were not at all sure what to think. What we all knew and were agreed upon was that the game of cricket would never be the same again.

Throughout the storm that raged, Tony Greig, all six foot seven and a half of him, stood tall as the winds of public opprobrium buffeted him. He must have expected criticism but the level of invective caught him off balance. He was branded a traitor and the implication that he was never fully committed to the role of England's captain because he was a South African hurt him deeply. The problem in the minds of officials, committee men, club members, supporters and the general public was that he had sold his soul to the devil and acted as his recruiting sergeant during the Centenary Test, an occasion that was promoted as a celebration of the legacy and continued good health of Test cricket, not its demise. The press whipped up public opinion into a frenzy of denunciation. Greig had to go. Accordingly, to nobody's surprise, a week later he was relieved of his duties by the selectors. Mike Brearley was appointed England captain in his stead but to his eternal credit refused to allow Greig to be dropped from the team. The English public was not so forgiving. Greig was booed every time he went to the wicket that summer. He had a quiet time in the series, quite unlike him, and after the final match at the Oval, he bowed out of Test cricket for good. His future now was inextricably bound up with Kerry Packer and World Series Cricket.

The thing is, I am not at all sure that the bad press he suffered was entirely justified, even at the time. I felt that the majority of players agreed and were not altogether happy at his being cast as public enemy number one. The disruption it caused in the dressing room we could all have done without – after all, professional cricketers have to go out there and perform, individually and collectively, and disharmony in a team never helps. But for decades players had been complaining about being poorly paid and any talk about money – for that is what the Packer Revolution was all about in our eyes – could never be a bad thing. Of course Tony Greig was motivated by personal gain – he could hardly be blamed for that – but he was shrewd enough to understand that the formation of World Series Cricket would, in the long run, benefit everybody in the game. He went on record to make this very point. Asked for a statement after he had been sacked as England's captain, he said, 'Obviously I am disappointed. The only redeeming feature is that I have sacrificed cricket's most coveted job for a cause which I believe could be in the best interests of cricket the world over.' Some scoffed at these words. But who can claim now that he wasn't right?

A few figures might underline the point. In 1977, the average annual salary for a capped player in county cricket was £3,500, though the uncapped players, such as me, earned considerably less. Today, a senior player for his county can expect to earn something in the region of £80,000 per annum. It does not take the insight of an economist to make the obvious comparisons, even taking into account the effects of inflation. The lot of a county cricketer today is a comfortable one. It was never an attractive career option back in 1977. None of us seriously believed we were playing county cricket for the money; we played for the love of it and made do with what we were paid. And what of the Test player? How much has his income increased? Tony Greig, when he was captain of England, was paid £210 per Test. Joe Root, as the current England captain, has just signed a contract worth £1 million. He might well whisper to himself as he takes guard in his next Test match, 'Thank you, Greigy.'

Of course, it was not all down to him but only his most curmudgeonly critic would deny that he played a significant role. He just didn't do insignificant roles. Even had he been a bit-part player in a Shakespearean drama, the third spear carrier at the back of a battle scene, he would have stood out and it wouldn't have been long before he thrust himself forward centre stage to take on the major part. Once he had nailed his colours firmly to the mast of WSC, he quit these shores for good. Packer famously offered him a 'job for life' for his commitment and loyalty to the cause and he was as good as his word; for the rest of his life, Greig acted as a commentator and media pundit for Channel 9. He was still working for the organisation when he informed his colleagues of his diagnosis of advanced lung cancer in October 2012, with the typically laconic comment, 'It doesn't look good.' It wasn't. Two months later, he succumbed to a massive heart attack and died at the shockingly young age of 66.

We in England had largely lost sight of him, apart from his occasional forays over here to commentate for Channel 4. We still heard him, however. His distinctive style and recognisable tones were heard on Sky and whenever the Poms were Down Under tilting for the Ashes and we began to miss him. Perhaps it was a case of absence making the heart grow fonder. Perhaps time allowed a more dispassionate review of his career and influence. Perhaps the very fact that what had seemed so dangerous and revolutionary at the time had since become commonplace helped to change people's perceptions. Certainly I sensed a softening of attitudes in this country, where he had his harshest critics. In Australia, he suffered no such reproof. As if to make the point, the MCC invited him to present the 2012 Cowdrey Lecture at Lord's. The delicious irony of the venue cannot have passed him by. But typically he eschewed any temptation to score points, to scratch old sores, to signal his own fours, which he used to do as a player. It was a fascinating speech, as you would expect of a man with such a rich vein of experience; many of his comments bear close scrutiny. But that can wait until later. I only want to quote one sentence here: 'I have never had any doubt that I did the right thing by my family and by cricket.' Doubts? Tony Greig? Never.

Chapter 1

The unveiling of the monument dedicated to Bomber Command – 28 June 2012

'At last, after 67 years of waiting, our comrades have finally been honoured.'

The words of one veteran

I N the event it was a bit like an Ashes Test match at Lord's; the demand for tickets far outstretched the supply. The ceremonial opening of the memorial to Bomber Command and the 55,573 aircrew of its squadrons who lost their lives in the Second World War had been eagerly anticipated and attendance at the event had necessarily been strictly limited. There was room for 6,000 veterans and their families but as at Lord's, a mere couple of miles away from its location in Green Park, there would be considerable numbers of people who wished to be present but were unable. The war had finished some 67 years previously and veterans of the conflict in the air were now thin on the ground but their relatives were not.

Sixty-seven years before a memorial is built? That is an unconscionably long time. How come? The somewhat shambolic preparations for the event – many veterans had been late in applying and missed out on tickets, only placated by others who benevolently returned theirs so that they could attend – had been a symbol of a wider controversy swirling around the entire project. Successive governments over the years had prevaricated and postponed erecting a memorial to those who had lost their lives serving in Bomber Command, a dereliction of duty which many found shameful. Yet it is as well to remember that of all the top brass tasked with prosecuting the war none was a more divisive figure than Air Chief Marshal Sir Arthur Harris, Commander-in-Chief of RAF Bomber Command. He was dubbed Bomber Harris by the press and known as Butcher Harris within the ranks and that probably sums up his reputation at the time and latterly. His hotly disputed policy of area rather than precision bombing of German cities, resulting in hundreds of thousands of civilian fatalities, still stirs the bubbling pot of discord. His supporters believed he was a hero; his detractors labelled him a war criminal. As a result, the building of a memorial for his fallen airmen was put on the back burner.

To put the whole thing into perspective and leaving politics aside, it should not be forgotten that the men who served in Bomber Command were the bravest of the brave. Their average age was 22. All were volunteers and almost half would lose their lives. A further 8,400 were wounded and 10,000 taken prisoner. They were never given a campaign medal, let alone have a memorial dedicated to their sacrifice. Winston Churchill did not even mention them in his speech at the end of the war. The campaign to establish them permanently in the nation's memory was long and bitter.

Finally, after endless wrangling, political obstruction and financial difficulties, the monument was completed. On 28 June 2012, the Queen, accompanied by the Duke of Edinburgh, arrived to unveil the statue of the seven-man crew of a heavy bomber in front of a host of dignitaries and veterans and families. The day had dawned warm and still, a perfect midsummer's day, with the prospect of the temperature soaring later on. As is often the case on these sorts of occasions, there were numerous surreptitious glances and whispered asides as those in attendance strove to identify the great and the good as they arrived in their limousines. The royal family were out in force: the Prince of Wales and his wife, Camilla, Prince Andrew, Prince Edward and his wife Sophie, the Duke and Duchess of Gloucester, the Duke of Kent and others less easily recognised. Politicians in the main were conspicuous by their absence but Philip Hammond was present in his capacity as Secretary of State for Defence.

One young man leant across to the elderly lady at his side, perhaps a grandson and a widow of one of the veterans whose name was inscribed within the memorial.

'Robin Gibb would have loved to have been here.'

'Who, darling?'

'Robin Gibb, one of the Bee Gees.'

'Why would a pop singer want to be here?'

'Because he donated a lot of the money to have this monument built.'

'That was very sweet of him. So why isn't he here?'

'Because he's dead, mother. He died of cancer a few weeks ago.'

'Oh, that is a shame. Poor chap.'

'Do you see that fellow over there? The tall guy with the sun hat?'

'Yes.'

'Do you know who he is?'

'Er … the sculptor?'

'No! Let me give you a clue. England cricket captain.'

'He looks a bit old to be … whatshisname … that nice boy … Andrew something or other.'

'Andrew Strauss. No, not the current one, a former captain.'

'I'm afraid you've got me there, dear.'

'It's Tony Greig.'

'Oh yes, I'm sure I have heard of him. He's the one on the television who always wears a hat, isn't he? Rather like the one he's wearing now. Or am I mixing him up with Geoff Boycott?'

'I don't think it's possible to mistake Tony Greig for Geoff Boycott, mother. Chalk and cheese, I should say.'

It was Tony Greig. And he was also right that the two, Boycott and Greig, could not possibly have been mistaken for each other. You could say that they came from two different planets but oddly enough, the two got on, both professionally and privately. As we shall see, most of Greig's contemporaries – as opposed to some of the game's hierarchy –

got on with him; he was just that sort of bloke. Many people there did of course recognise him but as he now lived in Australia and was but an infrequent visitor to these shores they did not immediately take note of his drawn and haggard features and the perspiring brow under the rim of his hat. His sister, Sally Ann, who was at his side, was aware that he was ill but had no idea of the seriousness of his condition. Neither did he, it appeared. 'He was on antibiotics for a chest infection,' she told me. 'This was his second course of treatment and the infection was proving to be stubbornly resistant to the drugs. We didn't know at that stage that he had cancer.'

The other question that might have intrigued onlookers had they asked was what Tony Greig and his sister were doing at the unveiling of a memorial to those who had served in Bomber Command. Greig had faced the fury of Lillee and Thomson on that famous, hair-raising tour of Australia in 1974/75, which had left experienced England batsmen demoralised and in some cases emotionally scarred for the rest of their careers, but the usual grim banter in the England dressing room about going to war and taking flak from the enemy would have seemed totally out of place at a solemn occasion such as this. He was not there for cricketing reasons, clearly.

Friends of the Greig family would have known straightaway. Alexander Broom Greig, known universally as Sandy, was born in Bathgate, West Lothian in Scotland in 1922, and educated at George Watson's College in Edinburgh where he excelled in games, notably rugby. Had war not broken out in 1939, who knows, Sandy might have emulated other alumni, such as Ian Robertson and the Hastings brothers, who went on to represent Scotland in the sport.

However, Herr Hitler had other plans in mind for the young Sandy. Family history has it that, two hours following the announcement by Neville Chamberlain that Britain was now at war with Germany, Sandy Greig signed up for active service. Furthermore, he lied about his age; he was only 17 and a half and the official age limit was 18. He had no intention of joining the army. Like many of his peers, he had studied enough recent history to have a horror of the dreadful conditions and loss of life suffered by soldiers in the trenches of the Great War. He chose the RAF. His father had done the same, lied about his age so that he could enlist to fight in the Great War. When he remonstrated with his son about joining up before he was old enough, Sandy replied, 'You did the same, Dad.' Reluctantly, Greig Senior went along with the plan and did not spill the beans to the authorities. Already, one can sense in Sandy's personality elements of decisiveness, conviction and indeed stubbornness, which his son in turn undoubtedly inherited.

It took a surprisingly long time to train pilots for combat duty in wartime. Two hundred hours of flying was the norm, together with instruction in mathematics, navigation and the principles of flying, over an 18-month to two-year period. During his training, Sandy was sent to Rhodesia for flying instruction. There he crashed his aircraft. Details of the accident – a not infrequent occurrence for rookie pilots but on this occasion without the all too inevitable fatal consequences – are sparse but it is understood that he was dissuaded from continuing on the pathway to gaining his Pilot's Wings and instead switched to a navigation course. In this discipline, it could be said that he found his true vocation. Tony's mother once remarked that her husband rewrote the handbook of navigation in the RAF. Subsequent events were to prove that to be no idle boast.

The role of a navigator on a long-range bombing sortie is patently crucial and never straightforward, given the constantly changing variables of weather, visibility and enemy action. It has often been compared to a maths exam and having to get 100% every time. Actually, it was more than one exam because the examiners would keep on asking different questions. You might be diverted by unexpected circumstances. Your pilot would very often not take the same course back home. You might be attacked by enemy fighters, your pilot then taking evasive action, perhaps diving down to rooftop level in an attempt to escape. After a hair-raising period of violent manoeuvres, he would come on the intercom and casually ask you to set a course for home when you have no idea where you are. Put like that it is a wonder that any of them got back home. Many did not.

It is undeniably true that if Sandy Greig was a first-rate navigator, he was also extraordinarily lucky. The general rule of thumb was that a bomber crew would do a 'tour', that is 30 missions, before being stood down having done their bit. Medical and psychological researchers had come to the conclusion that if anybody survived a tour he would more than likely be suffering from 'battle fatigue' and his effectiveness severely reduced. Sandy Greig flew on 54 missions and somehow beat all the odds. Two extraordinary statistics bring into sharp relief how much fate was kind to him. Only one in six crewmen survived a tour of 30 missions. One in 40 survived two tours of 60 missions. I use the word 'survived' advisedly; Sandy did not escape unscathed. As his grandson, Mark, explained to me, 'When he was shot down over the North Sea, he was burned as he attempted to rescue his pilot from the aircraft. In another crash, he lost feeling in the lower part of his face on one side, something that stayed with him for the rest of his life.' Something else that stayed with Sandy for the rest of his life, deeply hidden from view, from even those who loved him, were the emotional scars of his experiences. Today, we would recognise them as symptoms of post-traumatic stress disorder. Back then they might have been described as shell-shock or battle fatigue – if they had ever been properly diagnosed at all.

In my research into Sandy Greig's war record, I am indebted to Air Commodore Graham Pitchfork, MBE, now retired from the RAF, who has forged an impressive career as a military historian, author and a writer of over 500 armed services obituaries for *The Daily Telegraph*. He whistled in disbelief and admiration when he told me of what he had unearthed. 'Squadron Leader Alexander Broom Greig was awarded two gongs while on active duty, the Distinguished Service Order and the Distinguished Flying Cross. The DSO is awarded for "meritorious or distinguished service by officers in the armed forces during wartime, typically in active combat". The DFC is awarded for "an act or acts of valour, courage or devotion to duty while flying on active operations against the enemy". So Greig had what would have been known as a "good war". It wasn't uncommon for a navigator to attain the rank of squadron leader and captain an aircraft. But it *was* unusual for a navigator to be awarded both the DSO and DFC. Now, under normal circumstances,' Pitchfork continued, 'the captain on board was the pilot, in sole command of his aircraft. Greig must have been some leader to have been granted that responsibility as a navigator.' I was puzzled about the split roles of navigator and pilot and the possibility for confusion in the chain of command and wondered what it must have been like for the crew. He explained. 'The pilot was of course in charge of operating the aircraft; he flew the damn thing. If he said bail out, everybody bailed out. But Greig, the navigator and captain, was in charge of all operational and strategic decisions, for example whether to press on or turn back.'

Greig first joined 218 Squadron, which by September 1941 were flying four-engine Stirlings, the first of the heavy bombers. Targets included ports, railways, industrial sites, gun batteries, petrol installations, infantry columns, even V-weapon sites. In October 1942, the citation for Greig's recommendation for a DFC read:

> This officer has proved himself to be one of the most successful navigators in the squadron. During an attack on Poissy on April 2nd 1942 his aircraft was badly damaged by light anti-aircraft fire. Flying Officer Greig requested his captain to make a second run to enable him to release his five remaining bombs. These he dropped directly on the target.

Pitchfork added some further details of the raid. 'Poissy is just north-west of Paris. It was the location of a major factory operated by Ford France, requisitioned by the Germans in the war and produced light trucks.'

In October of that year, Greig was posted to 101 Squadron, flying Lancasters in specialised airborne radio-jamming operations to disrupt interceptions being made by German night fighters. These adapted bombers were fitted with distinctive large vertical antennae rising from the centre of the fuselage. In order to jam enemy radio traffic, the operator had to break radio silence, making his aircraft easy to detect and vulnerable to attack. 'Thus the hunter became the hunted,' Pitchfork added drily, 'and it was no surprise that 101 Squadron suffered the highest casualty rate of all bomber squadrons.'

In short order, Sandy had been promoted to squadron leader, and this, let us not forget, was a month after his 21st birthday. The words of the air vice marshal in his letter to Bomber Harris recommending the promotion make interesting reading:

He is an exceptionally able officer and moreover has an outstanding enthusiasm for flying, particularly operational flying, in which he has shown great ability not only as a navigator but also as an officer. He possesses pronounced organisational abilities and has powers of leadership which mark him as fully qualified for the post ...

The following year, 1943, Greig was recommended for the Distinguished Service Order. The citation says it all:

This officer who has completed many sorties since being awarded the DFC is a fearless and courageous captain. His great navigational ability and fighting qualities have inspired all with whom he has flown and have played a large part in the many successes obtained. His record of achievement is worthy of the highest praise.

You might be interested to know that the motto of 101 Squadron is *mens agitat molem*: mind over matter. Does that remind you of anyone?

Whoever it was that decided Sandy Greig had done his bit, and much more, for king and country and took him off operational duties, did it not a minute too soon. It seems trite to say that he was surely due to run out of luck and no doubt he was as aware of that as anybody. The mental stress endured by these bomber crews each time they took off can only be imagined.

By all accounts, Squadron Leader Greig did not go quietly into 'semi-retirement'; he felt his duty remained on the front line, so to speak, and did not take kindly to being removed from operational duty to the role of navigational instructor. But that was the decision taken by his superiors and no doubt a wise one, given his already exceptional service and his undeniable knowledge of, and experience in, his specialised subject. In September 1943, he was sent to South Africa to train future navigators of the RAF and their brothers in the SAAF the art of plotting a course for a bombing raid. He was posted to No 47, Air Navigation School in Queenstown where he met his future wife. And this is where our story truly begins.

Before we do, let us briefly return to that sun-kissed, midsummer's day in 2012. Before the dignitaries arrived to witness the unveiling by the Queen of the new memorial in Green Park, the veterans who had survived were being interviewed on a specially erected stage. Sally Ann Hodson (nee Greig) happened to take her seat just as 101 Squadron – the few who were left – were strutting their stuff on the boards. 'How I wish Tony had been with me,' she told me, 'he would have been thrilled to listen to all the old stories being recounted of our father's old squadron.' *I thought he was with you.* 'No, he came later. He had a number of interviews to do for Sri Lankan television and he wouldn't miss that for anything.' Indeed not. Greig's love affair with Sri Lankan cricket began during the 1996 World Cup. He was almost alone in believing that the minnows might triumph and trumpeted their silky skills and uninhibited cricket to all and sundry. As it happened, he was proved right, a minor miracle he called it, and thereafter he became a tireless champion of that island and its people. Yes, Tony Greig was big in Sri Lanka, very big.

'He arrived a bit later,' said Sally Ann, 'and as he strode through the crowd wearing Daddy's medals, with his signature hat, towering above everybody else, I was aware of heads turning.' Apparently, luck had played a part in their being there at all. Sally Ann had applied for tickets through 101 Squadron but no joy – their allocation was exhausted long before. Nothing daunted, she appealed to a higher authority, none other than Field Marshal Lord Bramall, formerly Chief of the General Staff. 'If you go high, you may as well go to the highest,' she added cheerfully. She might also have added that Lord Bramall was also a former president of the MCC and her husband, Phillip Hodson, was the current MCC president. They knew each other well. 'Hey presto!' she grinned, 'two tickets landed on our doormat.' Well, nobody could begrudge her pulling strings on this occasion; the privilege was right and fitting. 'Tony came in Phillip's place and he was honoured to have the opportunity.'

The service of dedication and remembrance was led by the Chaplain in Chief of the RAF, thanking 'those who had laid down their lives in the cause of justice, freedom and peace'. One veteran, interviewed at the time, made this telling remark: 'At last, after 67 years of waiting, our comrades have finally been honoured.' Before the sounding of the Last Post, five Tornados flew past in formation. Then a hum, which became a roar, and then a familiar rattling in the ribcage, signalled the arrival overhead of the last airworthy Lancaster. Amidst gasps from onlookers, its bomb bays were opened and great clusters of red poppies were released to flutter downwards, scattering on the ground beneath. 'It was a spellbinding moment,' said Sally Ann. 'Tony and I just sat there and reflected on our father's life, his wartime experiences and the sacrifice all those young men had made on our behalf. Very poignant, just him and me. Tony turned to me and said, 'Dad would have loved to have been here. Do you think he would have been proud of us, here, honouring his memory?' Of course he would. He worshipped Tony. And to think my dear brother only had six months to live makes it even more poignant now, whenever I think of it. The end, Andy … well, it was just heartbreaking.'

Before an end, there must be a beginning. That was in Queenstown, a small town in the Eastern Cape of South Africa.

Chapter 2

Queenstown:
The Greig Clan 1943–68

*'The voice of parents is the voice of
gods for their children*

They are heaven's lieutenants.'

William Shakespeare

THERE is a theory that ability at ball games is handed down the female line. I know of no empirical evidence to support this hypothesis but if there is any truth in it then the genes were providentially aligned in the Greig family. Joyce, Tony's mother, was a fine games player, proficient at hockey, tennis, squash and golf and it was inevitable that ball games would be at the centre of family life. Apart from a love of sport, Joyce Taylor possessed an enormous strength of character and inner resilience, which matched that of her future husband, Sandy. And when you slowly uncover her history, you realise what an extraordinary woman she was too. The life she led and the hardships she endured are every bit as remarkable as those of Sandy. No medals were struck, no citations recorded, no decorations bestowed but for keeping a family together and functioning as a tight, loving unit against all the odds, she deserves similar respect and acknowledgement.

As with so many of her generation, war had played havoc with her early life. It seems strange to those of us born and bred in Britain, whose parents were willy-nilly caught up in a European conflict, that families as far away as South Africa would be similarly affected. Old ties to the Mother Country were still emotionally strong and many a call to arms was answered within the English-speaking communities of the former colonies. Joyce was caught up in its web as much as anyone. Her father had fought for the British in the Boer War. The family moved to Queenstown when she was three and that is where she grew up, in a God-fearing and devout family that attended the local Methodist church. After leaving school, she joined the Standard Bank. It was not long before she met and fell in love with Charles Barry through their mutual love of dancing. The outbreak of the Second World War put paid to their dancing; in common with many young South African men of English descent, Charles immediately enlisted. The pace of life rapidly accelerated. Very much aware of the fact that he would soon be posted overseas, Charles proposed marriage and Joyce accepted. Her parents were initially opposed to the union – there was a war on and what on earth was she doing getting married when the future was so uncertain – but she was insistent and they relented. What else could they do? While Charles was on leave in August 1940, they were married. She was barely 21. Following an all-too-brief honeymoon, they parted as he embarked on a troopship bound for the Western Desert in North Africa. What the future held, she had no idea. Nobody did. We know the war lasted for six years. They had no such assurance. For all anybody knew, this could have presaged the end of civilisation.

In light of which, the moral dilemma that confronted Joyce at this stage of her life was quite understandable. In one of Rommel's advances in Libya and Egypt during the Western Desert Campaign, Charles was captured by the Germans at Tobruk. He and other combatants were turned over to the Italian Army as prisoners of war at whose hands they endured terrible privation and ill treatment. They were transferred to Italy and as the Allies slowly and painfully advanced up the peninsula, in the ensuing chaos as the Italian Army capitulated, he and others escaped and joined the Partisans fighting in the hills.

Eventually they were rounded up by the Germans. Charles was lucky. Some 200 Partisans, including a dozen South Africans, among whom was a brother-in-law of Joyce's, were shot by the Germans in an orgy of reprisal killings. The atrocity became known as Il Massacro del Grappa. Charles was apprehended by another German unit and was spared summary execution. He was loaded into a cattle truck, packed in so tight it was standing room only, and was transported by rail to a prisoner of war camp in Germany where he would remain for the rest of the war. He suffered badly, of that there was no doubt. News of Charles's whereabouts and well-being was sparse. Letters via the Red Cross were few and far between. As the days turned to weeks and the months to years, what happened next was as predictable as it was all-too-familiar. Into Joyce's life strode a handsome man in the light blue uniform of the RAF, a charismatic figure with a compelling personality and a war hero to boot. He was irresistible and she was unable to resist.

Not immediately, you understand. She fought her feelings, pushed him away and never made any secret of the fact that she was married. But it was a futile defence. If the full force of the Luftwaffe could not deter Sandy Greig, neither would her protestations; he was indefatigable in his pursuit of her. It was not long before she accepted the inevitable, that she had fallen hopelessly in love, and there was little else but to admit as much to her parents. Needless to say, they were horrified. This was Queenstown, a conservative little town in a deeply conservative country in a conservative age. Furthermore, the family was a scion of the local Methodist church. Their dismay and her torment can only be imagined.

She never made any bones about the stark fact that she betrayed her first husband. She suffered agonies of guilt and remorse, deepened by her Christian faith, which sets great store by the sanctity of marriage and the indissolubility of its vows. Yet her love for Sandy was overwhelming and uncontainable. Shakespeare knew a thing or two about matters of the heart: 'They are in the very wrath of love and they will go together; clubs cannot part them,' concluded Rosalind in *As You Like It*. Charles was a prisoner of war 5,000 miles away in Germany. Who could possibly know when, or indeed if, he would ever return?

She stopped writing to him – a conscious act that betokened in her own mind the end of the marriage. She was mindful of the pain she must have been causing him and the moral minefield that she had to negotiate but she accepted the inevitable. She and Sandy Greig were in love. Meeting Sandy was fate, becoming his friend was a choice but she firmly believed falling in love with him was out of her control. 'There are some things in life that are hard to fight,' she later said.

The war eventually ended. Against the odds, Charles had survived his time as a prisoner in Germany and was eventually repatriated back to South Africa. She went to meet him off the ship as it docked in Cape Town. She had no choice really. It was the right thing to do and besides, they were still legally man and wife. Once he had set foot again on home soil and they had been reunited, she was shocked at his physical appearance, thin as a rake, gaunt of face and hollow-eyed, with boils covering his skin. Bowed he may have been but broken he was not. One cannot help but have the most enormous respect for Charles Barry, who had survived unthinkable hardship as a POW, as he now faced the psychological torment of his wife's defection with remarkable generosity of spirit. To say nothing of old-fashioned chivalry. When Joyce unburdened herself to him of the truth – under the stern eyes of Cecil Rhodes at his memorial on the slopes of Table Mountain – he immediately understood the hopelessness of his position and assured her that all he ever wanted was the best for her. To that end, he arranged to meet Sandy. Not pistols at dawn but for the time-honoured British answer for all crises – tea! He withdrew and left the field free for Joyce and Sandy to marry. Which they did in December of that year, 1945, once all the legal details of Joyce's divorce had been settled.

There is a poignant postscript to this sad tale. In 1990, after 45 years of marriage to Joyce, Sandy Greig died. At the time, they were living in Australia, the reasons for which shall concern us in a later chapter. The following year, she decided to return to her roots, back in Queenstown, to be near her sister. But her sister then moved, so Joyce relocated to a splendidly appointed, gated community in East London, called Parklands, further up the coast in Border. While her daughters had been clearing out some stuff and personal belongings after Sandy died, they had found a medal, a sporting one, not military. Joyce racked her brains and concluded it must have belonged to Charles Barry. The girls were insistent that it should be returned to him. By a circuitous route the medal found its way back to Charles, who was still alive, and by an even more circuitous route, Charles was thereby able to track down his former wife. One thing led to another, a meeting was arranged and Tony, who was in South Africa at the time commentating on the Australian tour, drove her to meet him. It was as if the years had fallen away; the two hit it off immediately. They became close once more and together they stayed right up until his death in 2001.

By now, Sandy Greig, still an RAF officer, had received his orders from London. He was to return forthwith to England; his job in South Africa was done. As is the way with bureaucracy in any large military organisation, little thought had been expended on the likely domestic ramifications of such orders. What about my wife, would have been Sandy's first reaction. But orders were orders. He was to return alone; his wife could follow later. Clearly his superiors did not know their man. They should have. After all, they knew all about his war record, a man who had flown 54 sorties ... and there were not many of those still alive to tell the tale. My wife accompanies me or I don't travel, he made plain. From that stance, he would not budge. Neither would the RAF. Sandy promptly resigned his commission and remained in South Africa. 'And thank God for that!' Joyce wrote with feeling.

At the time of their wedding, they had but four shillings to their name. That mattered not a jot to Joyce; she had her man, a large weight of guilt had been removed from her shoulders and she could not have felt happier. And to all intents and purposes so did Sandy. What could possibly blight the future for Queenstown's most exotic and glamorous couple? They had no money, that was true, which was a besetting problem for periods of their married life as Sandy moved from job to job, house to house, town to town, province to province and even to Scotland and back. One gets the impression that he never really found himself in his work, as if his life's achievement had been telescoped into his RAF career. If you confront death on every mission and rejoice in having escaped its ugly clutches every time you successfully make it back to base, the rest of your life, no matter how agreeable, must seem at the very least humdrum and lacking in intensity.

Joyce bore this peripatetic existence stoically, even cheerfully. The money would come from somewhere and it usually did. What did it matter if they had no home they could truly call their own as long as she had her husband and, as they arrived, her children? Her confidence in the power of love, buttressed by her strong religious convictions, never wavered, even when the going got tough. And my word did it get tough.

Sandy Greig had a problem and as was the way in those days, he was unwilling to admit it to his wife. He was probably unwilling to admit it to himself. He took to drink. Not copiously, not uproariously, not disgracefully or embarrassingly, not so much that he was ever three sheets to the wind, but steadily, numbingly ... and in secret. Before he joined the RAF, he touched not a drop. It is his family's belief that his destructive relationship with alcohol began when he started flying. If that were true, he wouldn't have been the first; one can imagine flight crews winding down in the mess after a mission, probably taking more on board than they ought, especially after a hair-raising assignment. After the war, when he had returned to civilian life, he was already hooked. Furthermore, the demons continued to assail him; he suffered nightmares until the day he died. Of course he would have benefitted from counselling, psychotherapy, medication, help of some description, but alas, none was available. He suffered alone and in silence.

He drank, so it seems, to forget, to anaesthetise himself. Sally Ann made this point: 'He was never obviously drunk, never out of control, never abusive or anything. Apparently, when he came to South Africa in 1943, he contracted jaundice, which could have been exacerbated by his heavy drinking, we were later told. But my mother suspected nothing. Of course he would go to the club and have a drink after work – everybody did. But she was unaware of the extent of the problem.' Clearly, Sandy Greig was a functioning alcoholic or what we used to call a secret drinker, someone who used alcohol as a means of suppressing his grim and horrifying memories, but was able, after a fashion, to hold down a job and keep a lid on his problem.

With this in mind, everything falls into place. Sally Ann remembers several significant episodes later explained to her by her mother. 'On long journeys, we would make the odd pit stop for refreshment and toilets. Apparently my father would disappear for a while. He was, I subsequently discovered, topping up on the booze.' There was another fact, something that would not have occurred to me, unaware that South Africans of British stock remembered the fifth of November. 'We never celebrated Guy Fawkes Night in our household,' she said: 'Dad used to say that he had heard enough explosions in his life and didn't want to hear any more.' She remembers – it must have been the period of their lives when they were in Scotland because television was not introduced in South Africa until 1976 – watching a war film featuring a scene with German civilians fleeing for their lives as bombs rained upon them. Sandy fled from the room in tears. At a reunion of 101 Squadron in 1984, at which Squadron Leader Sandy Greig DSO DFC was guest of honour, he suffered similar grim flashbacks.

The crisis when it came was harrowing. In 1961, Sandy took an overdose of sleeping pills. Together with the alcohol already in his bloodstream, the effect was calamitous, potentially deadly. Molly Joy remembers her father's hand dragging on the floor as the ambulance men carried the stretcher towards the waiting vehicle. 'I tucked it in,' she said, 'I was convinced he was going to die.' *Was Tony there?* She nodded. 'He was about 14 or 15 at the time. He became a man that night.'

Not for the first time in his life, Sandy survived but even then, his problem was not in any way ascribed to alcoholism. The episode was passed off as a heart attack to friends and the wider family, even if Joyce may well have harboured private misgivings about her husband's mental state. Tony knew that something awful had happened to his father but in a vague sort of way. Adolescent boys are not prone to deep, analytical assessments of cause and effect.

Recovered and back at home, Sandy carried on drinking. And still those closest to him remained in ignorance. 'He was known as a drinker,' said Sally Ann, 'but not a drunk. He fooled people because he was hugely intelligent, very articulate and well respected. Nobody saw him rolling about making a fool of himself because he was sensible enough to avoid becoming an embarrassment and take himself off to bed.' She also has a mental image of his gait: 'He used to walk with his feet wide apart so he wouldn't sway.' She was adamant about one thing; Sandy never used the war as an excuse for his heavy drinking, even after his secret had been uncovered. To do so would have meant admitting to weakness of spirit 'and my father was a strong man'.

Joyce claims that the scales finally fell from her eyes in 1964, in the most banal of circumstances. The family doctor had been called to attend to Sally Ann, suffering from flu-like symptoms, and after he had diagnosed the illness and prescribed the treatment, he took Joyce aside and confided in her that it was her husband, not her daughter, who was worrying him. Sandy was an alcoholic, he said. Joyce was not so much in denial at this news as completely flummoxed. She had no idea what being an alcoholic meant; she knew that Sandy drank, sometimes a lot, but was ignorant of the fact that it was a serious, sometimes fatal, affliction. The doctor was insistent however, and slowly the full realisation dawned and its ramifications came into focus. This was another battle Sandy would have to fight but this time, he would not be alone. She would loyally remain by his side, prepared to do anything to keep the family together.

Sally Ann reckons that it was in Scotland of all places that everybody finally faced up to the truth. Sandy's father, who ran the family firm up in West Lothian, a retail department store by the name of … no, not Grace Bros but Greig Bros, suffered a heart attack and Sandy was persuaded to move back home to help out in the business. Eastern Province to West Lothian – what a culture shock that must have been. Tony, by this time, had decided to try to make his name in English county cricket and was already in the country; the other Greig children had no such desire to up sticks and wrap up warm. As usual, Joyce did her best to make the best of a bad job. It was not all doom and gloom at their home in Edinburgh – at least Tony was able to come up regularly from south of the border to visit them – but Sandy's continuing problems with drink made working with his relatives in the business more and more unmanageable. Finally, enough was enough. The Greigs moved back to South Africa, at the end of 1968.

Now Joyce, finally and not without considerable heartache, took the decision that was really the only course of action open to her. She agreed to have her husband legally sectioned to an institution for alcoholics – for three years.

We are consistently informed by experts in the field that there is no cure for alcoholism before a measure of self-appraisal has been achieved. An alcoholic first has to admit to himself, critically and honestly, that he has a problem and needs help. It cannot be done by willpower alone. And then he has to be willing and able to accept that advice, no matter how painful it might be. Then the real battle can commence. During his time in the drying out facility, it seems that Sandy did not wholly buy into the principles that were being laid down. In short, he managed to pull the wool over everybody's eyes; so much so that he was discharged as 'cured' well before the three years were up. On reflection, this should have been no great surprise. He had been in the services and anyone with half a brain who wants to survive in that sort of environment swiftly learns how to play the system. On his return to his old life, he resumed his drinking. For Joyce, the 'hard times' as she termed it never let up. Only her profound Christian faith and the support of her family sustained her. Financially, this was a time, if not of austerity, then certainly of belt-tightening.

The climacteric, after so many false dawns, came sometime in 1973. Sandy was packed on to a train headed for a clinic in Boksburg, hundreds of miles away in the Transvaal, this time by Sally Ann as Joyce was away in England visiting Tony. Sally Ann remembers pressing a 20 rand note into the guard's hands 'to make sure he kept Dad drunk and on the train'. It was the only way; alternatives had dried up. She likened it to the launch of a sputnik, convinced it was the right thing to do but not at all sure he would come back.

He did. Not for the first time, Sandy Greig had defied the odds. They all sensed a change in him after this latest course of drying out. The transformation was not immediate – there were still potholes in the road – but now he was serious about seeking help. On the advice of their Methodist minister, he joined Alcoholics Anonymous. It was, as Sally Ann said, the saving of him. From that day until the day of his death, he did not touch another drop of alcohol. Sally Ann, in common with the rest of the family, believed that this, his second campaign, the Battle of the Bottle, was every bit as grimly heroic as his first against the Luftwaffe.

Heroes, rather like saints, are not always the easiest of bedfellows. Few of us are blessed with the same bravery and certainty, which sets such men apart. Reading about Sandy Greig's fascinating public and private life, I became intrigued to know what sort of man he was. His family revered him, not through rose-tinted glasses but with clear eyes, cognisant of his faults but respectful of his achievements. His contemporaries, flight crews and golfing partners alike, have long since had their final debrief and joined him at the nineteenth hole but we do have the memories of those who knew him by reputation or through personal contact. I have a friend who grew up with the Greig family in Queenstown. She knew Joyce better, 'a lovely, kind lady who would help anyone who needed it' but Sandy, though a more distant figure, was well known in the town, a larger-than-life figure who seemed to dominate civic affairs and local society. At the time he was editing *The Daily Representative*, Queenstown's district newspaper, one of the oldest in South Africa. Allegedly, he wrote most of it himself. That would not have surprised Sally Ann, who told me that he was a stickler for correct grammar and accurate expression in everything he wrote. The family were instructed to read and comment on every leading piece or editorial that had his name at the top of the page and some of his political analysis was forthright and, given the repressive nature of the apartheid regime that was in power, very brave.

For an insight into Sandy Greig as a boss of a well-respected newspaper, I was dispatched in the direction of Alexandra Broom, known by all and sundry as 'Chux', who worked at *The Daily Representative* from 1976, first as a proof-reader, then slowly working her way up the chain of command. She's still there. *That's an odd name. Why Chux?* 'It's pronounced Chooks, as in Aussie for chickens. My dad called me that when I was little but he couldn't remember why. It seems to have stuck.' She revered her editor. 'In all the years since Sandy resigned from the paper – I was devastated when that happened – I have never worked with anyone I admired more.' *What was he like as a boss?* 'He was brutally frank and honest at all times, sometimes to the point of brusqueness and there were some who thought he was positively rude. But he was always meticulously fair and handled most situations with a dollop of humour.' She cited one or two examples. A certain journalist on the staff could write brilliantly but spelling was not her forte. In one copy, she wrote 'definite' as 'deafnit'. 'Do you know what a deaf nit is?' he thundered, 'it's a bloody fool that can't hear!' Nobody was spared, according to Chux. One of his most frequently used phrases was: 'Do you have any bloody brains in your bloody head?' Not behaviour in the workplace that would be tolerated today, she admits, but people accepted it because they knew he was passionate about the paper and wanted to produce a flawless edition every day. 'Misplaced commas used to send him into a towering rage.' Another bugbear of his was what we in England humorously refer to as the 'grocer's apostrophe' on account of solecisms such as 'tomato's' and 'potato's' as plurals. 'I remember an argument arising about an apostrophe, so much so that I thought that blows would be exchanged – not with me, I hasten to add! Some of the men in the technical department had been working there for more than 40 years and were very knowledgeable. They all had an opinion, resulting in a real shouting match. In the end, I offered to mediate by ringing my English professor at Rhodes University for his ruling. Only then did Sandy relent. "OK, he should know," he said, "we *must* get it right."'

Were you aware of his drinking problems? 'He had given up drinking for the umpteenth time not long before I started but never hid the fact he was an alcoholic. He showed me where he had two desk drawers adapted to form one deep one and told me it could hold six flagons of Lieberstein [a cheap, white win].' Apparently, Sandy also needed regular infusions of coffee. Chux remembers Sally Ann coming to the office to say goodbye to her father as she and her new husband, Phillip Hodson, were leaving for England a few days after their wedding. 'Tears were streaming down her face. She said to me, "Please, just make him plenty of coffee."' *You must admit it was admirable that he managed to curb his demons and give up the drink, finally and for good.* Chux agreed. 'I know he helped many others with the same problem but only if they asked him for help. And then he would speak about his own alcoholism matter-of-factly. "I've told many people what they could do with their well-intended advice," he would say, "so I'm not having them tell me the same.' But if they did ask, he did not hesitate to drop everything and go to them, even if it was in the middle of the night."

Her respect for her old boss was unambiguous. 'His loyalty to his staff was phenomenal and he would defend us with his last breath if he believed it was necessary, no matter who was attacking us or how influential they might be.'

What about his views on apartheid? 'Politically, he was very critical of the National Party and was very vocal about his views. This was never well received by the powers-that-be and I believe he was very brave to air his thoughts in editorials and in person openly as he did.' She told me that she still works for *The Representative*. 'I quote Sandy often,' she said, 'all the junior staff know many of his quotes, as I use them when training them.'

It is instructive to know that Donald Woods, of *Cry Freedom* fame, was at the same time editor of *The Daily Dispatch* in East London, a sister paper of *The Daily Representative*. The two men held similar anti-apartheid views, became close associates and good friends and shared advice and tactics on treading the fine line between freedom of expression and being flung in gaol for sedition. Woods it was who befriended Steve Biko, the freedom fighter and political activist who was murdered while in police captivity in 1977. Woods exposed the official cover-up and had to flee the country in fear of his life. His friendship with Sandy and the Greig family endured until his death in 2001. Tony's younger brother Ian, likewise a county cricketer and England Test player, persuaded Woods to contribute an article to the brochure for his benefit year in 1992, which he was pleased to do. With Ian's permission, I quote Woods's words because they shed light on the regard in which Sandy Greig was held in his hometown and further afield:

> An outspoken individualist, Sandy never left anyone in any doubt about his views and when as a newspaper editor I came under governmental pressure from time to time, Sandy was usually the first to phone his support with disdainful disregard

of the fact that the telephones were tapped by the state security police. To his proud Scots blood such matters were a provocation rather than a threat.

The government censors might not have approved of Sandy's liberal views, so eloquently expressed in his editorials, but they could have had no quarrels with the probity of the newspaper's finances. 'Dad had an amazing head for figures,' Sally Ann reminded me. 'He was excellent at maths.' Of course. A navigator had to be proficient at so many facets of the subject: calculus, trigonometry, geometry, quadratic equations, aeronautics and all the rest of the complicated business of plotting an aircraft's course to a designated destination. Keeping *The Daily Representative*'s books in order must have been a doddle in comparison. And with a methodical brain goes a tidy mind. 'He was, unlike most South Africans who have got used to maids picking up after them, very tidy; he liked things to be neatly put away and in apple-pie order.' Once again, his early training in the services would have been hard to shrug off.

Was he a stern disciplinarian? She puffed out her cheeks. 'Daddy was always in charge and insisted on good manners, etiquette, polite behaviour. And if you did wrong, you certainly knew about it.' When Tony nearly burnt the house down, she pointed out with a grin, 'he got a hiding he never forgot.' *Like a true South African father.* 'Scots!' she retorted, 'don't forget where he came from.' Apparently, among the Xhosa servants and employees Sandy came into contact with, his nickname was The One With The Loud Voice. 'Our cousins were scared of him,' she continued, 'though we his children could never really understand why.'

A boyhood friend of Tony's, who grew up almost in the next street to the Greigs and who was a regular participant in fiercely contested, impromptu games of cricket, Paul Ensor, remembers Sandy thus: 'He often visited our house to borrow books – he was a prolific reader – so I got to know him quite well. I liked and admired him but he had a quick temper. He was opinionated and forthright in his views, which left little room for ambiguity.' Another close friend of the family was Kenny McEwan, who played with great success for Eastern Province, Essex (and would surely have played Test cricket had his career not coincided with the years of South Africa's sporting isolation). He came across Tony's father on many occasions. With his close interest in rugby and cricket, it was no surprise to find the editor of *The Daily Representative* reporting on school matches involving Queen's College (Tony's alma mater, as we shall see). McEwan as captain of the school first XI came under considerable attack in Monday's newspaper report of Saturday's match. Apparently, the *Representative*'s reporter had been critical of McEwan's captaincy and several tactical decisions he had made. Kenny takes up the tale: 'Being an immature schoolboy, I took exception to this …. The following Saturday – the match took place over two Saturdays – we batted, chasing about 280. Batting at No 4, I scored a hundred and we won the game quite easily. In his report on the Monday, he praised us, especially me, but he reminded me of the previous week, again saying that my captaincy was bad and deserved criticism but that I had made up for it …. That incident always remained with me. Sandy taught me to accept the downs as well as the ups in life.'

Coincidentally, at the time, Ian Greig was McEwan's fag at school. Fagging might have started to die out in the UK by now but in South Africa the practice was still seriously endorsed. Both fag and prefect laugh at the memory. 'Jeez, I had a hard time of it for a while after Dad wrote that about him,' said Ian. 'Ah, but he had a much easier time of it after I got my hundred,' countered McEwan. It might be speaking out of turn here but at Queen's a fag was known as a 'skunk'. The origin of the word 'fag' can easily be traced. In Middle English, a 'fagge' was a loose or broken thread of cloth, resembling a thing drooping, tired. From there it evolved to describe something that made one weary, tired, entailing drudgery, toil. The menial tasks of a fag for his prefect were indeed wearisome. The origin of the term 'skunk' I shall leave to your imagination.

It does not take a tremendous leap of imagination to imagine a World War II Lancaster bomber, named Greig, rumbling down the runway and taking to the skies with a tremendous roar of its four Rolls-Royce Merlin engines. On board is the commanding officer, Squadron Leader Sandy Greig, poring over the maps, deciding when, where and how they should go. The children will have their eyes peeled in the defensive turrets, on the lookout for enemy fighters, their fingers poised on the trigger of their Browning machine guns. The aircraft of course needs a pilot to keep it on an even keel, no matter what the anti-aircraft barrages might throw at it. Joyce, in everybody's opinion, miraculously kept that plane in the air in spite of close shaves and near misses. Sandy may have been awarded all the medals but she deserved the plaudits. Mark, her grandson, put it succinctly: 'Sandy's alcoholism brought great heartache to the family, particularly his wife.'

Joyce Greig's loyalty to her husband was unyielding and non-negotiable. There must have been times during their eventful marriage when she was sorely tested but there was never any doubt in her mind where her duty lay. She remained steadfastly constant as a wife when others might well have buckled and fled. Her religious convictions would have told her all about devotion but it must have been more than piety that kept her at Sandy's side. No minister, no pastor, no priest could have blamed her if she had thrown in the towel. She loved Sandy unconditionally. There isn't a single person who has ever suggested otherwise.

The fact is that Joyce Taylor was made of sterner stuff than she has been credited with. I was not aware of this incident until the family told me; she survived a shark attack. When I heard the tale, that chilling theme music from the film *Jaws* – the menacing, alternating pattern of just two notes played on the tuba – rose up through my intestines to meet my jaw which was dropping in the opposite direction. Kei Mouth is a resort on the Wild Coast of Border, a delightful spot much favoured as a holiday destination for families. The Greigs were there *en famille* for the Christmas vacation, as tradition dictated. It was 1956. Ian had just been born which would have made Tony ten. The cottage, which they had rented, was called Malvern, an uncanny coincidence for me, for Malvern is where I live in England. As usual, the river mouth and lagoon were full of swimmers; the Indian Ocean is warm and South Africans love the surf. This particular day was different in that the water was cloudy, not its usual clear, ultramarine colour. There had been recent heavy rainfall and the Kei River was in full spate, churning up the mud and sand. Not wholly enthusiastically, Joyce was persuaded to join the swimmers.

All at once she felt a tremendous blow to her leg, 'as if two rocks had closed over it'. She knew immediately what it was; a shark had locked its jaws on her. She had little recollection of what happened next but family wisdom had it that she fought back instinctively and frenziedly, landing a flurry of blows with her fists on her assailant. The shark let go of her leg and fastened its teeth upon her arm. Her sister, who had been swimming alongside her, thrashed to her aid, grabbing hold of her to keep her from going under the water. Who knows why the shark relaxed its grip, disappearing in the murky water as quickly and as stealthily as it had attacked, but remarkably it did.

The experts maintain that most shark attacks are the result of mistaken identity. This one fell squarely into the category of a typical hit-and-run, which is the most common of attacks, occurring where the surf boils or the water is murky, as it was that afternoon in Kei Mouth. Statistics attest that most such attacks are, in themselves, non-fatal, though that would have been of scant solace to a wounded Joyce and her horrified helpers. She may have seen off the shark but her life was in grave danger from shock and loss of blood. Those in attendance battled to stem the flow of blood with swathes of beach towels, whilst doing their best to keep her awake with brandy as she was rushed to hospital. The trouble was that the nearest hospital was 80 miles away in East London along an apology for a road, more accurately a bumpy track.

The lacerations to her leg in particular were horrific and for some time the doctors were not at all sure that they would not have to amputate. In the event, they did not but the healing and rehabilitation were long and painful. Her family reckoned it was a good 12 months before she fully recovered. Physically, that is. Like her husband, the mental scars were harder to deal with. It took a long, long time before she ventured into the water again. Mike Selvey, who played for England under the captaincy of Tony Greig, recalls a pleasant stay with the Greigs during the long summer vacation of 1973/74 while he was playing for Border in the Currie Cup. 'I remember something in particular. "Listen buddy," said Greigy, "you need to get on this tour of India. It'll be magical." I did and it was.' More of that famous series in a later chapter. 'Another thing I remember,' Selvey continued, 'was that it was the first time that Joyce had ventured into the water since her confrontation with the shark. Everybody was remarking on it and congratulating her.' Seventeen years later!

For the rest of her life, Joyce remained anxious every time any of her children went swimming in the sea. 'I was not a good swimmer,' Ian told me. 'I always had a healthy respect for the water and rarely strayed out of my depth. Unlike Tony. He loved it and would swim for miles. He wasn't one bit put off by my mother's accident. He took the view that an attack was unlikely and if it did occur ...' Ian gave the Greig shrug – what will be, will be. He said that Tony even went to a fancy dress party not long afterwards as a victim of a shark attack. Today's thought police might condemn that as a bit tasteless. Nobody took offence; it was Tony's usual response to bad luck or misfortune, to laugh in the face of baleful fate.

Although the story of Joyce and Sandy Greig does not end with the birth of their eldest child, for the purposes of this book the spotlight now shifts from them on to their son Tony and his formative years in childhood and at school. The pair of them moved lock, stock and barrel to Australia to join Tony when he put down his roots in Sydney after Kerry Packer had offered him a job with Channel 9 for life. Sandy died in Australia in 1990. A year later, Joyce returned to South Africa, to be closer to family and friends, and there she remained until her death in 2017, five years after Tony died. Before they move aside as Tony takes centre stage, I wanted to know how their remaining children viewed their childhood in the Greig clan.

Respect, admiration and undeniable love for their father; praise, adoration and unconditional love for their mother. That was the message from all of them.

Sally Ann rummaged through the boxes of letters belonging to her mother that she had kept after her death. She emerged with several, one of which said it all. It was from Tony on the occasion of Joyce's 90th birthday and as the eldest, he was speaking for them all. 'The bond of love ran through the middle of Anske (the name we all called him) like a stick of Brighton Rock,' said Sally Ann. 'We know this because we all grew up in the same knowledge of being loved by her.' She then quoted from Tony's letter:

For as long as I am able to remember, you will feature in so many of the special aspects of life, not least of which is the ongoing knowledge that your love is, and has always been, unconditional … You have been the guiding light in our family and your great love for all of us has resulted in a family that loves and cares for each other. To adequately thank you for your role in our lives is very hard but I am sure that you know we will try to continue with the wonderful example you have set for all of us.

Happy 90th Mum!

We love you dearly,

Anske xxx

'You see,' continued Sally Ann, 'Mum was ever present with her gentleness, serenity, humour and unconditional love. A true child of God with an unfailing faith and a powerful sense of family. Mum is the lady I aspire to be … when I grow up! She was a keeper of our secrets, many of which have gone with her to her grave. She was the backbone of the family, the magnet to which we were all drawn.' At this point, her husband, Phillip Hodson, chipped in: 'Joyce was the undoubted matriarch of the family.'

Ian reminded me that Sandy was incontrovertibly the head of the family but given his problems with alcoholism, their mother took on the role that would normally be associated with the paterfamilias. She was 'our rock', as he described it, 'the home builder, the centre of family love and forgiveness and true Christian spirit'. He recognised the force of nature that was his father but he did not always have an easy relationship with him. There was little respect there while he was growing up, unaware of the reasons for Sandy's erratic behaviour but not liking it anyway. As an example, he points to an incident in early 1967, when he was 12. 'It was a big match for Selborne against Dale College. I had taken eight wickets for 19. But hard as I tried, I just couldn't get those last two wickets to take all ten. And suddenly there was this gruff voice coming out of the undergrowth around the boundary, 'Bowl on the bloody wicket!' No, if you wanted praise, you didn't go to Dad.' He guesses, being the youngest, that he was protected from the truth by his mother and elder siblings. He didn't become aware of the nature of the problem until they got back from Scotland, sometime in 1968. 'I remember playing indoor rugby and diving on to a bed to score a try. I was aware of the tinkling of glass under the bed. On investigation, I discovered a half-empty bottle of booze. In disgust, I threw it away in the dustbin but my mother saw me. "Don't do that, son," she told me, "he'll only go and buy another." It sort of all fell into place at that moment.'

However, once Sandy joined Alcoholics Anonymous and started to sort himself out, their relationship changed. 'My respect for my dad returned when I realised what he had been through and how bravely he was combatting his demons. When I was young, God help you if you disturbed his Sunday afternoon nap – you'd get your head chewed off. When he became a leading light in AA, our telephone number, anonymous of course, was in the paper as a helpline for alcoholics in trouble. Every so often the phone would ring and I would gently wake him up to tell him that somebody was in trouble. He'd be straight on his feet, saying, "I'm on my way," and he'd drive off to wherever he was needed. Sometimes, he'd be gone for hours. He never refused a plea for help. You have to admire someone enormously for that, especially in view of what he had been through.' *You might say you rediscovered your father.* 'Indeed. We all did. It brought us closer.'

However, he is in no doubt that during the times when his father was 'absent on parade', so to speak, it was his mother who held things together. 'She was there for all of us in times of heartache, need, support and celebration, for Dad and her children. She nursed us, encouraged us, mentored us …. Each one of us will have our memories of her and what she meant to us, both growing up and in adult life. For my part, I will never forget them and will treasure them always.'

In researching the background to Tony Greig's family and his childhood, it has struck me how remarkably honest and forthcoming his brother and two sisters have been about those early years. All families have dark secrets hidden away and skeletons rattling in cupboards. Few of us are prepared to share domestic pain and household strife so willingly. Of course, in their case, final redemption rose up from the ashes of a life that had practically self-immolated, rather like new plants and shrubs shooting up after a forest fire, but most families, surely, would prefer privacy. Not so the Greigs. That is how they were, and continue to be. Somehow, we know now from what cloth England's future captain was cut.

Chapter 3

Queenstown 1946–66

'Tony Greig would dive on concrete for you.'

Mike Buss, Sussex all-rounder and cricket
coach at Queen's College

ANTHONY William Greig first took guard on this earth on 6 October 1946. 'It was a long birth,' wrote his mother, with unconscious irony. Furthermore, the baby had a mop of black hair. Tony Greig with black hair? That simply doesn't fit. It would be as incongruous as a clean-shaven WG Grace, a slim Colin Milburn or a bespectacled Ian Botham. It was not long before the natural order of things was restored and the blond hair and the fair skin of his Scots ancestry reasserted themselves. But where did the enormous height come from? 'Me,' proclaimed Ian. Two facts cast doubt on this assertion. Ian was born nine years after Tony. *Wisden* records Ian Alexander Greig's height as 5ft 11in. 'Ah, but my dad was a tall man,' he added, by way of justification. That may be so but there is a family photograph in existence, which shows a young Tony, resplendent in his striped school blazer, not far off the size of his father on the other side of the portrait. The boy was already, clearly, head and shoulders above his contemporaries.

He was raised in a liberal, English-speaking family. Perhaps this description needs some explaining. In a country that comprised the white as well as several native tribes, it is often assumed by outsiders that the 'whites', for want of a better definition, were one and the same. Nothing could be further from the truth. A casual encounter with South African history will inform you that the Dutch arrived in the Cape before the British and even after the Boer War – perhaps *especially* afterwards – the Afrikaners, as they were known, fiercely maintained their customs, language, independence and ultimately their hegemony over the country. Generalisations can be misleading but I think it fair to say that, by and large, the Afrikaners, who by this stage held a majority in Parliament and were the ruling party, were more dogmatic and xenophobic in their policies, especially when it came to apartheid. Their English neighbours tended to hide their misgivings because they were wealthier and the system was to their advantage. They adopted a more liberal outlook because they could afford to do so, thus laying themselves open to charges of hypocrisy. But when has hypocrisy ever hampered Britain's desire to trade? Many were uncomfortable with the system and did their best to ameliorate apartheid in its most nakedly discriminatory form. In this regard, the Greigs were of the genuinely liberal disposition, though in no way, as the children have pointed out, could Sandy Greig be termed liberal in his family values.

This strange, anomalous, paradoxical situation that the majority of English-speaking South Africans found themselves in was never easy. On the one hand, they felt that apartheid was unworkable and ethically wrong. On the other hand, what could they do about it? Foment protest and ultimately rebellion? Most peace-loving, law-abiding, home-owning families would abhor, and probably be aghast at, such social upheaval. So they did their unobtrusive best to ameliorate the iniquities of apartheid where and when they could.

The Greigs were no different. Sandy wrote trenchant editorials in *The Daily Representative* critical of the government where and when he could get away with it. According to her children, Joyce could not exactly be described as liberal in her politics, such as they were. She had an inner conviction, buttressed by her Christian principles, that all men of whatever colour, creed or social status were worthy of respect and did her best to inculcate these values in her children. It was a lesson they all took on board. But they suspected that when she disappeared behind the screen to cast her vote in general elections, despite her public statements, she probably put a cross next to the ruling Nationalist Party. This would be understandable. She had enough upheaval in her domestic life without wanting to upset the status quo in the country at large. This did not make her a racist. By the same token, the very idea that Tony Greig was in any way a racist makes anyone who knew him laugh out loud with scorn. He spent his career playing with and against cricketers who were black and to him they were merely cricketers. There wasn't an ounce of prejudice in his body. The comment he made as England captain before the series against the West Indies that he would make them 'grovel' – something that followed him like an albatross until his dying day – was a mistake, an infelicitous choice of words, rather than an intended smear on the racial inferiority of his opponents. As he cheerfully admitted at the end of the series which England had lost 0-3, his words had had the opposite effect of that which he intended. He could be criticised for a lack of sensitivity; his friends remain adamant that he could never be accused of racism. It just wasn't in his nature. Joyce's upbringing had seen to that.

Charity begins at home, as the Bible did not, as a matter of fact, say but it was a proverb enthusiastically endorsed in the Greig household. Joyce had two maids, one who cooked and the other who was the housekeeper. A young lad who went by the name of Tackies, for the sole reason that he was wearing little else other than a pair of shorts and plimsolls, known as 'tackies' in South Africa, when he first appeared at the front door, was given the titular role of gardener but he soon became a net bowler for the young Tony. According to Ian, the description of Tackies as a bowler is taking the name of that honourable trade in vain. He was in truth nothing more than a blatant chucker, not ever having played the game or been versed in its arcane laws and practices. But that was all right. He threw the ball at the young batsman – at considerable pace and much closer than the stipulated 22 yards – which had the beneficial effect of sharpening up Tony's reflexes and no doubt preparing him for the physical onslaught of fast bowling in the Test match arena. Tackies also had another precious asset. He did not much fancy batting so Tony was free to perfect his batting technique without the chore of having to reciprocate in the bowling duties.

The point is that Tony grew up with Africans in close proximity. If not exactly speaking their language, he knew and understood them and made sure he remained on the friendliest of terms. In any case, he was a youngster and the maids were adults and he was brought up to respect their position and authority. Tackies became a sort of mate. There is a lovely story of his being flown to England to appear on *This Is Your Life* when Tony was the guest. The surprise and pleasure on Tony's face when Tackies strode on stage was genuine and touching. The look on Tackies' face when Tony showed him the sights of London was equally memorable. The fact that the show, aired in March 1977, was excruciatingly embarrassing for England's captain who was at the time engaged in secret recruiting for Kerry Packer's World Series Cricket will concern us in a later chapter but here it goes to show that Tony Greig never forgot where he came from. Old friends were greeted as enthusiastically when he became famous as they were when he was a lad. Tackies was no different. The fact is that he and maids were regarded as 'family', sharing in the trials and tribulations, the successes and celebrations, as one. They even went on their annual Christmas holidays to Kei Mouth together. 'The maids and Tackies were well looked after,' said Joyce, 'and felt part of the family.' It might not seem much in the face of state-sponsored repression of a whole people but it was something. And who are we to judge in any case, who never lived in such an oppressive environment? 'Every little helps,' as the Tesco slogan said, pinched unashamedly from a Danish proverb, incidentally which continues, 'as the sow said when she snapped at a gnat.'

The Greigs were not well off. Of course, one has to add the codicil that all things are relative; compared to the average Xhosa family, they were rich. But among their peers and social equals, they were not, by professional status, income or assets, very wealthy; at times they were what used to be called in my parents' era 'hard up'. Many people had an idea back then that all white South Africans led the life of Riley, in large properties, with manicured and well-watered grounds, swimming pools, tennis courts, a couple of Mercedes in the double garage, with drinks at sundown on the *stoep* (Afrikaans for verandah), waited upon by a small army of black servants. Of course there were rich families – there are in any society – but the Greigs were hardly in that category. Money was a problem at times and more than likely that informed Tony's firm intent, once he had made his name as a professional cricketer, to provide for his and his family's future. He was not grasping or obsessed but he was determined when he had the cards in his hand to play them shrewdly. Much in life is about timing. That is why, when Packer came calling, Tony Greig seized the moment … and he can hardly be blamed for that.

In researching his childhood, I was intrigued to discover whether, at an early age, anybody had him marked down for future stardom or at the very least a successful career as a professional cricketer. The answer seems to be not necessarily so. He was, from the outset, an active, energetic, fearless boy who loved playing games and hated to be cooped up indoors. In that regard, he was lucky to be born in South Africa. I have a South African friend and he tells me that he never wore shoes until he went to school. The point is that the climate and culture lent itself to an outdoor life. Furthermore, playing ball games was almost *de rigueur* for boys and a special place has always lain in the affections of the South African public for its sporting heroes. If rugby was king, cricket could regard itself as a favoured prince. Both Tony and Ian can remember quite vividly tuning in to a crackly radio to listen to SABC Radio, following the fortunes of the South African team overseas. That is, when they weren't playing outdoors.

There were endless games of cricket in the garden, with specific and peculiar laws, all fiercely contested. The girls joined in and they more than held their own in the hurly-burly of familial rivalry. Even when he found himself alone, Tony devised games to amuse himself, either by throwing a ball against a wall and hitting the rebound or tying a sock with a ball inside to a branch of a tree and whacking that. He built some rugby posts out of bamboo and would practise his place kicking for hours on end. The ingenuity, patience and determination of ball-playing children know no bounds. The ball becomes their friend, ever present and ever obedient.

A glimpse into the childhood of Tony Greig was provided for me by his boyhood friend, Paul Ensor. They were near neighbours in Queenstown, Tony about six or seven years old and Paul a year younger. There was a variation of French cricket played on their front lawn, the small size of the garden precluding any other, more expansive form of the game. Ensor told me that Tony soon worked out that if he threw the ball hard, bouncing just before it hit the bat, the chances were that it would rebound in the air, allowing him to make spectacular, sprawling catches. Shades of things to come: the tactical nous of a future captain and the penchant for throwing himself about in the field.

Ensor was keen to stress one aspect of Tony's personality that informed everything he did, even at this tender age. In due course, the two families moved houses into larger properties but still within striking distance of each other and – crucially – with more space to play 'proper' games of cricket. 'These were intensely competitive Test matches,' Ensor said, 'played for the most part with a tennis ball although occasionally we would switch to a cricket ball.' No pads, gloves or any other form of protection, note, but the intensity levels did not drop. If Ensor was proving to be a bit more stubborn than usual when batting, Tony found ways to dislodge him. 'He would switch from off spin to a much faster delivery, always short, that I did not much like. I complained that this should be regarded as a no-ball and therefore would not count if I got out. He said this was "rubbish" and that it was "just a quicker off break". Even then, his competitive streak was striking.'

This combative instinct was not confined to cricket. 'What distinguished Tony from his peers,' Ensor added, 'was his desire to succeed in any contest he was involved. This extended to games of tennis, table tennis, rugby, golf, even canasta, which was a regular occurrence in the Greig household.'

Roy Taylor, a cousin, told me an interesting story about Tony. There was a two-year gap between him and his younger relative, not that you would have noticed, he pointed out, because Tony was tall for his age and 'held back at nothing'. When Tony was about ten, the two of them went along to the recreation ground in Queenstown where the local team, Swift Rugby Club, were playing. 'Tony and I were acting as ball boys. Our full back sent up an almighty up-and-under, which faded off the pitch in the breeze. Tony, on the sideline, stood under it and caught the ball to the roar of the crowd who were amazed at the skill of this youngster. The papers were full of it the next day.'

Taylor too found himself playing innumerable games of rugby and cricket with the irrepressible young lad. Taylor's father was coach of the Swifts and Queen's first XV rugby teams and would often bring back the match ball for the boys to play with. 'Tony and my brother would play against me and another friend. This was always a tough match with no quarter given. Although younger than us, Tony was always in the thick of it and would never give up.' During the summer, it would be cricket, on the street, on the lawn, wherever and whenever they could find a pitch. 'I did not enjoy playing him at his home,' Taylor recalled with a smile, 'because he had a dog called Flossie. Whenever he was out, he would refuse to go. If I insisted, he would set his dog on me, so he always had a longer innings than me.'

Whenever the formative years of Tony Greig's cricket career are discussed, the prominence of his school, Queen's College, and its justifiable reputation for coaching the game, is always cited. That this is true is beyond question but there was an earlier influence not so well recognised, as Paul Ensor explained. 'When I visited my first teacher, Audrey Walden-Smith, in Cape Town a few years ago, she told me that she was responsible for starting up this little cricket game at our prep school following repeated requests from Tony and other boys. She said she showed Tony how to stand properly side-on and how to hold the bat so that it didn't look as if he was holding an axe.' I wonder if she taught him to stand upright in his stance, all six feet seven and a half inches of him, with his bat already raised in the air, a unique stance at the time though much copied these days. No, that change in his technique came later but in all other respects, the doughty Miss Walden-Smith clearly did a good job. The young Tony was apparently 'a very insistent little boy'. Well, perhaps not that little.

Another interesting insight was vouchsafed to me by the discerning and ever-helpful Ensor and this concerned Tony's growing tactical acumen, which I suppose at that early stage of his cricket development could be simply summed up as a quick appreciation of the best way to get somebody out so you can get hold of the bat. The two boys loved playing a table-top game called Test Match, which they took very seriously with elaborate scorecards to record the progress of each match. 'We both became very adept at the game, developing good hand/eye co-ordination to strike the ball where we wanted.' Tony soon saw possibilities and was the first to work out the best tactics to his advantage. 'He reckoned that he could improve the odds of having someone caught if he bowled just wide of the off stump with eight catching fielders set on that side of the wicket, with just a leg slip, a silly mid-on and a mid-on on the leg side. Of course, after a while, I adopted the same tactic but he was always a step ahead by better co-ordinating the speed of his selected "bowler" with adjustments to the field.'

The outdoor life, espoused by Tony in his later years as the ideal grounding for a fit and healthy existence, did not exclusively consist of ball games. Being naturally fearless and full of curiosity, as any young lads are, he and Paul Ensor explored the wide, open spaces of undulating veld around Queenstown, which leads up to the base of Madeira Mountain. The veld is criss-crossed with furrows or 'dongas' as Ensor called them. The word is a derivative of the Xhosa or Zulu word *udonga* and was commonly in use by both the British and Afrikaners in the Boer War. Whenever it rained, Ensor told me, these dongas would be transformed into rivulets running across the escarpment. He takes up the story: 'One day, after a particularly heavy rainfall, we were watching the water run through these dongas. One of us tossed a small twig into the water and we followed it as it disappeared in the flow. "Let's have a boat race," said Tony. Within a short while we were captivated as we engaged in boat races, experimenting with twigs of different shapes and sizes. We later tried racing our chosen boats in the roadside gutters but went back to the dongas which were much more fun due to the unpredictability of the natural obstacles and hazards.'

This native passion for wide open spaces was further nurtured by another cousin of Tony's, Rodney King, who was 15 years his senior. King ran a farm in the Tarkastad region of the Eastern Cape, about 50 miles from Queenstown. As a boy, Tony regularly spent school holidays at the farm and he loved every minute of it. Horse riding, shooting, driving farm vehicles (it's funny how the legal age to take hold of a steering wheel never seems to apply on farmland) – all of the usual pursuits to be found in a rural location were eagerly embraced. King, almost a god to the young Tony, took it upon himself to toughen up the lad and designed various ingenious tasks and ordeals to test his mettle. Some of these, comprising games of capture, imprisonment and escape, might sound to us these days as bordering on bullying but Tony never saw it like that. In the same way that he unquestioningly endorsed the system of fagging later on at Queen's College, both as a first-year and as a prefect, he believed this patriarchal discipline was educative, instructive and good for the soul. He reckoned it prepared him for the hurly-burly of competitive cricket at the highest level. His brother Ian felt that sledging Tony was a waste of time, 'water off a duck's back', he said; it was only a masculine form of banter, never to be taken seriously, and easily put aside over a beer after close of play. Besides, as we all know, Tony Greig could dish it out with the best of them. So, no, he never considered the scrapes he got into on the farm anything other than a form of tough love, one that he remained grateful for during the remainder of his life. Besides, it was so much fun.

It is tempting to ascribe what was probably the most significant event in his early life to one of these teenage escapades but the truth is a little more prosaic though no less shocking for all that. It is a fact that the accident happened on a farm, but not Rodney King's farm; it was a neighbour's. It did involve a car accident on a deserted track but no high jinks were involved. When he was 14, he attended a party in a nearby village. The foreman of the farm drove them home afterwards. There had been recent rain, the track was mountainous and treacherous and the Chevrolet skidded, overturned, toppled down a slope and hit a tree. Tony remembered hitting his head on the dashboard but was not knocked unconscious. He and his friend scrambled free, apparently unharmed, from the wreckage but the driver, the foreman, was badly hurt. He recovered and in time all seemed well. They had been lucky. It is true that several days later, Tony complained of dizziness and was forced to take things easy for a while but nobody considered the passing inconvenience to be anything other than a perfectly understandable reaction to the accident. The dizzy spell was soon forgotten.

Less than one year later, he suffered an epileptic seizure, the first of several that were to recur from time to time in his life; in fact it was a fit that finally caused his death, though the incident was of course complicated by the advanced stage at that time of his lung cancer. Two questions occupy my mind at this juncture, both prompted by my footing as a layman in medical matters: did the car accident bring on the epilepsy and how well did Tony manage the affliction for the rest of his life, a part of which he served as an international sportsman?

As sometimes is the case with diagnoses of illness, there is no clear answer to the first question. Usually, epilepsy sufferers have some sort of genetic predisposition to the disease. But it is also true that a structural change in the brain, such as that caused by a brain injury, can lead to the onset of epilepsy. Quite possibly, in Tony's case, epilepsy owed its existence to *both* structural change in the brain and a genetic tendency. That would make sense if you take into consideration that many people suffer brain injury but not all develop epilepsy afterwards. For clarification, I sought the opinion of a GP friend whether he thought Tony's accident and his epilepsy were connected. 'Hmm, possible but not likely. Don't forget, 15 is the age when it usually manifests itself.' And that was all. The point to bear in mind, however, is that Tony himself was convinced of the connection.

It happened in a school tennis match with an old friend and adversary in the annual scrap between Queen's and Dale Colleges. As with all the Greigs whom I have met, Tony was searingly honest and open about his affliction and how it affected the rest of his life. At first, he started to feel giddy, which soon made him confused and disorientated. He tried to shrug it off, threw up the ball to serve ... and then blackness. I have witnessed first-hand an epileptic fit and it is not a pretty sight, altogether disturbing in the violence and loss of physical control involved. The reaction of the other players, teachers and spectators can only be imagined. He regained consciousness and was driven home, feeling distinctly ropey. Of course, there was no question that proper, expert medical advice would not be sought, to which end he was referred to a specialist in Cape Town, at the famous Groote Schuur Hospital. He was just 14 and understandably scared and anxious. Tests confirmed that it was indeed epilepsy. Tony understood little about the diagnosis nor its probable ramifications but he was aware that it represented a severe risk to anyone who played sport. And sport was all that he lived for.

It went without saying that he resolved, there and then, that this bad news would not stop him leading a normal life. But it was never as simple as that. Epilepsy cannot be dismissed by an effort of will; it needs careful monitoring, watchful supervision, sensible precautions and a cocktail of drugs, none of which comes easily to an active and impatient teenager. But slowly, by dint of painful experience, he learned how to manage it. He was never going to chain himself to a safety-first regime and a long list of banned activities to keep him from harm's way. His parents sensibly realised this and let him off the leash. He would have slipped it anyway. That is not to say that they did not keep a close and fearful eye on him but they allowed him his wish, to live his life just the same as any active young lad.

For a while, he kept a lid on the news with friends and peers at school and relied on the support of his family to negotiate the tricky adolescent years. Even his great mate, Paul Ensor, was kept largely in the dark about his condition. 'I recall an incident when I went to his house,' Ensor told me, 'and I was informed that Tony could not come out to play because he was resting after having "fainted". I remember being a bit surprised but we did not discuss the incident subsequently.'

I wondered what effect Tony's epilepsy had upon the rest of the family. Sally Ann laughed. 'He was definitely Number 1! He could do no wrong. Perhaps that was because, as the eldest, he had taken on the role of leader and protector at times of family crisis. But there wasn't an ounce of malice in him. We didn't mind his special status at all. In fact, we probably put him up there as much as our parents.' Ian is in complete agreement. 'Tony was the one who Mum and Dad most worried about, because of his epilepsy. His health was of major concern within the family. Later it became a family joke – you know, who was the favourite, who was Number 1, Number 2 and so on.'

Carefree about his condition he may have been but reckless Tony was not. He began to recognise the warning signs if an attack was imminent and was diligent about taking precautionary action. Sally Ann explained. 'He always said that an "aura" would come over him.

He would start to feel dizzy with sickness. So he would take himself off to bed with sleeping pills. If that didn't work, the doctor would give him something to knock him out.' As time went on and adolescent growth spurts slowed, the doctors managed to balance his drug intake, always considerable and high duty, and he managed to stabilise things effectively.

There were mishaps along the way. When I started out on my cricket career at Hampshire in the early 1970s, I remember the Sussex boys telling us about Tony Greig and his epilepsy. They said that as youngsters on the staff, they were surprised by the amount of time he slept in the dressing room. Now, all professional cricketers are adept at falling asleep in a crowded, noisy dressing room, a habit which most of us have carried on into middle-age and beyond, so 'having a kip' during a match was no big deal. But Greig seemed to spend more time than most with his head down. The new boys at Sussex were soon put right by their seniors about the captain's need for sleep. Paul Phillipson, a young student on the staff at that time, told me that Greig's ability to sleep in the dressing room, no matter what was happening all around him, was remarkable. 'He would lie down wherever there was room with his pads on. "Tell me when it's time to go in," he would instruct, close his eyes and he'd be away. And then, when a wicket fell, we'd give him a nudge, up he would get and walk out to bat.' Thus it was no secret on the 'circuit', as the band of brothers of professional cricketers was known. But further than that, the chatter did not spread. Though most of us would have pooh-poohed the very idea as fanciful, there was in fact a strong bond among cricketers. Some things were fair game for gossip and wider circulation and some things, usually personal matters such as this, were not. I doubt many people outside this inner circle of players, officials and cricket, as opposed to news reporters, were aware of Tony's ailment. In light of which, what happened at the Wanderers Cricket Ground in Johannesburg in November 1970 went largely unrecorded.

Earlier that (English) summer, Tony Greig had made his debut for England in a five-day international match. I choose my words carefully here, omitting the adjective 'Test', something that causes me, cricket lovers and historians of a certain age intense irritation and dismay.

To replace the cancelled South African tour of these shores in 1970, owing to nationwide anti-apartheid protests, a series against the Rest of the World had been hastily organised. At first, they were designated by the authorities as full-blown Test matches, with caps and blazers distributed accordingly. And then, retrospectively, the status was removed; they were no longer regarded, for statistical purposes, as Test matches. How anyone could consider hard-fought, two-innings games against players of the calibre of Garry Sobers, Clive Lloyd, Graeme Pollock, Barry Richards, Lance Gibbs and Eddie Barlow as anything else left many shaking their heads in consternation. It still rankles. However, it was in this series that Tony Greig had first donned the sweater with the crown and three lions on its chest. As I remember, the irony of a South African-born but British-naturalised player representing England in a match against a World XI dominated by South Africans, as it happened, which in turn had replaced a South African tour cancelled because of politics, largely escaped the British public. It did me. I doubt it escaped Tony. How he got there will wait for later.

At the conclusion of that season's county cricket programme, Tony had found himself at a bit of a loose end. He had not performed with any great distinction in the three 'Tests' he played and had been left out, to his intense disappointment, of Illingworth's MCC tour party to Australia that winter. He decided to return to South Africa to take up coaching responsibilities in the Eastern Cape as well as representing Eastern Province in the Currie Cup. A brief look at the scorecard of the match I am referring to, Transvaal versus Eastern Province, tells us immediately that something was amiss. In EP's first innings, down there at No 11, is *AW Greig, absent hurt.* How come? Presumably he was not batting at the time when he was hurt otherwise it would have read, *retired hurt.* And he wouldn't have been batting at No 11. The only explanation must be that he hurt himself in the field, when Transvaal were batting. Note the words, *absent hurt*, not *absent ill.* And that single adverb 'hurt', not 'ill', tells its own story, as I discovered.

Geoff Dakin was something of a legend – still is, I beg his pardon – in Eastern Province cricket. He had a successful career as a player and later captain of his province. After retirement, he featured large in the administration of the game, both provincially and nationally. Following the collapse of apartheid and the election of Nelson Mandela as the country's president, the two boards of South African cricket, the white and non-white governing bodies, were amalgamated and Geoff Dakin became its first president. He watched with close interest the burgeoning career of Tony Greig, later becoming a firm friend. He it was who persuaded Tony to play for Eastern Province while he was on sabbatical leave, so to speak, from the England side. Dakin explained to me what happened. 'I was manager of the team and at seven o'clock on the morning of the match, Tony suffered a terrible fit. Peter Pollock was his room-mate. Against doctor's orders, Tony pronounced himself fit to play and took the field when Transvaal won the toss and batted.' Much later, Tony admitted to friends and family that this was an ill-judged decision. Youthful self-assurance and misplaced stubbornness won the day. Besides, he did not want to let his new team-mates and the selectors down. He thought he could buck the odds and instead of retiring back to the hotel to sleep it off, he ambled, somewhat dizzily, towards the slips, his usual haunt. A couple of edges flew his way and he managed to cling on to them, the second of which was a blinder, according to Dakin. 'Within seconds, he hit the ground with another fit. Ali Bacher was at the non-striker's end and went down the pitch to assist. I ran on to the field and after a while, Tony came round.' Bacher, the Transvaal and South African captain, was a doctor and he supervised Tony's immediate treatment. All the players gathered round, not out of unseemly curiosity but in order to shield the distressing scene from prying eyes. To the spectators lining the boundary, it must have seemed for all the world that one of the EP fielders had injured himself.

That the press kept a lid on the affair was largely down to Dakin. 'In return for my honesty about what had happened,' he said, 'I begged them never to write about his condition, that from a young age he had suffered from epilepsy, which, to the credit of the South African press, no one ever did.' *Why were you so keen to keep it under wraps?* 'Because if it had become public property, it may well have ruined his future career in playing the game he loved so much.' Of this prudent intervention, Dakin remains justifiably proud. After some time in hospital, Tony was able to resume playing for Eastern Province and within 18 months he was back in the England side – this time officially – and Dakin's worst fears had not been realised.

All that of course came later. First, Tony had to complete his education and in Queen's College he could not have chosen, or rather, his parents could not have chosen, a school better suited to his character and talents. For the time being, epilepsy was something that he largely kept to himself and his family. He did not zealously hide his condition nor did he shout it from the rooftops. The time for opening up about it publicly would come later, once he had established himself as a *bona fide* cricketer on the international stage. In the meantime, he had to tackle a much more pressing problem. He had to pass an examination in Afrikaans – a language with which he was not altogether conversant – before moving on to the next stage of his education. In his final year at Queen's, he failed it, which felt like a catastrophe because he had already secured a place at Rhodes University in Grahamstown, conditional of course on his having fulfilled all the necessary entry requirements. A pass in Afrikaans was a prerequisite. That he had not fully complied with the stipulated conditions meant that he had to return to school for an extra year and retake all his subjects. The syllabuses having changed, there needed to be a lot of extra cramming in the Greig daily routine, something he took as an unwelcome distraction from his sporting commitments. However, there was a silver lining in this particular cloud. He was able to mature as a person and as a games player and more success on the playing fields of Queen's and further afield lay in wait. The extra year was a blessing in disguise, one that was to change his life. The path of university followed by a return to his *alma mater* as a history and games teacher, which had been mapped out for him, was abandoned and a cricket career in England beckoned instead.

Before we leave his education, I want to make it clear that Tony Greig was no fool in the classroom. This fact is confirmed by Paul Ensor. 'He had a good intellect and probably underperformed at school due to a combination of domestic issues, sporting distractions and a resulting lack of application. Although his academic record was not outstanding, he certainly would have had the capacity to undertake university study if motivated to do so.' Had it not been for the Afrikaans hiccup, Tony would have gone to Rhodes, no doubt achieved a reasonable degree and more than likely had a respectable career as a teacher of history, promised by his headmaster.

There is no doubt that Tony had a whale of a time at Queen's. Paul Ensor told me that he was popular with his peers and admired by many of the younger boys. 'He had a terrific sense of humour and enjoyed telling jokes and recounting stories in a humorous way. I can recall instances when he was the centre of attention surrounded by a group of other boys.' *How did the staff view him?* 'I think the majority admired and respected him. There were times when he did the wrong thing and got a caning but ....' *Who didn't in those days?* 'Quite. He was never resentful about it, accepting that it was a reasonable punishment. Knowing Tony, I suspect he would have enjoyed describing in exaggerated detail how well or otherwise, the punishment was administered.'

A reliable gauge of how anybody regards his schooldays is usually indicated by his attitude to his school in later years. In this regard, Ensor is quite adamant. 'Tony looked back on his education at Queen's with great fondness. Like me, he believed he had a privileged upbringing and schooling there.' Apparently Tony was invited back to Queen's on a couple of occasions to address the pupil body at assembly. Ensor said that Tony told him once 'how moved he was to look out at a sea of black faces and how emotional he felt listening to them singing the school song.'

The image of those black faces prompted me to ask the question that would have exercised any other pupil body in schools the world over – except perhaps in South Africa. *Was apartheid, its morality and repercussions, ever discussed, either formally in class or informally amongst yourselves?* 'You may find this strange,' answered Ensor, 'but during our schooling, there was little discussion among students of the apartheid situation.' In actual fact, I did not find it strange for the simple fact that Barry Richards, a contemporary of Tony's give a year or two, had given more or less the same answer when I asked him. He reminded me that there was no television in South Africa until 1976. The first TV screen he ever saw was at Heathrow when an SA Schools team – he was captain – landed there on their tour of England. 'There were black people sharing buses, trains, public toilets, even stands at cricket grounds. We'd never seen anything like it.' He explained their ignorance in these terms. 'I guess we had gone along with the sort of brainwashing that we had grown up with. There was no means of knowing what was happening in the outside world other than what we read in the papers. And of course, even those were censored.' Sandy Greig would have given a shudder of recognition. Back to Ensor's take on the question. 'I think there may have been a feeling that the system of segregated facilities was discriminatory but the overall feeling at the time was probably an acceptance of the status quo. We knew no better.'

Tony Greig lived in a family that was broadly liberal in its political outlook – Sandy had made sure of that – and as a later story told Ensor recounts, both he and Tony, young and uninformed as they were, felt perfectly well-disposed to the native Africans, more so if they liked sport. But the complex ethical, political and socio-economic conundrums of apartheid would have passed them by. They were only boys. 'It was only after we had left school,' continued Ensor, 'that we started to understand the injustice of it all.' Tony's eyes were to be opened wide when he landed on these shores soon after, though I think it fair to say that racial integration was only one of the many surprises.

It is an uncomfortable fact for some educationalists that prowess at sport often greases the wheels of a pupil's progress through boarding school. But it was more than his talent for games and the opportunities that Queen's afforded that brought Tony happiness and fulfilment. He relished the hustle and bustle, the sheer exuberance that a busy existence brings to a fit young boy with energy to burn. He loved the friendships, the camaraderie, the banter, the boisterous fun and games to be had in a communal environment. The unique, claustrophobic culture of a county or Test match dressing room would hold no terrors for him. He would slip easily into any fraternity, set, company, clique, team, whatever you like to call it, in any part of the world and immediately fit in, feeling completely at home. For this ease of manner and social mobility, he largely had to thank his schooling.

Tony was made of the sort of stuff that could cope with adversity and hard knocks. Probably, the more difficult the task set by older boys, the more he would rise to the challenge, if only to prove that he could. He firmly believed that the tough, early years at school prepared him for the inevitable challenges and setbacks that would confront him in Test cricket. So what if he was ordered to polish his prefect's shoes or squeeze toothpaste on to his toothbrush or sit on the lavatory seat to warm it up on cold mornings? The time would come when it was his turn to have a fag and if he was a half-decent human being, he would remember what it felt like to be down on the bottom rung of human life and behave with a modicum of restraint and generosity in his turn. Qualities, incidentally, which Tony displayed time and time again when he was a captain.

The way Tony would have treated his skunk is exemplified in his relationship with his younger brother. 'He would set me challenges,' Ian told me, 'and he had a way of making it fun. For example, he set up a hurdle course around the house in a very imaginative way. He would jump over the hurdles and because I was so small, I would run underneath them. Everything was so exciting when he was around. When we were in East London, Peter Kirsten—' *Peter Kirsten, the Peter Kirsten who later played for South Africa? How did you know him?* 'We were living in East London at the time and Peter and I attended Selborne Primary together … well, he was in the year above me. But we were in the same school cricket and rugby teams and we struck up a close relationship, both on and off the field. We were practically inseparable and he spent all of the holidays with us. We would often play backyard cricket with Tony when he was home. We hero-worshipped him.' *What about that story you tell of Tony bowling you bouncers when you were a kid?* He grinned. 'The other boys were concerned that he was bowling too fast at them. "Rubbish!" he said. 'My six-year-old brother can face that speed. Just watch this!' I never usually got a bat but he came up to me and quietly whispered in my ear, "Just do as I say, hey. First ball is one for you to cut. Second ball will be a half-volley – just close your eyes and hit it. Third ball will be a looping bouncer. Don't worry, it'll just sail over your head." Thus was my face saved.' For the most part, Ian was a ball fetcher and carrier. 'Anske would kick a rugby ball over the house and I would have to fetch it. If I ever complained, he would hoist me on to the roof and tell me he would get me down when I stopped crying. He was my big brother and I adored him. I couldn't wait for him to come home whenever he was away.'

No wonder. What young boy wouldn't miss the company of his elder brother if such exciting adventures as this one were on the cards? One evening, Ian was instructed by Tony to go to bed at the normal time, not to argue or make a fuss, to do exactly as he was told but 'keep your dressing gown and slippers close by'. The reason became clear later. After Sandy and Joyce had themselves gone to bed, there was a discreet tap on the window and, sure enough, there was older brother ready to hoist younger brother out of his bedroom, into the night air and into the waiting car. 'The car was pushed out of the driveway and further down the road out of earshot, Tony started the engine and off we went.' *Where was the secret destination?* 'The fun fair down at the sea front! We had a marvellous time riding on the bumper cars, the big wheel and the octopus until the early hours of the morning before being snuck back into my room.' *Did your mum and dad ever find out?* 'Not until we told them much later in life.' *I heard that the Surrey boys employed similar night-time tactics on away trips under your captaincy.* 'Certainly not! Remember, Murts, it takes a thief to catch a thief.'

The high-spirited, fun-loving, devil-may-care temperament was the standout attribute that anybody who knew Tony as a boy remembers. A friend of mine whose family knew the Greigs in Queenstown and who often met the mischievous elder boy of the family, remarked to me when I mentioned him, 'Tony Greig! Gosh, he was a terrible tease! He never took anything seriously, always laughing and joking and pulling your leg.' This impishness was remarked upon by many in later life when reminded of him. One will suffice for now. In 1975, Greig was captain of England and in an effort to blunt the fearsome Australian pace attack of Lillee and Thomson, he and the selectors decided to take a gamble and pick someone from left-field. 'You'll never guess who it is,' he teased and challenged his team-mates in the Sussex dressing room before the team was publicly announced. They all spent the rest of the afternoon picking out increasingly unlikely candidates. 'Greigy just grinned at us,' John Barclay, who was there, told me, 'hugely enjoying the joke. "So who's the mystery man?" he kept on badgering us. Of course, none of us got it.' By now I had guessed, but this was 43 years later. It was of course the grey-haired, bespectacled, 33-year-old David Steele.

Tony would not have agreed that life was just a breeze, not to be taken totally in earnest. His sport he took very seriously but it was fun as well. He played games with a smile on his face. It was not in his nature to keep a low profile, every contest a grim battle of animosity and rancour. Keith Fletcher told me a story of that infamous tour of Australia in 1974/75, when the England batsmen were terrorised by Lillee and Thomson. 'Greigy would hit a four off Thommo, run towards him where he had pulled up after his follow-through and, just feet away from our principal tormentor, he would signal his own four to the crowd with a huge grin splitting his face. "For f***'s sake, Greigy," we would tell him later, "do you have to do that and get him all riled up? We've still got to go out and bat!" Greigy keep a low profile? He was a showman. He loved it.' Paul Ensor pointed out to me that this element of showmanship was always part of Tony's character even at school. 'The bigger the stage, the more focussed he was in lifting his performance beyond the everyday. I was not surprised that he would always perform well in the big inter-school matches and in the representative year groups provincially. He always enjoyed the big occasion which allowed him to display his talents and acumen to best effect.'

Kenny McEwan remembers the effect the charismatic Tony Greig had on the younger boys at Queen's. 'When the first XI were practising in the nets, we juniors would watch him and I would dream of being there one day myself. Tony always stood out. He was always so neatly turned out, even for practice, and *so* competitive, even in the nets.' Not just at cricket, it would seem. Geoff Dakin told me, 'Tony was also a very fine rugby player. In the first XV he played at lock and his main thrust was to win the ball at the line-out. Quite natural for a guy of 6ft 5in.' Still growing! He had another two inches to go before he stopped. There are two stories of his rugby career at school that I unearthed, both when he was captain. Amazing to recount, the school rugby matches at Queen's were attended regularly by crowds in excess of 2,000. Everybody who ever knew Tony always refers to his 'big match temperament', something he never denied. That was why these derbies against rival schools always appealed. A previous match at Selborne College from East London had been a humiliating 15-0 beating. This rankled with Tony, not so much that they had lost but more because he believed his side had betrayed a shameful lack of spirit. For the return fixture, he was determined that there would be no repeat. As captain, he worked on his team's confidence and resolve in the days leading up to matchday. As usual, the grandstand was packed, the motivation to succeed in front of their home crowd was ever present and Queen's ran out as creditable victors by 11-3. Once again, it was the performance rather than the result that pleased. Ian described the other match. 'The last match of the rugby term was always the traditional Leavers v Non-Leavers (those who were expected to comprise the following year's first XV). Of course, no one gave the younger team, the Non-Leavers, a price; the bigger, older team always won. But not this time. Tony was captain of the Non-Leavers. He destroyed them in the line-out and led from the front. It was quite a shock that result, I can tell you.'

Roy Taylor had this to say about his cousin at school: 'I was in Matric, two years ahead of him when he first got into the school XI. I was the wicketkeeper that year and I so enjoyed watching his talent from my position behind the stumps, as he could swing the ball both ways as well as having the ability to roll his huge fingers across the ball to great effect.' Aha! I often wondered when and how Tony had learned to bowl those off-cutters that he used to such surprising effect in the West Indies; he had been bowling them all along, since he was at school. Taylor continued: 'He was a tall and aggressive batsman and seemed to intimidate the opposition yet he was the first to shake their hand at the end of the game, win or lose. He was certainly one of Queen's College's greatest all-rounders. He was a born leader, a wonderful, wonderful sportsman, who led from the front and simply did not know the word, "lose".'

The game of golf – so I'm told – oft proclaims the man. Nothing tells us more about Tony Greig and his concept of human relations than the stories Paul Ensor tells us of their regular tussles on the course at the Queenstown Golf Club. Two or three times a week, he reckons, after school and in the school holidays. The two of them, for a while, 'were well and truly bitten by the golfing bug'. The caddies employed by the club were all local black kids and Tony was hugely popular with them. 'They would run down the street as we approached, jumping up and down animatedly in an effort to be selected as our caddie,' Ensor recalls, 'I say "our caddie" because we only had one bag between the two of us.' One of their favourites was a lad not much older than them called Jackson. It was clear that Jackson was no mean golfer himself and was keen to show the two boys how good he was. Provided no one saw them, of course. The strict apartheid laws, to say nothing of club rules, would never have countenanced such a brazen contravention. This troubled the intrepid rule-breakers not a jot. Having completed the first hole and now well out of sight of the clubhouse, the twosome became a threesome, on the condition that Jackson carried the bag, which he was happy to do. If anybody hove into view during the round, Jackson would immediately resume the role of caddy only to be offered choice of club when they were alone again. 'Jackson added considerable value to our threesome,' Ensor said. 'In addition to carrying the bag, he had an uncanny ability to track the flight and mark the spot of our balls when they flew off into deep rough. When we would be about to give them up as lost, he would invariably raise his arm and shout, "Over here!" Little he could do when we dropped our shots into the water at the 13th but he always had a few replacement balls in his pocket that we would buy from him at a "discount".'

Quite willing to flout the rules of the club, the laws of the land and the social conventions of the time, Tony was more than happy to play golf with a black kid not much older than him – provided he was good enough. Jackson clearly was, so Tony afforded him the respect of competing with him furiously. 'Naturally, when Tony was playing,' Ensor observed, 'the games would be highly competitive with Jackson being given cigarettes if he won and being relieved of a golf ball if he lost.' *So Tony's smoking habit was formed at an early age?* 'Er ... well, let's just say that Jackson ended up with a great many cigarettes. I often wondered if Joyce or my mother missed those cigarettes carefully removed from their packets.' *Did you have to pay to play? Was it cheap?* 'Actually, because we were playing so often, our pocket money was running out. So one of us had the bright idea of bypassing the clubhouse and starting our round on the 14th tee. We thought this was an excellent idea.'

As I had Paul Ensor to hand, so to speak, a primary source of Tony's boyhood, I couldn't resist plumbing his memory of the two obvious facets of his friend's personality that were to shape his future life. *Did you have any intimation at the time that Tony was destined for cricketing stardom?* 'Back then it never occurred to me that he would be destined for great things. I recognised he was better than me but attributed this to the fact that he was a year older, thus bigger, quicker and more capable.' However, as they got older, hints began to manifest themselves. 'We were having a game of cricket on Rodney King's tennis court on his farm just outside Tarkastad. We were about 15 or so at the time. He was in top form that day, smashing my reasonable bowling to all parts. As I was picking the ball up from the edge of the court, I heard Rodney say to a friend that he was sure Tony would play for South Africa one day.' Ensor admitted being a bit surprised by this. Hylton Ackerman, more or less a contemporary of theirs, had already played some remarkable innings for Dale College against Queen's and Ensor believed at the time that Ackerman was the more gifted cricketer. Only later, when Tony was selected for the Border Schools XI and subsequently South African Schools XI, did the realisation sink in that Tony Greig was every bit as talented as Hylton Ackerman. Mind you, Ackerman was a fine batsman in his own right and would have played for his country had not apartheid and sporting isolation intervened. As we know, Tony Greig's career took another path.

Talking of future careers, could you ever have imagined Tony as a television commentator? The answer was unequivocal. 'Oh yes. My fondest memory of those innumerable games of cricket was the accompanying commentary as we played. Tony would use a mixture of John Arlott to set the scene and Charles Fortune to describe the action .... He would use his commentary to try building pressure, going something like this: "Sobers goes right through Harvey's defence with a superb delivery that crashed into his stumps .... And now, in fading light, O'Neill is about to take his first delivery from Sobers, unsure whether it will be a sharp off-cutter, a short ball or a swinging yorker ...." Riveting stuff.' It seems that if anyone was born with a microphone in his hand, it was Tony Greig.

Girls. Many a promising sporting career has been stymied at the onset of puberty and its accompanying rush of hormones. Little of Tony's earlier experiences with the fairer sex can be gleaned from any of the recollections of brother and sisters. Hardly surprising really. What adolescent boy confides such intimacies with family members? No, the person to ask would be his boyhood friend and once again I am indebted to the detailed and affectionate reminiscences of Paul Ensor. 'Tony had an engaging personality. He was an extrovert, easy-going, an entertaining raconteur, with a good sense of humour and a steady stream of jokes. At some point, he realised that he was attractive to many of the local girls and quickly learned to develop budding attractions into more meaningful exploits. As usual, he shared many of these with me.' *The girls, you mean?* 'Ha ha. No. I mean what happened. A bit boastful perhaps – well, you could hardly blame him, lucky fellow – but never in a demeaning or offensive way.'

The stories that Ensor shared with me would give any mother kittens; it is just as well Joyce is no longer here to read this, though she probably guessed what her high-spirited son would get up to of a Friday night. There would usually be a dance at the local youth club. 'Afterwards, there was the customary car ride,' Ensor said, 'at very high speeds, bound for the Bongola Dam about five miles away. A couple of the guys who were not yet old enough to drive (18 in our country) somehow had access to their parents' cars. The cars would be filled to capacity and with tyres screaming round each corner, they would race each other recklessly to the dam.' *What were your feelings?* 'Terrified. I hated every minute. Tony loved the excitement, laughing and joking all the way, one hand on the wheel and the other arm round one of the girls.' All I can say is that Tony's rapid driving skills never left him.

The discovery in one's teens that there might be more to life than those endless games of cricket in the garden can be perturbing and disconcerting. Before, nothing would distract from the 'Test' match underway, irritatingly interrupted by a call to lunch from a parent. Now, the boy is turning into a man and the new thrill – pub, dance, party, disco, club, whatever – becomes a serious rival to sport.

Sometimes the attractions prove too enticing and one ball eclipses the other. 'When I became a man I put away childish things,' St Paul informed us. Ah, but he never played cricket. If he had, he might have come to a realisation that a balance can be struck; cricket and a social life are not mutually exclusive. Certainly Tony Greig believed the two could be combined. He fully embraced the notion that cricketers needed down time, opportunities to relax and unwind. He enjoyed a party. Those hair-raising car chases to Bongola Dam could well have ended in disaster and tragedy – one remembers the crash, which he had been involved in – but they didn't. For someone as frolicsome and as gregarious as he, the straitjacket of prudence and self-denial would have strangled him. Life was for living. Cricket was a part, a large part, of that life but he was never going to turn himself into a Geoffrey Boycott.

Geoffrey Boycott would have loved to play in this game; Tony Greig, I suspect, would not. The longest Test match ever played took place in Durban in March 1939. Because the series against the visitors, England, was still in the balance come the fifth Test, it was decided to play it to a finish. It lasted ten days and had to be abandoned as a draw because the MCC were in grave danger of missing their boat home. By all accounts, the pitch was so dead that they could still have been playing on it at the outbreak of the Second World War, some six months later. William Morris, later Lord Nuffield, founder of Morris Motors, had been a guest at the third Test, also in Durban, in which the home side had taken a pummelling, losing by an innings and 13 runs. So dismayed was the noted philanthropist by the home side's capitulation that he decided there and then to set up a charitable trust to be used specifically for the nurturing of future South African cricketers. The upshot was the inauguration of Nuffield Week, in which representative school sides from all the respective provinces played against each other. The culmination of the week's festival was a selected South African Schools XI playing against the full senior side of the host province.

Nuffield Week was a huge event in the South African cricket calendar. Anybody who was anybody would be present, casting an eye over the future talent of the national team. The list of captains of the combined schools XI reads like a who's who of South African cricket: Clive van Ryneveld, Jackie McGlew, Graeme Pollock, Lee Irvine, Barry Richards, Hylton Ackerman, Kenny McEwan, Kepler Wessels, Daryl Cullinan, Gary Kirsten, Hansie Cronje *et al*. Hardly anyone who later on in his career played for South Africa had not played in Nuffield Week.

Tony Greig represented Border Schools for four years at this annual jamboree. For the first two years, he felt a little out of his depth, being younger than anybody else and playing against boys from senior age groups. By the third year he had found his feet and was selected for the South African Schools XI to play against the host provincial side, on this occasion Griqualand West, as the finale of the week. As it happened, he nearly missed out on selection; on his own admission, he would probably not have made the cut had not Mike Procter, already a rising star, blotted his copybook and been left out for disciplinary reasons. Nobody seems to remember what Procter had got up to. Tony did not disgrace himself. Batting at No 6, he scored 23 but only bowled five wicketless overs. Clearly he was not needed; the schoolboys beat their elders by 78 runs! The following year, having had to repeat his Matric at Queen's because he failed that pesky Afrikaans paper, he was a shoo-in for the big match, SA Schools versus their hosts, Western Province at Newlands in Cape Town. Number 6 seemingly now his favoured slot, Tony scored only 1 but took 2-42, the victims being the WP opening batsmen. The standard attained by these schoolboys can be deduced from the fact that the full WP side, captained by Peter van der Merwe, the South African captain at the time, only scraped a win by the thinnest of margins, two wickets. Tony was in his element; he began to believe he could cut the mustard at this level, which went some way to inform a decision shortly to be made that would change his life.

Serendipity bowled a gentle half-volley to Tony Greig at this stage in his life. Mike Buss, the Sussex all-rounder, was the coach at Queen's at that time. He and Tony struck up a rapport. It would have been hard not to. Someone as gifted and as enthusiastic as Tony is manna from heaven for a school cricket coach. I played against Mike in the early 1970s and decided to track him down to discover whether he would be willing to share a few memories of his former protégé. 'What stood out a mile,' he told me, 'was the wholeheartedness of the boy. Everything he did was done with such keenness. I've never seen anyone who made more use of his talent. He never thought he would lose. As a player, he perhaps wasn't the most gifted but he made 120% of his ability.' At the time, before returning to school for that extra year, Tony was playing for Border in the B section of the Currie Cup, 'playing in the men's league and holding up well'. Buss remembers being invited to spend time with the Greigs in East London over the long Christmas holiday and enjoying the relaxed informality and the generous hospitality of his hosts. 'Tony was very polite,' he smiled, 'as all South African kids are brought up to be. He always stood up when my wife came into the room.'

Another who remembers the hospitality and friendship of the Greigs is John Snow, later to become Tony's team-mate at Sussex and of course England. He first came across Tony when playing a few games in the area during the Christmas holidays, on leave from a coaching and playing contract. The team was billeted with local players and it was Snow's good fortune to stay with the Greigs. 'Tony in his late teens seemed to be all arms and legs,' said Snow, 'but the bright-eyed, positive outlook and the large degree of confidence and ambition marked him apart. His career path was obvious even then.' This self-assurance manifested itself to Mike Buss as well. 'They're just like that, South Africans, aren't they? Not just on the field of play but generally, socially. Those old-fashioned courtesies. Yes, he was a charmer.' Buss left me with this telling comment of the young Tony: 'He would dive on concrete for you.'

How come then that the idea that he should try diving on the soft, green grass of England rather than the concrete hard pitches of South Africa took hold in Tony's mind? A place awaited him at Rhodes University now that he had finally cleared the hurdle of that missing Afrikaans qualification. A post as history and games teacher at Queen's had been virtually assured him once he had come down from university. His future was pretty well mapped out. However, a year's National Service, compulsory at the time, had first of all to be factored into any young South African man's plans. But the army had rejected him – hardly surprising given his medical record. What to do therefore in the intervening period between school and university? What better way, he reasoned, than to spend his 'gap year' playing cricket in England. He spoke to Mike Buss about it. 'I saw something in him,' Buss said, 'so I wrote to the Sussex committee and recommended him.' It should not be forgotten at this stage that Buss was a youngster on the staff at Sussex, a 22-year-old, hardly a senior pro, so his action must have taken some gumption. Evidently the powers-that-be at Sussex HQ trusted the judgement of their all-rounder and offered Tony Greig a six-month contract at £15 a week. Parental, or more specifically, father's, permission was sought and granted – after all, their son would be back in time to enrol as an undergraduate at Rhodes and Mike Buss would keep an eye on him – and all was set for the big adventure.

The one fly in the ointment was that the cost of his passage – by boat in these early days – would have to be funded by him. Sandy was in no position to find the money. So Tony took up a temporary post as a messenger boy for South African Railways in East London. You will be unsurprised to hear that he managed to scrape together the money without actually doing much work. Already he was learning that charm and cricket was an irrepressible combination in certain company; once his work mates discovered he was a 'famous' cricketer, they seemed to do most of his duties for him.

He departed from East London with Mike Buss bound by boat for England in late March 1966. His family were on the dockside to bid him farewell. Ian can recall the scene as if it were yesterday. 'It was a formal handshake,' he said of his brother's goodbye. 'I was very sad to see him go, as you can imagine.' *Is that when a teardrop landed on Tony's hand?* 'Actually no, that was the following year. On this occasion, we knew he would be back in six months, though that was long enough. The next year he left us we believed we weren't going to see him for three years, the time stipulated for him to qualify as an English player in the County Championship. That was when the tears flowed. As it happened, three months later, we were in Scotland, though we were not to know that at the time.' The bond between two brothers, as it was with the others in his family, was close and this farewell emotional.

The Greigs were a tightly knit unit and Tony was the first to flee the nest. His heart would have been made of stone if he had not viewed his enterprise with some trepidation and, as we are coming to appreciate, Tony was nothing if not all heart.

Chapter 4

The County Player 1966–72

*'Greig sort of filled the screen, like a film star. Well,
that was what he was in cricket terms, wasn't he?'*
Alan Mansell, Sussex wicketkeeper

U NFORTUNATELY, the heyday of passenger journeys
by sea for English professional cricketers bound for South
Africa in the off-season had passed by the time I made my
first trip to that country. In the early 1970s, the oil crisis and the
advent of mass tourism by air had put paid to all that. Nonetheless, my
team-mate, room-mate and erstwhile landlord, Mike Taylor, recounted
numerous stories of his very sociable trips on ships of the Union-Castle
Line fleet, keeping me entertained on many a long car journey. If his
accounts were only half true, I reckon I missed out.

Union-Castle Line was a fleet of passenger-carrying mail ships,
all of which were named with the suffix '*Castle*', distinctive with their
lavender hulls and red funnels topped with black. RMS *Pendennis
Castle*, whose gangplank Tony Greig ascended that day in March
1966, accompanied by his minder and future team-mate, Mike Buss,
made her maiden voyage in 1960 and was now in her prime. She had
already been voted 'Ship of the Year' in 1960 and was known by her
regular passengers as The Fun Ship. I have seen photos of her (she was
sold in 1976 and scrapped in 1980) and she was indeed a magnificent
looking liner, built for speed, the fastest of the fleet, without losing

any of the traditional elegant lines of her sister ships. Mike Taylor sailed on her several times. 'We used to have our air fares paid by the clubs and schools that were employing us,' he explained, 'but we could swap them for berths on these mail ships. So we had 14 days at sea, full board, a pleasant way to relax and recuperate after a hard season's grind in the Championship. We would arrive in South Africa fresh and rejuvenated having had a sort of a holiday on board, so to speak.' *Rejuvenated? From what you told me, the social scene was pretty hectic.* 'You're referring of course to all those table tennis matches we played!' Further than that, he was unwilling to be drawn, on the record at any rate. *What was your accommodation like?* He laughed. 'Well, we were above the Plimsoll line!'

Mike Buss's recollections of the voyage back to England with his ward, Tony Greig, are similarly fond. 'It was fantastic fun. There were always a few other pros on board, so we didn't lack for company. Let me see … who else was with us? Oh yes, Barrie Meyer, Jackie Bond, Dennis Amiss. They were of course senior players to me but everyone got along well. There was a fancy dress party, I remember now. Mrs Meyer and Mrs Bond were accompanying their husbands and they made the costumes.' *What was the theme?* Buss started to laugh. 'It was *Snow White and the Seven Dwarfs.* And Greigy went dressed as Snow White! Well, he could hardly go as a dwarf, could he?'

There was another incident that occurred not long after slipping their moorings at East London, which had its tragi-comic nuance. 'We were in three-bunk cabins,' Buss said, 'can't remember much about our cabin mate but we didn't mind. As a pro cricketer you're used to sharing rooms.' A passenger had been spotted jumping overboard from one of the upper decks. A roll call was immediately ordered to ascertain who it was. The identity of the jumper was narrowed down to the third member of their cabin. 'We'd only just met him,' said Buss, 'it seemed from his letters and personal effects that it was clear he was going to take his own life. Anyway, the rest of the voyage was not quite so eventful.' *And gave you more room in the cabin?* 'Actually no. He'd only booked a passage from East London to Cape Town.' Obviously, if his intention had been to take his own life by jumping overboard. His place was taken by another passenger who made it all the way to Southampton without giving his 'roomies' any further anxiety.

They were met dockside by Mike's brother Tony. The elder brother told me, 'It was snowing! First time Greigy had seen snow. His eyes were wide open as we drove along the south coast to Brighton. My immediate impression of him was of a very tall and very pleasant young man. I liked him immediately. It was obvious he had a strong personality but that was fine. South Africans are like that, aren't they? We became firm friends. Our two families became close. I remember us looking after nine-month-old Samantha when he was in the West Indies.' *Where did you drop him off? I mean, he must have had digs or something arranged for him?* Tony was unsure. 'This is 50 years ago. For a while, he may have stayed with Alan Oakman. He had been a coach at Queen's and remembered Tony. After that, I think he stayed with Mrs Cooper.' Ah yes, the legendary Mrs Cooper. She was a splendid Yorkshire woman who lived about 200 yards from the Hove ground and many a young cricketer at Sussex boarded with her.

That April was unseasonably cold and wintry with occasional widespread snow showers. In the middle of the month, the south was covered with a blanket of snow to a depth of six inches. Tony had to be persuaded that pre-season practice was not always so inclement. He was anxious, impatient to get out there and play. He even took a few balls and loosened up in the nets. Quite what he discovered about the behaviour of English cricket balls, different to the Kookaburra used overseas, on a surface of snow is unrecorded. His future team-mates thought he was mad. Eventually, the snow melted and the cricket started in earnest.

Life in second XI cricket is a strange, hybrid existence. Rarely did counties have 22 full-time pros on their staff in those days, so whoever was in charge – usually the coach – had to augment his team, known as the Dinky Doos (Cockney rhyming slang for 'Twos', never 'reserves' or 'stiffs') with available club players or university students after exams. Thus the team would effectively be split between professionals and amateurs, long after the distinction had officially been abolished. The difference in ability and experience was often marked, sometimes humorously so. Furthermore, the professionals in the ranks could more or less be divided between the keen young thrusters on the way up and the disenchanted old-timers on the way down. A potent recipe for compelling, competitive match play it not always was. Certainly there were occasional passages of play that were keenly contested but too often games drifted without meaning. The whole point of second XI cricket was not to be there. If a player languished too long in the Dinky Doos, he became too comfortable and the edge of battle would be dulled.

As we know, Tony Greig relished a battle. I was intrigued how he coped with the less than cut-throat culture permeating these matches between counties that were neither first-class nor recreational. There was no chance of his being promoted to the first XI, as there was with some of his team-mates, because he was there only on trial. Besides, he was categorised as an 'overseas' player and the qualifying period for them to become a naturalised English player was three years. The most he could hope for was to be picked for a match outside the County Championship, against one of the universities, for example, or against the visiting tourists. And there were plenty of his young team-mates vying for a place should such a vacancy ever present itself. And county pros, ever mindful of the precariousness of their position, were notoriously disinclined to stand down in favour of a potential rival. No, Tony could expect not much more than a season spent learning his craft in the second XI.

Was he happy to do so? What little of him I encountered in my playing career and how much of him I have learned during my research for this book, I would not say that patience was one of Tony Greig's enduring traits. He was anxious to take wickets, eager to score runs, fretful if the game was drifting, intent on getting ahead and winning the match. It was the same with his career. Once he decided that this was the profession he wanted to pursue, Test cricket was the ultimate goal. He didn't want to languish in relative obscurity, eking out a peripatetic, hand-to-mouth existence as a journeyman on the county circuit. He craved the smell of the greasepaint and the roar of the crowd. The loudest roar you would hear at an average second XI game was the occasional bark of a dog, accompanied by the proverbial two old men.

He always said that he enjoyed his apprenticeship in the ranks at Sussex. England was a new and fascinating country and there was much to take in, both on and off the field. He often told the story of when he took himself up to London to visit Lord's, strolling through the Grace Gates, exploring the Tavern Stand and casually jumping the low, white, picket fence to feel the famous turf of the playing area under his feet. Anybody who has ever visited Lord's will tell you that security and officialdom are on a par with those in the Forbidden City in Beijing. How he was not frogmarched out of HQ can easily be explained by one simple fact. He was South African. I don't know whether it has got anything to do with an unconscious sense of entitlement that their upbringing has imbued in them or whether it is just a case that, as a race, they are more confident and self-assured than their Anglo-Saxon cousins but I have found that they are the past-masters of blagging their way in anywhere. Have you ever known a South African cruising around town looking for a parking space? No, they tend to park right outside the front door. Spaces seem to open up for them. Tony would have behaved as if he owned the place – there would come a time when, as England captain, he more or less did – so he was never challenged. He was free to wander … and to dream.

Back at Hove, Sussex's HQ, detailed menial tasks on first XI matchdays must have reminded him of his days as a skunk at Queen's and the dream of playing at Lord's would have seemed a distant one. Contracted players who were not in the team when the first XI were at home were treated like skivvies in those days, expected to pick up litter, clear rubbish from the stands, act as gatemen, help the groundstaff, pull covers on and off the pitch, mop up surface water, run errands, work the scoreboard. The only answer was to get into the first team and avoid the drudgery of a bondservant.

Second XI players had a lot of nets. If no match was scheduled – owing to financial restraints, there were fewer matches on the fixture list than for the first XI – then all contracted players would be expected to turn up every day for nets at 10am. At weekends, they would be farmed out to play club cricket in the local league to obtain match practice and to improve the standard of cricket at the top level of the recreational game. I find it ironic that the modern county player complains about life on the road and the constant diet of car journey, hotel and match, repeated almost without respite during the season, with little or no time for practice. In the second XIs of the 1960s and 1970s, there were more net practices than you could shake a stick at. The question is whether, during the 1966 season at Hove, Tony Greig became bored and stale with this regimen. There is no hint from anybody who knew him that he did. First, his boundless enthusiasm for cricket would not have allowed any such apathy or cynicism to enter his soul. Besides, everything was so new and exciting and talented player though he was, he had a lot to learn about English conditions, English techniques and English ways. Also, he had a bevy of young team-mates, as well as older pros, to get to know and to rub along with. Had he not broken through to the first team, if not now then soon, his enthusiasm might well have waned and he might have decided, after a suitable amount of trial and error, to abandon his dream of playing county cricket and return home. For the time being, he watched and learned and soaked up the atmosphere.

Looking at his record in the second team that season, it has to be said that Tony did not exactly set the world alight. He played well enough and certainly did not disgrace himself but others who would have regarded themselves as contemporaries made more of an impression and some were promoted to the first team. In his defence, we must remember that he was still young, not long out of school – it took him some time before he felt able to drop his habit of calling Mike Buss 'Sir' – and he found the conditions, especially early on in the season, alien. As was pointed out to him, he had 'a lot to learn'. The coach at the club, the man entrusted with keeping a paternalistic eye on the youngsters on the staff, was Jim Parks Snr, so dubbed to differentiate him from his son, Jim Parks Jnr, also of Sussex, the club captain and the England wicketkeeper-batsman. Parks Snr was one of those pros with a distinguished and long-serving career for his county behind him who sort of fell into the role of club coach, as if the post were a cushy little number kept warm for loyal servants. Coaching qualifications and an ability to communicate, especially with the young lads, were not necessarily considered prerequisites.

It seemed to many of us who went through the system that the word 'sinecure' was coined with county coaches in mind.

Of course, there were inspirational and energetic coaches dotted around the counties but Parks Snr was definitely of the old school. A tracksuited trainer and mentor he certainly was not. He took a largely passive role, said little, watched closely and expected his charges to learn by experience. After all, that was the way he, and others like him, had learned to play the game. He was not a nanny; his lads were old enough to change their own nappies. Tony found him impenetrable, though he liked him well enough and respected his experience and knowledge. Happily, Tony was of the type, as Mike Buss had observed at Queen's, who soaked up know-how like a sponge. What the senior pro, resplendent in MCC sweater and blazer, watching impassively as practice went on in the nets, made of him, Tony never knew but he hung on every brief word, every succinct observation that was vouchsafed, and tried to put it into action.

If figures are your thing – and I'm not sure they ever were Tony's – he played in 19 second XI matches that season, had 24 innings and scored 452 runs at an average of 25.11. He also bowled 387 overs, had 1,095 runs scored off him and took 55 wickets at 19.88 apiece. Not spectacular by any means but it is interesting to note that he was having more success with the ball than the bat at this stage of his career. Contemporaries Denis Foreman, Mike Buss and Peter Graves were promoted to the first XI and did not return. Would Tony have accompanied them had he not been on a six-month trial and a South African to boot? Possibly, but it has to be remembered that Sussex were a pretty settled side at the time. In batting, they had seasoned players such as Ken Suttle, Jim Parks, Alan Oakman, Les Lenham and the Nawab of Pataudi. Even Ted Dexter made a brief return from retirement to play in two matches. On the bowling front, they had John Snow, Tony Buss, Don Bates, Alan Oakman and Mike Buss, once he had forced his way into the side. Established players were not for standing down voluntarily, especially if the young Turk (well, a young Springbok anyway) was seeking to supplant any one of them permanently. Such was the curse of county cricket. There was not a lot of movement in a settled XI. It was predominantly a dog-eat-dog environment and if your chance presented itself, you had to make jolly certain you seized it with both hands. Tony Greig would have to bide his time.

Glancing through the pages of the Sussex Handbook for the 1966 season, from which I gleaned Tony's figures, I was struck by something that would become central to Tony Greig's prominence in the national consciousness at a later date. The sheer amateurishness of the bureaucratic administration of the English game cries out from each page. The artlessness of the publication might give rise to the odd affectionate smile but listen to this report of the season's deeds: 'The hospitality shewn [sic] to us was of the usual high standard for which we express our sincere thanks.' Charming, but no player is mentioned by name. And how about this for taking the biscuit? Four pages are devoted to second XI results and averages but 30 pages are devoted to club cricket! Little did the members of the various Sussex committees realise at the time that the 'young South African' they had in their midst would soon be instrumental in flushing away a tired and inefficient management structure in the English game with the tidal wave of the Packer Revolution. It would hardly be apt to compare him to Lenin who was smuggled into Russia in a sealed railway carriage during the Bolshevik Revolution of 1917 but Tony Greig was to cause the establishment much conflict and disharmony and he was already embedded, so to speak.

That is for later. For now, let us pause and amuse ourselves with a typo on page 29 of this edition of the Sussex Handbook. Tony's surname is written as Grieg. Or perhaps it was no typo at all. Maybe the editor knew more than we give him credit for. Family folklore has it that Sandy Greig was a direct descendant of the great Norwegian composer Edvard Grieg. There is some credence in this claim. Grieg's great-grandfather, Alexander Greig (spelt the Scottish way – keep up there at the back!) had fled Scotland after the Battle of Culloden (1746) in which the Duke of Cumberland brutally and finally put down the Jacobite Rebellion. Sensibly, once settled in Norway, Alexander Greig changed his name to the more Scandinavian-sounding Grieg. One assumes, being Scottish and a naturalised Norwegian, he did not play cricket but obviously he could bash out a few Scottish jigs and reels. The music gene never made it to South Africa.

Back to Tony. He did score a maiden hundred on English soil but it was in a Club and Ground match against the schoolboys of Lancing College, hardly earth-shattering in its significance if no doubt pleasing personally. But there was one match in the season when the cricket committee felt it was appropriate to test out the triallist on the grand stage. If you can call the annual match against Cambridge University a grand stage. Still, it was a first-class fixture, which meant he was making his debut for the full Sussex team.

The Oxford and Cambridge university cricket sides had enjoyed first-class status since the early 19th century and for a long time nobody questioned their right. There were periodic golden eras when the England team comprised many who were educated at these ancient institutions. By the mid-1960s, rumblings of discontent about their protected status had started to surface, which swelled into a chorus until matches against either of the universities were no longer designated first-class. That is not to say that very fine cricketers – even those who went on to play Test cricket – did not represent Oxbridge anymore but the increasing reluctance of admissions tutors to take on games-playing undergraduates meant that there had been a steady diminution in standards. A glance at the Cambridge side that faced Sussex in early July 1966 underlines this point. Largely unknown outside the rarefied limits of amateur cricket, the team did include two players of undoubted class who would later become household names: David Acfield, the Essex off-spinner and captain Deryck Murray, the West Indies wicketkeeper.

By this stage in the history of Oxbridge cricket, county players had stopped taking these matches entirely seriously. Many now regarded them as useful opportunities to boost their averages. The less than competitive nature of the game was given endorsement by the Sussex captain, Ken Suttle, who used nine bowlers in Cambridge's second innings in a successful attempt to prolong the game into a third day. One or two Sussex players may well have been going through the motions but you can bet your bottom rand that Tony Greig was not one of them. He contested a game of cards against his grandmother as fiercely as he approached an Ashes Test match. He performed creditably, taking 3-27 in Cambridge's first innings (we can discount the long list of bowling figures in their second), scored 26 batting at No 8 and 25 not out, to see the side home by five wickets. I have known worse debuts.

Tony always maintained that it was in the festival games at the season's end that he started to make a name for himself, which convinced the Sussex committee that it was worth taking a punt on him in the longer term. I am not so sure. I believe that the more knowledgeable members in the committee room at Hove had their eye on him long before. The message I got from the Buss brothers was that Tony had already got tongues wagging with his boundless energy, competitive spirit and insatiable appetite for the game and this had so impressed the powers-that-be that it was a foregone conclusion that he would be invited back on a more permanent basis. For all that, he did play well in these end-of-season games. He scored a century in both innings for Colonel Stevens' XI (captained by a future England team-mate, Mike Brearley) against Cambridge University and took the wickets of Rohan Kanhai and Conrad Hunte for Arthur Gilligan's XI against the touring West Indies. The committee at Sussex had seen enough. At the conclusion of his six-month trial with the county, the secretary called him into his office and offered him a three-year professional contract. The secretary was forced to reach for his phone with his left hand to dial 999 for an ambulance because Tony had bitten off his right.

As it happened, three years was about right. He agreed with his father that if he hadn't 'made it' within that period of time, he would come home and take up a serious profession. In truth, the life of a county journeyman, content to eke out a pleasant if uninspiring existence plying his trade around the shires, never really appealed to Tony. It was the high road or no road at all for him. He loved playing for Sussex and was forever grateful to the club for allowing him to learn his craft as a player and captain but it was on the international stage that he wanted to strut his stuff. He raised his game for the big occasion. Playing in front of a sparse crowd on a windy day at Hastings was not his idea of the grand stage. It is no coincidence that his batting average in first-class cricket (31.19) is inferior to his Test average (40.43). His old friend and Sussex team-mate, Peter Graves, told me a story about the young Tony Greig that is to the point. During that first season of 1966 when Tony was on trial, Graves had been promoted to the first XI. 'Tony was still in the second XI and not playing that day. He came over and sat by me for a chat. "Gee," he said in that Sarf Efrican accent of his, "'All ah want to do, man, is to be out there like you." And it was not long before he was.' Within the three years he had given himself, Tony was in the England side.

The residential qualifications in operation at the time meant that the three years would have to be spent in England, holidays abroad excepted. Thus Tony had to find a job for the winter months. One was waiting for him up in Scotland, at his grandfather's store. As was the Greig way, just because he had the family name did not mean that a cushy number on the board of directors, with a plush office and a company car on hand, was afforded him. Oh no, he was bunged into the electrical department to work more or less as an errand boy. The best thing that could be said about his experience there was that he did not insert the wrong plug into the wrong socket and burn the place down. He survived the tedium and the cold with his customary good humour but it was a mighty relief to escape the British winter for a couple of months to return home for the long Christmas holidays.

Ian remembers his brother's arrival back home with poignant intensity. 'In the months he was at home we did so many simple but exciting things together. He made things happen. He was an ideas man and he did not just talk about it – he did it. He always had time for us – whether it was cricket in the garden with my mates, Peter Kirsten and Neil Fraser, going to the beach and swimming with him, way out of our depth, learning to body surf but always knowing he was there for us.' The ability to get people whom he led to trust him was a characteristic that many who knew him were keen to emphasise. Ian corroborated my understanding that money within the family was 'tight' but that didn't matter; 'the exciting things he initiated did not cost much'. Whatever they got up to, 'there had to be a winner'. As an example of his older brother's intrepid sense of adventure, Ian recounted an adventure, which involved hitching a ride to Kei Mouth (60 miles away) with some very dodgy personnel and being 'dropped off in the middle of nowhere'. In the middle of nowhere in South

Africa is not the same as in England, where the next village is usually only a mile or two away so Ian was justifiably anxious. 'Anske was unworried. "It'll be ok," he said. And it was. Of course it was.'

It was a delightful hiatus, over all too soon. Ian remembers seeing his brother off at East London Airport when it was time for him to come back to England. 'It was a very emotional moment. I loved having my older brother back home and was distraught to see him go. We thought we wouldn't see him for three years. It was going to be a wonderful adventure for him but he was, like all of us, very family orientated and knew he would miss us as we would miss him. I shook his hand – all very formal – and my tears were falling on his wrist. He turned abruptly and walked away.'

1 April 1967. Traditionally, county players reported back to their clubs on April Fool's Day, which always amused me. Who in his right mind would want to don cricket whites and try to catch a hard ball when the temperature is close to freezing, as it often was? I felt sorry for the overseas players returning from warmer climes – those who had not wangled a stay of execution, that is – who had to be dragged kicking and screaming from the warmth of the dressing room for cold and windy nets. There was one occasion when we all gasped in astonishment at the sight of a bulky Barry Richards waddling down the steps, shocked at how much weight he had put on during the winter. In fact, all he had done was swathe himself in layer upon layer of sweaters, many nicked from our bags. Tony was perhaps more used to an English April than most, having spent the past couple of months in Edinburgh; besides, he was raring to go. He *had* to get into the first team and there was no time to waste.

Beneath the noisy banter and relentless jocularity of pre-season practice at any county ground, there is always an underlying tension as jockeying for first-team places takes place. The atmosphere would have been even more strained at Hove in early spring of 1967 for here was a team in flux. Several of the older players, stalwarts of the team for many years, were coming to the end of their careers, the previous season had been a disappointment, and the captain, Jim Parks, had early on intimated that change might be in the air. Parks kept his cards close to his chest as the regulars in the team gave guarded glances at the form and performance of the fringe players and those in with a shout of promotion looked about and wondered who among them was catching the captain's eye.

Tony was catching the eye all right. It would be hard not to. It was not so much his height, his blond locks, his handsome profile and his obvious talent ... it was more than all that. He had that indefinable manner about him that so many South Africans seem to exude. Some call it arrogance. Those of us who have played with and against them and have lived and mixed with them on their home turf, so to speak, would prefer to call it self-confidence. How or why they manifest such poise and assurance, both on and off the field, is a subject for another time but it is true that to their detractors they can appear brash and a bit cocky. Love 'em or hate 'em, they were not to be ignored. Self-assured? Assuredly. Cocksure? Probably. Decisive, positive, audacious? Usually. But loyal, friendly and generous – always.

This is what set Tony Greig apart from his team-mates. And who told me this? None other than his team-mates themselves. Alan Mansell was an exact contemporary of mine. Though born in Surrey, he played for Sussex in all the age groups and we played against each other regularly. He made his first-class debut before me but we remained on the best of terms, even when opposing each other in county games. He was, I suppose, my closest friend in the game, a relationship strengthened even further when we spent six months together coaching and playing in Eastern Province. It was a surprise when he was released by Sussex in 1975 in favour of the older wicketkeeper from Surrey, Arnold Long, and a devastating blow when I learned of his untimely death from Parkinson's disease, aged just 58. He and I shared many a Castle beer in the bar after games – this at a time when Tony Greig was in his pomp as player and captain in the England side – and I was intrigued to know from Alan what it was like having him as a leader in your team. Like a mediaeval warlord, was his answer. 'He led from the front and you had no option but to follow him. Perhaps his battle strategy was not always the wisest but it was the bravest. Honestly, you couldn't take your eyes off him. He sort of filled the screen, bit like a film star. Well, that was what he was, in cricket terms, wasn't he? A larger-than-life character, a huge personality.' We shook our heads at the low-key but insistent carping that revealed itself as an undertone whenever the subject of Greig arose, either in South Africa or in England.

While in South Africa, I could never quite get my head around the less than generous credit that Tony Greig was accorded, even at the height of his fame, by his countrymen, particularly in his home province. 'A prophet is not without honour but in his own country.' Could it be a case of resentment for his having abandoned the land of his birth to seek fame and fortune elsewhere? 'Not good enough for us but good enough for England ... tells you all you need to know about the standard of cricket in the UK, eh, Pommie!' Or, as Barry Richards pointed out to me, 'Look, buddy, we had half-a-dozen world-class all-rounders in the frame at the time. There's no need for me to tell you who they were.' But he did anyway. 'Trevor Goddard, Eddie Barlow, Mike Procter, Denis Lindsay, Tiger Lance, Clive Rice.' When Tony went to England, he was a virtual unknown. His career took off over here but I suppose cricket supporters in South Africa could be forgiven for not following his fortunes as closely as they might. The media was tightly controlled in those days and news was spasmodic and perfunctory.

If Tony Greig was not a prophet in his own land, why was it that he was never *wholly* taken to English hearts either? This I can ascribe to no other reason than residual xenophobia, particularly in the upper echelons of the cricket administration. When he 'defected' to Packer, there were those who said, well, what did you expect? He's not a natural-born Englishman, is he? This was not a view shared by team-mates of England or Sussex but I sensed it at the time, in the press, in the club pavilions and in the members' bars. That is why his record as a Test player has been shamefully overlooked and his influence as a captain, a shaker and mover of the status quo, has been underplayed. It is the reason for writing this book; his reputation needs a thorough dusting down.

County cricket as a workplace was a completely different environment when Tony Greig arrived at Hove in 1966 from what it was when he left 11 years later. Much, though not all, of this change can be laid at his door. A cursory glance at the teams competing in the Championship at this time will reveal counties almost exclusively manned by Englishmen. The scattering of players from other countries would have had to fulfil the statutory requirement – as did Tony – of a three-year qualification period resident in this country. So any overseas player would have forsaken the opportunity to play Test cricket for his own country, preferring the stability (such as it was) of a proper contract and the regular wage of a cricketer doing his job in the only country that had a professional set-up. All that changed in 1968 when, in an attempt to freshen up what was largely regarded as a stale and declining model, the game was opened up to the best overseas players in the world. It certainly revolutionised county cricket. Teams (with the exception of Yorkshire – of course) were by the 1970s augmented with the brightest and the best from around the world and the game was immeasurably the better for it. Not for nothing did it become known as the Second Golden Age of Cricket.

Greig could well have been seen as a trailblazer, arriving the year before the gates were opened. But the point about trailblazers is that they are not always fully appreciated at the time; often they have to negotiate and overcome antagonism and jealousy. Listen to the words of Barry Richards, who explained what it was like to walk into the Hampshire dressing room in 1968, one of the first overseas players, young, naïve and with a lot to prove. Particularly to the older pros who saw him as a threat and an upstart. 'I hadn't yet made my Test debut. I was largely unknown, no matter how good my references were. It was April ... gee, it was freezing. Too wet to play outdoors, so we went in the indoor school. You remember what the indoor school was like.' I do indeed. It resembled nothing like the modern, airy, well lit, superbly appointed sports halls of today. It was more like an aircraft hangar, gloomy, noisy, narrow, dilapidated and depressing. 'Butch White, who was mean, fast and nasty, greeted me with an over of bouncers, following through each time and making sarcastic references to my youth, my lack of experience and the different pitches I could expect over here from the shirt fronts in South Africa.' *Except that he didn't put it quite like that, I'm guessing.* 'Too right, buddy. But that was the way it was. Not an easy baptism for me. It took me a long time to be accepted.' Now, I understand that Tony Greig was a kettle of fish different from the shy, gauche Richards and that he would have made friends more quickly and more easily but even he sensed a certain friction in the Hove dressing room before the season got underway. Was this young nonentity from South Africa going to take the place of one of the regulars? It wasn't exactly animosity but there was an edge to proceedings.

Jim Parks remembers pre-season of 1967 well enough. 'There was no doubt in my mind that I was going to give him a run in the first team,' he said to me, 'his talent stood out a mile. A little raw perhaps but I thought he was worth a punt batting in the middle order and bowling a few overs. He was so tall. I mean he could take a great stride forward and turn a good length ball into a half-volley. And what a fine striker of the ball he was. Oh yes, I had my eye on him all right. Difficult to take your eyes off him, in fact.' Other team-mates were equally impressed, even if at times a bit grudgingly. Peter Graves was laughing as he recounted this story. 'When Greigy got in the first team, he performed some miraculous piece of fielding by diving full length and stopping the ball. 'S**t!' said Tony Buss, 'if he does that, soon we'll all have to be doing it!' Before him, only the best fielders would dive around all over the place. Now, everybody does it.'

Tony Greig's debut in the County Championship had the press purring with admiration as much as when he caught that rugby ball as a ballboy, which had drifted out of play at the local club in Queenstown. The match against Lancashire was at Hove at the beginning of May – a late start to the season by today's standards. Fifty years later, the County Championship is more or less at the halfway point by then. Parks was as good as his word; Tony was at No 5 in the batting order. He found himself strapping on his pads rather more rapidly than he would have wished. Early wickets tumbled and he strode out to the middle with the score at 34/3, soon to be 72/4. He was joined at this stage by Peter Graves, an exact contemporary, also starting off on a long and distinguished career at Sussex, a firm friend and colleague, later Tony's vice-captain, equally blond (they all seemed to be blond at Sussex, we thought) but not quite so tall. They made a contrasting pair. Graves, a leftie, was more conservative in his shot selection, preferring to nudge and push the ball into the gaps; Greig took the route of counter-attack, taking on the bowlers and putting bat firmly to ball. It was gripping stuff. The Lancashire bowlers smelt blood and they were more than equipped to exploit the conditions and the moment. Their seam attack – Statham, Lever, Shuttleworth and Higgs – were all England Test players and Savage, the off-spinner, was good enough to take 100 wickets in a season three times and might well have played for England had there not been a plethora of talented offies around at the time, namely Illingworth, Titmus, Allen and Mortimore. Two inexperienced youngsters, recently promoted from the Dinky Doos, stood between them and a complete breakthrough. Together, Greig and Graves put on 117 for the fifth wicket and turned the game around.

It was Tony Greig who took centre stage, however. This is in no way being disrespectful to Graves. How do I know this? Because Graves told me so himself. 'Tony reached the 90s and I was on 30 odd. I went down the wicket and said to him, "I'll talk you through the nervous nineties, mate." Well, that was a lot of help because I got out for 32 when he was on 99!' Tony soon got his hundred … but he wasn't finished. Jim Parks had this memory of the young man's innings: 'It was simply a marvellous knock. He was such a fine striker of the ball.' Mike Griffith, the Sussex wicketkeeper who took over from Parks as captain the following season, had this to say: 'I have vivid memories of that day. It was a *fantastic* innings and had a huge impact on how his career seemed to blossom from that moment.' John Snow was watching in admiration from the pavilion, side-on to the wicket at Hove. 'He smashed it,' Snow told me, 'it was fearless batting and don't forget this was his first game. I remember him hitting Statham on the up over extra cover for six. And not a lot of people ever did that. We sat there in the dressing room open-mouthed at that shot. Shades of what was to come in his Test innings. It was easy to see right then that he was going places.'

Brian Statham, one of the greatest of English fast bowlers, was now in the twilight of his career but he could still raise a gallop, that of the thoroughbred to which his bowling was famously compared. He took 5-70 that day, three bowled and two lbw, underlining his fabled accuracy, but he couldn't get Greig out. Tony eventually fell lbw to Savage for 156 out of a total of 324. It was the first of several innings in his career that, for different reasons, could be classified as 'great' and for that you would expect him to remember it in detail. Alas, not so for our hero. He always said he remembered very little about it, just the thrill of reaching three figures and the noise and excitement of the crowd as he launched himself into the attack even more vigorously thereafter. He did remember the delight on the faces of the two Buss brothers as he returned to the dressing room when he was finally dismissed. More than any others, they had shown great faith in him both before and after he arrived at Sussex and he was pleased, and relieved, to have repaid them.

Ian Greig told me the story that has been repeated many times but it was one that had escaped me. 'At that time, we were on the boat to England as a family to take up a new life in Edinburgh. Anske later recounted what had happened first ball of that innings. He was perilously close to being given out lbw. The umpire took a close look while they ran a leg bye but eventually said, "Not out". The umpire's name was Dusty Rhodes. "Is your name Greig?" he asked of Tony who was now down at his end. "Is your dad called Sandy, by any chance?" Tony replied that his name was Greig and that Sandy was indeed his father. "Good decision, then," muttered Dusty, "debt repaid!" Later over a beer together, it emerged that Dusty had spent a lot of time in South Africa and knew Queenstown well, having coached at Queen's. In those days, there was a tab system in operation at the club where he would spend time chatting and drinking. The idea was that you would settle up later but obviously Dad had picked up the tab, refusing to allow Dusty to pay. Not that that would have affected in any way the not out decision.' Of course not.

There was time enough that evening when Lancashire went in to bat for John Snow to leave his mark on batsmen and scorecard alike before close of play with the visitors on 21/4, all four wickets falling to the England paceman. Then it rained and rained and rained. No further play was possible on either of the two remaining days and the match was abandoned as a draw. Time and space for the pressmen to file reams of copy about the new golden boy of English cricket. Tony was besieged by the media, by supporters, by well-wishers and back-slappers, by the committee men, and of course he loved it. Whether he started to believe in his own PR or whether he kept a sensible head above the melee, he did not say. It doesn't really matter. The game of cricket is a great leveller. The following match was against Cambridge University. Tony was bowled by David Acfield for 0. For good measure, he was wicketless when he bowled in both Cambridge's innings. Nor did he fare much better in the next Championship match, against Essex, scoring 11 and 23.

Tony's ambition for the season was 1,000 runs. It was not accomplished with ease. In fact it became a struggle. He knew from his knowledge of county cricket gleaned from press cuttings and radio reports back home that the benchmark for a successful season in English cricket was 1,000 runs as a batsman and 100 wickets if you were a bowler. He was not at all sure at this stage of his development if his bowling was of sufficient potency to take 100 wickets but he was as determined as hell to prove to himself he could score 1,000 runs.

He admitted it became something of an obsession. He'd go back to his digs and work out his average and number of runs scored and look at the remaining fixtures to plot a course to realise his goal just as meticulously as any mariner in the English Channel just down the road. There were squalls and currents that threw him off course, as there are in any voyage, but he resolutely pulled himself back on course after every setback. That is another thing about Tony Greig that was never fully appreciated, then or later. He gave the impression that everything came to him easily. It had something to do with his effortless charm and cheerful demeanour. But it didn't. He worked hard at his game and his fierce ambition would never allow a slackening of effort to realise his potential.

There were moments of elation along the way, when everything, timing, confidence, footwork, concentration, all fell into place and he made the game look so infectiously easy and fun. For some reason, Gloucestershire seemed to float his boat. At Hove, he bowled Sussex to victory, taking 8-25, a career best incidentally, and down in Bristol, he scored 55 and 123 against the same opponents. If he had done little else that summer, he would have made people sit up and take notice. He did more than that. He totalled 1,299 runs and took 67 wickets.

He was awarded his county cap and was voted the Young Cricketer of the Year. A young man in a hurry had his foot to the pedal.

By now, the Greig clan were holed up in their northern fastness in Edinburgh, a long way from Hove it is true but not as far away as South Africa. *By now, you were in Scotland, Ian, so presumably your brother came up to see you all once the season had finished. Having resigned yourself to not seeing him for three years, you were reunited within six months?* 'Before then, Murt. Once term had finished at George Watson's College in Edinburgh, where I continued my education, I flew down to London and made my own way down to Hove, where I stayed for three weeks of the summer holidays.' It's worth pointing out that Ian was only 12 at the time, testament to different times, safer environments and the Greig trademark – self-reliance. *Where did you stay?* 'With Tony in his digs. With Mrs Cooper, his landlady. Amazing woman. She cooked, washed, ironed and looked after us. Everybody at Sussex knew her. Years later, when I started playing for Sussex, I stayed with her. 89 Lorna Road.' Never mind the amazing Mrs Cooper. What about the amazing Tony Greig? Not many older brothers would take kindly to a 12-year-old brother landing on his doorstep and queering his pitch, as it were, especially when in the first flush of manhood and eager to make his way in the world. Far from resenting Ian's presence, older brother made him welcome and took him into the bosom of the Sussex family, where he was embraced.

As Ian described his summer holidays in Sussex, for a cricket nut of 12 years it is hard to imagine a more blissful existence. If the first team were playing at home, he would spend the day watching and then, when stumps were drawn, he would go out on to the outfield with the other kids and play until it got dark. If the first team were away, he would take himself off to watch the second XI. And if there was no match, he would bring along his gear and bowl to the lads in the nets. 'I was a good little bowler. I remember bowling Peter Graves once with a "jaffa". Jim Parks Snr, the coach, was watching and he said, "Well bowled, son. I think we'll sign you up!" Ten years later, they did.'

Do you remember any of Tony's finest performances from this earlier stage of his career? 'I remember when he got that 8-25 against Gloucester. I missed most of it because I was involved in my own Test match at the back of the ground with the other kids. Also there was a warm-up match for the Rest of the World against Sussex. They were scheduled to play against England the following week in the Scarborough Festival. I ran round the ground taking pictures of all the famous players.' Reference to the archives reveals that the Rest of the World did indeed comprise famous names: Hunte, Barlow, Kanhai, Graeme and Peter Pollock, Bland, Nurse, Lindsay, McKenzie, Gibbs and captained by the incomparable Garry Sobers. Tony was mixing it with the world's best even now. He scored 42 in the first innings and snaffled the wicket of Graeme Pollock. 'They were wonderful times, great memories,' said Ian. 'Peter Graves was a great mate of Tony's and he looked after me a lot. I would play outside The Long Stop pub and every so often Joyce, the barmaid, would bring me out a Coke, then home for dinner at Mrs Cooper's and then maybe off to the Palace Pier for some fun.'

He saw Tony's hundred against Gloucestershire at Bristol. *Bristol? Presumably you didn't travel with the team. How did you get there?* 'You get the train to Victoria. Then the Tube across London to Paddington. Then—' *No, what I mean is … well, you did that on your own?* 'Yes. "When you get to the ground," Tony told me, "I'll either be in the field or at the bar. Trust me. It'll be OK." And it was. Of course it was.'

He recounts a delightful story, one you just couldn't make up. 'Sussex were playing Kent at Hastings. The family came down and we stayed in the Winchelsea Hotel in Rye. There was a family from Kent staying at the same hotel. They had a boy of more or less the same age as me and we played cricket in the hotel car park until it was dark. Years later we played against each other but this time not in a hotel car park but on a proper cricket ground. I was captain of Surrey and he was captain of Kent. His name? Chris Cowdrey!'

Before the advent of the Sunday League, sponsored by John Player, in 1969, the season's beneficiary would organise matches against local clubs as fund-raising ventures. You need ten other players to make up a team so the younger players on the staff would be dragooned into turning up in the place of the older pros who were disinclined to spend their one day off in the week having a busman's holiday. On one occasion, Sussex were short and the 12-year-old Greig, having thoughtfully put his cricket bag in his brother's boot, donned his whites and played. 'Graham Cooper, Ken Suttle, Richard Langridge, Don Bates, Jim Parks, Mike Griffith, John Snow ... they all were very kind and treated me as one of their own.' Once again, I have a hunch that they might not have been if his brother was less than popular in the dressing room.

Further evidence of the rapidity with which Tony Greig was integrating himself into English cricket is provided by the fact that he was invited on a world tour under the patronage of Joe Lister, the secretary at Yorkshire. You do not get asked on these unofficial tours of the outposts of the cricket world if you are not a promising, up-and-coming force in the game, an acknowledged team man and a good tourist. What exactly defines a 'good tourist'? Many different attributes and many different personalities make up a happy touring party in any occupation or walk of life but it is generally considered that the ideal tourist is one who knows how to use a knife and fork, tries hard and gives his all, remains cheerful even under considerable duress, is gregarious and sociable, remains fit and possesses a cast iron stomach and a forgiving liver. Clearly Tony fulfilled most, if not all, of these requirements. One fellow-tourist was Keith Fletcher. I contacted him and asked him about Tony, how well he had got to know him and whether the young man had enjoyed himself. 'Young man? We were all young men. It was basically a Young England side. Amiss, Arnold, Underwood, Denness. Mickey Stewart was our captain.' *How did you get on?* 'We were unbeaten. Mind you, some of the opposition wasn't the strongest—' *No, what I meant was how did you and Tony get on?* 'Washie? He and I—' *I beg your pardon?* 'Washie. That was Greigy's nickname. Have you never heard of it?' I had not. Fletcher's explanation for this moniker was just a little vague – something to do with a wash peg – but he was adamant that that was what everybody called him. For elucidation and clarification, I sought confirmation from Paul Ensor. Nicknames are usually bestowed at school and if they are good enough, they stick. 'Oh yes,' said Ensor, 'that was what we called him when we were younger. He'd grown so fast and he had these enormously long and gangly legs that we reckoned he resembled a wash peg, so we called him Washie.'

Sorry Keith, you were saying? 'Washie, me and Dennis Amiss became great mates. Later of course, we played in the England team together. It was a *fabulous* tour.' *Where did you go?* 'Where didn't we go? Africa, Pakistan, India, Sri Lanka – then known as Ceylon – Singapore, Bangkok, Hong Kong. Away for three months. We had a bloody good time and Washie enjoyed himself tremendously.' So successful were they that the story goes they (as an unofficial England B side) challenged Colin Cowdrey's MCC team, who had just returned from a successful series in the Caribbean, to a one-off, winner-takes-all challenge match. The gauntlet, if it ever was thrown down, was not picked up.

As happened the previous summer, Ian came down from Scotland as soon as term had finished to luxuriate in the warm glow of his brother's charisma and popularity, staying once again at Mrs Cooper's boarding house. This time he very nearly didn't make it; the rather vague travel plans went awry. 'I was a year older now,' he said, 'but at 13 still a minor. I got picked up by the police at Gatwick, having been put on the plane from Edinburgh. If Anske wasn't there – he wasn't – he told me to walk to the railway station and catch the train to Brighton. The police put me on the train under the watchful eye of the guard and was told that if nobody was there to meet me at Brighton, I was to be sent back to Edinburgh on the next plane.' *Tony was there, I guess.* 'He was there!' Of course he was. 'Another great holiday with my hero – much the same as the previous year.'

Apart from the continued thriving of their South African all-rounder's reputation, Sussex's 1968 campaign was largely undistinguished save for two events. The first was the return of Lord Ted. E.R. Dexter had retired from cricket to concentrate on his political ambitions. One would have thought that had he seriously contemplated seeing out his days in the House of Commons, he would have sought an easier entry into Westminster than challenging the incumbent MP for Cardiff South East, the future prime minister, James Callaghan, in a safe Labour seat. But Lord Ted always did it his way and never shirked a challenge. He contested the seat as a Tory candidate in the 1964 general election and performed surprisingly well, polling 22,000 votes, only 8,000 fewer than his experienced rival. And then in 1965 he broke his leg savagely in the most bizarre of circumstances. Having run out of petrol, he was pushing his Jaguar towards a nearby petrol station when it ran out of control and crushed his leg against a warehouse door. So far, so Lord Ted. Then, halfway through the 1968 season, he decided to answer increasingly shrill calls for his return to national colours by digging out his old cricket bag and playing for his old county against Kent. So far, so more Lord Ted. The mention of his old cricket bag was not a figure of speech. Tony and his team-mates remembered the smell when it was opened that morning in the dressing room at Hastings. Clearly nothing therein had been washed or disturbed since he had last played years before. But it was not long before Dexter was being remembered for what he was famous for – the quality and the ferocity of his strokeplay. With the same old brown bat that he had never thrown away and with no meaningful practice or preparation, he put the Kent attack, including Underwood, to the sword, rolling back the years with a breathtaking double century.

Tony's son, Mark, was not yet born but he remembers this innings as if he had been there in person because his father never stopped referring to it. 'Dad talked about Dexter's return to the team three years after he retired for two reasons,' he told me. 'It allowed him to see first hand what a brilliant batsman Ted Dexter was. It also had a huge impact on team spirit at Sussex, something Dad always emphasised.' Dexter's recall to the England team was but a formality. He played in the fourth and fifth Tests against Australia, performing adequately, but the MCC tour to South Africa that winter was cancelled, owing to what became known as the D'Oliveira Affair, so Ted Dexter once more packed his bag, this time for good, and Test cricket never saw his genius again.

The traditional finale of the season was the Gillette Cup Final at Lord's, at a time when limited-overs cricket was in its first flush of youth, with the grand old ground packed to the rafters and the BBC televising every ball. In fact it was Ted Dexter, when he was captain of Sussex, who had been the first to work out and implement the right tactics to approach this novel form of the game, carrying off the trophy in the first two years of its existence, in 1963 and 1964.

Now in 1968, Sussex were back at Lord's, without Dexter this time, to face Warwickshire. It wasn't in truth a memorable final. Sussex's total of 217, augmented with 41 from Tony, is a paltry score by today's standards (off 60 overs, don't forget) but it seemed enough before a remarkable innings by A.C. Smith saw Warwickshire home with three overs to spare. Tony called the innings 'lucky'. Perhaps it was. But I know Alan Smith well and he always says with a broad grin on his face that it is remarkable how many of his best innings were 'lucky'.

Despite the run in the Gillette Cup, 1968 had been a disappointing season for Sussex, doubly so as they had set out with such high hopes and good intentions, none of which had been realised. Tony was still a junior player but he was as aware as anyone of the rumblings of discontent at the club. This was the first time he had encountered internal politics and its damaging effect on a team within a professional environment. The captain of the side was the captain; you followed him come hell or high water. That was how he had been brought up and that was the way he was used to playing. Now everybody was muttering in corners. Was it time for Jim Parks to go? And if so, who would replace him? In the event, Parks saved everybody the trouble by standing down voluntarily. Or was he sacked? People have differing views, differing memories. I talked to Jim and he was unequivocal about the sequence of events.

'I stepped down from the captaincy after the 1968 season,' he told me. 'I was keeping wicket, batting at four and captaining the side and it was all too much.' *As well as playing for England.* 'Actually, I'd played my last Test on Colin Cowdrey's tour to the West Indies that winter, when I had lost my place to a certain Alan Knott. And the rest is history,' he added with a laugh. His successor as captain was Mike Griffith, Marlborough College and Cambridge educated, a fine all-round sportsman (he gained Blues for hockey and rackets as well as cricket) but on his own admission short of talent at the highest level. In one sense, he was an ideal fit as captain of Sussex, a role traditionally filled by ex-public schoolboys who were, it was believed, to be made 'of the right stuff'. He was also, and remains, a cultured, intelligent, urbane and affable man about whom team-mates and opponents struggle to find a bad word. He later became president of the MCC in 2012, which gives you a clue of the measure of the fellow. He was unfailingly helpful when I asked him to contribute to this book and was quite honest and open about his limitations as county captain.

'I was too young,' he reflected ruefully, 'and I never really cemented my place in the team as a player, other than that I was captain. It was a difficult situation for me, my father being who he was and all that.' Indeed. I could see the potential problems, the conflict of interests and the veiled charges of nepotism. His father, Billy Griffith, having gained a DFC as a glider pilot carrying airborne troops at the Battle of Arnhem, was appointed captain of Sussex in 1946, made a century on his debut for England on the 1947/48 tour of the West Indies, played two more Tests in South Africa the following winter, took up the post of assistant secretary to Ronnie Aird at the MCC, and finally became secretary of the club in 1962 where he remained *in situ* until his retirement in 1974. By any yardstick, Billy Griffith was a considerable figure in the game at a time when his son was captain of his old county. The old school tie as a system was working well, would have been the muttered curse of disenchanted critics. In fact, the distinction between amateurs and professionals had been abolished years before, in 1962, but there were those who believed that vestiges of the old ethos still lingered. Tony Greig, amongst others, did not feel that the appointment of Mike Griffith was in Sussex's best interests. He would have preferred the elder Buss, Tony, as captain. Still, the choice had been made and as is the way with professional cricketers, they simply got on with it.

Taking into consideration, Mike, that you did not have the wholehearted support of Tony, how did you get on with him? Was he a menace to handle? 'No, not at all. We were good friends and remained so until he died. He wasn't always the easiest to handle on the field but when I say that, I don't mean that he was disruptive or anything. It was just that he had this burning passion to get on top, to win the battle. So he would go out with all guns blazing when perhaps more caution was required. You can't attack *all* the time. But what a player! Always cheerful, great company, popular in the dressing room, with members and supporters and the general public. We were cut from different cloth, I suppose. I was more reserved. I preferred to do things quietly, more understated, if you like. Greigy was never understated!' *Was he ever impatient to take over from you? I mean was his ambition obvious and all-consuming?* 'Well, it was clear that he was ambitious and the captaincy of Sussex was a role that he thought he could do well. But it was never a problem between us. He never made life difficult for me.'

In spite of reservations about Griffith's youth and inexperience, Sussex didn't have a bad year in 1969, finishing a creditable seventh in the Championship table and having another decent run in the Gillette Cup cut short at the semi-final stage. And what of Tony Greig's season? He did not score 1,000 runs this time; he fell agonisingly short by two runs. However, his bowling was coming along in leaps and bounds, if you will forgive the description of his run-up and action. He took 69 wickets, more than anybody else, and his bowling average remained satisfyingly lower than that of his batting. I say 'satisfyingly' because the benchmark of the effectiveness of an all-rounder's contribution to the team effort is traditionally gauged by the batting average exceeding the bowling average. If the numbers are reversed, you are in trouble and wonder about next season's contract. However, Tony would not have been satisfied with his tally of 998 runs at an average of 23.37. He knew he would have to do better than that if he was to progress, which he was determined to do.

Again, I am indebted to the Sussex Handbook of the 1969 season for providing an interesting morsel of information, meant no doubt as a casual throwaway remark but one that was about to have enormous significance. 'Tony Greig captured the most wickets,' wrote the club chairman, 'and his likely inclusion in the proposed visit of South Africa next season would leave a gaping hole.' Questions, questions, questions. Was the writer totally unaware of the political ramifications of the D'Oliveira Affair, the cancellation of the MCC tour to South Africa the previous winter and the Stop The Seventy Tour campaign organised by Peter Hain to disrupt South Africa's visit to these shores the following season? (It was never going to happen and sure enough the tour was called off not long after the publication of this yearbook.) And was Tony Greig really pencilled in by the South African selectors as a possible Springbok? Wasn't he now 'English'? Furthermore, what were Tony's views on his nationality and choice of country to represent? Was he ready for Test cricket, whichever team wanted to pick him?

Let us put away, swiftly and once and for all, which country he was going to play for. It was Mike Griffith's father, Billy, who raised the subject and gave him good advice. He told Tony at the end of the season that he had fulfilled his three-year qualification period and that he would be available to play for England the following year. Tony was astonished. Not that the three years had slipped past almost without his realising it but that the possibility of his playing Test cricket had not entered his mind. In his view he was not nearly good enough – yet. However, there was another consideration to take into account. That winter, he was asked to go on a tour of the Caribbean with the Duke of Norfolk at the helm. The possession of a South African passport would not ease his passage from island to island so he scooted off to avail himself of a UK passport, to which he was fully entitled, given his father's Scottish nationality. Now he was a fully registered Englishman playing in the English professional game, qualified to play for England if and when his country came calling. Sussex wanted to remove him from their list of overseas players – obviously, because they wanted to draft in another top-class cricketer from abroad, which, to be frank, they had dire need of. Simples! Ah but no, they had reckoned without the arcane workings of the Registration Committee at Lord's. Even until 1973, by which time he had played 19 games for England, Tony was still classified as an overseas player.

'Bureaucracy is the death of all sound work,' said Einstein. I never understood his theory of relativity but that observation would have been reason enough in my eyes for his Nobel Prize.

To fill in a gap before he set off for the Caribbean, Tony returned to his *alma mater*, not as a history teacher but as cricket coach, playing a few games for Border in the B section of the Currie Cup. By now the 'Scotland experience', as Ian described the family's less than harmonious time in Edinburgh, had ended and they were back in Queenstown. Ian was in the under-14 side at Queen's and Tony was in charge. A match had been lost that should have been won. He asked the team who had dropped catches. Two boys put up their hands, one being Ian. 'Using a stump,' he told me, 'Tony gave the other bloke one and then me one – twice as hard.' Inwardly I winced. This was 1969, don't forget, and anybody with anything about him would have got the cane in a less forgiving era than now – but with a stump! Ian was hurt, physically and emotionally. 'How could he do that to me? His own brother. I cried myself to sleep that night. He came up to me next morning at breakfast and discreetly said, "Sorry, *boet*, but I couldn't show the rest of the team that I was favouring you. And you took it well!"' I guess Tony thought he had overstepped the mark, even for those days, and felt guilty at doing so. Ian's love for his brother, and his respect, remained undimmed. 'That was Anske. Hard but fair and never accused of favouring his own.' Possibly the mortification of a beating by his own brother was soothed by presents of a new bat, gloves and pads every year. 'One year he bought me new Garry Sobers boots, crepes and spikes – no wonder I adored him.' Slowly the young boy was growing up. He could now begin to understand the difficult circumstances that obtained at home and could see for himself the role that his brother had now assumed as the family rock. 'I saw how Tony supported Mum. He adored her and was there for her. She probably worried more about him throughout the whole of his life than the rest of us put together because of his epilepsy. She felt he was vulnerable and this was his only weakness.' It is instructive to point out that at no stage in any of our conversations about their elder brother have Tony's siblings betrayed the slightest hint of jealousy at Tony Greig's favoured position in the family hierarchy. Family members are notoriously judgemental about their upbringing and have long memories. Tony, it seems, was loved unconditionally.

There were still opportunities for high jinks, even if Tony was the school cricket professional. Ian was in hospital with a deep and badly infected boil. 'Paul Ensor was doing some holiday work as a part-time nurse at the hospital,' Ian recounted. 'Anske was an inveterate prankster. He and Paul dressed up as doctors in theatre gear, with masks covering their faces. They came into the ward announcing they were going to "remove said boil". They rolled me over, removed all the dressings and with huge tweezers in hand, one of them (Paul) said, "This is going to hurt." I was beside myself. Petrified. Then I heard Tony laugh!'

There were plenty more opportunities to laugh once Tony had made the hop across the Atlantic to join up with the Duke of Norfolk and his peripatetic band of young, promising, English professionals, captained by Colin Cowdrey, who was no longer young, no longer promising and certainly no professional. In the touring party were characters whose careers were to become inextricably bound up with his over the next few years: Underwood, Old, Ward, Sharpe, Denness, Birkenshaw, Hobbs as well as his county captain, Mike Griffith. The duke, England's premier peer, a lovely man, a cricket enthusiast and a gentleman to his bootstraps, caused great amusement in the party when he first addressed them. 'I want this to be a totally informal relationship,' he told them, 'please don't call me Your Grace or anything like that. Sir will do.' The matches were deemed first-class so it was no holiday interspersed with a few desultory exhibition matches. Tony performed tolerably well. He scored fifties against St Lucia, Trinidad and Tobago and Barbados and chipped in with useful wickets from time to time. However, someone accompanying the party had sat up and taken notice. Not just anyone but the *eminence grise* of cricket journalism, E.W. Swanton. He saw something in the tall, gangly young man that his experienced eye recognised as untapped talent. 'Greig showed a glimpse of great all-round potential,' he wrote, 'above all that he had a big heart in that enormous frame.'

Glimpses are seductive. Was Tony Greig ready for Test cricket in 1970? He was of the opinion he was not. His county form seemed to bear that out. His bowling average for the season had outstripped that of his batting – not a good sign. Sussex had another season of mid-table mediocrity, though their enduring love affair with the Gillette Cup had meant another trip to Lord's in September, where they lost disappointingly to Lancashire. Tony's contributions in both three-day and one-day cricket had been mixed; certainly not the stuff of which public clamour would demand his inclusion in the England side.

Yet there was something about him that attracted attention and it was not only Jim Swanton who was tantalised. After a heavy defeat against the Rest of the World in the first Test of the summer, the England selectors made wholesale changes for the second at Trent

Bridge, jettisoning five players in all, with A.W. Greig making his international debut as one of the replacements. Tony had arrived!

Well, not quite, not really. There are two shades of meaning for 'to arrive'. In the first sense, it is true that he had reached the destination – Test cricket – of a journey on which he had embarked four years earlier. But in another sense, he did not think he had arrived at all. He had accomplished nothing at this level, he had not pulled it off, made the grade, 'nailed it'. As he strode into the dressing room at Trent Bridge, he may well have affected confidence and nonchalance but he was acutely conscious that his South African accent set him apart from the outset. He would have to make a big impression, and quickly too, to feel comfortable and accepted in this environment.

Perhaps he put too much pressure on himself to make a mark. Perhaps he was not quite ready. 'It might well have been a bit early for him,' Peter Graves admitted to me. 'No doubt the selectors wanted to see how he adapted to the bigger stage.' The team selected for Lord's did not excite and were roundly thrashed. 'England have seldom been represented by a duller side,' wrote John Woodcock in *The Times*, a point taken up by Graves. 'Like most sports, cricket wanted an exciting star and Greigy was approaching that.' Worth a punt, in other words.

Trent Bridge is a ground where traditionally the ball swings, especially if conditions are favourable. On a damp and cloudy morning, Garry Sobers would probably not have wanted to win the toss but win it he did and no doubt with a wry smile chose to bat. Typical English conditions in which the typical English seamers prospered. But hang on a minute. Bowling at one end was not an Englishman but a South African. 'Greig was soon making an impression,' reported *Wisden*, 'taking 4-59.' He had snaffled Richards caught down the leg side, Kanhai caught at slip and Engineer caught behind. And, wonder to behold, he persuaded Sobers to drag on a wide long-hop. 'Amazing how many wickets he got like that,' laughed John Snow when I quizzed him about Tony Greig's 'golden arm'. I have heard this argument many times, that some bowlers seem luckier than others. I would counter that – as would any bowler – by asking the question, what about all the magical balls delivered that somehow don't get a wicket?

Snow recalled one incident in particular that illustrated this very point. He was bowling to the Middlesex No 11, Dennis Marriot, in a one-day game when 'they were getting dangerously close to our total. He heaved a couple of good length balls from me over the midwicket boundary. Tony took over from me. First ball a long-hop. Dennis hit it straight up in the air. All part of the plan, Tony would grin.' John Barclay was another who told me all about Tony's ability to get wickets with long hops and full tosses. 'He had such self-belief. Every ball he thought he would get a wicket.' *And as a batsman?* 'Terrible! I'd get him out loads of times in the nets.' Barclay wasn't being entirely serious here. He pointed out that Ian Botham was another who seemed to get wickets by sheer force of personality alone and he too was never regarded as a dedicated netter.

'With the ball now swinging freely,' continued *Wisden* in its report on the Trent Bridge Test, 'the medium-pace bowlers soon got on top.' And who was the England medium-pacer at the other end? None other than Basil D'Oliveira, another South African. All right, his back-story was significantly different to that of Greig's but the paradoxical twists of the situation were becoming more and more delicious. England never relinquished their grip on the match, winning by eight wickets and thereby squaring the series one-all. With a further three wickets in the second innings, seven in all, Tony could have been forgiven for feeling thoroughly satisfied with his international debut. But he wasn't, still worrying whether he really belonged on this stage. Scores of 55 and 22, but no wickets, in the third Test and 5 and 0 but 4-86 in the fourth provide no conclusive evidence of a glittering career in the making but neither do they represent failure. However, he was dropped, harshly, I think, for the fifth and final Test that summer, a fact that did not entirely surprise him. I wonder why. Perhaps *Wisden* can provide a clue. 'The turning point came when Greig at second slip dropped Intikhab off Snow. Had that chance been accepted soon after the last day's play began, the teams could well have gone to the Oval all square.' Oh dear. Greig had dropped the series in effect. That is what our correspondent seems to be conveying. But everybody drops catches. And Greig dropped fewer than most. 'Don't forget those big bucket hands of his for catching,' John Snow reminded me, 'he was brilliant in the slips.' This from the man off whose bowling Tony had dropped that all-important catch. All that needs to be said, I think, is that selection processes for England teams were a lot more capricious back then.

Peter Lever of Lancashire took his place for the final Test at the Oval. Talk about *carpe diem*. Lever certainly seized his chance by taking 7-83, admittedly in a losing cause but thereby he cemented his place on the forthcoming MCC tour of Australia, under the captaincy of Ray Illingworth. However, a touring party is made up of more than 11 players and surely Tony Greig had done more than enough to be included in the 17 places. He had not. As he freely admitted, the failure to be selected provided the single most disappointing moment of his cricket career.

As it happened, being overlooked might well have been a blessing in disguise. Lever was part of a very effective fast-bowling attack, spearheaded by Snow, in Australia that winter. Illingworth's team regained the Ashes and if Tony Greig had been a member of the touring party it is perfectly possible that he would have found himself on the fringes of the side, a bit-part player, not much more than a net bowler. Far better he take the winter off, recharge his batteries and rethink his game. As it was, he was present at one of the most heartening – and humorous – moments of Sussex's season. Two bowlers were vying for the distinction of being the first to take 100 wickets; one was the aforesaid Peter Lever and the other was Tony's team-mate, Tony Buss. By the middle of August, both were in touching distance of the honour. The prize this year was a brand new Ford Capri. At the Oval, where Lever was playing for England, Illingworth won the toss and elected to bat. Lever had no option but to put his feet up for the day. At Blackpool where Sussex were playing Lancashire, Sussex were in the field and Buss had the ball in his hand. First round to the man from the south coast resort. But Lever's team-mates at Lancashire did him proud by putting on 265 for the first wicket. Buss's goal of four wickets was seemingly out of reach. Second round to the man from the north-west seaside resort. Buss, however, was indefatigable. With Greig filling in at the other end, similarly lacking success, he bowled and bowled and bowled. Eventually, he broke through, dismissing

David Lloyd for 124 and Barry Wood for 138. In a marathon spell of 42 overs, now practically on his knees, he secured his 100th wicket and the prize of the Capri. Peter Graves held the all-important catch and remembers Buss chasing him around the infield, his exhaustion suddenly forgotten, finally catching up with him and jumping on him. The spectators were bemused by this outbreak of frenzied delight; Tony Greig and the rest of the Sussex team were highly amused. Peter Lever, feet up in the Oval dressing room, probably reflected on what might have been, calculating whether an England cap (later to be taken away of course) was worth more than a Ford Capri.

Rather than twiddle his thumbs – he was no good at inaction – Tony Greig took up a coaching post back home, this time at St Andrew's College in Grahamstown and accepted Geoff Dakin's offer to play for Eastern Province, marking his debut, you will remember, with that epileptic fit at The Wanderers in Johannesburg. A member of the St Andrew's first XI remembers clearly the effect a coach wearing his England sweater had on the boys in the nets. Antony Clark opened the batting for the school team with Robbie Armitage, with whom I played for Eastern Province several years later. Armitage had a successful career in the Currie Cup and sadly died of cancer at the relatively young age of 45. Antony Clark became a teacher and successively headmaster at his old school, St Andrew's, Gresham's School in Norfolk and Malvern College in Worcestershire. I too taught at Malvern but Antony took over as head after I had retired, to his immense relief. He was keen to share with me his memories of Tony Greig as his cricket coach. 'He was like a god to us. I was 13 or 14 at the time and like all the other guys in the team, I found him inspiring and hugely enthusiastic. Our school was renowned for its cricketing prowess. We had 12 members of staff who had played first-class cricket. Far from being slightly irritated by this young chap who'd just played for England, everybody was simply bowled over by him. I think he bought my parents' Opel Kadett to drive around in.' Two incidents in particular remain firmly lodged in Clark's mind. His team, the U15s, were on tour in Cape Town. He was batting at No 3 and had got off to a good start. 'And then I nicked one to second slip and walked. Tony was furious with me when I got back to the pavilion.

I thought the guy had caught it – he certainly claimed it – and as the umpire said nothing, off I went. Tony said it was a bump ball and *never* was I to do that again! He took me round the back of the pavilion and gave me a sharp whack on the backside with a bat.' At least it wasn't a stump. The point is that both Ian Greig and Antony Clark did not resent corporal punishment, it was the way things were done in their day and both reckoned it did no harm and possibly some good, but neither of course (both being schoolmasters) would endorse the practice. The other occasion was when Clark and his school chums went to Port Elizabeth to watch Tony playing for EP. 'I was strolling past the players' enclosure and a voice called out, "Clark! Come up here!" So I did and he introduced me to all the EP players, including Graeme and Peter Pollock, Chis Wilkins, Lorrie Wilmot and others. Then some bigwig came in and demanded to know why this kid was in the dressing room, and not in the politest of language either, I might add. "He's my guest!" exclaimed Tony, "so show him a bit of respect." I was only 13 at the time.'

When St Andrew's toured England in 1973, with Clark now in the first team, Tony arranged for the boys to use the nets and all the facilities at Hove. 'It was a great honour for us. He was marvellous and took a great interest in our progress throughout the tour. He got to know everybody, remembered our names and could not have been more helpful and charming. He was just a lovely, lovely man.' Finally, he had this to say about Tony Greig. 'St Andrew's were great rivals of Queen's College, where he went to school. Two of my favourite Queenians, as their old boys are called, happen to be cricketers. They are Kenny McEwan and Tony Greig.' I had no quarrel with either choice.

Another silver lining – though red might be more appropriate, given that the subject is love – was that Tony Greig married Donna Reed in March of 1971. Had he been in Illingworth's team touring Australasia that winter, he would have been in New Zealand by then. You can just imagine the response of England's captain had the young Greig asked permission to miss the second Test against the Black Caps in order to fly back to South Africa to get married. 'You're here to play creekit, son, not gallivant round world chasin' lasses.' Or words to that effect. Donna Reed? Who was she? When did she burst upon the scene? I need to go back a year or two.

The Greigs and the Reeds were not close friends but given that they both lived in the relatively confined white community in a small town like Queenstown, it would be surprising if they were not known to each other. Donna in fact was a classmate of Tony's sister, Molly Joy. Donna and Tony, as they grew up, were acquainted but there was no hint at that stage of any romantic attachment. Suddenly, according to all accounts, Donna bloomed into a beautiful and confident young woman. When Tony's eyes fell on her when she returned to Queenstown after attending a finishing school in Switzerland, they lit up as if he had just spotted a half-volley. It could be said that the finishing school had certainly done its job. In that winter of 1968/69, he was coaching at Queen's College. Sally Ann takes up the story: 'Donna was camping with her family in Gonubie, a seaside town just north of East London. Mum and Tony were on a drive in the vicinity and Tony saw Donna walking in shorts and bare feet. And that was it!' In the words of Mark, Tony's son, who was not there at the time, obviously, but his father had told him the story often enough, 'My mum really blossomed into a stunner after leaving school. When he saw her in Gonubie, she raised his eyebrows .... I don't know the details of their courtship but I'm sure Dad didn't waste any time.' Indeed not. Half-volleys were there to be hit.

Half-volleys are easily dispatched but a long innings takes care and patience to construct. The life of a cricketer is a peripatetic one, not the ideal bedrock for a sustainable relationship. Tony came back to Sussex for the 1969 season and Donna accompanied him. He played cricket; she did some modelling work. I quote Mark's words again: 'They had fallen for each other but with Dad's cricket commitments and maybe because they were still young, they had not settled down into a serious relationship.' Tony returned to Queenstown to coach once the season had finished and Donna went off to Switzerland, working as a fashion designer and attending a cookery course. Mark itemised his mother's attributes: 'She had a great sense of fashion and was an amazing cook. It's easy to see why Dad fell in love with her ... beautiful, intelligent, confident and a domestic goddess. She even ironed Dad's underpants.' I wish to record at this juncture that the beautiful, intelligent, confident woman at the ironing board while watching her husband dismiss Tony Greig for a duck on the television, described in the opening chapter of this book, would not ever have ironed my underpants.

Whether the Duke of Norfolk had a patriarchal word with the young Tony Greig while on tour to the West Indies that winter is not recorded (from what I have heard about His Genial Grace I would not be surprised) but Tony was determined when he stepped off the plane at Heathrow after his homeward flight from the Caribbean that he was going to put his love affair with Donna on a firmer footing. But the bird had flown. She was in Switzerland, not waiting for him, slippers laid out, a glass of wine in hand and dinner in the oven. Undeterred, he hopped on a plane to Geneva, the way Tony did, sought out her whereabouts and rushed towards her to gather her in his arms, as they do in films. Comically, he slipped in the snow, took her out at the knees and they both tumbled in a heap on to the icy floor. Whether he decided, as he was already on his knees, to propose there and then or whether he waited for a more opportune moment remains unclear but what was as clear as the driven snow of the surrounding Alps to Donna Reed was that Tony Greig was not a man to be taken lightly. They were married on 20 March 1971.

The wedding was the social event of Queenstown's year. Most of the town's population were in attendance as well as many others from far and wide. Mark's description: 'Donna wore a beautiful traditional, long, white wedding dress with Tony and his groomsmen in morning suit, top hat and gloves. Tony's best man was Paul Ensor ... Ian arranged an impressive cricket bat guard of honour outside the church. Peter Pollock made the speech at the reception and hundreds of telegrams arrived from all over the world, including one from Donald Woods.' Sounds perfect. But like all professional cricketers, any thought of a long, languorous honeymoon was cut short by the necessity of reporting back for duty on 1 April.

Blissful married life may have been for Tony but the day job was proving more low-key. County cricket was settling into a pleasant enough routine; he was now firmly established in the Sussex team and his figures bore all the hallmarks of a player destined for a long and successful first-class career; 1,196 runs and 76 wickets represented a wholly satisfactory season. Sussex maintained their safe but uninspiring position in the middle of the table, though their love affair with the Gillette Cup came to a premature end in the first round. So far, so satisfactory. But was county cricket mediocrity motivation enough for the ambitious South African? Some thespians are perfectly content to tread the boards in a continual round of the provincial footlights; it is a respectable and agreeable existence if a little lacklustre. The stars of the theatrical firmament crave recognition in the more salubrious surroundings of the West End. Tony wouldn't have been happy or fulfilled to see out his cricketing days in the regional outposts of Hastings, Folkestone, Gloucester, Derby, Chesterfield, Colwyn Bay, Leyton, Westcliff, Huddersfield and countless other no doubt charming but humdrum venues. He might have been forgiven for remembering that occasion when he first came to England and visited Lord's, dreaming one day that he would play there. He could have been there – perhaps should have been – but taking his place that summer in the England changing room in the famous old pavilion for Tests against Pakistan and India was the Yorkshire all-rounder, Richard Hutton.

There being no MCC tour overseas that winter, Mr and Mrs Greig returned to South Africa so that Tony could resume coaching at St Andrew's. No sooner had he donned his whites, put on his England sweater and made his way to the nets than he received a phone call from Lord's. He had been selected for the Rest of the World team to tour Australia. Yet again, there is a certain irony in this turn of events. In spite of much diplomatic to-ing and fro-ing between Canberra and Pretoria, even at the highest level, the proposed tour of Australia by South Africa had been called off at the last moment, for pretty much the same reasons that the Springboks' tour to England had been cancelled a couple of years earlier. The straw that broke the camel's back had come during a last-ditch attempt to save the tour made by Donald Bradman in person, during a meeting with the South African prime minister, John Vorster. The mood swiftly turned sour as the two men spoke. Bradman wanted to know why blacks in South Africa were denied the opportunity to represent their country. Vorster replied that was because they were intellectually inferior and couldn't be expected to cope with the intricacies of the game of cricket. 'Have you never heard of Garry Sobers?' was Bradman's famously uncompromising reply. He knew there and then that the tour was dead in the water so he returned home to offer to the press this damning indictment: 'We will not play South Africa until they choose a team on a non-racial basis.' Nor did they, and neither did anyone else, for 21 years, until non-whites were at last able to represent South Africa.

Bradman was not one to sit idly by. He contacted the aforementioned Garry Sobers and asked him to compile a Rest of the World side to take on Australia in a five 'Test' match series to replace the Springboks. This time, the decision not to award these matches Test status was announced *before* the cricket started but that took away not one jot from the fierceness of the competition. To those taking part, it was Test cricket in all but name. And yes, you've guessed it. The Rest of the World comprised a number of South Africans, notably the Pollock brothers, as well as Tony Greig (now English) and his contemporary and great friend, Hylton Ackerman, playing alongside West Indians Sobers (captain), Kanhai and Lloyd. They gelled, as you would expect, beautifully. Tony was a great fan of Sobers. The greatest all-round player in the history of the game did not always get a favourable press as a captain. Tony was not in that camp. He thought Sobers's leadership qualities were remarkable; nobody else could have led that side full of superstars, he believed, and got them to play as a team.

But I run ahead of myself. Tony quickly packed his bags – cricketers are used to this – and hastily arranged for a replacement from Sussex, Alan Mansell, to take over his coaching duties. For Tony the call to arms was a godsend. For the boys of St Andrew's it was a catastrophe. Antony Clark reminded me, as if a reminder were needed, that the new Mrs Greig was a beautiful woman. 'The captains of all the school teams were regularly invited to their flat for tea. We all hoped that Donna would be there and were mightily disappointed if she wasn't. And then he went off to play for the Rest of the World!' How could he! The disappointment on Clark's face was clear to see 45 years later.

'Seize the day, put very little trust in tomorrow.' If I had to put my finger on the moment when Tony Greig took hold of this aphorism and shaped it to his own purposes, I would point to this tour of Australia with the Rest of the World. He grabbed his chance with both hands. The series, eventually won by the Rest by the narrowest of margins, 2-1, provided compelling and entertaining fare, including probably two of cricket's greatest performances. At Perth, in the second 'Test', Dennis Lillee announced himself on the scene as a giant of the game by dismissing eight of the world's finest batsmen for only 29 runs. The side was bowled out for 59. Farokh Engineer, who opened the batting, had the dubious distinction of being dismissed twice by Lillee before lunch as the Rest followed on. The second outstanding feat was provided by – who else – Garry Sobers. Up until the third 'Test', by his own standards, he had been having a quiet time of it, bothered as he was by personal problems, trying to reconcile with his estranged wife. Furthermore he had been dismissed for a duck in the first innings and had been angered by Lillee's persistent bouncers. With his team facing defeat and doubtless the loss of the series, he scored a majestic 254. Donald Bradman described the innings as 'probably the greatest exhibition of batting ever seen in Australia'. I wonder if he was taking into consideration any of his own.

As we are on the subject of Bradman – and Tony never wavered in his admiration for the man – I asked Mark for confirmation of an amusing story that his father never tired of telling. Sure enough, he confirmed that every word of it was true. When Tony landed in Adelaide to join up with the party after his flight from South Africa, he was met 'by an old bloke, a little man in glasses wearing a woollen cardigan', Mark recounted. 'Dad didn't catch the little man's name but was happy to give him his bags while he went to the bathroom to freshen up.' When he returned, together with other people who had met him, they repaired to a coffee shop. 'They started to talk about cricket and the little man seemed to be a bit of an expert on the subject. Eventually, Dad turned to him and asked whether he had "anything to do with cricket around here".' The little man admitted that yes, he did, a little. 'Dad had no idea who he was talking to.' At which point Garry Sobers arrived. Tony stood up, thinking that

Sobers was going to shake his hand but Sobers walked right past. 'He stretched out his hand to the little man, saying, "Good morning, Sir Donald, I'm so sorry I'm a little late. I was caught up in the traffic."' *How did your father cope with that? And more to the point, what was Bradman's reaction?* 'Dad nearly died when he realised the *faux pas* he had made. Sir Donald thought that the incident was hilarious ... and he never let Dad forget it either. Every time they met after that, he would come up to Dad and say, "Have you got anything to do with cricket around here?"'

Throughout that series, Tony revelled in the atmosphere, the competition, the gladiatorial contest, the best of the best standing toe to toe with each other and neither giving an inch. He was born to perform on this sort of stage and now he began to believe it himself. He didn't just hold his own; he shone as an all-rounder of the highest class: 4-94 in the second 'Test'; 66 in the third; 70 in the fourth; 6-30 in the fifth. These were figures that the England selectors, next time they convened, could not ignore. To put it all into context, Greig played in all five matches and flourished. His rival, Richard Hutton, played in the first, was dropped and never played international cricket again.

The England selectors could not, and did not, ignore Tony Greig any longer. The Australians were in town for the 1972 season and to nobody's surprise, A.W. Greig made his Test match debut – that sounds so bizarre as he had already played nine of them, in all but name – at Old Trafford on 8 June. Once in the team, he never left. That is until he quit of his own volition following the uproar surrounding the Packer affair. Australia were his opponents on his debut and in an unbroken sequence of 58 Test matches later, they were also his opponents in his last Test at the Oval in 1977.

His career in the England team will concern us in the forthcoming chapter; for the meantime, I wish to concentrate on his time at Sussex. 1972 was a disastrous season for the county. They finished second from bottom in the Championship, third from bottom in the John Player League and were knocked out in the first round of the Gillette Cup. Drastic changes had to be made. Mike Griffith, who had led the side since 1968, had clearly had enough. 'I no longer wanted to be captain,' he said, 'the job had ceased to be enjoyable.' Among the many problems that had assailed the young leader during his reign was the problem of John Snow. Now the undisputed spearhead of the England fast-bowling attack, he was beginning to find the daily grind of county cricket irksome. Some, team-mates included, inferred that he was falling out of love with the game. That wasn't true. He was criticised for not trying when he was bowling for Sussex and for turning it on whenever he donned his England sweater. Undoubtedly there were times when his pace dropped alarmingly and he would mooch around in the outfield, cutting a moody and disconsolate figure. I witnessed one of these occasions first-hand. I was at the non-striker's end when Snow was summoned to bowl by his captain, Tony Greig. The game was at Basingstoke, which has a considerable slope and unsurprisingly your fast bowler would usually bowl downhill. That is what Snow had done in the first innings. Hostile doesn't begin to describe the torrid time we had of it. We always believed that he found an extra gear whenever Barry Richards was playing and this day was no different. He took 6-62, including yours truly for a duck. By the time we were batting in the second innings, the pitch had gone dead and he had lost interest. However, Greig was insistent he bowl ... but from the 'wrong' end, that is, uphill. He was distinctly unimpressed. 'I dunno, Jack,' he complained bitterly to Jack Crapp, the umpire, as he handed him his sweater, 'reduced to a bloody medium-pacer now.' But he bowled. Sometimes he more or less refused, a downing of tools that would be a headache to any captain. In fact, he was disciplined and dropped by Sussex for 'not trying'.

In fact it was less a case of not trying than of pacing himself. He could not bowl fast, really fast, all season. He wasn't built for a heavy, sustained workload, like Fred Trueman, Butch White, Ken Higgs, Jack Flavell and others; he was more of a thoroughbred than a workhorse. In the same way you would not expect a potential Derby winner to take to the jumps at Aintree, so a lissom, whippet-like John Snow needed careful handling, which he did not always get. Mike Griffith provided an interesting insight into the mercurial John Snow, comparing him to the more gregarious and less temperamental Tony Greig. 'Snowy was very much a loner. He was not what I would call a "dialogue man". Basically, he bowled when he wanted to and generally you would give him his head. Greigy, by contrast, would bowl any time, even if the conditions didn't suit or if the batsmen were on top and the pitch was dead. He was willing to plug away even if there was nothing in it for him.' *You played under him once he had replaced you as captain. How did that relationship work out?* 'Fine. I was happy to stand down and let somebody else make all the decisions.' *How was he tactically?* 'All action. Always trying to make something happen. Nothing wrong in that *per se*. That's what you need sometimes. But at other times, you can't go out all gung-ho. There are occasions, especially in a two-innings match, when you need to defend and consolidate.'

Griffith wanted to compare Greig's captaincy with Mike Brearley, under whom he had played at Cambridge and who is regarded as one of the best post-war captains. That jogged my memory of a story about Brearley. Middlesex were playing Nottinghamshire at Lord's. Mike Brearley and Garry Sobers were the two captains. As the pair of them made their way out to the middle to toss, one of the Notts players (wild horses won't get me to reveal his identity) remarked from his vantage point at the visiting dressing room window, 'There they go, one with too many brains and one with none at all.' Hmm. Well, we can take it as read that Brearley, with a First in Classics, was the intellectual but Sobers won the toss. And the match! But it wasn't Sobers that Griffith wanted to compare Brearley with but Greig. 'One took the academic, forensic approach towards tactics. The other was the swash and buckle warrior. Now, some people react better to one type of leadership and others to the other. Personally, I thought Greigy was not so good with those players of lesser ability who did not share his enthusiasm and self-confidence. Brearley took time to analyse the flaws in less gifted players, especially chinks in their temperament. But perhaps it is a trait of all-rounders not to become bogged down with constant analysis.' A fair point. If you are constantly at the forefront of the action, as Tony was, there is less time for scrutiny and reflection. Griffith continued, 'Greigy got better at this the longer he captained the side. And then of course, he had to concentrate on captaining England.'

Chapter 5

County Captain 1973–77

'Well, that's Greigy!'

The usual response of his team-mates in the
Sussex dressing room to another over-
enthusiastic utterance or plan

TONY Greig was appointed captain of Sussex for the 1973 season, a post he held until 1977. In all that time he was a continual presence in the England team. Furthermore, he was handed the England captaincy in 1975, which must have provided even further distraction from his duties and influence on the south coast. Given that he was never totally involved with his club – by that I mean he never had a full season in county cricket as captain: when he was there, of course, he was totally committed – it is difficult to come to any definitive assessment of his reign as Sussex captain. In his time, the county won no trophy. In the County Championship, Sussex under his stewardship finished successively 15th, 15th, 17th (bottom), 10th and 8th. But can his captaincy be judged solely on silverware? That is what I was anxious to find out. Greig's team-mates were the ones to ask.

First, it is as well to remember what sort of environment he was operating in. County cricket in the 1960s and 1970s had changed very little, in culture and management, since the Second World War. The distinction between amateurs and professionals had been abolished in

1962 but ten years later you would have been hard-pressed to think of much that had changed in the meantime. Counties were still run on patrician lines; the players, believe it or not, were the 'servants' of the club and the various members of the committee were in charge. The system very much reminded me of a school. The *raison d'etre* of any school is the pupils but the teachers are in control. Of course, there are many committed, dedicated, kind and helpful members of staff, just as there were knowledgeable, approachable and supportive members of the committee but the over-riding impression as a player was that your fate was being decided by faceless laymen (no women, as I recall) whose only qualification for their role was an enthusiastic predilection for attending meetings.

On the first page of the Sussex Handbook for 1973 is listed all the officials of the club. There are no fewer than 102 of them. To keep them all busy, there are 21 functioning subcommittees. I doubt any of the other counties were much different in their governance, though Sussex did have a reputation at the time of being a bit more archaic than most. Tony Greig, a man impatient for success and restless for change, looked at this unwieldy management structure and his heart must have sunk.

It was not Greig's place, nor his intention, to reform the way Sussex was run. This would happen throughout English cricket eventually by osmosis, hastened by Packer and his revolution. However, Greig was not at all happy with the status quo. His predecessor as captain, Mike Griffith, had this to say about Tony's relationship with the committee. 'Take this example. Mark Faber, a young batsman on the staff, would turn up to play in his Porsche. Hmm, thought Tony, why haven't I got one of those? Faber was part of a rich and influential family – the publishing giant – and he had a considerable private income. But Tony felt it right to push for higher salaries for the players. He was popular with the rest of the boys on the staff because of this but one can imagine his brash manner didn't go down so well with members of the committee. I wasn't so pushy. I never felt quite comfortable doing that. I couldn't see myself as a rabble-rouser.'

One or two former players felt that Griffith suffered unfairly in comparison with his successor. Paul Phillipson referred to the enormous pressure the young man was under, in addition to the millstone around his neck of having the MCC secretary as his father. 'Quite a few of the old guard, Parks, Suttle, Bates, the Buss brothers, with Dexter popping in for the odd game on his motorbike, did not provide him with unqualified support. They weren't all that easy to manage.' John Barclay agreed. 'Mike did his best. But Sussex at that time were not a very good side. Not all the blame for their poor showing could be laid at his door.'

What everybody was agreed upon was that the appointment of Greig as captain ushered in, if not a new dawn, then certainly a radical shift in mood. 'Suddenly, things felt different,' said Phillipson. 'There was an enthusiasm and anticipation around the team which I had not sensed before. He would do some crazy things but that was all part of his up-and-at-'em personality.' Another who took note of the new leader's attitude was Peter Graves, soon to be appointed his vice-captain. 'He led by example. This is what we're going to do, he would explain, now let's go and do it! The belief rubbed off on most of us. There was a feeling that you didn't want to let him down.' *How was he tactically?* 'OK. Well, he wasn't a Brearley but he had charisma and flamboyance. Bit naïve to begin with but he gradually grew into the job. If he made a mistake, he'd hold his hand up and apologise. Basically, he led and we tried to follow him. One in, all in. That was the team ethos.'

That Tony did not always get it right on the field seemed not to affect his standing within the team, particularly the younger players. This no doubt stemmed from his compelling personality and greater experience, especially once he had become England captain. His players were prepared to forgive the odd injudicious comment and the occasional eccentric decision in the field because he was so fiercely determined for the team to win. Take the vexed matter of man-of-the-match awards and other concomitant prize money on offer. Should they be kept by the individual or shared out on a pro-rata basis with the whole team at the end of the season? Tony Greig was firmly of the belief that all winnings should be shared and it was no surprise that his young acolytes were broadly of the same opinion. 'Greigy was always 100% for the team,' said John Spencer, an ever-present member of the

Sussex bowling attack in the 1970. 'He always felt we should share, even though he won more man-of-the-match awards than anyone else.'

Tony Greig was manifestly and wholeheartedly on the side of his players. Hence their forbearance when things went spectacularly wrong, as they were always likely to do from time to time with such a man in charge. Spencer points to one catastrophic misjudgement by their captain. Warwickshire were visiting during the 1975 season on the back of two successful run chases (259/3 v Surrey and 371/5 v Notts). Full of runs you might say. 'There's *no way* I'm going to declare against that lot,' Tony announced to his team before the start of play. 'Well, Greigy *did* declare,' Spencer recalled, 'and they knocked off the required 355 runs with an hour to spare for the loss of just two wickets! Jameson, Amiss, Kanhai and Kallicharran found the flat wicket and short, fast outfield at Hastings very much to their liking.' *How did he explain away that one?* 'He didn't. He simply told a very deflated team back in the dressing room, "Never again!" he said. "Until the next time," whispered someone near me!' The team never doubted him because his stated intent was to play positive cricket and if sometimes it went wrong, well, that was infinitely better than setting your stall at the outset to avoid defeat. 'That's Greigy,' was their usual, wry reaction.

Spencer bows to no man in his admiration for Tony. 'Even before he became captain,' he said, 'Greigy was a dominant and influential figure in the Sussex dressing room, taking a big part in the discussions and tactics and often at the heart of all the banter. He was refreshingly honest in team talks and said what he thought in open forum.' This candour amongst team-mates – no blame, no shame, as it is called in these more open days – was less conspicuous than you might think back then. There was a pervasive sense that survival in the professional game depended more than anything else on self-reliance; basically, you worked things out for yourself and looked out for number one. Cricket as a team game was a flexible notion. All right, there were 11 of you out there but all that seemed to count was individual performance. And never forget there was someone back there in the pavilion waiting and eager to take your place. Such an atmosphere did not always lend itself to free and generous sharing of ideas and opinions. The best teams, the more successful ones, it seemed to me, somehow managed to marry personal ambition with the collective good. Mind you, there were also sides that could not stand the sight of each other but still worked out how to win. It would seem from what I heard from Tony Greig's contemporaries that he banished selfishness, or at least its outward expression, in favour of the common bond.

'Greigy discouraged – and actively detested – those who preferred to air their negative thoughts behind his back,' continued Spencer. '"Stand up and be counted" and "If you can't say it to my face, don't say it" were two of his favourite sayings.' *Did you feel you could criticise him then?* 'He positively invited it, understanding that if an alternative view was put forward, then that implied a reservation about the way he was handling things. This was a new concept to county cricket in the 1970s and was indicative of his innovative style of leadership.'

Paul Phillipson was not so convinced that such a brutally honest approach suited everybody though he accepted it was a refreshing change. One or two of the more diffident characters in the team sometimes felt nervous around their captain. 'Jerry Morley was very intimidated by Tony to the extent that it affected his game. Alan Mansell, our wicketkeeper, a delightful but somewhat shy lad, was often told by Greigy to stand up to the stumps when he came on to bowl. Sometimes Greigy would bowl these off-spinners – cutters really – and if nothing was happening, they would get faster and faster. Against Yorkshire in 1975, the third-day pitch at Hove had deteriorated and poor old Manse had a nightmare time of it. The Yorkies chased down 195 and he let past 30 odd byes that innings. Greigy was unimpressed and Manse always thought his captain had lost faith in him that day, though in fact Alan Mansell is remembered as a top-class keeper.'

That Tony Greig may have been less sympathetic to introverted and under-confident team-mates – a point made earlier by Mike Griffith – found an echo in the recollection of Roger Knight, who played for Sussex from 1977/78, while he was a teacher at nearby Eastbourne College. 'Those in his team needed to be strong because he was always positive and never prepared to take a backward step. I do not remember him putting an arm round someone's shoulder.' That never bothered Knight personally because by then he was a senior pro, who went on to captain Surrey. Someone who later became a headmaster, secretary and ultimately president of the MCC was unlikely to be intimidated by anybody, even the England captain, but he saw that Tony expected, nay demanded, the same self-confidence from his team that he himself demonstrably possessed.

One former player and contemporary of Tony's I was anxious to interview was John Snow. This volatile but hugely talented fast bowler always had a reputation for being difficult to handle. With a ball in his hand he exuded menace and he was capable of devastating spells, seemingly able to instil in the best batsmen a sense of inferiority and helplessness. It seems extraordinary, looking back on his career, that he was only picked to go on three overseas tours with England, giving rise to the suspicion that the authorities at Lord's distrusted his uncommon and particular personality. The selectors saw fit to pick him for just 49 Tests in total; this for one of the finest bowlers to pull on an England sweater since the Second World War. It still leaves cricket supporters shaking their heads in bafflement. Allegedly he was left at home when lesser players were picked to go on MCC tours ahead of him because 'he was not a good tourist'. Yet Colin Cowdrey on tours of Pakistan (1968) and the West Indies (1969) and Ray Illingworth on the Ashes tour of 1970/71 had no problems handling him. In fact both lavished praise upon Snow for being the single most important reason for the success of the team. So, how did Tony Greig find him? How did he manage to motivate Mr Difficult?

You would have thought that it was a lot easier to talk to John Snow today than to Tony Greig but you would be mistaken; Snow is an elusive man who does not make himself readily available for nostalgic chats. It took the intervention of Sally Ann Hodson – a clear indicator if ever there was of the regard with which Snow held her brother – to persuade him that I was genuinely interested and to be trusted with his memories. We met in a West Sussex pub and, wonder to behold, the mercurial and moody John Snow was as affable, informative and helpful as it was possible to be. He looked a lot less menacing these days with a pint in his hand than he used to be clutching a ball. John Snow had mellowed. I could scarcely believe it. This is what he had to say about his team-mate and friend.

'The qualities of positiveness, confidence and ambition ran through Greigy like the wording in a stick of rock.' A stick of Brighton Rock, he could easily have said, having a literary bent himself with published poetry to his name. Tony's captaincy, he averred, was based on those same character traits, which 'led to some bizarre decisions at times, though he could usually make an argument in defence of them'. Snow, in common with all other team-mates of Tony's, defined his leadership style as 'leading from the front' which demanded a wholehearted response. 'He was the first to bring diving stops to the English game,' commented Snow, 'and invariably left the field covered in grass stains.' It is Snow's contention that the fielding at Sussex, and later England, improved immeasurably as a consequence. 'You have to remember that county cricket in the 1960s was a very staid affair,' Peter Graves explained. 'By that I mean that certain players, usually the fast bowlers or the elder brigade, were not expected to, and never did, throw themselves around in the field. All that changed with Greigy,' said Graves. 'I remember once he chased a ball to the boundary, dived and attempted to scoop it back from the rope. In fact, he was unsuccessful but all the naysayers in the team, such as Ian Thomson, Don Bates, Tony Buss, looked at each other, shook their heads and muttered, "Christ, if he's diving around all over the place, soon we'll all be expected to be at it." And they were!'

'Tony had a mystical thing called charisma,' Snow continued, 'and he brought its shining light to brighten and liven up the Sussex dressing room. The older ones watched slightly warily and then, somewhat bemused, shrugged shoulders, smiled and said, "Well, that's Greigy for you." While the younger ones were given the freedom and encouragement to be themselves more and follow him.' *Was he a force of nature from the first minute he entered that dressing room?* 'Not really. He was suitably respectful at first but as time went on, his natural gung-ho attitude and exploits led to him being more vocal and forceful over time.' This reminded me of something Barry Richards had told me about the younger Greig. 'He was always respectful and polite but articulate, forthright and sensible. Mind you, there were lots of great players around at the time so he didn't really stand out as the next big thing. That is, apart from his height. So the course he chose, to seek fame and fortune in the UK, was undoubtedly the best thing for him. I liked the guy. I got to know him better when he came to Sussex and we always enjoyed each other's company.'

Another point Snow made, about giving the younger players a free rein, resonated with those under his command to whom I spoke. John Barclay was particularly impressed with the new regime, 'Probably because I was one of the first to benefit from it,' he said with a wry grin. To his great surprise, Barclay was thrust in at the deep end for the first Championship match of the 1973 season, Greig's debut as captain, against Kent at Hastings. 'He brought me on to bowl early on, even though there was no suggestion that there was any spin in the wicket.' *But John, you always told me, a claim borne out by my experience of facing you, that you didn't spin the ball.* 'Very funny, Murt, but listen up. Graham Johnson played all over a perfectly flighted yorker and then Colin Cowdrey clipped a half-volley straight to Greig at mid-wicket. Two wickets. A good day, eh?' *What happened then?* 'Ah, a certain individual by the name of Derek Underwood bowled us out twice, for 67 and 54. Yet Greigy wasn't downcast. He took the view that nothing much could have been done about it, so let's put it behind us and think of the next one.' *Who else did he bring into the side from the Dinky Doos?* 'Groome, Morley, Spencer, Phillipson, Mansell.' *Just like a kindergarten, John.* For all our joshing about the old days, Barclay was keen to make this point: 'I liked Greig and admired his spirit. He was great with us youngsters, a bit like an inspirational teacher. He made you feel good about yourself and keen to do well so as not to let him down.'

Barclay's reference to Tony's youth policy was given endorsement by his recollection of a match in which we both played and remembered clearly. Sussex v Hampshire at Hove in 1975. Batting first, Hampshire declared at 401/5. On this occasion, Snow did not have it all his own way as Barry Richards and David Turner both made big hundreds. Then Andy Roberts ran amok, scything through the Sussex batting, taking 2-24. Scything through the Sussex batting by taking only two wickets? That sounds like nonsense. But as was often the way with Roberts, the queue of injured cricketers at the A&E department of the local hospital should be taken into consideration. Sussex only totalled

153 and were asked to follow on. It was the evening session and I shall never forget the intensity of the cricket as we, or rather Andy Roberts, strained every sinew to make inroads into Sussex's second innings. We were held up by two Old Etonians, M.J.J. Faber and J.R.T. Barclay, not the most recognisable opening pair in the country at the time. Barclay explained. 'Greigy took me aside and said, "John, I want you to open. You're as good a player of fast bowling as there is. Just the man for the job." Against Andy Roberts! Well, of course I had to do it. Couldn't let him down, could I?' Sussex were short of another opener, with Jerry Morley now *hors de combat*. Apparently, Greig spun the same line to Mark Faber, so out they came to open, these two unlikely heroes, to face the most hostile bowler in the world, with the wind and the slope in his favour and the light of battle in his eyes. I was terrified and I was on the fielding side! I was positioned at silly mid-off, barely half a dozen yards away from the batsman, the only man in front of the wicket. Two things I remember about my station. First, I had to ferry the ball by hand back to Roberts after each ball because he wasn't a great catcher and if the ball didn't land accurately in his outstretched hand, he wouldn't move a muscle to gather it. Secondly, I had a box seat, as it were, as two very brave youngsters fended off everything that Roberts could fling at them. They defied us – him – until stumps. As they trudged off the field unbeaten, Peter Sainsbury – not one to dispense praise freely – clapped them off with the words, 'Well played, lads. Got to hand it to you – that wasn't very pleasant.' The point of the story, apart from the heroism of our two Etonians, is that Tony Greig believed in his youngsters … and they repaid him. The footnote to it all was that Faber & Barclay (sounds like a firm of solicitors) did not prevent Hampshire winning by an innings on the following day. Sussex were all out for 113. Actually, they were not all out. Only eight batted; the other three were 'absent injured'.

Barclay and I fell for a moment into silent reflection over the sad and premature death of Mark Faber, a contemporary, fellow cricketer and friend, at the age of only 41. If ever anybody could be said to have been born with a silver spoon in his mouth it was the Fabulous Faber, as we called him, or Fabes as he was known to his team-mates. His grandfather was Harold Macmillan, he went to Eton and Oxford, he was an obscenely talented all-round sportsman and he played cricket as a professional for fun, a throwback to the old amateur days. For all that he was a genial fellow who hit the ball hard and drove his Porsche even harder. There were many amusing stories about him that did the rounds but the best has gone into Sussex folklore and concerned Tony Greig, his captain at the time. It was at Trent Bridge and involved an irritating last-wicket stand by the Nottinghamshire tail-enders. Bill Taylor, a renowned rabbit, took a shine to a short ball, swung at it and skied it in the direction of Faber in the long grass. John Spencer filled in some detail. 'Fabes, bless him, was a bit slow off the mark so Greigy shouted at him, "Catch it!" But Fabes didn't quite get there in time. The ball bounced and sailed about five feet over his head.' John Snow took up the story. 'Faber was known as "Racer" because he wasn't the quickest over the ground and Greigy gave him some almighty stick for what he perceived as slack fielding. Racer would have none of that. "Greig," he shouted back in his best Etonian accent, "If you swear at me like that, I'm going to get in my car and drive home!" Of course we all fell about laughing.' Spencer added a further ingredient. 'Greigy bellowed back, "No you won't! I arrived after you and I've blocked your car in!" Of course he apologised afterwards. Nobody took offence at these outbursts because it showed how much our captain wanted to win. We wouldn't have wanted him any other way.'

Tony was charismatic but a hard taskmaster in pursuit of success. 'He was a tyrant around the ground,' said Phillipson. 'All of the younger players were in awe of him and not a little scared of him as well.' He remembers when Tony grabbed him around the middle, pinching his flesh and telling him to "get rid of this". Phillipson was outraged. 'I wasn't fat. I was at my fighting weight for a pace bowler and a good deal fitter than most in the squad. In hindsight, I now realise that Greigy was telling me I liked my beer too much, being a typical student, and needed to change my lifestyle. Anyway, we just laughed off things like that and took it on the chin. "That's Greigy" was our customary response.' These occasional outbursts of passion, even temper, were regarded as merely symptoms of a tremendous desire for improvement. 'His comments were usually fair,' said Snow, 'and if there was any slight, there was invariably an apology afterwards.' Roger

Knight had this observation on the relationship between Greig and Snow. 'He and John Snow had their arguments on the pitch but both respected the other. You see, as a captain, Tony had confidence in his own ability and expected the same from his team. When someone leads from the front, there will always be someone behind with his own views but he was a popular character with an open and friendly disposition. Actually, I rather suspect he enjoyed a good argument.'

Man management. Leadership always boils down to that one, all-important attribute. Geoffrey Boycott did not always get on with his captains (and neither did everyone get on with him when he was a captain) but he was firmly in Tony Greig's camp when he was England's skipper. 'He was clever enough to realise his strengths and slight weaknesses,' he wrote once, 'he was never a man to let his own ego get in the way of doing his job properly.' Part of this was an honesty and straightforwardness in his dealings with his players. Spencer remembers being dropped from the side for a Gillette Cup match at home and being acutely disappointed not to be playing in front of a large crowd. 'Greig's explanation was quite simple,' he said, 'I was told I was dropped because I was not bowling well enough. "I can only pick 11 players and you're not in the best 11 for today." No fancy words about "rest" or "rotation" or "squad system"; there was no scope for misinterpretation. But it was followed by words of encouragement.'

Sussex always seemed to play with a smile on their faces during those years and we, their next-door neighbours and local rivals just along the south coast, always enjoyed playing against them. There were not many cheerful, vivacious captains around at that time but Greig was one of them. He played hard on the pitch and would do anything to win but once hostilities had ceased, he could be the life and soul of the party afterwards. 'He had a great sense of humour,' Spencer told me, 'and a fund of stories to entertain us with and his quick wit produced plenty of smart one-liners. Intervals and rainy days were never dull as he recalled incidents on the road, especially from his England tours, and he was never afraid to allow himself to be the butt of his jokes and stories.'

One of these stories resonated with me because it involved the 12th man, a role I was more than familiar with at Hampshire. Once you had received the fateful tap on the shoulder from the captain, accompanied by an apologetic smile and a few regretful words, you became the team's dogsbody for three days. Occasionally, the opposition would have no 12th man, for whatever unaccountable reason, and your duties would be doubled, though to be fair, it was a good way to hear all the gossip in another camp and you were rewarded at the end of the day with a few quid from grateful opponents. Such a divine decree fell upon Paul Phillipson one day up in Blackpool when Sussex were playing Lancashire. 'It was the last day of a Championship match at Old Trafford and we were chasing a fair total,' he recalled. 'A44s Lancashire had no 12th man, I found myself fielding for them when one of their players was indisposed. When Greigy came to the wicket, he looked as if he meant business. Jack Simmonds was bowling and I was stationed at deep long-on. Greigy hadn't even got off the mark but he charged down the wicket and hit one like a tracer bullet to my right. Somehow I clung on to it just in front of the boundary. It was a hell of a catch, even though I say it myself.' If you have never been put in that unenviable position, it is difficult to imagine the contradictory feelings that overwhelm you at such a moment. There is the elation at having pulled off something remarkable; at the same time, you have done it *against your own team*. It seems like treachery and nobody should ever have to be put in that position. You can't drop the ball deliberately because that goes against every instinct in your body as a professional cricketer. All you can hope for is that the ball doesn't come anywhere near you. 'The Lancashire lads were cock-a-hoop,' Phillipson went on. 'Greigy was incandescent, especially as Sussex fell two runs short of the target. At the end of the game, the Lancashire boys were ribbing me, hailing me as a hero and sticking a Lancashire cap on my head. "You don't want to go in there," they said, pointing to our dressing room, 'You should come and change in here with us.' But as usual, once Greigy had calmed down and I felt brave enough to go back in, he generously congratulated me on a good catch.'

It is remarkable that so few 12th men have gone on to take up a career as a butler or *maître d'* as the training has been done as a drinks waiter on most cricket grounds in England. John Barclay's story will raise knowing eyebrows of those who have felt the captain's hand on their shoulder before start of play. It fell to him as team lackey one day at St Helen's, Swansea, to make up the drinks list for his team and to fetch them, precariously balanced on a tray, from the bar in the pavilion to the dressing room at the close of play. 'When I reached our dressing room door, I found it shut. I gave it a couple of taps with my foot whereupon it was opened by a grim-looking Tony Greig.' His grim face could possibly be explained by the fact that Sussex had just been hammered by Glamorgan by nine wickets. 'I think it was then that I missed my footing. I tripped on a pad, lost my balance and tipped the entire tray of drinks into Greig's cricket case. To watch the contents of his case swimming about in a mixture of beer, milk, orange juice and the scorer's whisky was just about as bad as it got in my entire cricket career.' Perhaps it was no coincidence that Barclay had to wait a further two years before he was picked for Sussex again.

In all these conversations with team-mates, the subject of Tony's driving seemed to crop up a lot. Not the cover drive, not the off drive, not the lofted drive but the automobile drive. Sussex may have had a tired-looking and dilapidated pavilion but they were one of the first to have their own bus. Or van, I should say. It certainly took the load off the designated drivers whizzing around the country – cricket equipment is notoriously commodious – but a van needs a pilot. Tony took it upon himself to take the joystick and occupying the co-pilot's seat was usually the reliable Senior Aircraftman Graves. Occasionally, one of the junior members of the team would be invited on board for a spin he would never forget. Jerry Morley nearly failed to make it back to base on one of these journeys. John Snow told me the story. 'Greigy took one corner a bit too fast. The door of the van slid open and Jerry, on the passenger front seat, shot out into the ditch. Fortunately the corner was so sharp that they weren't going all that fast. They stopped and picked him up unharmed and went on their way.' *Thank heavens for that!* 'Yes, it could have been—' *No, thank heavens they didn't leave Jerry there in the ditch.* 'Sussex was a team, Andy, not like other counties I can mention.'

Peter Graves could scarcely stop laughing when he recalled these hair-raising journeys. He knew about Tony's epilepsy, was well aware of his need for rest and sleep and was concerned about his captain driving long distances, often after a hard day in the field. So they compromised; they shared the driving. 'We had a mattress in the back so he could take a kip while I took over the controls. But he wouldn't stop so I could get up and move over into the driver's seat. I would take hold of the wheel, he would do a backflip on to the mattress and instantly fall asleep and I would have to manoeuvre myself across the wheel shaft and into the seat to take over the controls. All this at 70mph on the motorway.' Paul Phillipson confirmed that these high-speed changes of bowling were true all right. He was in the middle seat on one occasion when Graves clambered over him to take hold of the wheel while their captain gently fell backwards on to the mattress.

Snow was convinced Tony had a guardian angel perched on his shoulder. 'We were motoring home once when he overcooked a corner … not to say he wouldn't have got out of it … but whereas a normal person would have been faced with a brick wall or a tree, Tony was presented with someone's nice smooth driveway to ease the problem.' Angels – guardian, avenging, messenger, guiding, comforting – usually take care of their own. Even Snow, not one to eulogise particularly, described him as 'a blond, blue-eyed, six foot seven Adonis – difficult to miss – no ordinary man, one whom committee men and members tripped over themselves to meet'. John Barclay's mother instantly fell in love with him. 'Let's be honest, John,' she told her son, 'he's like a Greek god.' Paul Phillipson remembers queueing up to get his autograph. *But Phillipo, no need to queue, you shared a dressing room with him.* 'I was a Sussex supporter as a kid and he was one of my heroes. There he was, a six foot eight Adonis.' There seemed to be a doubt, a confusion, amongst his friends, an inexactitude shared by the records, whether Tony Greig was six foot six, seven or eight inches. 'Between six foot seven and six foot eight!' his brother pronounced. So there we are, confirmation that he was closer to the gods than the rest of us.

There were times when he played as if he were a god. Though he never wavered in his commitment to Sussex, it was clear to team-mates that he had bigger fish to fry. 'It was obvious Tony wanted to succeed at whatever he was doing; he never wanted to be just an "ordinary" player,' John Snow said. 'Of course he was destined for greater things for which Sussex cricket and captaincy were just a stepping stone,' added John Barclay. Naturally, the longer Tony played and the greater success he had in England colours, he would have had to be remarkably modest if the possibility of captaining his adopted country had not from time to time crossed his mind. And, as we know, even his best friends would not count self-effacement among his personal attributes. The fact that his record at Test level surpasses that of his county career tells its own story. It wasn't that he became disenchanted with the daily grind of professional cricket, though he did wonder why so much cricket was played in this country. But he found it easier to respond when the limelight shone, which it didn't at Derby or Bradford, let's say, on a windswept day in early May in front of the sparsest of crowds. 'He possessed BMT!' proclaimed John Spencer. *I beg your pardon, Spence. BMT?* 'BMT. Big Match Temperament. The ability to produce the goods when it really counted.'

Tony Greig chased victory, not records. Undoubtedly he was an exceptional player who could, and often did, seize a game by the scruff of the neck and shape it to his own ambition. But Sussex were never a great team in the 1970s and there were times when he felt the pressure, occasionally frustration, of not having other, similarly gifted players around him. He put his faith in the younger generation and they repaid him with their loyalty and commitment and, to be fair, team morale and results did improve under his stewardship. However, there must have been times when he yearned for an explosive batsman or one of the many fearsome West Indian fast bowlers who were around at the time or a mystery twirler from the subcontinent who would take the county up a level in order to compete with the best. It always puzzled me what sort of policy Sussex had for signing overseas players in that decade. At a time when players of the calibre of Richards (Barry and Viv), Roberts, Procter, Zaheer, Majid, Holder, Kanhai, Kallicharran, Gibbs, Lloyd, Bedi, Mushtaq, McEwan, Daniel, Intikhab, Asif and others, not forgetting the incomparable Garry Sobers, were gracing English cricket, Sussex were employing as their overseas players ... Geoff Greenidge and Uday Joshi. Both were fine players and delightful people but neither name struck fear into an opposing team when they read the Sussex team sheet. The mention there of Kenny McEwan in the list of wonderful overseas players reminded me that McEwan tried his luck first at Sussex when he came over from South Africa. *Why did they not take you on, Kenny?* 'Well, they already had their quota of overseas players – Geoff Greenidge and Uday Joshi,' he explained modestly. Hmm. That patently underlines my point. 'Tony was not captain at the time,' McEwan continued, 'so he had no say in the matter. But I am indebted to him for recommending me to Keith Fletcher, who was captain at Essex, when they were both in the England dressing room. That was how I ended up north of the Thames.' Sussex's loss was Essex's gain, illustrating two points: Sussex's muddled recruitment policy and Tony's generous nature that was always willing to help out old friends. He was the star player at Hove but he could have done with another world-class cricketer to share the load, especially as he was often away on England duty himself.

The fact that he was an England player did not mean that he stinted in his efforts when he returned to the day job. Some cricketers found no problem in combining their enthusiasm for the county game with regular Test match involvement. I am reminded of two subjects of former books of mine, Tom Graveney and Colin Cowdrey. Both had their roots deeply embedded in the county game and loved playing day in, day out in familiar and cherished surroundings. However, they were exceptional. Consider this. Following a five-day Test match, with all its attendant physical and mental pressures, an England player was expected to climb into his car on a Tuesday evening and drive halfway across the country to turn out for his county on the following morning. You could forgive him, especially if he was a bowler, for hoping and praying that his captain would win the toss, elect to bat and provide him with the opportunity to put his feet up for a few hours.

Now, was Tony Greig ever allowed to put his feet up? No chance. He was the captain spinning the coin for a start and win or lose he would soon be in the thick of it. His enthusiasm and energy never wavered, to the amazement of team-mates. Take this as just one example of many. The Ashes series in Australia of 1974/75 was perhaps one of the most taxing and punishing (for the English) in modern times. Some players returned from that tour mentally and physically shot. Not Tony Greig. Back in England for the 1975 season, he was being lined up to replace Mike Denness as England captain. He, more than anyone, surely, needed time to rest and recharge his batteries for the coming challenges. But no. In mid-May, he bowled 70 overs, taking 7-164, in a Championship match against Leicestershire, followed by 46 and 48 overs in the next two county matches. This in advance of the first World Cup, scheduled for June. No peace for the wicked, as my mother used to say.

Paul Phillipson told me about Tony's relationship with cortisone. 'Not a lady,' he said, 'but a new drug. He swore by it. Being a tall chap who bowled quick, he suffered more than most from rib injuries, specifically to the intercostal area. So he sought the advice of a famous surgeon, Bill Tucker, who specialised in sports injuries.' Ah yes, Bill Tucker, the legendary orthopaedic surgeon. He it was who had operated on Denis Compton's knee, an operation that had assumed soap opera notoriety in the British press in the 1950s. Tony was an unapologetic champion of Mr Tucker's methods. 'I recall his descriptions of his visits to his Harley Street surgery,' said Phillipson, 'and Tucker's use of this massive needle which he used to inject cortisone in the affected area.' It was Phillipson's contention that Tony would not have played in several Tests had it not been for these interventions. 'He was convinced they worked. When I got the same injury, he suggested I have the same treatment.' *And did you?* 'No way, Jose! But you have to admire Greigy's determination to get out there and play.'

Phillipson also remembers an unusual tenth-wicket partnership he had with Tony Greig against Hampshire in 1972. 'He walked down the wicket to me when I took guard,' said Phillipson, '"You hang in there, buddy," he said, "and give the strike to me." We were only 230 runs short! He was on 15 at the time. Anyway, he started to slog and the ball kept on going everywhere. The fielders were laughing because it became so outrageous the way he was "farming" the bowling. He got to 88 and then I was run out. Greigy was furious with me. He wanted a hundred and even thought we could win it. What was worse, I wasn't out! I think the umpire had had enough of the shenanigans and wanted to get home.' *By the way, Paul, what was your contribution to this last-wicket stand of 79?* 'Er, one.'

Then Phillipson gave another example of Tony's never-say-die attitude on the field. 'It was a Sunday League game at Southampton. I was bowling. The batsman top-edged it and the ball flew over Greigy's head at midwicket. He turned, chased after it, dived full length and caught it with his fingertips. It was an astonishing catch. Nobody else in the country could have done that.' *Nobody else in the country was tall enough to do that.* 'The point is that he was so pleased with himself. He ran up to congratulate me as if we'd just won a Test match.'

Tony's fielding. People tend to forget about it these days. His team-mates don't. 'His catching was phenomenal,' said Spencer. 'Those bucket hands,' said Snow, 'he caught pretty well everything at second slip.' The best catch Phillipson has ever seen was taken by Greig at slip off his bowling. 'It was Mushtaq,' he proudly told me, 'first ball!'

What set Tony apart, it is John Barclay's contention, was that he didn't play like a professional cricketer. 'He was far too dashing for that,' Barclay told me, 'and yet, deep down, he was as fiercely ambitious as anyone, both socially and as a cricketer.' Some people turn heads as soon as they enter a room. Bill Clinton was one such famous example. Alexander the Great, Julius Caesar, Napoleon, Abraham Lincoln, Gandhi, J.F. Kennedy – they all had that aura, that magnetism, that star quality that attracts, like a candle does a moth. Tony Greig was a bit like that. He was not self-consciously cocky or vainglorious but he was aware of his attractiveness and enjoyed being in the public eye. Once he became England captain, the spotlight was turned on him and he never dodged its beam.

'You have to understand,' Peter Graves told me, 'that previously all-rounders, particularly English all-rounders were a staid breed, doing two jobs tolerably well, not excelling in either but useful players to have in a team nonetheless. Greigy wasn't like that. He was different. He batted, bowled and fielded with gusto. There was nothing understated in what he did.' Paul Phillipson was in total agreement. 'When Greigy was around, there was this feeling of excitement. He captured the imagination. He was good fun. People liked him. They came to watch him in droves. He drew attention to himself and pulled in the crowds.' He was also a pressman's dream. Not for him the bland cliché and the commonplace observation. Many are the examples of a Greig quote that made the headline, sometimes to his advantage, sometimes not. Martin Johnson, the journalist, put it better than most: 'He had a tendency to make the verbal journey from brain to mouth without the safety valve of a filter system in between.' Tony's friends and supporters loved this; his detractors – and I suppose there were a few – used it to wound him. There is no doubt in which camp his team-mates resided. That's Greigy, they'd laugh. John Spencer speaks for them all. 'If someone took five wickets, Greigy would suggest that he could be in the next England squad, even if it was a county plod like me who would never have made it to the longlist. It was part of his charm, these spur-of-the-moment comments given without too much thought.'

One of these moments caused Tony Buss an enormous amount of grief, though he laughs at the memory now. At the time, Buss Snr was coach at the club but was totally unaware that his captain had made a public promise, via his weekly column in *The Sun*, to unearth some fast bowling talent in the country. England were currently being hammered by a quartet of West Indian pacemen. He wrote that the Sussex coach, viz Tony Buss, would be holding nets at Hove for any youngster who fancied his chances to come along and turn his arm over. The winner would be offered a full-time contract at Sussex. 'I had hundreds of replies!' Buss grimly recounted, 'and it was my job to go through them all and sort them out for a series of nets at the end of the season. Bloody nightmare!' *Did anything come of this exciting initiative?* 'We whittled 'em down to half a dozen. The winner was a chap by the name of Chris Fletcher, I think.' *Was he any good?* 'Actually, he was a useful bowler but sadly injuries took their toll and he was unable to make the mark he might have. Delightful bloke though. Thanks, Greigy, I thought when all those letters came in. Still, it made a good headline.'

Tony's gregariousness and penchant for sharing his thoughts at will was part of his charm, certainly to those who knew him well, but sometimes, as we shall see in later chapters, it could land him in hot water. For the time being, let me share two delightful vignettes of his time at Sussex. The first concerned yet again Paul Phillipson. The Long Stop was a favoured meeting spot at the Hove ground for opponents to share a beer and a chat after the day's play. Phillipson was sipping his half of shandy with Adell, his girlfriend from Cape Town, when Tony Greig, club captain, hove into view. 'Hell then, Phillipo,' he announced in those fiercely clipped South African tones, 'When are you two getting hitched, hey?' *Well, did you?* 'What?' *Get hitched?* 'We did, as it happened, a year later. But Adell was fearfully embarrassed.' *That's Greigy, eh?* 'Just what I told her.'

The other was recounted to me by a lifelong Sussex member and current archivist, Mervyn Brown. It took place in The Long Stop. He believes it was during that chastening 3-0 thumping by the West Indies in 1976. 'A couple of my mates were sitting there after a day's play in the County Championship discussing team selection for the next Test. Tony, by then the England captain, was sitting at a nearby table and overheard them. He came across and joined them and wanted to know what ordinary supporters thought about the selections. Together, they proceeded to pick the team literally on the back of a fag packet.' *Any surprises?* 'They all wanted Boycott. This was during his period of self-imposed exile. Greigy said he had personally implored Boycott to come back, even offered him the vice-captaincy, but to no avail.' Hmm, Geoffrey Boycott. He will feature in later chapters. Brown tells this story because it was one of many; Tony Greig was popular with the members at Sussex because he was willing, anxious even, to engage with them.

Peter Graves has given the legacy of his old friend and captain some thought down the years. It is his contention that people are always attracted to powerful men and Greig, at the height of his fame, captain of England, rescuing his country from the doldrums with an unprecedented successful series in India, immediately followed by possibly the most famous cricketing encounter in history, the Centenary Test in Melbourne in 1977, was for a while the man whose name was on everybody's lips. 'Successful athletes are firmly in this bracket,' said Graves, 'and are particularly attractive to the opposite sex because they are young, fit, energetic, full of life and more often than not well built and good-looking. Greigy had more than his fair share of admirers.' Lucky fellow and all that. But the true measure of a man is not the adulation he inspires but the legacy he leaves behind him. All his friends and most of his contemporaries remain intensely loyal to Greig. John Spencer again … 'Greigy was a great influence on my cricket career and beyond. His ability to manage people taught me lessons I took forward into my teaching career at Brighton College and whenever I "stood up to be counted" or confronted someone to "say what he meant" I always thought of my former captain and mentor. He was a great man, respected as a captain and as a person.'

Sadly, the grand project that was the rejuvenation of Sussex cricket, with the aim of securing the County Championship, fizzled out in 1977, doused in a tsunami of post-Packer recrimination and an expensive legal case. At the forefront was Tony Greig and it was a moot point whether Sussex or Tony himself was the bigger loser. Winning the Championship pennant would be put on hold for 25 years, after which came a decade of Sussex domination. By then, Tony was living on the other side of the world. How nice it would have been if he had been president of his old club during those heady years but that was never going to happen. His association with Sussex came to an end, abruptly and unhappily, during one week in July 1978. He had played only a handful of games for Sussex up until that point and I had always believed that his absence in the earlier part of the season was bound up with the Packer affair and the court case. Not so apparently. Well, not directly anyway. He had been sacked as England captain once his involvement in recruitment for Kerry Packer's World Series Cricket had come to light; he had expected that. He had remained in the England team during the 1977 Ashes series, mainly at the instigation of his successor as captain, Mike Brearley, but he had taken it as read that his Test career had come to a close at the Oval that summer in the final match of the series. But he was still a Sussex player and their captain. The unhealthy atmosphere that obtained in county dressing rooms at that time will be discussed later but he still resisted any attempts by the diehards on the Sussex committee to get rid of him. They had no right to do so, he maintained, a stance later taken in the High Court, with success. However, he had inadvertently tangled with the aforesaid Geoffrey Boycott during the court hearings. The details do not concern us here; suffice it to say that Tony did not take too kindly to being criticised by Boycott who was in the commentary box during the Centenary Test when England's captain firmly believed that Boycott's place was out in the middle, with his England team-mates. He wrote as much in a newspaper article: 'Boycott has the uncanny knack of being where fast bowlers aren't.' Ill-advised, certainly, but there you are, that's Greigy. It was after all no more than what was being whispered on the circuit. He was hauled over the coals by the Test and County Cricket Board and suspended for the first two months of the 1978 season, which explains his absence. In his place as county captain was appointed the ex-Surrey wicketkeeper, Arnold Long, known universally as 'Ob'.

Following his suspension, Tony returned to the Sussex dressing room and found it, if not an inhospitable place, then certainly uncomfortable. His youth policy had been abandoned and the team featured a preponderance of older pros, with all the attendant cliques that had plagued the club when he had first arrived. 'I had to get out,' he wrote simply. The fire still burned but he was aware that his presence had become a hindrance, not a help. Mervyn Brown, a keen spectator of events at his beloved Sussex, sensed that all was not well with the ex-skipper. 'Tony had got out cheaply,' he recalled. 'As he approached the pavilion on his way back to the dressing room, a member shouted, "Rubbish, Greig!" There was a lot of ill-feeling around that time and Tony was in the eye of the storm. He stormed off to the dressing room, removed his pads and came back to find his critic, who was eagerly pointed out by other members. Greig was clearly trying to restrain himself but loudly and at length he reminded the member that he had given many years of his life to the club and didn't appreciate the insinuation of disloyalty.' *What happened to the member?* 'He slunk off rather sheepishly but this small incident did show that Tony, even in his later years at the club, was still passionate about Sussex.'

I think the jibes of 'traitor' and 'mercenary' hurt Tony deeply. Things were getting nasty. The press were on his back, public intrusion into his personal life was affecting his family, old friendships and alliances were breaking down, he had lost the England captaincy and now even some of the Sussex faithful were turning on him. Not one to prevaricate, he made up his mind swiftly and decisively. He would seek an immediate release from his contract. Funnily enough, just along the south coast, Barry Richards was telling a shocked Hampshire dressing room that he too was packing his bags forthwith. It was a strange and unsettling time.

Where was Tony Greig bound? Australia. It seems inevitable looking back on it now, with his Packer connections and his contract signed for World Series Cricket. He was about to tread the boards of a bigger stage than Hove or Hastings but he never forgot whence he came. Everybody to whom I have spoken has said that he always went out of his way to greet old friends from England who visited him in his Sydney home and to make sure they were well looked after. But as he said at the time, he had signed on the dotted line and he was now, fully and committed, a Packer man. 'I rang Kerry that night to explain my decision. "The tickets will be waiting for you in the morning," was his reply.'

This is the way the world ends
Not with a bang but a whimper.

T.S. Eliot

Chapter 6

England 1972–77

'Where did he get that streak of showmanship?'

Mike Brearley of Tony Greig

BACK in 1970, when Tony had been selected for the unofficial Test series against the Rest of the World, he had entered the England dressing room if not quietly and unobtrusively – Tony just didn't do quiet and unobtrusive – then at least with a palpable sense of not quite belonging. Now, in 1972, following his successful winter with the Rest of the World team in Australia, he believed he was worthy of selection and was not surprised to learn that he was in the team for the first Test of an Ashes summer at Old Trafford. He was, incidentally, the only new cap in the room, surrounded, as he was, by old campaigners such as Boycott, Edrich, M.J.K. Smith, Knott, his Sussex team-mate Snow, and of course the captain, Ray Illingworth. This time he claimed a peg in the England dressing room as of right and his name remained on it until he stopped playing for his country in 1977, not missing a single Test in that time. One imagines that the significance of the occasion did not curb his natural ebullience on that first day but the nerves must have been jangling nonetheless, soothed by the obligatory cigarette. It seems bizarre nowadays to contemplate the fact that cricket dressing rooms, professional as well as recreational, were often fugged up with cigarette smoke. I don't know how many smokers there were in that England team but Tony was certainly one of them. It is well known that he puffed away nervously before going in to bat.

This being Manchester, it was raining. The start was delayed by 90 minutes. Illingworth had resisted the temptation to bowl first in typical English conditions, cold and damp, relying on his experienced batsmen to combat the swinging ball. Well, they didn't, not very well anyway. Tony was soon at the crease, joining his fellow South African, D'Oliveira, as the pair of them fought hard to turn the tide. It would have been fascinating to eavesdrop on their conversation between overs. I wonder if the incongruity of their situation, playing in the same side (for England), an opportunity that would have been denied them for their home country (South Africa), ever occurred to them or whether their attention was wholly focussed on the job in hand. For it was a battle, one that D'Oliveira for once was not up to, but Tony fought his way through until stumps, 23 not out. Sometimes an innings like that is worth double what it says on the scoreboard.

The next morning was no easier but the stand of 63 with Alan Knott proved significant in a meagre England total of 249, Greig top-scoring with 57. It was now up to the England seamers to exploit the conditions and put the Australians firmly on the back foot. This they did, Snow and Arnold to the fore with four wickets apiece, dismissing Australia for 142. It would have been an even more decisive lead had England not had a crisis in the slip cordon. They were without regulars to fill those positions so Illingworth asked for volunteers. Tony, never slow to put his name forward, took his usual place at second slip. Usual for Sussex but don't forget he was the debutant in this side. Snow too put his hand up in the dressing room but he omitted to do so out there in the middle, or not quickly enough anyway; a catchable chance at head height was palmed away for four to third man. Another chance hit him on the ankle. His recollection of the dropped catches is slightly different. 'The one that hit me on the boot Knotty should have gone for and the one over my head was travelling like a tracer bullet.' Tony now caught the bug. Uncharacteristically, he too put down two reasonably straightforward catches. 'Much easier than mine,' grinned Snow. Illingworth, by now in a state of some indignation, put himself in the slips, to 'show them boogers 'ow to catch', only for the ball to fly straight at him and rebound painfully off his chest. Later, after play had finished for the day, he announced on television that Old Trafford was 'worst ground in coontry to see ruddy ball'! Illy was fondly regarded by his men but his excuses for getting out or dropping a catch were legendary and gleefully recounted around the circuit. He once told me on the balcony of the Leicestershire pavilion that the car park was disadvantageously placed at Grace Road for right-handers such as he. Why, only the previous day he had been dazzled by the sunlight reflecting off the car windscreens and been dismissed when well set.

Notwithstanding these mishaps, England prevailed in the match, winning by 89 runs. It should have been an even wider margin and seemed to confirm the view of many onlookers, no doubt swayed by a pessimistic press, that this was an unusually weak Australian side. I wonder if the Australians themselves would have agreed. For a number of reasons, not the least that he later became Tony Greig's agent and best friend, I was urged to contact Bruce Francis, a hard-hitting opening batsman from New South Wales who played in three of the Tests that summer. 'I knew Greigy from my time playing for Essex the previous year,' he told me, 'and we had some merry old tussles before I retired in 1973. I first came across him at Hove in 1971. He dismissed me for 94 and gave me quite a send-off! When he got out for 99, he walked past me and I pretended to suppress an exaggerated laugh. I got 121 not out in the second dig and as I walked off he said that he supposed now *I* had the last laugh.' *So there was a fair bit of banter between the two of you?* 'All in the right spirit. We always had a good chat in the evenings.' *Were you a weak side, as everybody said?* His snort spoke more loudly than words. However, Tony had had a thoroughly satisfying debut, scoring two fifties and taking five wickets. 'He had made the biggest contribution to a winning England side,' said Francis. 'Our players rated his fighting qualities on an extremely difficult, seaming wicket.' As for Tony, he agreed with Francis's assessment of this Australian team and did not share the general scepticism of their ability. He had seen them at first hand the previous winter and he knew they were a far better outfit than the general British public believed. The extraordinary events in the second Test at Lord's were to bear him out.

What came to be known as Massie's Match encapsulated a story that could have been lifted from the pages of a *Boy's Own* Annual. Bob Massie, an unknown fast-medium bowler from Western Australia, with minimal first-class experience, bamboozled and befuddled the England batsmen with late swing in his debut Test to take 8-84 and 8-53, thus securing for Australia an historic and unexpected victory by eight wickets. Massie's 16 wickets in the match was the third highest haul in history of wickets in a single Test, bettered only by Sydney Barnes's 17 for England against South Africa at The Wanderers, Johannesburg in 1913 and Jim Laker's 19 for England against Australia at Old Trafford in 1956. The mystery man played only five more Tests before losing form, health and confidence and within two years he was no longer even playing state cricket. The parable of this fleeting rise and precipitous fall bore all the hallmarks of a Greek tragedy.

Who was this Bob Massie and where on earth had he come from? And, more poignantly, where did he go? As in many of the best stories, the truth is slightly less improbable. Tony Greig knew who he was all right. He had encountered him in Australia a few months before. Massie had been selected for the third 'Test' of the series against the Rest of the World and taken 7-76 in the fourth. It had not gone unnoticed by Tony that Massie had managed to trouble Garry Sobers on occasions, even during his magnificent innings of 254 at Melbourne. Tony remembered that series and the way Massie had bowled to Sobers. 'Any bowler who can occasionally baffle Garry Sobers wins my vote,' he wrote later. 'Sobers never tried to pick seam or swing, preferring always to use his remarkable eye to play it as it came. But Massie had him puzzled.'

Massie puzzled England too. In fact, he dismantled their brains. Tony believed it was the finest exhibition of swing bowling he had ever faced. I watched a compilation of all of those 16 wickets on YouTube recently and despite the fuzzy quality of the footage, I was struck first by the easy rhythm of Massie's approach and delivery – a sure sign that a bowler is 'in the groove' – and secondly by the absolute control he had over his line and length, whether delivering the outswinger or the inswinger, with no discernible change of action. Furthermore, he did not waver an inch from his line of off stump when he went round the wicket and, as any swing bowler knows, that is difficult when you switch your line of attack from over to round with the ball swinging all over the place. The conditions, overcast and heavy, were in his favour certainly but the mark of a supreme practitioner of his art is how well he exploits those conditions.

Something else I noticed while viewing those 16 wickets on YouTube. The Greig stance, still at the crease as he awaited the ball's delivery with his bat held high above his head – one that has been copied extensively over the years – was nowhere to be seen. He stood at the crease with the toe of his bat resting alongside his right (ie, his back) foot in the conventional manner. When, and why, did he change? Extensive questioning among his contemporaries yielded no clear answer; nobody could remember. The most plausible theory advanced was that it was brought about by the extreme pace of Lillee and Thomson in the Ashes series of 1974/75 in an effort to avoid playing the ball too late. He was a tall man and by the time he had lifted his bat up and brought it down, his stumps had been rearranged. Or so the theory went. In fact, that was not the case, not the reason. I discovered the truth by accident. All shall be revealed shortly.

The irony was that these conditions at Lord's were quintessentially English and you would have expected the England bowlers to exploit them better than the two Western Australians (both Lillee and Massie came from that state). Unfortunately, Geoff Arnold, who would have loved to play in conditions which suited him down to the ground, pulled up lame on the morning of the match and was replaced by John Price who had a disappointing game, despite the fact that Lord's was his home ground. Furthermore, England went in with two spinners, usually a bit of a luxury when playing at home, so they only had Greig as the third seamer, with D'Oliveira no more than a useful, stop-gap medium-pacer. John Snow, with 5-57, alone excelled in Australia's crucial first innings, held together with a matchless century from Greg Chappell, who openly admitted that his experience of playing two seasons for Somerset had ably prepared him for batting in English conditions. In actual fact, it was not so much the England bowlers who had let the side down but their batsmen. No one, with the exception of Greig, who scored his third half-century in succession, the highest score of the innings, and Knott, who with Greig put on 96 for the sixth wicket (while Massie was being rested), showed the necessary technique and strength of mind to combat the swing of Massie and the pace of Lillee. The contribution of Dennis Lillee to Australia's dominance in this match is often forgotten, overshadowed as it was by Massie's feats. Tony was quoted later as saying 'Lillee was bowling as well as Massie, fast and hostile, but we didn't touch anything although we were beaten all ends up time after time.' It can sometimes happen like that. One bowler of a pair has all the luck and the other doesn't. It was simply Massie's day, Massie's Match.

If anything, he bowled better in the second innings. Once Lillee had knocked over the prize wicket of Boycott, the Australians were inspired in the field and Massie unplayable. Listen to his own words. 'The wicket of Edrich was very important. I planned to go round the wicket because he was so good at leaving the ball. I thought if I could get an inswinger at his off stump going away, it would be harder for him to judge the line. And that is how I got him.' The ball caught the edge of the bat and wicketkeeper Marsh did the rest. What joy and satisfaction it brings to a bowler when his plan is perfectly executed and has the desired effect. England were doomed. They were skittled for 116, no fewer than six of their batsmen failing to register double figures. Interestingly, Massie persisted with bowling round the wicket to both right- and left-handers and nobody had an answer to him. The 81 runs needed were knocked off as a formality and Australia had levelled the series. It was a vital win too, not just in terms of the Ashes but also as a symbolic turning point of Australia's fortunes in world cricket, which they were to dominate for the next half-dozen years. 'We showed we could mix it with the best,' observed Greg Chappell.

For England, it had been a chastening experience. Only Snow and Greig, and possibly Knott, had emerged from the game with much credit. Tony, as ever, was sanguine about the experience, preferring to give all the credit to Massie's inspired performance. 'He was a nice, quiet guy,' he wrote, 'who had the ability to make the ball "talk". He did it naturally and it was almost impossible for the batsman to differentiate between the one that left him and the one that dipped in late.'

Massie was not able to reproduce his heroics of Lord's in the rest of the series; his only figures of note were 4-43 in the third Test. He returned to Australia, played in two Tests against Pakistan that season, went on the tour of the West Indies, where everything went wrong ... and that was it. Not only did he not play again for Australia, he played only five more matches for his state before disappearing into obscurity. Plenty of cricketers have shone brightly but all too briefly on the international stage and then dropped out of the limelight but usually they have returned to the more comfortable and familiar surroundings of first-class cricket and continued with worthy careers. Massie's fall from grace is easily the most rapid and spectacular of all shooting stars. So what happened? Or rather, why did it happen? Opinions for his demise vary widely. The art of swing bowling is as elusive as a will o' the wisp, here one minute, gone the next. Some days the ball goes round corners, other days it stays stubbornly on the straight and narrow. For a while, in a season or a career, it can be a reliable friend and then for no apparent reason it deserts you, sometimes for good. As usual, John Snow gives an incisive opinion on Massie's demise. 'John Edrich said at the time that Massie had bowled a lot of overs in that Test and wouldn't be the same bowler again. How true. Basically, the conditions were exceptional at Lord's and Bob was a laid-back West Australian who wasn't chasing fame.' In other words, he lacked the drive and the ambition to do it again, and again, and again, as all the great cricketers do.

Tony Greig, who *was* prepared to do it again and again, was in no doubt what happened. Massie was aware of a series of press photos, alleging to have uncovered slight changes in his action when he bowled the outswinger and inswinger. That, Tony believed, led him to worry about his bowling and to analyse what was going wrong. So he started to tinker, to over-analyse, to deconstruct what had come naturally, with consequent loss of rhythm, control and ultimately confidence. Massie himself took a different view. 'It was on that tour [to the West Indies] that the outswinger deserted me. I found that pounding the ball into the slow tracks impaired my action and I was never the same bowler again.' It was a personal tragedy as well as a huge loss for Australia. Tony believed that Massie and Lillee could have led the Australian attack for years. As it happened, the firebrand Dennis Lillee was joined by another unknown, to form the most fearsome pace attack the world of cricket has ever seen. But not yet, not quite yet.

The third Test at Trent Bridge was an uneventful draw. Bruce Francis, however, has one vivid memory of the game. Well, not so much of the game itself but an incident off-field, so to speak. 'I was fielding at third man,' he said, 'and a number of people were sitting in chairs between the fence and the rope. I started to chat up the girls – there were about half a dozen of them. They gave me an ice lolly. I asked one of them out for dinner that evening. She said she'd love to but had other arrangements. After play, Greigy came into our dressing room and asked me what Donna was doing that evening. I said, 'Who is Donna?' He said, "My wife – the one you asked out!"' *How did you manage that embarrassment?* 'I stuttered and said, "Er … well, you must admire my taste!" We got on much better after that. Donna was sitting with the England wives.' Francis and Tony later went on a tour of Rhodesia with the International Wanderers and found themselves naturally drawn to each other. 'Tony was a light drinker,' Francis said, 'and I was a teetotaller and we had dinner together most nights and became good mates.' A deep friendship that lasted up to Tony's death.

The fourth Test at Headingley was anything but uneventful. The previous weekend had been wet, with the square under water. When both teams arrived at the ground on the day before the match, they were surprised, to say the least, to find a pitch that had dried and was totally devoid of grass. The official explanation was that the surface had become infested with fusarium, a fungus that had killed the grass. Australians were sceptical. 'It was uncanny that it only attacked a strip 22 yards by 8 feet and the rest of the ground was perfectly healthy,' Greg Chappell later wrote. Uncanny too that England had called up Derek Underwood to play, not having picked him for the previous three Tests, arguably the finest exploiter of a drying and crumbling pitch in the world. Despite the official protestations of innocence and blamelessness, let us listen to the traditional voice of fair-mindedness and impartiality, John Woodcock, writing in *The Times*: 'It might have been made for Underwood … it does no one any credit.' Even E.W. Swanton was moved to remark, 'It was an embarrassment.'

Ian Chappell won the toss and, with some foreboding, elected to bat first. He could hardly have done otherwise; nobody would have fancied batting last on that pitch. Australia reached lunch without undue alarm but once Underwood was introduced into the attack, they sunk without trace, subsiding from 93/2 to 98/7 and 146 all out. Underwood, bowling his left-arm spinners at a quickish pace, almost medium-pace cutters, was nigh on unplayable, taking 4-37 off 31 overs. Tony had bowled ten fruitless overs. The conditions did not suit his type of bowling and he had yet to experiment with his own form of off-cutters. Besides, in Underwood and captain Illingworth, England had ammunition enough, and the experience, to exploit this unusual, but very English, surface. England still had to bat on it, mind you, and when Tony was out for a hard-fought 24, they were perilously positioned at 128/7, with only the bowlers to bat.

'What do you mean, "only" the bowlers to bat?' John Snow looked offended when I reminded him of this fact. He had every reason to be, for together with Illingworth, he fashioned a match-winning eighth-wicket stand of 104. His contribution was 48. 'I used the lap a lot,' he laughed. And why not? Illingworth said that he was used to batting on slow turners in Yorkshire and the lap is a perfectly legitimate stroke to use in the circumstances, despite all the oohs and aahs coming from bowler and close fielders at the cross-batted swipes.

Bowlers win matches, Boycott always asserts; we batsmen merely put them into a position to win. That was certainly true in this case. Underwood was expected to bowl England to victory and it is a measure of his standing as a Test match player of the highest class that, given these conditions, he invariably did. Australia had no answer. By this time, the ball was starting to lift from the worn patches and bowling at this pace and with this accuracy he was lethal. Not for nothing was the nickname 'Deadly' bestowed, one to which he answers universally to this day. Australia were rolled over for 136 and lost by nine wickets, Underwood taking 6-45.

The pitch was doctored? No, claimed the Yorkshire authorities. 'It wasn't a good wicket for starters,' said Ian Chappell afterwards through gritted teeth, 'but more than that I cannot say.' The *Yorkshire Post*, in the form of their cricket correspondent, Bill Bowes, wrote,

'I hadn't seen a Leeds pitch like it in 40 years.' John Snow offered a typically brief and trenchant take on the controversy: 'Same for both sides.' Who cares, seemed to be Tony's response. England had taken an unassailable 2-1 lead in the series, thus retaining the Ashes. He found the beer during post-match celebrations much to his taste, the more so as it was Australian and it was in their dressing room.

The Australians had their revenge though in the fifth Test at the Oval, which they won by five wickets. Tony had a quiet game. To the victors went the spoils. Lillee took ten wickets in the match and both Chappells in their different styles, Ian all bustle and intent, Greg elegance personified, scored hundreds, and they were the difference between the two sides. The series may well have ended 2-2 but somehow it felt that the balance of power had shifted, a view borne out by Australia's dominance over the next few years. It had been an enthralling Ashes summer, full of memorable performances and positive cricket and, if nothing else, answered two questions. Actually, it was the same question but posed by two different voices. The first came from the mouth of the British cricketing public: did we possess in the person of Tony Greig a true, world-class all-rounder in our team? The answer was an unequivocal yes. He had scored more runs in the series than any Englishman (288) at a higher average than any other of his team-mates (36.00) and furthermore had taken ten wickets. Not breathtaking figures, it has to be admitted, but it was more the manner in which he had performed that had caught the eye. No less an authority than E.W. Swanton sang his praises, writing that England could be satisfied with 'the emergence of Tony Greig as an all-rounder of higher potential than anyone this country has produced in a long time'.

The same question had resided in the mind of Tony Greig himself and this too had been answered in the affirmative. He belonged on this stage and he had loved every minute of it. A cricketer he had wanted to be, ever since he was a kid, and a cricketer – of some standing – he had become. The only query was how far he could go. All the way – hell, why not? You can almost hear him telling himself that.

If the 6ft 7in (and a half) blond, Greek god that was Tony Greig had made such an impact in England, one might well wonder what sort of a ferment he would stir up in India, where MCC were bound that winter. Apparently there are 33 deities in the Hindu religion. Or 33 million. It depends, as everything does in that country, on what you mean by a deity. Whatever … surely they had room for one more. Unquestionably, by the end of the series, the Indian public had taken Tony Greig to their hearts, if not yet into their temples.

All tours of foreign climes provide different charms and challenges. The Indian subcontinent throws up its own peculiar trials and vexations, which makes a long tour in that part of the world a test of morale and endurance. In a culture where members of the family live together in the same room, there is little understanding of what is personal and what is private. The teeming millions is the first surprise. Massive poverty sits side by side with conspicuous wealth. The crazy roads, the mad driving, the wandering livestock, the noise, the smells, the heat, the dust, the dirt and the startling sight of people urinating and defecating on street corners – all of this is unsettling.

Embrace it or shun it? Several senior England players decided on the latter course of action and made themselves unavailable for this tour, which seems unimaginable these days, but was not uncommon at a time when the financial rewards for touring were not of the measure that makes declining practically impossible. For various reasons, Illingworth, Boycott, Snow, Edrich and M.J.K. Smith let it be known they would rather stay at home. The selectors were unimpressed, particularly with Illingworth. He was after all the England captain and now, following his late withdrawal, they had to find someone else to lead the side.

In Tony Lewis they lighted, or perhaps stumbled, upon the ideal man for the job. In many ways, from an establishment point of view, he fitted the bill. A double Blue at Cambridge (rugby and cricket), he had captained Glamorgan from 1967–72, winning the Championship in 1969, and was clearly trustworthy enough to uphold the highest traditions of the amateur ethos of the MCC, an attitude that still obtained in the corridors of power. But Lewis was no ex-public school popinjay. A product of Neath Grammar School, he was also a talented violinist and already had a burgeoning second career as a journalist, reporting on rugby for *The Daily Telegraph*. In other words, he had interests outside cricket and was therefore willing to take on board the wider political and social implications of a gruelling tour to a part of the world where the MCC had not always covered themselves in glory. In this regard, it was generally accepted that he was a success, even though, at the age of 34, he was never going to be considered more than a stop-gap appointment.

Just as importantly, he managed to gel a young and inexperienced squad into a happy and tight-knit group. He proved to be an enterprising captain, his players liked and respected him, he was an excellent ambassador for English cricket and his team were popular tourists. 'He got the best out of his players,' said Keith Fletcher, 'bit inexperienced at the highest level but he was a good bloke and people respected him.' The success or failure of any England tour of India or Pakistan (or both, on the occasion of this long and arduous trip) has a lot to do with team spirit, group loyalty, the common bond. That should be true of all touring parties but it is particularly applicable in the subcontinent. 'Because, let's face it, aside from the cricket there's not a lot to do, is there?' Chris Old told me with a wry grin. 'So you are thrust more into each other's company and if you don't get on … well, it's a long time to be getting on each other's nerves.' *So, it was a happy tour then?* 'Yes, we all got on, enjoyed being together and we played some damned good cricket too. A lot of this had to do with the captain.'

Chris Old, who rejoiced in the simplest, and to my mind the best, nickname on the county circuit, 'Chilly' (C Old) was anything but in his regard and respect for his England colleague. 'Greigy too was great for team morale,' he was at pains to point out. One thing the selectors could be sure of – they could have mortgaged their houses on it – was that Tony Greig would not shun the experience. He was an 'embracer'. Was he ever in the frame to captain the side, I wondered. All to whom I spoke shook their heads. No, not yet. And probably just as well. He had enough on his plate, still establishing himself as a Test player of proven class. In that respect, he succeeded beyond all expectations. Man of the Series, you might say, had such an award existed back then. Even more than that, he warranted his position, among the cricketing public of India at any rate, as the Overseas Personality of the Year, once again a fictional award but not so fanciful in the amazed opinion of his team-mates. 'He was the star of the show,' Chris Old told me. Old was on his first England tour, a shy young man from Middlesbrough who had only travelled abroad a couple of times before this, and at first found it all a bit intimidating. 'Tony was quite different to me,' he said, 'he loved the limelight. Whatever he did, you noticed him. Look, I'm here, he seemed to be saying and the Indian crowds loved it.' Another member of the party who was amused and dazzled in equal measure by Tony's antics was Keith Fletcher. 'He was the complete showman,' he said of his friend, 'and great with the crowds. Gosh, he had to be! They were loud and volatile and we needed to get on the right side of them. This Greigy did, simply by acting the fool sometimes and … well, communicating with them, like an actor on a stage.' But he believed there was method to Tony's madness. 'Greigy was the ultimate competitor. Anything that would give him, and therefore the team, an advantage was fair game. He was a winner and if he believed that getting the crowd onside gave us that 5% advantage, he was up for it.' *So his antics were calculated?* 'You bet!'

Mind you, all his play-acting would have counted for naught had he not backed it up with peerless performances on the field, which he did, emphatically. Nobody ever accused Tony Greig of being all dinner and no gong. His gongs for the tour were impressive. In five Tests in India, he topped the batting averages (382 runs at 63.66) and came second in the bowling (11 wickets at 22.45); in three Tests in Pakistan, he came second in the batting averages (261 runs at 52.20) and was third in the bowling (six wickets at 42.33). Those are the figures of a top-quality batsman and if the bowling statistics look a bit meagre, do not forget that Indian, and especially Pakistani, wickets are notorious graveyards for fast-medium seamers. If he went to India as a nascent talent on the world stage, he came back a superstar.

The assignment ahead of the MCC tourists was daunting. England had not won a Test there, let alone a series, for more than two decades; furthermore, this was an inexperienced side. Nobody had played in India before, the captain had not played a single Test, Alan Knott and Derek Underwood were the only ones with 20 caps to their name and only Knott had a Test hundred in his locker. Their preparation was far from ideal as well, with just three matches of dubious value as practice before the first Test after a three-month lay-off. They could be forgiven for approaching that Test in Delhi with trepidation, hoping to escape with a draw to keep the series alive while they found their feet. Except that 'trepidation' was not a word in Tony Greig's vocabulary.

The long and the short of it – and with the Blond Beanpole on one side and the diminutive Gavaskar and Viswanath (5ft 5in and 5ft 3in respectively) on the other, the metaphor is apt enough – is that England surprised their hosts by winning a famous Test by six wickets. Tony Lewis thus became the last man to captain his country on his debut, with a victory to boot. The shockwaves reverberated around India, who had come to believe in their invincibility at home. When you remember their bowling attack comprised almost exclusively of spinners – after all, why bother to bowl fast in that heat, an Indian friend of mine once remarked – you can understand their confidence. England had Underwood but India had at their disposal Chandrasekhar, Bedi, Venkataraghavan and Prasanna. Has there ever been a more formidable spin quartet in one team in the history of the game?

Ironically, the pitch on the first day, as well as the overcast conditions, suited the England seamers more than was expected and India were bowled out for 173, Arnold taking 6-45 with Greig chipping in with two wickets. In reply, England were soon in trouble, especially when the ball lost its shine and the Indian spinners came into play. Chandrasekhar in particular was wreaking havoc. Nobody seemed to have a clue how to play him. Lewis came in with the score at 71/3. Shortly, it was 71/4, Lewis departing lbw for 0. 'It wasn't out!' he later complained about a ball that had pitched outside off stump, which he was in the action of sweeping. 'It was a huge disappointment,' he said, 'because if the ball pitches outside the line of the off stump and the ball hits the pad, you can't be out.' But he was. A glance at the scorecard confirms this: A.R. Lewis, lbw b Chandrasekhar 0.

Ah yes, Indian umpires. Was the criticism – voiced by many an England player down the ages – that they were inordinately accommodating to the home side justified? I sought the opinion of Keith Fletcher, as fine a player of spin as there has ever been who had plenty of experience of batting in India. 'Don't forget, lots of wickets in Essex turned and every county had a couple of spinners who knew their trade,' he reminded me. 'Were Indian umpires more dodgy than anywhere else? I would contend that New Zealand umpires were worse. The thing is that, except in England, umpiring was not professional so it was more inept than biased. And let's face it, if you were a poor umpire in India and you gave out the national hero, say Gavaskar, lbw, you'd be lucky to get home in one piece. And if you did get home, you'd probably find it burnt out.' Was there any truth in the belief that it was almost impossible to get Gavaskar out lbw in India? Difficult but not impossible. He was dismissed lbw at home ten times out of 101. The same was said of Javed Miandad in Pakistan. Once again the figures are interesting. He was only given out lbw eight times out of 73 dismissals in his home country. Coincidence or were they both simply masterful players who did not allow the ball to hit their pads? 'That's why the introduction of neutral umpires was such a good thing for the game,' Fletcher offered, by way of bringing the subject to a close. Tony Greig was not so easily appeased, as we shall see.

I read in a report of the game that 'Tony Greig was reading Chandra better than his team-mates.' That may have been so but the crucial word is 'better'; he was still ill at ease, employing his long stride and judicious use of the pad to combat Chandra's turn and bounce. Chandrasekhar was an unusual, not to say unique, bowler. Polio had withered his right arm at an early age but he recovered the use of hand and fingers to develop an unusual array of leg-spinners, googlies and top-spinners, delivered at something approaching medium pace. Not dissimilar to Derek Underwood in speed and trajectory, though Underwood was a finger spinner and Chandra obviously a wrist spinner. On dusty Indian wickets, with a cluster of predatory close fielders, he was quite a handful. Greig hung on and slowly but surely the Indian total was overhauled. England were still perilously placed when last man, Bob Cottam, not known for his batting prowess, joined Greig at the crease. He may not have been much of a batsman but he was a fine bowler, in the typical English tradition of fast-medium, who could make the ball bounce because of his height. I know this to my cost, having faced him in the nets at Hampshire, suffering bruised ribs

Squadron Leader Sandy Greig (at the back) together with his crew in front of their Avro Lancaster bomber.

Squadron Leader Sandy Greig is presented with the DSO by Rt Hon Gideon Brand van Zyl, the Governor-General of the Union of South Africa, on behalf of His Majesty King George VI.

At one stage in his boyhood, Tony caught the golfing bug and seriously contemplated giving up cricket to concentrate on the game. From this early picture of him as a child, you can see he certainly had the talent.

The Greig clan: standing: Molly Joy, Joyce, Sandy; below: Ian, Sally Ann, Tony. Flossie, the Rhodesian Ridgeback, keeps a watchful eye.

England bound. Tony bids farewell to his family at East London on SS Pendennis Castle, bound for England and a life as a professional cricketer. Is that a stick of Brighton Rock in his hand? He is, after all, going to play for Sussex.

A fine action photo of Tony Greig's bounding approach and high delivery.

Tony Greig bowling
against Middlesex for
Sussex in 1966. A
bounding action full of
youthful promise and
expectation.

Ouch, that hurt! Nobody played the
fearsome pace of Lillee and Thomson
on the 1974/75 tour of Australia with
better technique and more courage
than the 42-year-old Colin Cowdrey.
Here Tony Greig at the non-striker's
end cannot bear to look as Cowdrey is
struck in the ribs by thunderbolt from
Jeff Thomson.

Wherever he played, Greig made a point of engaging with the crowd. Here he is waylaid by two scantily clad fans in Melbourne on the 1974/75 tour.

Tony Greig made no bones about his ambition to become the first cricket millionaire. It looks as if he is well on his way as he is captured taking possession of his (sponsored) Jaguar.

Tony Greig salutes the crowd – dressed in MCC blazer, of course – after victory over India during the 1972/73 tour of that country. 'What's Greig doing leading my team on a lap of honour while I'm stuck doing media duties?' muttered his captain, Tony Lewis.

Pre-season training at Hove in early April can be pretty chilly but what on earth is Tony wearing?

Tony Greig awaiting his turn to bat. On this occasion, he is not puffing nervously on a cigarette.

Greig always took his captain's responsibilities seriously. Here he is presented to the Queen at Lord's in 1976. Clearly he is in the middle of an innings, as he is wearing his pads. Next in line are Brian Close and Bob Woolmer. The West Indians opposite, smartly attired in their tour blazers, stare on impassively.

Greig bowling at Lord's in the second Test against Australia in 1975. During the tour of the West Indies in 1974, he had experimented with bowling a form of off-cutters, with considerable success. Judging by his grip of the ball, between first and second fingers, he is using this form of attack rather than his usual fast-medium style. Umpire Bill Alley keeps a close eye on the bowler's front foot.

Who's grovelling now? Greig bowled neck and crop for a duck by Andy Roberts in the first innings of the first Test against West Indies at Trent Bridge in 1976.

Greig uses his considerable reach to clip a delivery through midwicket. Behind the stumps is his old friend and faithful team-mate Alan Knott. This is a Benson and Hedges match between Sussex and Kent at Hove in 1977.

in the process. *Give me your take, Bob, on this match-winning partnership you had with Tony Greig.* 'Before I do that, let me tell you a story about Greigy, one that I never tire of re-telling.' *Please do.* 'I can tell you exactly where and when he first started using that bat held-high-in-the-air stance of his.' Eureka! *I've been trying to find that out for months. Go on.* 'Well, it wasn't in Australia in an attempt to combat their quicks, as everybody thinks. It was during that last-wicket stand we had in Delhi … Chandrasekhar and Bedi were bowling when I came in. At the end of the over, Greigy came up to me and asked me whether his head was falling away to the off side when he was playing a shot. I said I'd have a look and damn me, it was! Miles on the off side. Right, watch this, he said. Next over, he stood bolt upright with his bat raised above his head.' *Did it work?* 'I should say! Thereafter, he played it with a stick of rhubarb.'

No self-respecting book on cricket should pass without reference to the ubiquitous 'stick of rhubarb'. Beloved of batsman who feel they are in form, middling it, seeing it like a football, in the zone, the stick of rhubarb was even on occasions used by Geoffrey Boycott's grandmother, so the term has been around for a while. 'So impressed was I by the technical adjustment,' continued Cottam, 'that I adopted it too.' *With success?* 'I survived an over!' Together, they put on 20 valuable runs, Cottam's contribution being 3, which did not quite match his eventual Test average of 6.75. Tony carried his bat for 68. A lead of 27 may seem paltry but in a low-scoring game, which this one was shaping up to be, just edging ahead of your opponents' score can be an important psychological advantage.

Cottam, who went on to have a long career in coaching, was always fascinated by the technical side of the game. That is why he was so intrigued by Tony thinking on his feet like that and making such a crucial modification. 'I loved that,' he said, 'that Greigy was thinking about his batting and how to combat the challenges laid down by the Indian spinners. And to have the courage to back his instincts. He never looked back.' This anecdote reminded me of a conversation I had with John Barclay. He too admired Tony's self-belief. 'People thought it all came so naturally and so easily to him,' he said. 'No it didn't. He was continually thinking about his technique and making small modifications when problems arose.' Barclay used Derek Underwood as an example, or, to be more specific, how best to deal with him on uncovered wickets. 'Greigy was always up for trying something. He couldn't abide just doing nothing and eventually getting rolled over by Deadly. He tried taking an off stump guard. We said it wouldn't work. "It'll be fun trying," he said. So he did and he got 90 on a turning wicket. It *was* fun too and in the end, he had us all trying it. He made you think about your own technique.'

By now, in India's second innings, the Delhi pitch was taking considerable turn and the England spinners set to work, Underwood taking 4-56 and Pocock 3-72. India all out 233; England needing 207 to win. The victory was anything but a formality, particularly when Amiss and Fletcher were dismissed cheaply in swift succession. But to everybody's relief and considerable satisfaction, Tony Lewis played a captain's innings of 70 not out, aided and abetted by Greig, also undefeated on 40, to secure an historic victory by six wickets. 'They probably underestimated us,' said Lewis later, 'we probably underestimated ourselves.' The difference between the two sides in a match in which nobody scored a hundred was Tony Greig, who made 108 runs over the two innings without being dismissed, as well as taking a couple of wickets and fielding fearlessly close to the bat. But what about the impressively named Bhagwat Chandrasekhar, the man with the withered arm and fizzing deliveries? Not many bowlers can have taken eight wickets (for 79 runs) in the first innings of a Test match and ended up on the losing side. He was, however, to play a pivotal role in the series.

Oh dear. 'Dashed hopes and good intentions. Good, better, best, bested,' as George remarked in *Who's Afraid of Virginia Woolf?* England came so close, an agonising 28 runs short, of beating India in the second Test in Calcutta, thereby spurning the chance of taking a 2-0 lead, one that could have been decisive in the series. Twenty-eight runs! It seems a pitiful few in a game which deals, by and large, in triple figures. Where did it go wrong? Had one English batsman made a significant contribution in either innings, victory in another low-scoring match would have been secured. Tony Greig, of all the England batsmen, could be absolved of any blame. Indeed, in the fourth and final innings, with England chasing 191 to win, he was batting well, even magisterially, before he was dismissed for 67 – the highest score by either side – and the visitors subsided from 114/4 to 163 all out. England did have a long tail, with Old, Pocock, Underwood and Cottam filling the last four places in the order. You will be unsurprised to hear that Chandrasekhar and Bedi had done all the damage. Tony, by the way, had taken 5-24 in India's second innings to set up the chance of victory. Alas it was spurned and the feeling was hard to ignore that the balance of the series had significantly shifted.

Before we move on, Bob Cottam suggested to me that he might have been actively present at another epochal moment in the development of the game of cricket. My ears pricked up. What could this be? The raised bat stance was one thing. What else could Tony Greig have thought up? 'You've heard of reverse swing, Murt, haven't you?' *I have but I don't really understand it. Any more than I understand the physics of conventional swing. Reverse swing? Never existed in our day, did it?* 'No. Well, yes, it might have. During that second Test in Delhi, we might have stumbled across it inadvertently.' I was intrigued. He went on, 'During the game, the ball had gone out of shape and we requested another one.' *Had it really turned into an oval or was it because it wasn't swinging?* He laughed. 'Whatever. We wanted it changed. So they brought out a box of balls and the umpires chose one that looked as if it had been chewed all night by a dog.' My memory jogged. Chris Old had made the same comment about this change of ball. 'So bad was the condition of the replacement ball,' said Old, 'that Knotty threw it in disgust into the crowd. But unfortunately and unusually, it came back. So we were stuck with it.' Cottam took up the story. 'Greigy said, "Give it to me. I'll make it talk. And he did!"' Old agreed, 'The first two balls of the next over bowled by Greigy came straight down to me at long leg, huge wides that Knotty couldn't get anywhere near. He couldn't control it because it was swinging so much. At the end of his over, he came up to me and said, "Turn it round the other way, the reverse of the way you usually hold it." And, lo and behold, it swung. He was very generous in that regard, sharing information with you.'

And so, reverse swing was born, although nobody knew it at the time. 'I don't know whether we were the first,' said Cottam, 'the

Pakistanis had allegedly discovered it earlier. But that was the first time we had encountered it.' He explained, 'There was so much sweat on the one side of the ball which we were trying to shine up, the way you always did. But it was the weight of the sweat on the one side that was making it swing. Freakish really.' *Did you go away and plan to use the same method for the rest of the tour? For the rest of your career?* 'No, that was the strange thing. We never did. We put it down to an accident, just an odd ball. You know I played a lot of cricket with Sarfraz Nawaz at Northants, supposedly the father of reverse swing and we never talked about it.' Clearly keeping it up his sleeve to use in Test matches for Pakistan. 'So, no,' Cottam ruefully admitted, 'it was not one for the history books – England players discover reverse swing.' Pity. They could have done with some magic during the rest of the tour.

By now, the Blond Beanpole had firmly established himself as a crowd favourite. 'Where on earth did he get that streak of showmanship?' Mike Brearley asked me (as if I was the psychoanalyst!). 'He had it as a commentator too. Something in the family perhaps?' I assumed that was a rhetorical question. I can point to Tony's irrepressible charm and self-confidence but what had prepared him for the role of public jester he assumed on the field of play? I remember vividly the photo that appeared in the papers of a prone Tony Greig, poleaxed on his crease as if he had been shot, while the umpire is signalling a no-ball and Roger Tolchard at the non-striker's end is typically halfway down the pitch looking for a quick run. A firecracker had gone off in the stand and Tony was playing up to the crowd. They loved it. His team-mates were at first bemused and then began to find it all rather funny. 'The ultimate showman – we all thought he was mad,' said Keith Fletcher, with a genial smile. 'He was the first to wave to the crowd,' Alan Knott observed, 'and build up a rapport with them.' 'Star of the show,' was Chris Old's slightly envious take, 'quite unlike me, a shy boy from Yorkshire.' 'He was certainly a target for the crowds,' commented Bob Cottam, 'at Calcutta, there must have been 120,000 in the ground. They said that it was a sell-out crowd of 70,000. Well, I can tell you there were far more than that. Imagine the noise and when Greigy stirred them up, they went bananas.' *Talking of bananas, didn't they throw fruit at you?* 'Greigy went over, picked up a couple of oranges, stuck 'em up his jumper and pretended to be a woman.' *Not the sort of behaviour that one would expect at Hove, is it?* He laughed. 'But that was Greigy.'

Another tourist whom I quizzed was Roger Tolchard, an old friend and colleague with whom I worked when I was master-in-charge of cricket for 30 years at Malvern College. 'I wasn't in the original tour party,' he told me, 'but Bob Taylor failed his medical – ear infection, I think it was, which could have been problematic in the hot climate – so I was called up as reserve wicketkeeper-batsman. It helped that I had the same initials as Bob (RWT) and as I was more or less the same size, I inherited all his kit and bags!' *What about Greigy as a tourist?* 'Life and soul of the party. He loved playing up to the crowd and wherever we went, even the up-country games, the grounds were full to capacity, overflowing in fact and he'd go over to the ladies' stand and blow 'em kisses. They loved it.'

The question posed by Mike Brearley, left hanging in the air, about where Tony got his showmanship from – 'Something in the family perhaps?' – led me to ask his brother Ian. He gave the matter some thought before answering. 'Hmm, good question. My father was not a showman. He was very proud of his war record but he never talked about it. He was always wryly contemptuous about other people, family or friends, who boasted about what they had done in the war when he knew for a fact that their involvement in actual fighting had been minimal.' *Certainly compared to his experiences of active service.* 'Exactly. So, no, he was not a showman. Nor was my mum. That is not to say that they didn't have a good time whenever the occasion presented itself but they were not the type to push themselves forward.' *So where did Tony's theatrical streak come from?* 'The thing is that he was not so much an extrovert as an enthusiast. He had ideas, adventures, endeavours, exploits. We had a simple life in South Africa but he would come back and say, let's do this or that. He made things happen. He built dreams.'

A dream that he almost certainly might have had was winning the third and crucial Test in Madras. Once again England fell agonisingly short, losing by four wickets. If only someone in the batting order had found the necessary technique and concentration to stay with Keith

Fletcher for a reasonable period of time as he compiled a masterful 97 not out in England's total of 242. By now, following a shaky start to his England career, Fletcher was building for himself a reputation as a batsman of the highest class. Even he found no answer to Indian spin in the second innings; this time the tormentor-in-chief was not Chandra but Bedi, aided and abetted by Prasanna. The total for victory was a mere 86 for the Indians, a formality, or so it seemed. Tony had had a quiet match. That was about to change. After Engineer had fallen cheaply to Old, Wadekar, the Indian captain, slashed at an outswinger hard and low to Tony at first slip, which he pouched jubilantly. Wadekar stood his ground. The umpire made no signal. Tempers rose and Tony's boiled over. He ran down the pitch, holding the ball aloft, in the direction of the umpire. Versions of what he uttered to the umpire differ as to which side you listen to but the fact remained that it was not altogether a becoming scene. Eventually, the umpire was persuaded to consult with his colleague and after some deliberation, it was deemed that the ball had carried, Greig had made a clean catch and Wadekar was given out. Justice, if not good manners, had prevailed. In Tony's defence, it has to be said that it was a tense and crucial period of play when the result of the series hung in the balance and feelings were running high. In the event India squeaked home by four wickets but the damage to England's reputation had been done. Tony was rebuked publicly and privately by the tour manager, Donald Carr, and later on his return home was forced to attend a disciplinary hearing at Lord's where he was given six-of-the-best from the head beak. The whole unseemly business did not seem to curb his natural enthusiasm, however, or his popularity with his adoring Indian public. He always took his punishment stoically and rarely bore a grudge.

India now had a 2-1 lead, one they were never going to relinquish. It was felt that England had missed the boat; their chances had come and gone and so it proved. The fourth Test in Kanpur was drawn, the only event of significance being the captain's maiden, and only, Test century. He was a popular skipper even if, in the minds of the senior players, likely to make way for Illingworth on their return home. 'A good bloke; he got the best out of us,' was Keith Fletcher's opinion. 'Handled us well,' said Chris Old, 'a good player of spin bowling.' 'Not a great batsman,' was Roger Tolchard's verdict, 'but a charming man.' The only person to whom I spoke who had reservations about his captaincy was Bob Cottam. 'He was OK with me but not really my cup of tea. I thought he was tactically limited.' It would be fascinating to get Tony's views of his captain. All we have is a rather bland comment later, saying that Lewis had done a 'splendid job' and that his captaincy had been 'careful and intelligent'. But there, Tony was always a loyal and energetic lieutenant to his skippers; not for him the backbiting and the forming of cliques that he so despised in the English county game. When it was time for him to assume the England captaincy, he accepted it eagerly and graciously but it was not something he had actively worked towards. He was ambitious but not at the cost of trampling over others in his climb to the top.

There was one final pyrotechnic burst for the MCC in their tour of India and as in all the best fireworks displays the best was saved for last. The fifth Test at Bombay was drawn, thus securing the series 2-1 for India, something that had not been in much doubt, but Tony Greig scored his maiden Test century and left an indelible memory in the minds of the hordes of his admirers. Some might have said that a three-figure score from him was overdue but it was bound to come sooner or later, taking into account the increasingly confident and authoritative manner in which he had been playing throughout the series. It was particularly satisfying for him that it took place in partnership with his friend and ally, Keith Fletcher, whose hundred was also his first. England were struggling at the time, 79/4, in the face of a large Indian first innings score of 448. When they were parted, Fletcher going for 113, the good ship England had sailed into calmer waters, the score being 333. Tony was finally out for 148. 'I remember that partnership well,' Fletcher told me. 'Washie was a much cleverer cricketer than people give him credit. He learned quickly that you shouldn't just lunge at spinners. He used his pads a lot and with that great reach of his, he could smother the spin. Mind you, with the use of Decision Review System these days, he'd have been given out lbw a lot more.' *That could be said of a lot of batsmen back then, Keith.* 'Indeed. Deadly always claimed he would have had another 100 wickets if he'd been playing now.' Fletcher had this to add to his impressions of his team-mate. 'He was an excellent tourist. Me, Greigy and Amiss became great mates on this tour, often sharing rooms, a friendship that would last throughout our England careers and beyond, one that couldn't be broken even after the Packer affair.'

Tony's reputation with the teeming crowds of India, already firmly fixed, rose to almost adulatory heights with his unusual form of congratulation to the diminutive Gundappa Viswanath when he reached his hundred in India's first innings. He took up the story himself in a later interview. 'I had spent most of the day fielding at silly point. As you know Vishy is very short and even bent in half I would find myself staring right into his eyes. Apart from being a really good player, Vishy is also a very nice man. When he reached his hundred, I spontaneously picked him up and rocked him like a baby. The Brabourne Stadium absolutely erupted – they loved it. It was the sort of involvement that they looked for, since cricket had long been perceived as too prim and proper. Wherever I go in India, I am reminded of what happened that day in Bombay. It is an extra-special memory I have of a special cricketer and a wonderful ground in a great city.'

He might have added that when he duly completed his century later on in the game, the two smallest men on the pitch, Viswanath and Gavaskar (brothers-in-law, incidentally) attempted to do the same to the Blond Beanpole but found the task of hauling him off his feet beyond them. These gestures were a fitting symbol of a successful series that had been played in a competitive but chivalrous atmosphere, one that sealed a lifelong love of the country in Tony's heart.

Would that the tour had ended there on a celebratory note but no, there were still three Tests in Pakistan to be negotiated. Following a short sojourn in Ceylon, they crossed the border into Pakistan where the conditions and the type of opposition were completely different. A campaign too many? A bridge too far? Undoubtedly. The team found it a slog after the long and arduous trek around India and now, instead of combatting the great spin trio of Chandrasekhar, Bedi and Prasanna on turning wickets (incidentally in the five-match series they had taken 70 wickets between them, the rest of the Indian bowlers only five), they had to face up to the might of the Pakistani batting line-up on wickets that were so dead they could still be playing on them now. The statistics of the three-match series say it all. The three Tests were drawn. Five Pakistani batsmen averaged over 40 (Mushtaq, Asif, Intikhab, Sadiq and Majid) and only Norman Gifford, with ten wickets, got into double figures. Tony was equal third with six. Of the batting, Dennis Amiss filled his boots, narrowly missing out on three successive hundreds, with an average of 81.20, with Tony second, with an average of 52.20. It was a batsman's series, one of unrelieved tedium. Chris Old no doubt spoke for them all. 'Pakistan was as dull as ditchwater. The wickets were just rolled mud. All I remember was the heat and the dust. Hyderabad was in the middle of the desert. The wicket *shone*, it was that bright. Knotty and Fletch, between overs, would walk to the other end via square leg to give their sore eyes a rest.' Keith Fletcher reckoned he never again played in heat like it. 'The temperature never fell below 115 degrees. It was like an oven. You could feel the heat rising off the dark pitch of rolled black mud.' It was with some relief when the team at last touched down at Heathrow.

As for Tony Greig ... he had quit these shores as a talented all-rounder; he came back a superstar. It was late May during the following English season of 1973. Hampshire were playing Glamorgan at Swansea. I happened to be sitting next to our captain Richard Gilliat, sipping a cup of coffee before proceedings got under way, when we were joined by Tony Lewis. He and Gilliat were old friends, captains of their respective Oxbridge and county teams, and they fell into conversation. They were discussing the recent tour of India. Shamelessly, I earwigged. Gilliat wanted to know all about Greig and his exploits. Lewis was adamant that Greig was 'the real deal'. Ignore all the histrionics, the theatrical appealing, the playing up to the crowd, he was saying, Greig was a seriously good Test batsman. The wickets didn't suit his bowling out there but no doubt he would 'strangle' a few on green, English pitches. And his fielding! Fearless. He had buckets for hands. No, he couldn't fault him at all. Needed reining in from time to time but his enthusiasm was infectious. It was an interesting and informative glimpse into the personality of his erstwhile team-mate.

'If you ignore the histrionics,' I think were Lewis's exact words but then he went on to say that sometimes you couldn't. He hadn't been greatly impressed with Tony's insistent and prolonged appeal and the furore it caused over the Wadekar 'bump' ball and he was irked when Tony took the team on an impromptu and triumphant lap of honour around the ground at the completion of the fifth and final Test in Bombay. Lewis at the time was busy giving post-match interviews. 'What the hell is Greigy doing out there with my team?' he later waspishly wrote. But Lewis was too much of a realist, to say nothing of his good nature and generosity of spirit, not to recognise the star quality of the South African in the ranks. On Tony's death, Lewis paid him this thoughtful tribute: 'We sat down for a long chat over a glass of wine at the end of the tour. One thing we had in common was that we were both always looking ahead of the game, not back on it. We both believed in trusting your luck and obeying your gut instinct.'

As I remember, the subject of the England captaincy cropped up. Not for me, boyo, was Lewis's response, I have other fish to fry in the media. Actually, that is a lie. He did not say 'boyo', but he was right about the captaincy. Illingworth was back in charge for the three-match series against New Zealand, with normal service being resumed as England beat the traditionally weak Black Caps 2-0. However, as we shall see, that score was deceptive; New Zealand could, and probably should, have won their first series in the Mother Country. What happened to Tony Lewis? He scored 2 and 2 in the first Test at Trent Bridge, withdrew from the side for the second, owing to a knee problem, and never played for his country again. The following year, he retired from cricket for good. Unlike Massie, whose Test career had an equally brief period of sunshine, he did not disappear into the gloom and apparently off the face of the earth. Lewis had long cultivated a career in the press: he was appointed as the cricket and rugby correspondent for *The Sunday Telegraph* before moving to the BBC, where his soft Welsh tones became familiar to millions of viewers as a cricket commentator. Later, he became president of the MCC, unusually serving two years in the job, so it would be fair to say that he did not regret for long his stint as caretaker captain of the England side.

As for Illingworth, I am sure that he was aware as anybody that the 2-0 result flattered his team. After having been bowled out for 97 in their first innings in the first Test at Trent Bridge (Greig 4-33), New Zealand were set a mammoth target of 479 to win ... and very nearly made it. They fell a mere 39 runs short. Their heroic chase owed much to their captain, Bev Congdon, who scored a brave and memorable 176. All the plaudits went to Congdon, and deservedly so – New Zealand were, after all, the underdogs – but nobody who was there would forget Tony's innings of 139 which did so much to set up the final innings run chase. Even hardened critics in the press room were purring at the majesty of his driving. Comparisons were made with the finest that Ted Dexter and Colin Milburn had served up in recent years, praise indeed. A century and seven wickets in the match, in a winning cause to boot. Was there anyone in the country to match Tony Greig as the darling of the English cricketing public?

The New Zealanders should have won at Lord's too. They were ahead by 298 runs as England started their second innings but were unable to ram home their advantage on the last day. Arnold was dropped with eight wickets down and only 70 runs ahead with two hours left for play. Fletcher (178) stood firm, Arnold survived with 23 not out and England escaped with a draw. They won the third at Headingley comfortably, by an innings, but this served only to paper over the cracks appearing in a team in which the England batting, with the exceptions of Greig, Boycott and Fletcher, looked brittle. The West Indies, already warming up against the counties, would provide a sterner test in the latter part of the summer.

Sobers, Boyce, Julien and Holder, supported by the ageless Lance Gibbs – the West Indies had a more than useful bowling attack. But it was the batting that did for England in this series. No fewer than six of them, Sobers, Lloyd, Fredericks, Kanhai, Julien and Kallicharran, averaged more than 40 in the three Tests. It had been suggested by press and informed onlookers that Sobers was now in the twilight of his career. I would have liked to hear anyone suggest that to the England bowlers. He averaged an astonishing 76.50 for the series. He bowled less these days but he was as predatory as ever close to the bat with his catching. The gulf between the two sides was made glaringly obvious in the final Test at Lord's. Not even a bomb scare could dislodge Sobers; he was left undefeated on 150 as West Indies racked up a mammoth 652/8 declared. England subsided to their worst ever defeat on home soil, by an innings and 226 runs, thus losing the rubber 0-2.

Tony Greig had a quiet series. His top score was 44 and he took only seven wickets. His sense of humour was not dented, however. It is a strange fact that cricketers set great store by three figures. After all, it is only a number, one more than 99. Batsmen cherish the magical 100 after their name; bowlers dread it. When the England bowling figures were read out on the Tannoy at the completion of the West Indies' huge total, five of them had conceded more than 100 runs, one of them being Tony. As his figures (3-180) were announced, there was a great roar from the large West Indian contingent in the ground. Tony raised both arms high in the air and the roar grew louder.

Despite Tony's playful relationship with crowds both at home and abroad, this was a shattering, ruinous defeat. Someone had to pay the price, take the rap, fall on his sword. Illingworth as captain was very much in the firing line but he was a Yorkshireman and hardened professionals like him are disinclined to accept personal blame when the fault is corporate. The problems with the English team were not down to one man, he would have argued, and besides, in this mood, with the talent at their disposal, this West Indian side were unstoppable. Most sensible critics would have accepted this. Illingworth was an experienced and respected captain, his players followed him loyally, he had had success in the past and in any case, who else was competent enough to do the job? However, the selectors felt they had to act swiftly and decisively and Illingworth was unceremoniously dumped.

Players usually take these upheavals to the team in their stride; they are much more sanguine about the vagaries and the whims of selectors, managers, chairmen and administrators than one might imagine. Besides, there are usually one or two in their midst, or lurking in the wings, with their eyes on the main job. The king is dead; long live the king. Nevertheless, Illingworth had been a popular captain in the main. The best players in the country – for that is what the England team were, despite recent reversals – admired his tough, no-

nonsense approach and his tactical acumen. Tony said that among the players it was a 'move that enraged a lot of people'. Why? Not so much why was it an unpopular decision but why had it been taken at all? John Snow was not in any doubt. 'Illy was in the bad books of the powers-that-be ever since he refused to go to India,' he told me. 'He had always been independent minded and had not made himself popular with the game's administrators. He was on the players' side, you see, and was not afraid to speak out when he thought our interests were being compromised. The selectors, the administrators were looking for a way to change this, so they sacked him.' He did admit that it was true that Illingworth, at the age of 41, was not getting any younger. He had, after all, made his Test debut back in 1958.

So, who was the natural successor? There was none. Well, there was Geoffrey Boycott who was not in any doubt who was the natural successor but probably in that regard, he was in a majority of one, outside of his native Yorkshire, that is. Was Tony ever in the frame, if not in his own eyes then in the opinion of his contemporaries? 'Greigy was probably viewed as one for the future,' said Snow, 'but considered a bit too young.' Tony seems not to have considered the possibility, not yet at any rate. He remained shocked and bewildered by the departure of Illingworth, whom he regarded as the best tactical captain he had played under. 'I believe that it was a premature decision.'

Premature because no obvious plan had been made for a successor. Geoffrey Boycott was Geoffrey Boycott's choice. The vacancy was too soon for Tony Greig. Colin Cowdrey had played what he thought was his last Test back in 1971, since when he had suffered a severe bout of pneumonia and in any case his age – he was now in his late thirties – militated against him. Tony Lewis had given up on his Test career and was soon to retire completely. He would have refused had he been asked; he was set on his new career. No other name in that England team heavily defeated at Lord's leapt from the page as a contender, so the selectors had to look to the shires to lead the team on a potentially inflammatory tour of the Caribbean that winter. Their choice was Mike Denness, who had not played in any of the six Tests that summer. Tony's reaction to the appointment was publicly diplomatic but we can read between the lines. 'Mike was a nice fellow and a good cricketer but his Test experience was very limited.' That seemed to be the general impression of the man. An elegant batsman and a fine cover point, he lacked the necessary steel to succeed as a Test player of the highest class and his gentle and sensitive nature did not make him the ideal person to deal with the stubborn and egotistical personality of a Geoffrey Boycott. Tony, unlike his Yorkshire team-mate, was prepared to give Denness the benefit of the doubt and once he had been appointed Denness's vice-captain for the tour, his loyalty was never in any doubt.

For another opinion of Denness as an England captain, I sought out Keith Fletcher who played under him enough times and who must have got to know him even better once Denness had joined him at Essex after Kent dispensed with his services. 'Yes, he came to us at Essex and helped us win the Championship and the Benson and Hedges Cup in 1979. My take on him was that he was a better captain in the one-day game than in the three-day game or Test matches. His record in limited-overs cricket speaks for itself.' One gets the impression that, yet again, the captain foisted on the team was felt to be no more than a stop-gap, one whom the authorities at Lord's could trust to handle the tricky political and social headaches that always seem to arise in a tour of the Caribbean. And, my word, there was no shortage of those.

As usual, Tony Greig was centre stage, with bat, ball and controversy. Denness, who had a wretched time with the bat, was simply overshadowed by Tony's exploits on the field and his sheer charisma he exuded every time he stepped out of his hotel room. Consider this, a tall, imposing, blond haired, white man from South Africa by turns enchanting and infuriating the volatile West Indian crowds. He was, like it or not, the star of the show. It was impossible, according to onlookers, to take your eyes off him, whatever he was doing. As for performances on the field, he was doing a lot. At times, he seemed to be carrying the team on his shoulders. Figures do not always tell the whole story but on this occasion, they are hard to ignore. He finished second in the averages as well as second in the number of runs scored, 430 at 47.77. Only Dennis Amiss outscored him, 663 runs at an extraordinary 82.87. Furthermore, Tony was the leading wicket-taker, with 24 wickets at 22.62. Nobody else got into double figures. And let us not forget his electric fielding, close to the wicket or indeed anywhere on the park. Just one point to ponder when considering the status of Tony Greig in the pantheon of great all-rounders. Ian Botham never had figures like that in any series against the West Indies.

That England drew the series 1-1 came as a bit of a shock, a welcome one no doubt, but it could not wholly disguise their shortcomings. In cricketing parlance, they 'got out of gaol' but West Indies must bear their share of responsibility for so carelessly leaving the keys to the prison lying about. In the first three Tests, they had a lead in excess of 200 going into the second innings and it was only in the first of these games that they managed to convert their superiority into a victory. At every stage, they were thwarted by courageous fightbacks from the England batsmen; in the first (to no avail) by Amiss's 174, in the second by Amiss's mammoth 262 not out and in the third by Fletcher's 129 not out. The less than unequivocal praise that Dennis Amiss was accorded among some people as a Test batsman of proven class has always bemused me. On this tour, he was masterful and it should not be forgotten that his two Test double hundreds were made against the formidable pace attack of the West Indies, giving the lie to his perceived weakness against fast bowling. In the fourth Test, both he and Tony scored centuries and for once England seemed to be scrapping on equal terms with their opponents before rain put paid to an intriguing contest.

The *denouement* of the tour was at Port-of-Spain in Trinidad, with England just about hanging on to their last chance to square the series. Was this Tony Greig's finest hour? It certainly was with the ball in his hand. The match was played over six days on a low, slow turner of a wicket. Early on in the tour, he had worked out that medium pace was ineffective on the wickets being prepared. You either had to have extreme pace to succeed or have the ability to spin the ball. He started to experiment with bowling off-cutters and discovered that, providing he could exert enough control – easier said than done – he could make the ball turn and bounce, using his height and a good pivot of the body at the moment of delivery. Furthermore, it had not gone unnoticed that there was a fair number of West Indian batsmen in the side who were left-handed – four in the top five – so attacking them with off spin from around the wicket made a lot of sense. Here in Trinidad he came into his own. He took 13-156 in the match and bowled England to an unlikely victory by just 26 runs. 'I have never bowled better than in that Test,' he later said. 'Everything was right, the run-up, the loop in flight and the length.' Alan Knott gave me a fascinating insight into Tony's bowling on this tour. 'For two or three Tests, his off-cutters were beyond belief and in that Trinidad Test, he produced the best spells I've ever seen. You'd think it was going to be a full toss then it would dip, turn and bounce. Magical!'

It was an irony lost on nobody that Underwood was bowling equally well at the other end but he only took one wicket to Tony's 13. 'That's just the way the cookie crumbles,' my old mate Mike Taylor would say at the arbitrariness of fate, the cruel disbursement of luck by the cricketing gods. 'It was extraordinary how lucky a player was Greigy,' he told me, 'he'd play and miss, play and miss and then hit a four!' John Snow was equally dumbfounded on occasions. 'The long-hop that trapped a well-set batsman was not at all embarrassing – it was always part of the plan,' he laughed. Roger Tolchard told me, 'Deadly would bowl maiden after maiden, wheeling away, *hating* to concede a run. Then Greigy would come on and bowl long hops and full tosses, go for runs and get a wicket! It used to drive Deadly mad.' No doubt it did here, too, at Port-of-Spain, but Underwood's frustration must have been assuaged by the satisfaction of victory. These criticisms were offered with a generous and knowing smile. Great players make their own luck, was their agreed conclusion. Snow probably speaks for them all. 'It was because of his positiveness and confidence that he more or less willed things to happen ... and they did!' The competitive instinct and the single-minded pursuit of success were noted by *Wisden* in its report of the tour: 'His driving influence on this side was apparent; it was even more apparent when he was not present.'

Which begged the question among the press why was he not captain. He was leading the side, even if Denness was in charge. Ironically, Tony's exploits, particularly that match-winning haul of 13 wickets in the final Test, had probably saved Denness's bacon. How can you court martial a captain who has just returned from plundering in the Caribbean towing a prize ship with the booty of a shared series? The reservations remained but so did they about Tony's candidature. Why? It all boiled down to the Kallicharran Incident, one that haunted Tony throughout his career. As memory served me, Tony had received a bad press both at home and in the West Indies for an act that at best was described as ungallant and at worst downright unsportsmanlike. He had run out the non-striker, Alvin Kallicharran, on the last ball of the day as the batsman was making his way back to the pavilion, believing that stumps had been drawn. In fact, Alan Knott, unaware of what was happening, had in fact removed the bails, as you do in order to hand them to the umpire on your way back to the pavilion. There was hell to pay, not least among the crowd, Kallicharran being the local hero, and the whole episode threatened to get out of hand. Hurried discussions between both teams' management resulted in Kallicharran's reinstatement at the crease the next morning and an apology and public handshake between him and Greig before the start of play. Common sense, it seemed, had prevailed.

Or had it? In order to refresh my recollection of the exact sequence of events, I watched a video on YouTube of the whole incident. It transpired that my recollection was defective. It happened nothing like I had been led to believe. Bernard Julien was batting, Underwood was bowling and Tony was fielding very close in at silly point. He could have leant forward and picked Julien's pocket; in fact that is just what he was attempting to do. Julien pushed the ball, the last of the day, past Tony towards silly mid-off. As usual he hared after it, looked up – after all, he was facing that way – saw Kallicharran, the non-striker, backing up five yards out of his crease, so he hurled the ball at the stumps, spread-eagling them and appealing in the same instant. The umpire raised his finger. Out! Nothing could have been more cut and dried. Kallicharran had been caught napping and he had paid the price.

As a batsman, you guard your crease with your life. You venture forth at your peril and if something happens that threatens your safety you scurry back home as quickly as you can. As for wandering up the wicket to do a bit of gardening, you make damn sure the ball is dead before your do your reconnoitring.

Although it could be argued – and it was, exhaustively – that the spirit of the game had been impugned on both occasions, I am convinced that the decision to reverse the decision was wrong. Kallicharran was out. There is no doubt about it. The ball was not dead and he was remiss in not making sure he was safely back in his ground. Thus no blame should be attached to the fielder concerned, whatever the two management teams decided retrospectively. But poor old Tony Greig got it in the neck, from spectators, onlookers, press, media and public opinion. For the life of him he could not see what he had done wrong. In the immediate aftermath, with tensions running high, Garry Sobers – typically – came into the England dressing room, sat down next to Tony, put his arm round him and said, 'I'm with you on this one, man. And you'd better be with me tonight!' Derek Underwood, meanwhile, was more peeved that Tony might have missed and the ball would have gone for four overthrows … off his bowling! Deadly gave runs away as willingly as John Paul Getty gave away ransom money.

Never one to bear a grudge or to let disagreements fester, Tony acquiesced in the hastily cobbled together compromise and willingly shook Kallicharran's hand – in the middle – and the crowd were happy. The threat of a riot had faded and the tour could continue. The West Indian crowds bore no grudge either. The Blond Beanpole soon won them over – as he seemed to do wherever he played in the world – with his presence, charm, charisma, love of the game, appetite for a contest and talent for showmanship. Flair as well. There was now considerable evidence building up to hail him as the current leading all-rounder in Test cricket. What about Garry Sobers, you might ask? He had finally dropped the curtain on his illustrious international career in that same match in Trinidad that Tony had taken 13 wickets. In his last innings he had been bowled by Underwood for 20, Deadly's only wicket in the match while Tony was wreaking havoc at the other end.

How about the other Scotsman in the side, Captain Denness? He had his supporters and detractors but the general feeling seemed to be that the jury was still out as far as the England captaincy was concerned. The twin tours by India and Pakistan in the summer of 1974 provided little in the way of convincing evidence either way. The

Indians were dispatched with minimum fuss by 3-0, providing far less of a threat in English conditions than they were at home. Tony got himself on the honours board at last at Lord's in the second Test with a century, one of three from England, the others being Amiss and Denness. The captain for good measure scored another ton in the third at Edgbaston, thus becoming the second England captain since Peter May to score successive Test hundreds. Nobody ever queried his class and elegant style against bowling not quite out of the top drawer. In this regard, he was probably the polar opposite of Tony, who thrived on pressure and who seemed to unfold his best innings against the very best.

The Pakistanis provided stiffer opposition. Their array of talented and resourceful batsmen provided plenty of runs and headaches for the English bowlers, none more so than the prolific Zaheer Abbas, who emulated his feat of 1971 with another double hundred against England (he was to score two more against India). Although the series was squared with neither side recording a victory, Pakistan did emulate the Invincibles, Bradman's side of 1948, by going through the tour unbeaten. As for Tony, it could be said that he had a quietish time of it throughout the summer but Greig being Greigy, he was never far from the action, literally so in the first Test, when he equalled the world record of six catches in an innings by an outfielder.

Who was going to captain the MCC on their Ashes tour that winter? That was the question that filled the cricket columns of the newspapers, more so than the actual cricket. Two candidates were mooted, Denness and Greig. Where was Boycott? Nowhere to be seen. After the first Test against India, he absented himself from the England team, a self-imposed exile that lasted until 1977. The official reason was that he had taken time away from international cricket to sort out a technical flaw that had been plaguing him against left-arm medium-pacers (Eknath Solkar of India being his main tormentor). Everybody within the game knew the real reason; he felt he had been slighted by the England selectors by the appointment of Denness over his head, a man whom he did not personally dislike but one whom he felt was not his equal as a cricketer. Tony Greig may well have thought the same – he would have had just cause if he had – but he chose to keep his opinions to himself and in the meantime offer the incumbent his full support.

The choice was a simple one, if not exactly straightforward. Did you want your captain (of the MCC, as it still was on overseas tours) to be an agreeable fellow, a tactful diplomat, an honest ambassador, a soother of troubled brows and indignant egos, a reasonable tactician and a stylish player, a man to keep a cool head in a crisis, a calming influence on and off the pitch, a thoroughgoing good egg? Or did you want somebody who would ruffle feathers, take the fight to the enemy, lead by example and inspire his men by deeds of derring-do? In short, did you want someone to direct the charge or lead the charge himself? That is not to denigrate the respective qualities of either man; it just seemed to me at the time to encapsulate their different temperaments. It was not at all clear that Tony Greig was the obvious candidate. That view smacks of retrospective thinking, knowing what we now know lay in store for them in that fateful Ashes series of 1974/75. No less an authority than *Wisden* was still voicing reservations about Tony being entrusted with the job. Their correspondent referred to his 'explosiveness' and wondered whether 'his desire to succeed seemed to overwhelm his judgement'. Time would tell. If time can be measured in chunks of six months, then it can be said that it certainly did.

In the end, the selectors went with the 'safe' choice, as everybody knew they would, and Mike Denness was appointed captain of the MCC tour Down Under in 1974/75. His vice-captain was John Edrich. John Edrich! Nothing wrong with him *per se*. He was a vastly experienced campaigner and would no doubt prove to be a loyal and committed lieutenant but he had been unavailable to tour the West Indies the previous winter where Tony had acquitted himself well in the role. Tony felt snubbed and wondered whether the Kallicharran Incident had played in the minds of the suits at Lord's who had a big say in these sorts of things. Privately, he shrugged his shoulders and vowed to make the best of it. After all, who would not relish taking on the Australians in their back yard?

Some Ashes series stick in the memory, for a variety of reasons. Close encounters, outstanding individual performances, victories against all the odds, great teams, controversy .... The 1974/75 visit by the MCC to Australia falls into this category and its slogan is unforgettable:

> *Ashes to Ashes, Dust to Dust,*
> *If Lillee don't get you, Thommo must!*

Australia won the six-match series 4-1 but it was the emergence of arguably the fastest pair of opening bowlers in Test match history that caught the eye of onlookers and various painful and brittle parts of the anatomy of the unfortunate batsmen. Reputations were made and reputations were broken. For England, it was a disastrous tour, effectively finishing the Test careers of several players and leaving others with mental scars that took a long time to heal. For Australia, it was of course a satisfying riposte to defeat on home soil by Illingworth's team four years earlier, underlining their status as unofficial world champions and sealing the fame of Lillee and Thomson.

But it was the making of Tony Greig. He alone, with perhaps the exception of Alan Knott, emerged with his reputation enhanced – if that were at all possible. The tour could justifiably be said to have changed the course of his life, leading as it did by a circuitous route to World Series Cricket, a job for life with the Packer organisation, a career in television commentary and permanent residency in Australia. All will be revealed in due course; for the time being, the only thing that was on Tony's mind was standing up to Australian bullying and making sure that in so doing he did not take a backward step. Would that some of his team-mates had shown half his courage. This is what contributed to his success and popularity with the Australian public. The Indian crowds loved his flamboyance and play-acting; the Australian crowds admired his courage under fire.

England sailed into a perfect storm. They had a captain who was not everybody's choice and whose batting, though pleasing on the eye, was suspect against fast bowling. Two of their best players were left at home: Geoffrey Boycott, of his own volition, and John Snow .... *Tell me, John, why were you not selected for this tour? You were still in your prime – I can personally vouch for that.* 'Blackballed! No way was I going to be selected after making myself unavailable to go to India.' Dennis Lillee had spent weeks encased in a plaster cast the previous year following a stress fracture of the lower vertebrae and it was feared he would never bowl fast again. As it transpired, by a supreme effort of will and with expert medical care, he returned as fast and as hostile as ever. Jeff Thomson was practically an unknown. He had played one Test, against Pakistan two years previously and taken 0-110. David Lloyd has always said that the boys on the tour when they heard that Thomson had been picked for the first Test mistook him for 'Froggy' Thomson, so called because he had a whirlwind action and bowled off the wrong foot.

They were soon to be put right. In the words of the *Wisden* correspondent, 'Watching the two [Lillee and Thomson] in action, it was easy to believe that they were the fastest pair ever to have coincided in a cricket team.' He went on to speculate that *any* England batting line-up would have struggled against those two. As it was, their technique and mental frailties were to be sorely tested and found wanting. Furthermore, the two fast men left a trail of physical devastation in their wake. Amiss, Lloyd and Edrich (twice) suffered fractures, Dennis Amiss, the highest run-scorer in Test cricket for the calendar year of 1974, was blasted out of form and out of the side, David Lloyd had his box turned inside out by a savage ball from Thomson and unsurprisingly had to retire hurt (subsequently making his name as an after-dinner speaker by virtue of his amusing recollections of the incident), Keith Fletcher was hit on the head, the ball ricocheting off the badge of St George on his cap to be nearly caught at cover, Brian Luckhurst, a stoical and reliable opener under Illingworth on his previous tour to Australia, was shattered by the experience and never played for England again, and Mike Denness was so shorn of runs and confidence that he dropped himself for the fourth Test. In short, the England batting was blown away. Furthermore, the wickets were not up to scratch. The only true surface they played on was at Perth, the rest were up and down and there is nothing a batsman more fears than an unreliable pitch when the bowling is fast and nasty. The Australian catching, particularly in the slip and gully cordon was outstanding. Nobody could remember a single chance that went down. Greg Chappell was in a class of his own as a batsman, for England also had one or two fast bowlers, but his aggregate runs for the series (608) and his average (55.27) eclipsed everybody else on both sides. Last but not least, Australia provided only two umpires, Brooks and Bailhache, for the entire series and neither seemed able or willing to curb the excessive use of the short ball, which Lillee and Thomson employed to brutal and terrifying effect. And need I remind you that these were the days before helmets.

All of which serves to underline Tony Greig's heroism on this tour, something for which he has not, in my opinion, been granted sufficient recognition back in this country. The Australian crowds recognised it all right. Not since 1958/59 had they been able to see at first hand the English being so comprehensively demolished and they rather enjoyed the spectacle, turning up in their droves and breaking all records for attendances at Test matches. The noise, especially when Lillee and Thomson were bowling in tandem, was as hostile as it was intimidating and must have resembled for all the world, certainly in the view of the *Wisden* correspondent, the Colosseum as the Christians faced the lions. Christopher Martin-Jenkins, the BBC cricket correspondent covering the tour, described it all as 'so fearsome that even hardened campaigners in the press box were seen to blanch'. This is what Tony had to face up to and it was how he reacted that earned the admiration of the crowd and the grudging respect of his opponents.

Show me a batsman who claims that he is not frightened of fast bowling and I shall show you a liar. Tony Greig was no different from other mortals. It would be easy, he said after he had stopped playing, for anybody on that tour to claim that he had not been frightened facing those two but in truth he believed that everybody was, at some stage or other. His method for combatting nerves was a cigarette before he went out to bat, a fierce whirling of arms as he walked to the wicket and an aggressive demeanour when he was out in the middle. In the game of cricket, the role of batsman and bowler is a polar opposite. One runs in; the other waits motionless. One delivers the question; the other tries to answer it. One can physically hurt you; the other cannot. One has ten accomplices to support him; the other only has the non-striker as a friend (quite possibly in no hurry to take his place). It can be a very lonely place at the crease, knowing that one mistake, one small error of judgement, will send you on your way.

Most batsmen of true class respond to intimidation in the only way they know how, by hitting the ball to the boundary. Thus they accumulate runs, score a century and give their answer in the scorebook. Nerves have been conquered, problems solved, pressure eased, runs scored, the team helped without saying much. Quietly, they have put the bully boys in their place. Needless to say, this approach never suited Tony's temperament. He felt compelled to stand up to them, literally as well as metaphorically. He started to play-act, in an attempt to rile them. He would theatrically signal his own fours, often taking a pace or two down the wicket to do so right under his tormentor's nose. No doubt words were exchanged. That wouldn't have worried him. He was South African, after all, and he could give as much as he got. He saw it as a gladiatorial contest and he was resolved to come out on top. Of course, for a batsman it is impossible to be the victor every time. Even Bradman was now and then dismissed for a low score. But the point was, in Tony's eyes, not to betray weakness, fragility, apprehension, fear. All right, he seemed to be saying, you may get me out but you're not going to scare me out.

This was no better illustrated than in his century in the first Test in Brisbane. Australians have given the ground known as the Gabba the nickname 'Gabbatoir' on account of its less than pleasing architectural design and its less than welcoming atmosphere. So intimidating is the place that England to this day has an unenviable record there, with only two Test victories since the Second World War. There was a familiar feel to this match for pessimistic England supporters. Australia won comfortably by 166 runs. The stage was set, the script written, the actors given their parts for the story to be played out over the summer, brittle English batting bruised and broken by fearsome fast bowling. A new star was born, Jeff Thomson, with his unusual but effective 'slinging' action, who dismantled England in the second innings, with 6-46 (plus three in the first innings), a bowler of terrifying pace, steep bounce and a method of delivery, with his cocked wrist behind his back which was difficult to pick up and which no England batsman successfully countered throughout the series. Lillee, not long recovered from his back operation, no doubt spurred on by the speed of his partner at the other end and by the baying chorus of

'Lillee, Lillee!' from the crowd as he ran in, bowled faster and faster as the series went on. Only Greig it seemed was able to stand up to them.

Australia had scored 309 in their first innings. Towards the end of the innings, England had been held up by one of those irritating tailender partnerships, with Lillee in particular taking liberties with the England pace attack. Tony suggested to his team-mates that a short ball would not go amiss. They seemed strangely reluctant. 'Hell, man, give me the ball,' he said, thinking they were taking the unwritten law of the fast bowlers' union – that neither should bounce the other – too literally, 'I'll give him one then.' Which he promptly did. Lillee got himself into a terrible tangle and offered up a dolly to Knott behind the wicket. Lillee was furious and made it known to Tony on his way back to the pavilion that he could expect a hot reception when the time came for him to bat.

It was said at the time, and continues to rumble on today, that Tony started the bumper war with that delivery. Nonsense! Lillee and Thomson were fast bowlers. The bouncer was a principal weapon in their armoury. Is there any way on God's earth that they would have reined in their aggressive intent with a batsman wearing the dark blue cap of England 22 yards away, with the crowd baying for blood and the scent of fear in their nostrils? You would have had as much chance of calling them off as a pack of wild dogs circling a stricken wildebeest. The only two men with the authority to curb the bouncer war were the umpires and they did nothing. No, the short ball was going to be the staple diet of the series and nothing Tony did, or did not do, would have made the slightest difference.

He expected retaliation when he came to the wicket in England's first innings, with the side in considerable trouble, four wickets having gone down for 57, and retaliation is what he got. 'Lillee tried to hill me,' he later said. His first ball whistled past his nose, evaded a leaping Rod Marsh way back behind the stumps and cannoned into the sightscreen first bounce. Many batsmen would have been intimidated, and many were on that tour, but Tony played the only way he knew. He took a step, not backwards, but forwards, taking on the bowler and doing his best to rile him. He succeeded, too. Lillee lost his rag, tried to bowl quicker and quicker, attempting to hit Tony instead of getting him out.

It wasn't pretty but it was effective. It was also very brave. Tony rode his luck – you had to have slices of luck from time to time against such bowling – but he also played some stirring counter-attacking strokes and reached his hundred in typical fashion, signalling his boundary to the crowd. He rated the innings as not necessarily the best of his Test hundreds but certainly the most satisfying. It was his first against the Old Enemy and it had been achieved in the midst of a crisis against the finest pair of fast bowlers that he had ever faced, before or after. It did not, alas, prevent an Australian victory but singled him out as one player, perhaps the only one, in the team who would not be cowed.

Notwithstanding Tony's heroics, the fact could not be ignored that England had suffered a shattering defeat. In more ways than one. Rather like camp followers sifting through the piles of bodies following a mediaeval battle, the selection committee sat down after the match, counted the wounded and considered their options. Reinforcements were desperately required. On his return home, Alec Bedser, the tour manager, admitted that the list of illnesses and injuries besetting the touring party exceeded anything he had ever known. Send for the cavalry! That would normally have been Tony's response (he had been overlooked as vice-captain but he had been co-opted on to the selection committee) but even he knew that was an impossibility – the cavalry were already there and had been routed. They all instinctively shied away from sending for an inexperienced youngster, someone who had shown promise in the county game but who had yet to be exposed to the brutal reality of fast bowling of such hostility. It just wouldn't be fair. Confidence could be broken for evermore. No, experience and a proven track record against fast bowling was what was needed. Even more so given that the next Test was at Perth, at the time considered the fastest and bounciest pitch in world cricket.

I had always believed that the surprising choice of Colin Cowdrey to come to England's rescue had a lot to do with the strong Kent cadre within the side – Denness, Knott, Underwood and Luckhurst. They all knew about their county colleague's familiarity with fast bowling over a 20-year career in Test cricket and, let's face it, they would have said, nobody possessed a better technique in the game than he. Put aside for one moment that Cowdrey was not currently 'in the game' –

he actually had his feet up in front of a roaring log fire with a gin and tonic in his hand when the call came – and furthermore he had more or less come to the conclusion that at the age of 41, his Test career was over. Strangely enough, it was Tony's voice that was the loudest in championing the old warhorse during that fateful meeting. He recognised Cowdrey's pedigree and class. He knew that his former England colleague in his career had faced the fastest, from Lindwall and Miller, to Adcock and Heine, to Hall and Griffith, had never flinched and had often prospered. Sentimentality rarely intruded into Tony's assessment of ability and he was sure that Cowdrey was their man even if it may have fleetingly crossed his mind that he had been his idol when playing those 'Test' matches in the back garden in Queenstown.

Cowdrey's arrival at Perth International Airport had all the ingredients of a 'story', eagerly seized upon by the press. The Australian media were largely scornful, not quite believing that England should turn to in their hour of need a 41-year-old with a Falstaffian figure whose last Test was three years ago. Corporal Jones in *Dad's Army* was one of the more acceptable jibes aimed in his direction. The English pressmen sensed a fairy tale bookend to the much-loved Cowdrey's career, though fearful for his safety and well-being. Opinions among the touring party, now his team-mates, were largely supportive. Tony's choice had been unequivocal. Denness was known to be a fan and it was he, as captain, who had picked up the phone to interrupt Cowdrey's gin and tonic. Derek Underwood said this to me: 'He was considered to be the best at playing the quicks, even at this late stage of his career.' Geoff Arnold offered this by way of a reaction: 'Kipper was as fine a player of fast bowling as there was. And let's face it, there were not many options.' Bob Willis said, 'Here were Lillee and Thommo peppering our batsmen and we needed someone with experience who could counter them.' The battle-hardened warriors such as Amiss, Edrich, Knott and Titmus had been his team-mates in recent England sides and knew all about his record and his courage. Keith Fletcher was a lone voice amongst those I spoke to who was not so sure. 'I dunno,' he said. 'To be honest, I felt sorry for him. I don't think he should have been put through that. It wasn't fair on him.'

Fair or not, Cowdrey had come prepared. When he arrived in the dressing room at Perth, Tony witnessed an amusing but telling incident. 'As Colin released the lock of his cricket case, it sprang open as if alive, then gradually, like bread rising in the oven, a mountain of foam rubber rose from the interior. This was his protection and he had obviously been well briefed. He padded almost every part of his body but nobody laughed – we had seen enough to convince us he was right.'

As it turned out, there was no fairy-tale ending to Colin Cowdrey's career. But neither was it a personal – or physical, as some had feared – disaster. His bravery was never doubted and his technique, tested as never before, stood up well. He could do no more to stem the tide than King Canute but he exhibited a calmness at the crease that was extraordinary. 'He set an example,' wrote Christopher Martin-Jenkins, 'to team-mates that ought to have been shamed by the way he was withstanding two of the fastest bowlers in the world after only five days' practice.' He was lbw to Thomson for 41 in the second innings, not the hundred that he would have liked and the romantics craved, but sometimes a score such as that is worth much more than it says in the book. Perhaps the same could be said of Tony's two scores of 23 and 32, promoted now to No 4 in the order but the fact remains that you do not win a Test match with such meagre scores and England were duly demolished by nine wickets.

Rather like an old man on his deathbed who suddenly opens his eyes, sits up and demands breakfast, the England team, 0-2 down and already a defeated side, did not play half badly in the third Test at Melbourne. They gave their opponents a run for their money at last, providing a more exciting finale than anybody had any right to expect. It would be untrue to state that Tony Greig single-handedly dragged the side up by its bootlaces – there were noteworthy performances by other players – but once more he set the tone. Unusually, it was more or less level pegging after the first innings, one run separating the two sides. England started well in their second, putting on 115 for the first wicket, but then Lillee and Thomson warmed to the task, blowing away the visitors' middle and late order. At 182/8, England were staring another defeat in the face. Not with Tony Greig still at the crease; oh no, he didn't do capitulation. His innings of 60, shepherding the tail to a competitive total of 244, was every bit as extraordinary as his hundred at Brisbane. 'Greig's massive confidence and showmanship, with studious help from Willis, added 56 for the ninth wicket and set up the match for its astonishing finale.' Chris Old put some flesh on to the bare bones of that *Wisden* report. 'Greigy came out to bat, arms whirling around, looking as confident as ever. And this to face bowlers whistling the ball past batsmen's heads. Suddenly, he launched himself forward and hit a screamer through the off side. He raised his hand to his forehead to shield his eyes as if to say, now, where did that go? They got fired up and tried to knock his block off but he would just pretend box, as if he was punching the ball as it passed. Or he would pretend to head it as it flew through to the keeper. Terrifying! But not for Greigy. He was the star of the show.'

Australia's target was 246, the highest total of the match on a wicket that had never played true. But England were without one of their strike bowlers, Hendrick, who had pulled a hamstring. With seven overs remaining and only 16 runs required with three wickets in hand, Australia were on the verge of their third victory. One hand on the Ashes, you might say, or perhaps one finger would be more appropriate, given the diminutive size of the urn. And who else would now take centre stage to prevent that happening? At this crucial juncture, Tony bowled a tight over (eight balls in Australia, remember) conceding just two runs and at the end of it he punched the air as if the Ashes were going the other way. Underwood bowled a maiden – he *loved* bowling maidens – and the impetus was lost. When Tony dismissed Lillee on the fourth ball of the final over, the chase was abandoned and the match finished as a draw, Australia falling short by eight runs and England by two wickets.

Sometimes a draw can feel like a win. Had the balance of power in this series shifted? The answer was probably writ large even before a ball had been bowled in the following Test at Sydney. Mike Denness had been having a terrible time of it, both through illness and woeful lack of form. He decided to drop himself. Opinion was divided on this. Some regarded it as a brave decision, one made for the good of the side; you cannot have a relative passenger in the team, even if he is the captain. Others thought it was the wrong thing to do, an admission of weakness at a time when strength of character was required. The Australians probably allowed themselves a quiet chuckle before settling down to the business of putting the Englishmen to the sword, as they had been doing all series, and reclaiming the Ashes. This they did by winning the match by the comfortable margin of 171 runs. Only Tony, with a swashbuckling 50 in the first innings, plus his four wickets earlier, and Alan Knott, with a typically impudent and improvised 82, could be exempt from blame. John Edrich too showed enormous courage in England's hopeless chase of 400 to win. He was hit in the ribcage by Lillee and retired to hospital. Later, he returned, strapped up and full of painkillers, to block out for two and a half hours for 33 not out in a vain attempt to save the match for his side. Even the Australian crowd was impressed.

Edrich's bravery was a hallmark of a long and distinguished career; his suitability as a captain was perhaps less evident. When Denness made known his decision to step down, Tony's feelings can only be imagined. Publicly, he supported his captain's judgement, saying it was the right thing to do but none would have blamed him if he privately believed that he, and not Edrich, should have been leading the side out at the SCG. But protocol had to be followed. Edrich was the named vice-captain and as such, he would be expected to take over the reins if the captain was indisposed. He did a workmanlike, if uninspired, job in difficult circumstances but who do you want leading you out into battle in a crisis – a sergeant-major or a charismatic commander? Edrich, for all his sterling work in his country's service, was not the coming man. Tony Greig was. Everybody knew it and Tony must have quietly believed it himself. He had to bide his time and hope that the powers-that-be back at Lord's would put prejudice aside and make the obvious, if brave, decision.

In the meantime, things for the tourists went from bad to worse. With the Ashes safely reclaimed, there was a school of thought that the Australians might tinker with their team and subconsciously take their foot off the gas. The Australian psyche is not built like that. In Adelaide for the fifth Test, England were again consigned to a humiliating 163-run defeat. Denness reinstated himself in the side once it became apparent that Edrich, with broken ribs, was unfit to play but it made little difference; the gulf between the two teams was now as wide as the Grand Canyon. Some pride was salvaged by England winning the sixth Test in Melbourne but the victory will be forever given an asterisk in people's memory. Thomson was unfit and did not play and Lillee limped off the field after bowling only six overs. It was as if the Puritans had been banished from court and King Charles II restored to the throne. All was jollity and light and the English batsmen made hay. Denness scored a magisterial 188, thus only fuelling the suspicion that, fine player as he was, he was not the same batsman against seriously quick bowlers. Tony scored a dazzling 89 to speed the declaration on and for once there was no Australian fightback. A Pyrrhic victory by an innings and 4 runs perhaps but the tourists felt that at least they had made a point; could *any* side have stood up to Lillee and Thomson on those wickets? The great West Indies side suffered similarly at their hands the following season.

The tour felt like a seminal moment. England had been comprehensively, even ruinously, outgunned. Though everybody realised that in Lillee and Thomson their opponents had possession of all the aces, a 1-4 hammering would inevitably result in a rigorous post-mortem and no doubt a thorough cleansing of the Augean stables. The Denness regime staggered on for the two Test series in New Zealand, with the usual sense of 'after the Lord Mayor's Show' that it engendered, but Tony believed, along with others, that Denness's days as captain were numbered. Incidentally, the first Test in Auckland (which England won comfortably; the second was ruined by rain) provided personal triumphs for both Tony and Denness. Tony took ten wickets in the match and Denness made another cultured 180 odd. But these were mere sideshows to the main drama that was to unfold back home.

So what of the 1974/75 Ashes series and its place in cricket lovers' memory? Who better to ask than those who were there? Keith Fletcher will always remember how Tony wound up the Australian bowlers. 'It was all right for him,' he complained good naturedly, 'he was six foot seven and they had to get it up pretty high to reach his head. We used to give him stick about it but it was water off a duck's back. He played his own way and phew, what a spectacle it was.' Chris Old told me an amusing story about Tony's on-field antics. 'I was 12th man at Sydney and I was called on to the field to sub. I was sent down to third man in front of the Hill.' Now the Hill at Sydney was as notorious for riotous behaviour and boorish barracking as the Western Terrace at Headingley or the Eric Hollies Stand at Edgbaston, though perhaps less humorous and forgiving. 'Greigy was at slip,' Old continued, 'and had been making convict signs to the crowd on the Hill, holding both hands out in front of him as if they were manacled. The crowd were going mad just as I arrived to field right in front of them. Thanks Greigy, I said to myself.' He also remembered the first Test at Brisbane. 'As the Aussies came out to field, Lillee sprinted past them. Thommo followed him. They were both fired up with murder in their eyes. The first ball whistled past Amiss's nose. The stage was set, you could say.' Fletcher was in no doubt about the influence and damage the Australian pacemen caused. 'They were awesome. Greigy played them as well as anyone. If we'd had Lillee on our side, we would've won 3-1.' Alan Knott reckoned that for four and a half Tests (before he injured himself), Thomson was a genius, the like of which he had not seen before or after, and he saw a few fast bowlers in his time. 'But the innings Greigy played in Brisbane – nobody else could have played like that. Great players love pressure and that was a pressure cooker. And what a catcher! I reckon he was the best slipper I've seen. Not close to the wicket for the spinners, funnily enough, but standing back he was supreme.'

I leave the final word to Geoff Arnold. 'Look, it was a great tour. We got hammered, true, and people say the team spirit was poor. Not true. Team spirit was fine. Some of us weren't too keen on Denness as captain but that was on the field. Off the field, although results were not going our way, we did our best to enjoy it.' *Ah, but you were a bowler, Geoff. You didn't have to face down Lillee and Thomson.* He quickly put me right. 'Look, mate, Thommo hit me on the elbow before I had even picked my bat up.' The barrage was relentless and even tail-enders were not spared. 'Lillee bowled me a ball,' he continued, 'that flew past my nose, over Marsh's head and disappeared one bounce into the crowd. They all said I could've been killed.' Which puts into context the bravery, as much as the elan, of Greig's batting on that tour. He alone seemed to thrive in the hothouse of those encounters. Arnold added by way of perspective, 'People are *still* talking about that tour. It was a famous series and we felt privileged to have been a part of it. Of course it was uncomfortable at times but what an experience!'

There was another event that took place during the tour, unremarkable in itself but significant in terms of Tony's long-term future. While in Sydney, several of the players and their wives were invited to dinner at the home of Bruce Francis's parents. Tony and Keith Fletcher were among their number and it was only natural that Bruce would get together with the two of them, given that he had toured with Tony in Rhodesia with the International Wanderers and that he already knew Keith from his time at Essex. It had not escaped Francis's notice that Tony had become a bit of a cult hero in Australia during the tour. The Australian public had a rather poor opinion of the Pommies for their insipid capitulation in the face of their fast bowling and had taken enormous pleasure in their discomfiture. The one exception to their Pommie-bashing was of course not a Pommie at all. Tony Greig had earned their respect and grudging admiration for his spirited displays with bat and ball. The reputation he had gained for stirring up the patrons in the popular seats was nothing more than muscular banter. Every crowd wants a pantomime villain and Tony was more than happy to oblige. There was method to his madness, however, as Keith Fletcher pointed out. It wasn't showmanship for its own sake. Tony was not a natural clown, in the way that a future team-mate, Derek Randall, was. If not exactly carefully choreographed, Tony relished any opportunity to engage the crowd in mutual joshing and mockery if it in no way interfered with his team's performance. Indeed, he saw it as a potential distraction for his opponents and any edge over them was something not to be spurned. And in a funny sort of way, the Australian public enjoyed the exchanges. He became popular when others riled them. Similarly, they took to their hearts Harold Larwood (but not Douglas Jardine), Freddie Brown (but not Wally Hammond), Ian Botham (but not Mike Brearley), Darren Gough (but not Andy Caddick). They seem to like those who resemble their own, in spirit, temperament and bloody-mindedness. Not like the archetypal aloof, effete, arrogant Englishman, the hated colonial master. Greig was not one of those, they decided, he was the kind of guy with whom you could crack open a tinny and have a manly chat whilst cooking the snags on the old barbie.

Tony felt comfortable with this relationship – after all, it was not a lot different from the way of life back home in South Africa – and he was far too canny not to seek to turn it to his advantage. Francis instinctively recognised this bond that had been forged between his friend and the Australian public and on a later meeting, when both played for a Derrick Robins XI against South Africa after the MCC had returned from Australasia, the two chatted about plans and possibilities. 'Tony had been well received in Australia,' Francis said, 'and he asked me to see whether there were any commercial opportunities for him in Australia.' As it happened, England were not scheduled to tour during the following winter and Tony, like all his team-mates, international and county, would have to shift for himself. 'Unbeknown to me,' continued Francis, 'my club back in Sydney, Waverley, was negotiating with Dennis Lillee to play for them. When negotiations fell through, I suggested Tony. The club lined up about $100,000 and Tony agreed to play for us. Thus started a sort of business association alongside our friendship. I looked after his affairs in Australia.' And continued to do so until Tony's death. There was one final point Francis was keen to impress upon me. 'Tony was subsequently appointed England captain (*that happened during the following summer of 1975*) and the club expected Tony to seek more money or drop out. But he said that a deal was a deal and came to Waverley for the agreed money.'

That of course would not, could not, happen these days, the England captain having to go to Australia to play grade cricket during a fallow winter as a means of making his living. And therein lay the fertile ground for the seeds of the Packer Revolution to take root. The cricket establishment had no clue what was in store. Neither did Tony Greig, to be fair. For the time being, his mind was concentrated on the next stage of his life.

Chapter 7

England captain 1975–77

'We called him the Messiah.'

Alan Knott when Greig first produced his
sponsored St Peter bat from his bag

IN the event, the England selectors played safe over the question of the England captaincy and settled for the status quo. Their reasons were two-fold. There remained a residue of doubt along the corridors of power whether Tony Greig, for all his admirably combative attitude on the field of play, was quite the right man for the job. There was a feeling that he was occasionally hot-headed and might let the side down (the establishment side, that is, not his own team) by behaving inappropriately, in a way unbecoming of the captain of his country and MCC's ambassador abroad. Besides, was it *really* his country? His South African roots were still regarded with suspicion in some quarters. There had of course been a handful of England captains down the years who were not English-born: Lord Harris (Trinidad); Sir Pelham Warner (Trinidad); Douglas Jardine (India); Gubby Allen (Australia); Freddie Brown (Peru); Donald Carr (Germany); Colin Cowdrey (India); Ted Dexter (Italy). But there was no doubt in anybody's mind that they were all true English gentlemen, in spite of their foreign birthplace, and they all spoke with a recognisable English accent. All right, we can add to the list Tony Lewis and Mike Denness, the former's lilting Welsh tones as unmistakeable as the latter's Scots burr, but they were regarded to all intents and purposes as part of the family. Tony's South African accent cut through the committee rooms like a sharp knife.

The second reason was the fledgling World Cup, held throughout June of 1975, the first ever limited-overs international tournament. As England were playing at home, they were considered to be one of the favourites to win — at the very least, they were expected to reach the semi-final stage — and as such it was thought that a change of captain at this late stage in their preparation was not a sensible idea. Besides, as Keith Fletcher reminded me, Denness was a good one-day captain and had proved to be an astute tactician in the shorter format of the game. So things were left as they were for the time being.

The Inaugural World Cup was an outstanding cricketing, financial and popular success, so much so that the staging of future tournaments was there and then set in stone. As predicted, England reached the last four, losing to Australia who in turn lost the final to West Indies at Lord's in a thrilling match that lasted from 11.00am to 8.43pm. On a stage that was custom built for him, with record crowds and intense media coverage, Tony Greig for once failed to shine. He bowled well enough but successive scores of 4, 9, 9 and 7 left his admirers distinctly short-changed. He was expected to be the star of the show.

England reaching the semi-final? Neither here nor there in the eyes of the British public. Nor the selectors, it would seem. Their indecision was amply displayed by the appointment of Denness as captain for one game only in the hastily arranged four-Test series against the Australians after the World Cup. (Originally the South Africans were scheduled to tour but the possibility of their coming to these shores for the foreseeable future was fast disappearing over the horizon.) If he was a dead man walking, Denness would have been climbing the steps of the scaffold at close of play on the third day (Saturday) of the first Test at Edgbaston. Once again, England were staring at a humiliating innings defeat, duly completed on the Monday, and the press, knives already sharpened, gleefully thrust them into the guts of the England captain. It was later claimed that Denness's fate was sealed by the toss of the coin. Inserting the opposition is always a gamble and this one backfired catastrophically. The ball for some reason did not move around as expected in the overcast conditions and Australia made 359. Barely an hour into England's reply, the heavens opened and the home players could only stare glumly through the dressing room windows as the pitch (in those days left open to the elements once play had commenced) was flooded. On resumption, Lillee and Walker gleefully exploited the sodden, treacherous wicket and England were bowled out for 101. Seven of their batsmen failed to register double figures. Following on was a no more comfortable experience. By the time stumps were drawn on Saturday evening, they had been reduced to 93/5 and Denness's fate was sealed. Incidentally, this was Graham Gooch's Test debut. He made a pair, the first England player to do so in his first Test since Fred Grace (WG's brother) in 1880. Tony fared not much better, scoring 8 and 7.

One assumes that Mike Denness resigned from the captaincy sometime that Saturday evening, which would explain the phone call Tony received from Alec Bedser, the chairman of selectors, on Sunday, traditionally a rest day. Tony was certainly resting when the call came, in a pub, pretty sure he was to play no further part in the match (he was right on that score). The content of the conversation between him and Bedser might not have come as a complete surprise but the timing – in the middle of a Test match – probably did. When offered the captaincy, he accepted with eagerness, excitement and not a little trepidation. The fact of the matter was that England were simply not a very good side, Australia had the whip hand – some might have said the hex – over them and it was going to be the devil's own job for them to emerge from this series with any credit. They were already 1-0 down and what difference was a change of captain going to make with a side that was so demoralised? This was a challenge all right and Tony loved a challenge. I have no first-hand evidence of what he said to the team as they gathered at Lord's in preparation for the second Test but I can bet my bottom dollar it went something like this: 'Look, guys, these aren't supermen we're playing here. Let's give it our best shot, hey, and not be bullied by those arrogant ….' You catch my drift. I'm sure his team-mates did.

What of the discarded Mike Denness? Tony felt sorry for him though he knew as well as Denness himself that a change was inevitable. Denness was an honourable man, affable and dignified, and refused to dish the dirt once he got his marching orders. Quietly, he returned to Kent for whom he continued to play and was never picked for England again. If nothing else, the abrupt change of regime brought home to the new captain that his position would ever be precarious. 'All political lives end in failure,' said Enoch Powell, 'because that is the nature of politics and human affairs.' Tony was perfectly aware of how quickly his fortunes could change. That is what probably informed him in his later, momentous decision, to be discussed in a later chapter. How he must have envied his opposite number, Ian Chappell, who had at his disposal currently the finest batsman in the world, his brother Greg, and a bowling attack of Lillee and Thomson, backed up by Max Walker and Ashley Mallett. What resources did Tony have at his disposal?

Not a lot, it has to be said. However, all new captains like to make their mark in selection and Tony was no exception. Out with the old (Chris Old was indeed one of those axed) and in with the … er, even older. Beyond cricket circles, few would have heard of David Steele from unfashionable Northamptonshire. He was 33 years of age, silver-haired, bespectacled, slightly stooped of gait, with an unremarkable first-class average close to his age. But Tony had seen in him something he liked ('David would have gone under a bus for me,' he said) and it proved to be an inspired choice. During the course of the rest of the series, the English public took Steele to their hearts for a succession of innings that revealed the very qualities that Tony Greig felt had been missing in the team – obdurate stubbornness, no little courage and a refusal to be cowed by the Australian pacemen. With scores of 50, 45, 73, 92, 39 and 66, he cemented his place as a national treasure when voted the BBC Sports Personality of the Year 1975. I was there when he went on stage to receive the silver TV camera from Jim Laker, the only other cricketer (at the time) to be so honoured, in 1956. The Hampshire team were invited as one of the teams of the year, having won the John Player League that summer. As Steele turned to acknowledge the audience's applause, the arc lights glinted off his spectacles and he looked, well, a bit bemused, for all the world like the 'bank clerk who had gone to war', as he was so memorably described.

If you will forgive the pun, he put the steel back into the England batting. On his debut at Lord's, he very nearly made a unique name for himself for a more unfortunate reason. On his way out to bat, he got lost and found himself in the pavilion basement, in the toilets in fact, before retracing his steps up the stairs, through the Long Room and out into the middle, narrowly escaping the embarrassing fate of being timed out. To those who knew him on the county circuit, this would not have come as a complete surprise; he had a reputation for being a little dozy. He also had the reputation of never letting the occasion get to him, no more put to the test than when Jeff Thomson famously and loudly enquired of nobody in particular as Steele was taking guard, 'Bloody hell, who have we got here – Groucho Marx?' It was water off a duck's back. The score was 49/4 when Tony joined Steele, all four wickets having fallen to Lillee breathing fire and brimstone, three of them lbw. Tony needed a little luck early on but thereafter he batted as only he knew how. Despite his poor run of scores in the World Cup, he was actually in the form of his life that summer. Shortly before, he had become only the third England player to score 2,000 runs and to take 100 wickets in Test matches, the other two being Wilfred Rhodes and Trevor Bailey. That season, he was to score 1,699 runs and take 56 wickets and this innings at Lords of 96 was full of his trademark shots and crowd-pleasing flourishes. Even he admitted he could not have played better. In Steele, he found the perfect foil. At the end of the day, England had amassed over 300, Steele making a thoroughly deserved half-century.

Another Englishman who enjoyed sticking it up the Aussies took centre stage the following day. Tony knew all about the mercurial moods of his Sussex team-mate, John Snow. All he needed, Tony maintained, was an encouraging hand on his shoulder, reassurance that he had everybody's full confidence, including most importantly his captain, and the sight of an Australian in the distinctive baggy green cap taking guard at the other end. Snow's fire was suitably stoked and he loped in with that deceptively easy run-up of his and delivered one of the most devastating spells of his life. In quick succession, he removed Turner and the two Chappell brothers and with Lever and Greig also chipping in, Australia were reeling at 64/6 when the teams went in for lunch. Graham Gooch told me many years later that nobody in that team would ever forget the rapturous reception they got as they trooped up the pavilion steps and through the packed Long Room back to their dressing room. The Aussies were on their knees and it was a very satisfying, albeit unfamiliar, feeling. If nothing else, it had exposed the folly of the selectors in having omitted Snow for that series Down Under the previous winter.

Alas, the Australians though down were not out. They rarely are. Ross Edwards (99) and – remarkably – Lillee (73*) came to their rescue and the Test was eventually drawn. However, pride had been restored in the England ranks and that was, in Tony's estimation, progress.

Down the years, pitches have from time to time assumed an importance in matches that almost superseded the action that took place on them – some of them have gained a mention in this book. Headingley 1975 was probably the most shocking, news of it transferring from the back to the front pages in all the dailies. A professional cricketer spends many long hours behind the wheel of a car and the number of motorway bridges he passes under is incalculable. *George Davis Is Innocent OK* as a slogan daubed on bridges and walls the length and breadth of the country was as familiar to drivers in the early 1970s as *Things Go Better With Coke* and *Opal Fruits Made To Make Your Mouth Water* and *For Mash Get Smash*. Like many others, I suspect, I took as little interest in George Davis (innocent or otherwise) as I did in Coke, Opal Fruits and Smash. But what happened overnight to the pitch at Headingley before the final day of the third Test made us all sit up and pay heed.

It had not escaped the notice of England supporters that their team were playing with more purpose and conviction than hitherto. Some of this had to do with the slowness of the pitches after 12 months of near incessant rain, which had to some extent blunted the effect of the sheer speed and hostility of Lillee and Thomson. But some of it too had to do with Tony Greig's invigorating leadership. In this match, his team had stood toe to toe with their opponents and as the Tuesday dawned, the odds were slightly in favour of England pulling off an unheard-of victory. Australia had been set 445 to win in ten hours.

They had made an impressive start and at the end of day four, they were 220/3. The game was delicately poised but with both Chappells out, Tony's confidence in his side prevailing did not seem misplaced.

The well-known photograph of Tony Greig and Ian Chappell on their haunches looking with dismay at the vandalised wicket, with crudely dug holes and large, disfiguring patches of oil, is as depressing now as it was then. It struck me when I first saw it – and continues to do so – how differently the two captains are attired. Tony, ever a natty dresser, is wearing his usual check jacket, shirt and tie, a little loud perhaps but that was the fashion back in the Seventies. Chappell, by contrast, looks as if he has just wandered up from the beach, casual sweater thrown on and wearing flip-flops. It was said that the early morning call from the ground authorities had caught him on the hop and he had no time to shower, let alone dress properly. I'm not sure about that. Tony would not have been seen dead in flip-flops. He was the England captain and he took his responsibilities seriously.

Here was a moment when responsibility rested heavily on his shoulders. Leadership had to be shown and the right course of action taken. To him, it was obvious. They couldn't play on that surface; it was impossible. To cut and prepare another wicket would not be fair to either side, whoever won. No, the match had to be abandoned. He said so to Chappell, who agreed, and reluctantly the two captains shook hands on a draw. It was all so bitterly disappointing. A cracking finale to the game had been promised and now vandals had snatched that possibility from everybody's grasp.

It was clear from graffiti daubed on the wall beside the main gates at Headingley who was responsible. Alongside the usual slogan *George Davis Is Innocent* were the words *Sorry It Had To Be Done*. George Davis, it emerged, was a London gangster who had been imprisoned for armed robbery. A campaign headed by his wife and friends to release him had now reached national consciousness. Frankly, most people couldn't care less whether he was guilty or not. If he wasn't guilty of that particular crime, went the small talk over pints in bars, then he was more than likely guilty of other, equally heinous crimes. Be that as it may, in the face of the continued campaign, the Home Secretary at the time, Roy Jenkins, ordered a thorough review of

Davis's case and he was released the following year after doubts had been expressed about the veracity of some of the original evidence. To nobody's surprise, Davis was soon back in gaol, this time for armed robbery of a bank. Four vandals were arrested in the wake of the pitch protest and the ringleader, Peter Chappell (no, not the third of the Chappell brothers – his name is Trevor), a close friend of Davis's, was imprisoned for 18 months. Incidentally, few people remember that it started to rain as everybody was packing up to go home and the game would have been more than likely abandoned as a draw anyway.

Aaargh, so close, was Tony's feeling as he made his way back down to the south coast. The Ashes were gone – victory in the series was now impossible – but there was pride to play for in the fourth and final Test at the Oval. Pride was eventually restored but only after a scare. Australia compiled a score of 532/9 declared and England were bowled out cheaply for 191, Steele top-scoring with 39. The pride was to be found in England's response to being asked to follow on. They scored 538 and a creditable draw was salvaged. Incidentally, Tony Greig had the dreaded three figures alongside his bowling analysis, 3-107. He never shirked the hard yards with a ball in his hand, which could not be said of other captains.

The measure of a Test captain, I have always thought, is how his team performs abroad. He has 16, maybe 17, players at his disposal, most of whom one assumes are his choice, or at the very least those he has no objection to, and he has to forge them into a coherent, effective, competitive band of brothers. Captaining a side at home is not quite the same. For a start, everybody is not living cheek by jowl with each other for months on end. A player who is dropped or injured returns to his county and does not tag along with the party for the rest of the trip, probably aggrieved, bored and a likely source of discontent. Furthermore, help, advice, encouragement and a sense of perspective are readily available from outside the group; on tour, it is the same old ears that you have to bend. But nothing can beat touring – that is if you are not being beaten yourself – for it provides unforgettable memories and a comradeship, often forged in adversity, that nobody else can share. It can make a team. It can also make, or break, a captain.

Often Test cricketers yearn for a winter off. They have become tired and stale with the endless international merry-go-round and require time and space to recharge batteries. Tony Greig thought differently. This England team, he reckoned, needed an overseas tour that winter to grow and ultimately to flourish, which was his stated ambition. Sadly, there was none and they departed south London after the series against Australia to go their separate ways, all in pursuit of gainful employment. As usual, Tony had already made plans; he had the contract to play for Waverley in Sydney, brokered by his friend Bruce Francis, and took his family, wife Donna and children, Samantha and Mark, with him. Tony being Tony, this was to be no restful sojourn in the sun, playing club cricket at the weekends and enjoying Sydney's large array of beaches during the week. Already he had his mind on a life after cricket and here, in Australia, there was scope and opportunity to explore possibilities and make plans and there was not a moment to lose.

Not to put it too bluntly, Tony put himself about. As an instantly recognisable figure with a toothsome smile, an engaging personality and a clean-cut image, he was an advertiser's dream. His pulling power had been immeasurably increased by his appointment as the England captain and he left no stone unturned in his quest to maximise his endorsements. One that he had already secured before he left for Australia was a contract with St Peter Sports and he started to use their bats with their graphically distinctive SP logo. He also wore their state-of-the-art, single mitt batting gloves, which more resembled boxing gloves than the traditional finger sausage gauntlets. Their bats, though stylish, were not as good as Gray-Nicolls'. Several contracted players I knew continued to use their original bats but steamed off the SP logo to stick them on their own. 'Only for TV,' they winked at us. I have no idea whether Tony Greig similarly employed the dark arts of sponsorship but it is undeniable, with a personality like his heading up their advertising campaign, St Peter were for a while impossibly glamorous before disappearing as quickly as they had arrived. Alan Knott told me that Tony's England team-mates used to refer to their captain as the Messiah when the St Peter bat was first produced from his bag.

Tony secured for himself appearances on a number of advertisements on Australian television – for which medium he was particularly suited – as well as some stints commentating on the Australia–West Indies series. The West Indies endured a humiliating 1-5 hammering, suffering a physical battering at the hands of Lillee and Thomson every bit as bruising as that suffered by England the previous year. West Indies were due in England the following summer and the England captain, as you would expect, was casting a more than cursory glance over their next opponents. He had much food for thought. Despite the shambolic manner of their defeat, Tony was not hoodwinked. He had seen enough of their potential, especially in the fast bowling department, to convince him that they would be no pushover.

On 22 May, while the West Indians were still warming up, Roy Plomley had as his guest on *Desert Island Discs* the England captain. Out of interest, I recently listened to a recording of the broadcast, thoughtfully provided by his son, Mark. Two things struck me. First what an aptly onomatopoeic name is Plomley; his voice was all plummy vowels and carefully enunciated consonants. That was how BBC announcers and interviewers spoke back then. How times have changed. Secondly, and this surprised me, Tony did not tell us anything during the course of the programme that was remotely striking or controversial. He chose to follow a conventional course, outlining his childhood and his career in cricket up to that point, without much that was thought-provoking or contentious. So unlike Tony. It was as if he was saving up controversy for another BBC broadcast a week or two later – and we know what that was all about.

This is not to say that the programme was without interest because it did inform the listeners about the man, his likes and dislikes, his priorities, his love of family, his pride at being appointed England captain, his ease in front of a microphone, his impish sense of humour ... and his undeniably 'square' taste in music. His chosen records included songs by Vera Lynn, Kenneth McKellar, The Seekers, Ken Dodd, Peters and Lee, Neil Diamond and Abba. Oh, and a South African singer by the name of Jeremy Taylor, unknown in this country. Not exactly The Who, Led Zeppelin, Rolling Stones, Deep Purple, Pink Floyd, Queen *et al.* 'Do you enjoy it here in England?' asked

Plomley. Back came the response, 'Love the cold!' Questioned as to whether he was ever lonely on tour, Tony replied, 'No way! Good to get away from the tax man.' Plomley then quizzed him on his captaincy of Sussex, currently not setting the County Championship alight (Plomley was legendary for his meticulous research). 'Nah!' cried Captain Greig, 'we're on the crest of a wave!'

He did touch briefly on playing conditions for professional cricketers and the state of the game in this country. Too much of a good thing was his opinion; cricketers, like everybody else, need time off to rest and recuperate, which they did not get in the county game. He was also worried about safety. Already in his mind was the need for helmets to protect batsmen 'or soon, somebody's going to get seriously hurt'. Both topics were to exercise him over the next 12 months or so. We learned that he supported Rangers and Scotland, Ken Higgs and Brian Statham were his heroes (strangely he did not mention Colin Cowdrey), he admired Mike Brearley and, as for the captaincy, he intended to 'hold on to the job as long as possible'. He did not mention epilepsy but he did say he was a rotten cook. His one object to take with him to his desert island would be a bed! And the book at his bedside would be – surprise, surprise – *Wisden*. 'On behalf of all of our listeners,' Plomley concluded, 'may I wish you a singularly successful summer.' Hmm.

Plomley was too polite to cross-examine Tony on his financial dealings but the press were not so delicate. The unwonted interest taken in his money-making exploits while he was in Australia faintly irked him. First, the amounts quoted were clearly plucked from somebody's over-wrought imagination and bore no resemblance to reality. And secondly, he could not understand why on earth it was of anybody's interest, let alone business. He was contracted to no club nor county during the winter and the TCCB had shown no signs of taking any interest in his welfare once the series against Australia had finished. Why shouldn't he seek employment where and howsoever he wanted? What was he supposed to do – hunker down and seclude himself from winter storms at home in Hove, waiting for spring to arrive? This became a central plank of his defence when everybody ended up in the High Court 18 months later.

In any event, the TCCB did sit up and take notice on his return and appointed him as captain for the five-Test series against the West Indies in 1976. He was under no illusions as to the magnitude of the task ahead. Although nobody knew it, the start of two decades of West Indian hegemony in world cricket dated from this moment and as a herald to usher in this period of dominance, the cricketing gods (or maybe it was just global warming) furnished forth the longest, hottest, driest summer that anybody could remember, conditions amply suited to the men from the Caribbean. It is undoubtedly true that a production line of fast bowlers underpinned their success. It used to be said that the England selectors only had to shout down a Nottinghamshire coalmine to unearth a fast bowler or two. There are mines in the Caribbean but it was more likely that West Indian fast bowlers were to be found on the beaches and in the bars and they were well stocked.

For this series, the West Indian spearhead was three-pronged – Roberts, Holding and Daniel. To say nothing of a batting line-up comprising Gordon Greenidge, Roy Fredericks, Viv Richards, Alvin Kallicharran and captain Clive Lloyd. Tony Greig racked his brains how best to counteract their superior firepower and came up with a plan, the only one that might work. If they were allowed to get on top, they would annihilate you. But if their cage could be rattled somehow, as had been borne out in Australia, they could turn in among themselves and lose focus. Or so the theory went. Best then to prime the cannon and get a broadside in first. After all, Tony was never a man to hang back and wonder.

I remember the interview well. It was broadcast by the BBC on the day before the first Test match. Tony had already sprung a surprise by announcing the recall to national colours of the veteran Brian Close. It was not as preposterous a decision as many claimed; Close was a brave and experienced campaigner, especially against the short ball, and Tony had long admired his spirit and tenacity. He was a man hewn in his own image, the sort of resolute warrior you would want with you in the trenches, just as David Steele had been, another of Tony's hunches and he had exceeded all expectations. However, it did not escape people's attention that although Steele had been 33 when selected, Close was now 45. In answer to the question how he intended to take the fight to the West Indies, Tony got straight on the front foot and unleashed what he thought was a perfect cover drive, a statement of intent that could not possibly be misunderstood.

'The West Indians, these guys, if they get on top, they're magnificent cricketers. If they're down, they grovel. And I, with the help of Closey and a few others, intend to make them grovel.'

That was the rallying cry, the call to arms, his team needed. Not a backward step, folks, we're not going to be bullied. We're going to stand up to them and we're going to be the ones doing the bullying. Well, perhaps the choice of the word 'grovel' was a little unfortunate but, hey, that's Greigy.

My immediate response, hearing these words, was to take a sharp, dismayed intake of breath. Oh dear. Somehow it sounded worse – though it shouldn't – coming out of the mouth of a man with a South African accent. We all knew what he was *trying* to say but, my goodness, it had come out all wrong. If nothing else, it would be used by the West Indians as prime ammunition in the forthcoming battle. No need for Clive Lloyd to give his troops any motivational speeches; Tony Greig had just done it for him. But leaving aside for one moment the opposite effect of what he had intended, it is important to analyse the wording of what he said and ask ourselves what he was implying, either consciously or subconsciously. The fact of the matter is that Tony used a word that was more than unfortunate. With its undertones of racial superiority, especially when directed at West Indians, with all their history of slavery, it becomes at best catastrophic, at worst deeply offensive. Unsurprisingly, it stirred a hornets' nest.

I do not believe for one moment that he meant to insult the West Indians, and neither does a single person who knew him believe that either. Reactions range from an indulgent chuckle (that's Greigy) to exasperation for his not having engaged brain before opening mouth. He certainly intended to ruffle his opponents, to raise their hackles, and in this too, opinions are divided. Not the best idea he's ever had, said some, but he had to try something. Nothing ventured, nothing gained, all part and parcel of the phoney war and if it backfired, he would take the flak in person (which he did). Others believed it was a serious misjudgement but at least he had the good grace to apologise and not hide from the embarrassment.

Whenever you make a mistake and seek to put the matter right, the efficacy of your expression of regret does rather depend on the reaction of the wounded party. Did the West Indians accept his public *mea culpa*? His comment certainly enraged and unified them. They used it as a tool to spur them on to crush England and in this their anger was effectively channelled, the very opposite of what Tony was hoping to achieve. Did they, in their heart of hearts, believe that Tony Greig was a racist and was therefore betraying his true roots as a product of a deeply racist society? I guess there were as many different views on that as there were members of the West Indian team. Clive Lloyd showed real leadership qualities here. He did not allow the issue to fester or to break out into sporadic bouts of nastiness during the series. Whatever they felt privately, they kept a dignified silence and resolved to make sure it was Tony who was grovelling at the end of the series, not them.

And to be fair to the England captain, he did, literally. Ever the showman, towards the end of the final Test at the Oval, he got down and crawled on his knees in front of West Indian supporters – and they howled with laughter. He always had the ability to turn things around; he rarely took offence and he believed that others should hold no grudges either. The British establishment – and the press – took longer to forgive and it is a sad fact that Tony Greig will always be associated with a crass comment that did not in any way define the man. Gerald Ratner saw the profits of his jewellery business plummet after he described his products as 'crap', Alf Ramsey did nothing for his reputation in Argentina by vilifying their footballers as 'animals'. Public life is littered with comments made in unguarded moments and nearly all are instantly regretted. Together with his epilepsy, it was just something Tony had to deal with and deal with it he did, in the only way he knew how, by concentrating on trying to beat the West Indies, just as he had promised.

It is as well to remember two things about the visit of the West Indians in the summer of 1976. They were by no means a team that inspired fear and trepidation when they first landed at Heathrow, though by the time they departed, they most certainly were. And the series was closer than people care to remember. They had only defeated India 2-1 in the recent series in the Caribbean, which had followed on from their humiliation at the hands of Australia earlier that winter. World champions they were not. And the series on which they were about to embark, which would establish them as world champions in all but name, was not all one-way traffic. England were well beaten 3-0 in the end but there were times during at least three of the Tests when they were competing toe to toe. It is true that Richards and Greenidge were in outstanding form with the bat and that Roberts and Holding were irrepressible with the ball but it is also true that England had worthy warriors of their own. Captain Greig, Amiss, Snow, Willis and Underwood all performed with honour, and no little bravery, at crucial moments during the series. Ultimately, however, West Indian artillery was too powerful and England were overwhelmed.

I use the imagery of warfare advisedly. Clive Lloyd's decision to wheel out the big guns as a deliberate and preconceived plan of attack was forged in the blazing heat of Australia and the pummelling they had suffered from Lillee and Thomson and drilled to perfection in the Caribbean in front of their own supporters. The series against India is not often recalled but it was a seminal moment in the development of the West Indian dreadnought. Going into the final Test, the teams were locked at 1-1, the Indians having just secured a memorable and wholly unexpected victory by virtue of scoring over 400 runs in the last innings. Lloyd now lost patience with his spinners – it could have been argued he had none anyway, seeing as Lance Gibbs had just retired – and vowed to use heretofore a four-pronged attack of fast men. They duly obliged their captain with a bouncer barrage that had the Indians incensed. After several of his batsmen had been hurt, captain Bishan Bedi declared his innings at 306/6, partly out of protest to 'protect' his tail-enders. He went even further in his second innings. India had slumped to 97/5 at which point Bedi declared again, leaving West Indies the formality of scoring 13 to win the match and the series. India as they departed the Caribbean, in the words of *Wisden*, 'resembled Napoleon's troops on the retreat from Moscow ... with a lot of them enveloped in plasters and bandages'. Lloyd, however, was quietly satisfied. Nobody was going to walk all over his team again. Later, Michael Holding regretted the overuse of the short-pitched stuff, pointing out that 'it was 1-1 and we were under extreme public pressure'.

The first Test at Trent Bridge was illuminated by an imperious innings of 232 from Viv Richards. He was, and had been all year, in the form of his life that was to persist throughout the summer. Mind you, those bowlers who had the misfortune to toil against him during his career reckoned he was *always* in the form of his life. A maiden hundred from David Steele and resolute batting from Edrich (76*) and Close (36*) on the final day ensured that England left Nottingham with a draw and morale reasonably intact. Tony's old guard had not performed too badly. The same could not be said about their captain. Some overs in Test cricket stick long in the memory. One thinks of that riveting first over of the match at Bridgetown in 1981 from Holding to Boycott – the Greatest Over Ever Bowled, it was dubbed. The seven balls Andy Roberts bowled to Tony Greig stand fit for comparison. The photo, with one stump cartwheeling through the air, says it all. Tony knew what was coming. 'They seemed to bowl faster and faster to me,' he said, 'but I was used to that.' It was not an unusual tactic for bowlers, particularly the pacemen, to target the opposing captain or best player and Tony was both so he had expected the onslaught. The difference in this series was that it was incessant; with four fast bowlers, two rotating their spells at each end, there was no let-up. Furthermore, he was not in the best of form and nothing does more to expose those tiny flaws in technique and confidence than a succession of 90mph thunderbolts.

It was clear that something about Tony Greig got up opponents' noses. He had infuriated Lillee in Australia and now Roberts and Holding seemed to bear him a grudge as they peppered him with short balls. With Lillee it worked, up to a point. He lost his temper and tried to kill Tony instead of trying to get his wicket. Roberts and Holding did not lose their rag. Their anger was cold and sharply focussed. They bowled faster and nastier at him but they did not lose control. The right ball, the *coup de grace*, was delivered at just the right moment. In nine innings during the series, he was bowled five times.

As in Australia, his team-mates looked on from the dressing room with understandably mixed feelings as they watched the West Indian fast bowlers gain a yard of pace the moment Tony came to the crease. The fact was not lost on the non-striker either. David Steele was alleged to have walked down the wicket to greet his captain none too enthusiastically, 'I wish you 'adn't come in. We were 'aving a good game up until now.' Dennis Amiss openly admitted, a little shamefacedly, that never was he so pleased to see an England captain bowled as happened at the Oval during Amiss's double century. Tongue-in-cheek comments no doubt, but nobody was in any doubt the West Indians were fired up all right.

Lord's. Not long ago, my companion who had never attended a Lord's Test match leaned across to me and said, 'Listen. What do you hear?' 'Er … just the hum of conversation.' He grinned. 'Exactly! Where else in the world would you get that in a Test match?' The answer is nowhere. Lord's is just, well … different. The tradition, the history, the restraint, the form, the custom, all combine to produce a special atmosphere, less raucous than at other grounds but no less intense and knowledgeable, a bit like Wimbledon really, in its attention to detail, distinction and excellence. International teams love playing there and often raise their game to perform at cricket's home and the privilege is never lost on the home players either. There is a lovely photo of the Lord's Test of 1976 with both teams lined up in their blazers to meet the Queen. Tony Greig, as England's captain, is bowing to his diminutive monarch, about to shake her hand and introduce her to his team. He has his pads on. I have often wondered how batsmen who are in the midst of their innings and usually hate having their peace and quiet disturbed during intervals, manage to switch on their smile to utter pleasantries at such a time but there you are … the duties of an international sportsman. Tony Greig always said it was an honour to meet and greet Her Majesty. Especially as England captain. First in line is the old warhorse, bald of pate and firm of expression, Brian Close. He had of course been in Tony's shoes, doing the honours, and it must have crossed his mind that he never expected to be here once more. After all, he had made his debut for England 27 years ago. The West Indians are lined up opposite, smartly attired, patient and expressionless. It is, frankly, an odd moment, as if the roar of the guns had briefly been silenced for a tea break while both armies donned mess kit, clambered out of the trenches and lined up in no man's land to meet the Kaiser.

It was an irony that in a summer of record temperatures and virtually no rainfall one whole day of the Lord's Test was lost to rain, thus robbing the match of an almost certain result. It wasn't beyond the realms of possibility that England could have been the winners; at the conclusion of play on the Friday evening, they had a first innings lead of 95, an advantage that Tony would have been delighted to press home. But on the resumption of play on the Monday, much of the fizz in the match had evaporated, restored briefly only by Her Majesty's arrival to meet the two teams, which had been postponed from the dismal Saturday. There was a desperate flurry in the last hour or so of the match when West Indies set off on an almost impossible pursuit of victory and it was only when Lloyd was out with just four wickets remaining that he signalled to his opposite number that he was calling off the run chase. Not so fast, cried England's captain, crowding the bat for the final 13 balls of the match. Only when it was mathematically impossible (ie, in the middle of the last over) did he too call it a day.

As he drove up to Manchester for the third Test, Tony could well have reflected, all things considered, that his team had so far performed not at all badly, better than might have been expected. If there were lingering suspicions that the West Indies had not yet hit their straps, he would have dismissed such negative thoughts from his mind. He was usually of an optimistic disposition and the series was still tied. In fact, he was about to face the biggest crisis of his career, one that had him seriously contemplating his future and, possibly for the first time in his life, doubting his abilities as a captain and as a player.

Some Test matches stick long in the memory for all the wrong reasons and Old Trafford of 1976 is certainly one of them. Who to blame? Well, the list is long, depending on your point of view and whether you were an England supporter or West Indian. The fact that England succumbed by the colossal margin of 425 runs seemed incidental to what happened on the Saturday evening during 80 minutes of play before the close. How apt that I should end that sentence with the word 'close' for it was Close who was to provide the story. The wicket did not look good. Tony Greig knew that. Clive Lloyd knew that – it was his home ground. Everybody knew that. Old Trafford in the mid-1970s was not the best track in the country by a long chalk, certainly not for a Test match. That much had become evident as England bowled out their opponents for 211, Selvey taking 4-41 on his debut. Their score would have been considerably less had it not been for Greenidge's 134, mixing cautious defence with his usual muscular strokeplay. It was about now in his career, Barry Richards always maintained, that Gordon, his opening partner at Hampshire, began to mature as a Test match batsman. 'He realised that quick-fire fifties and sixties were no good at this level,' he said. 'He needed to score big hundreds to make people sit up and take notice.' With another hundred in the second innings, a total of 592 runs and an average of 65.77 in the series, you could say that Greenidge had listened to his county team-mate's advice (though he never admitted as much).

Then Close was asked by his captain to open the innings. He hadn't opened the batting for many years. Why, he wanted to know. Tony told him that he and John Edrich were the most experienced players he had at his disposal and in his view were the best men for the job. 'You must be bloody crackers,' was Close's reported response, but he did it anyway. He was not known to duck a challenge. Of all Tony's bright ideas, opening with a 45- and a 39-year-old against Holding, Roberts and Daniel at their fittest and fastest, was probably not up there in the top half-dozen. Edrich made 8, Close made 2, England were rolled over for 71, the only batsman to make it into double figures (20) being Steele, the youngster of 34. The wicket was atrocious, it has to be emphasised; it is doubtful that any batting line-up would have prospered against that bowling attack on that pitch. Close spoke about it afterwards. 'That was the worst Test wicket, Old Trafford, that we played on at that time …. The ball went through the top surface and lifted and did all sorts of things.' Tony was incandescent about it. As captain, he had to bite his tongue, though he was scathing about it later.

In their second innings, West Indies piled on the agony, eventually declaring at 411/5, Greenidge 101 and Richards 135. England were chasing a target of 552 to win. Of course I am being ironic; the words 'chase' and 'win' could not have been further from the minds of Close and Edrich as they walked out to bat on the Saturday evening with 80 minutes until stumps. Survival, literal as well as metaphorical, was all that was on their mind. That they did so was nothing short of miraculous.

The passage of play until the two of them hauled their battered and bruised bodies off the pitch at the end of the day has gone down in infamy. They were subjected to a barrage of nasty, brutal and dangerous short bowling that went far beyond the bounds of what was justifiable. *Wisden* described it thus: 'Close and Edrich defended their wickets and themselves against fast bowling which was frequently too wild and hostile to be acceptable.' Alex Bannister in the *Daily Mail* went further: 'Such bowling should be outlawed before a victim is killed or maimed for life.' It was estimated that of the 73 deliveries bowled that evening, only ten would have hit the stumps. Edrich chose to duck and weave; Close stood tall, as he always did, and let the ball hit him on the body. His bruised and discoloured torso, revealed when he stripped off later in the dressing room, brought aghast utterances from his team-mates. Do not forget that this was in an age before helmets (though thanks to Tony Greig that was soon to change). Close didn't even wear a cap. Nor a thigh pad. Nobody had heard of chest protectors and arm guards. Mike Selvey, later a respected journalist, described it all as well as anybody. 'I can't speak too highly of Closey that night … what we saw was a brave man. He went up massively in my estimation, as did Edrich.'

Watching it unfold from the dressing room (at that time, the pavilion at Old Trafford was square on to the wicket, which is always a discomfiting viewpoint if you are about to go in to bat) was a horrified captain. He wrote later: 'On the Saturday evening, two of the bravest English batsmen of my time were reduced to wrecks by a short-pitched assault unparalleled in its danger during my experience …. How John Edrich and Brian Close survived with their wickets and their lives intact I shall never know.'

What were the umpires doing? Not a lot, it would seem. There was no restriction at that time on the number of bouncers that could be bowled in an over but they did have the power to intervene if they thought the bowling was unacceptably intimidating. Eventually, Bill Alley stepped in to warn Holding after he had bowled three successive bouncers. Close wanted to know why. Because he's bowled three bouncers in succession, Alley told him. 'It's not the bouncers that worry me,' Close told him, 'they sail harmlessly over my head. It's the ones that pitch halfway down and don't get up that's the problem.' One ball nearly took Close's head off. It was cricket in the raw and nobody much enjoyed it. Viv Richards worriedly whispered to Close, his county captain at Somerset, 'You all right, Cappy?' History does not record Close's response though it does not take much to guess.

Was the wicket to blame then? Not really, maintained Clive Lloyd. He believed that Close and Edrich were past it and no longer competent to deal with bowling of that pace. 'Our fellows got carried away,' he admitted and was actually not very happy with them. What was required on that wicket was to pitch the ball up, not to target the body. In this he was undoubtedly right, amply vindicated by the change of tactics unveiled on the following Monday morning. They pitched the ball up and England subsided to a catastrophic 425-run defeat.

Tony slumped back on his seat in the dressing room afterwards, dejected beyond measure. Defeat always upset him and this one was particularly hard to swallow. But it was more than that. He was unusually depressed and troubled. Alan Knott told me that Tony admitted to him that he didn't feel that he was up to it anymore. His old self-confidence had deserted him. He had let the side down and the country and he was all for chucking in the towel. He just wasn't good enough, the fast bowlers had exposed his frailties and he couldn't handle it. He intended to resign the captaincy. 'Not a good idea,' Knott said to me, 'and I told him so. I always remember the advice of one of my team-mates at Kent, Stuart Leary – never give up voluntarily, you never know what's round the corner.' Wise counsel. Tony listened and promised not to act precipitously.

He did not resign but he was severely shaken. In his own words, he admitted, 'I had been more concerned with protecting my life than my wicket.' When you fall off a horse, you must get back in the saddle as soon as possible. So I'm told – I have never been on a horse – but I have been on my backside a few times evading a bouncer. If you lose your nerve as a batsman, you might just as well pack your bag and go home. That is not to say you do not continue to feel anxious but you must get up, shake yourself down and take guard again. The true measure of bravery, I have always felt, is in direct proportion to the amount of terror endured. An infantryman who charges a machine gun nest, clearly off his rocker and not minding if he gets killed or not, can hardly be said to be brave. But if he has weighed up the slim chances of survival yet still charges forward because that is what he has to do, he is the true hero. For that reason, I believe Tony's century in the next Test at Headingley to be one of the most courageous and significant of his career. He was at his lowest ebb but he hauled himself up off the ground, stood up tall, answered his critics and banished his demons.

First, there was work to be done. Ian Greig takes up the story. 'I had been awarded a scholarship to Downing College, Cambridge, so I was in England by now and it was during the summer vac. Tony asked me to come into the nets with him so that he could practise dealing with the short ball. It was in the indoor school at Hove. He produced a box of black lacrosse balls, you know the ones – bit like composition balls. They're a bit heavier than cricket balls and they bounce more. He put the stumps up at 18 yards. I bowled half a dozen. "Waste of time your coming to England if that's the best you can do," he growled at me. So I moved the stumps to 16 yards and bunged them at him as hard and as fast as I could so he could practise ducking and weaving. Two days later at Headingley he scored 116 and 76 not out.' *So you were not entirely a waste of the British taxpayers' money?* His answer to that is not repeatable but another story of that hot summer of 1976 is.

'I was staying with him at Hove and on one of his rare days off, I suggested we and Donna and the kids go down to the beach. He wasn't keen. Why? Because he felt that the public image of the England captain would not be conducive to stripping off and lazing on a beach. "You don't understand, Ian, what it's like being England captain." In the end he agreed to go and off we set. We parked on the beachfront and within two minutes he was surrounded by 200 people. Donna and I supervised the two kids while Tony spent the whole time signing autographs and talking about the Test matches.' *I notice the autograph hunters left you alone, Ian.* 'Aw, look buddy, my greatest years were yet to come.'

Tony's greatest year was about to start, at Headingley, which had provided such disappointment to all cricket lovers the previous year when supporters of that repeat offender, George Davis, had dug up the pitch. The match was a magnificent contest, which England lost narrowly, and thus the series, but it did much to restore their captain's prestige in the eyes of the British public. More importantly for Tony himself, it helped to heal a few wounds and rebuild his self-confidence. As expected, wholesale changes were made to the England team. Both Edrich and Close were discarded, never to represent their country again, a sad finale perhaps for two battle-hardened warriors who had given so much loyal service to the cause over many years. John Snow was recalled – yet again.

Batting first, West Indies set off at a pace that would not be extraordinary now but back then it was unheard of, both Greenidge and Fredericks scoring hundreds and Richards joining in the fun. Their total of 450 puts Snow's 4-77 into context. Why was it that he was so frequently overlooked by the selectors? He wasn't the first 'difficult' character to play for England and there have been a few since. It remains an anomaly. With his side perilously placed at 80/4, when Tony put out his cigarette and strode to the wicket, arms flailing as usual, he would not have been human if 'here we go again' was not reverberating in his brain. In view of all that, his hundred was an extraordinary achievement. It was all the more satisfying that he shared a partnership of 152 for the sixth wicket with Alan Knott, his good friend and companion-in-arms for many years, with both of them scoring 116. Tony never forgot Knotty's words of encouragement when he was at his lowest ebb.

Willis (5-42) bowled with pace, movement and control to peg the visitors back to 196, a lead of 259, a target England firmly believed was within their grasp. But once again, the West Indian triumvirate of Holding, Roberts and Daniel had other ideas, thus confirming their total domination over England batsmen that summer. All except

Tony Greig, in this match at least. It reminded me of a poem I learned at school:

> *The boy stood on the burning deck*
> *When all but he had fled*

Hardly a boy anymore but we can imagine the scene as he was left stranded on 76 not out as England folded for 204, the last five batsmen scoring a mere ten runs between them.

The series was gone but respect had been restored. That was blown away in the final Test at the Oval, the memory of Michael Holding's 14 wickets and a West Indian victory by 231 runs, thus sealing the series 3-0, searing itself into the consciousness of cricket lovers up and down the land. Back in the Caribbean they were regarded as superheroes, an apt enough description in view of the two decades of world domination on which they were embarking. 'Who's grovelling now?' – a single released by the reggae group Ezeike – was blasting from the boomboxes and England's humiliation was complete. Tony was not at all sure what was going to happen next, to him or his team.

There were some, it has to be said, who were looking for excuses for him to be sacked. He had lost two successive home series to Australia and West Indies, both of which had been depressing and one-sided. Time for a change. Who would be the best choice to lead the MCC in their upcoming tour of India that winter? What about Mike Brearley? He's a good player of spin, ideally suited for Indian pitches. Furthermore, he has just led Middlesex to victory in the County Championship and by all accounts, he is a shrewd and popular leader. Just the sort of chap to be relied on not to let the side down by uttering crass comments to the press. In point of fact, Brearley's candidature was not seriously considered, not yet anyway. His reputation as a miracle man of leadership came later. It was generally recognised that England had simply been outgunned by superior opposition; if John the Baptist had been in charge, it would have made little difference. In addition, the team were behind Tony. What could possibly have been achieved by a change of captain at this stage? Moreover, Brearley wasn't even in the England side; he had been dropped after the second Test at Lord's and had not returned. It would constitute a huge gamble to appoint a captain who wasn't even in the first XI. For the time being, in the absence of any compelling alternative, Tony was given the go-ahead to plan for India.

This England side were on the cusp of a renaissance and he was the man to lead them on a serious quest to regain the Ashes the following summer. Confidence restored, he hoped for a good tour of India and for his team to acquit themselves worthily in a country where historically they have always struggled. To win the series might be beyond them but there was no reason they should not provide a few surprises. Could he ever have imagined that he was about to set out on a tour that was to define his career, his *annus mirabilis*? I doubt it, though from his previous experience in that country, I bet he was determined he was going 'to have a hell of a time, hey!'

Before we head east, I want to share an anecdote from Ian about his brother, humorous but revealing nonetheless. It occurred during this Oval Test. 'I was going to watch him play,' Ian said, 'and he was already in London in preparation for the Test match so he told me to drive his Jaguar up from Hove on the morning of the game. "Er, where is the Oval?" I asked. "Go up the M23 and turn left," were my wholly inadequate instructions. Anyway, I found it! Dressed in my jeans and t-shirt, driving a white Jag, I felt a million dollars as I drove up to the main gate at the Oval. Far from being waved through by the gateman, I was stopped, quizzed and disbelieved. I begged him to go and get my brother, "Captain of England" I repeatedly reminded him. Reluctantly he relayed a message and it was actually Alec Bedser, chairman of selectors, who came down to rescue me. He took me into the committee room, as it happened. Tony came down, took one look at me and told me in no uncertain manner that I looked like a scruffy bastard, dressed like that. He took me out on to the balcony and gave me the mother and father of all dressing-downs. He was quite ashamed of me, truth to tell. "Look, pal," he said, "when my family come to watch me play for England, they get the best treatment, eh? Well, I expect you to dress accordingly." So, I was sent back to school.' *I beg your pardon?* 'You remember Archbishop Tenison's School, alongside the Oval?' *I do.* 'That is where I watched the game from. Well, I watched the first session from the pavilion and then I went over to the school to have lunch. There I met Colin Milburn. He had been a coach of mine back home when I was about 11.' *Knowing Milburn's reputation, I imagine you had a few beers.* 'We made sure that we stayed pretty close to the bar. Fortunately there was a TV monitor close by so we could keep one eye on proceedings.'

If you were an England supporter, especially if you were the brother of the captain, there was not a lot to grab your attention, on that day anyway.

Chapter 8

Annus Mirabilis
Tour of India
1976/77 Centenary Test
12–17 March 1977

'Ah, happy days!'

Roger Tolchard's memory of Greig's tour

IS brother's attention may not have been fully focussed on the England captain that afternoon at the Oval but there were millions of Indians who couldn't take their eyes off him as soon as he stepped off the plane in Bombay at the head of the MCC party on their tour of that country. A large number of the team had been on Tony Lewis's tour four years previously and would have been known to the Indian public but by far the most recognisable was the Blond Beanpole and Tony being Tony, he was determined to exploit this popularity for all its worth. The fact is he often belied his reputation as one who fired from the hip. Yes, there were occasions when he did not carefully consider the ramifications of what he said but for all that, he was a planner. His brother said that he 'built dreams'. Before you build, you have to plan, and this he did throughout his life. The Indian tour was no exception. He remembered the lessons learned from the last trip and was determined not to repeat the mistakes.

The plan of campaign was pored over long before the team quit British air space. He was not one for sitting next to the tour manager at the front of the plane, producing pen and paper and suggesting they jot down the side for the first Test. Thought had gone into the likely composition of the side long before at the selectors' meeting when the touring party was chosen. Remember the conversation Mike Selvey had with Tony when they met up in East London. 'Greigy was talking about touring, its pleasures and challenges. "Get on the tour to India," he said, "It'll be a great experience." Sure enough, I was picked and he was right, it was a great experience. I often wondered why he had said that.' *He believed in you, Mike.* Selvey laughed. 'Maybe. He was like that, though.'

There were one or two unusual aspects for the selectors to take into consideration, over and above the usual 'unusual' happenings that take place on any tour of that fascinating country, for which no contingency planning can cater. First, what to do with Geoffrey Boycott? To 'boycott' has entered the lexicon of English as meaning to isolate. Our Geoffrey had not been isolated; he had isolated himself. It was mainly in protest at the appointment of Denness and subsequently Greig as England captain in preference to him. Tony offered him the olive branch of the vice-captaincy, which he refused, citing health risks on a tour of India. Never mind, was Tony's riposte, we have a ready-made alternative in Mike Brearley.

Horses for courses. This is a logical precept to bear in mind when selecting a party to tour overseas but one that is not always followed. Tony was insistent that good players of spin should be picked, given the pitch conditions expected in India. Here the selection committee faced an unwelcome choice. David Steele had done all that had been expected of him and more in the face of fast bowling against Australia and West Indies but he was not regarded as so reliable against the spinners. He was discarded as had been Close and Edrich. Tony wanted to put his faith in youngsters. He firmly believed that this team needed rebuilding after the morale-sapping reverses in those two series.

There was another fly in the ointment for the selectors to ponder. Tagged on to the end of the tour in March was the greatly anticipated Centenary Test in Australia, to celebrate 100 years of Test cricket between the two countries. Melbourne, for that was the venue, at the end of the Australian summer was likely to offer different playing conditions to the ones the tourists would have become accustomed to in India. Where did their priorities lie? Should they pick a side with one eye on Australia? Or should they fly out replacements to Australia to join the party for the one-off Test, sending the unfortunate spare bodies home? In the event, they concentrated on the five-Test series in India and calculated that the battle-hardened warriors would be in a better state to face the Aussies than others plucked from an English winter. It was a good call, as it turned out, but a brave one. The team that set out from Heathrow on 23 November, resplendent in their MCC blazers – Tony always insisted on a smart uniform – had a youthful and unfamiliar look about it; eight of the players had a mere three caps between them.

Of the many imperious shots Tony Greig reeled off on this personally satisfying tour, none was better than the one he played before even a ball had been bowled. 'We all staggered off the plane at Bombay at 4am after an 11-hour flight,' Chris Old told me, 'and Greigy said to us, "Look lads, the manager and I have got to do a press conference. You lot carry on to the hotel and we'll see you later." We got to the hotel and there was Greigy on the news on TV telling everybody that Indian umpires were the best in the world. Brilliant!' Some context is required here. In the eyes of many tourists, including a recent New Zealand side, Indian umpires were *not* the best in the world. Tony, at the press conference, had been asked by an Indian reporter what he thought about the standard of umpiring in India. This time, he was determined not to make a similar *faux pas* to the one he had made before the West Indies series. His reply sent ripples of pride throughout India and produced gales of laughter among his professional colleagues back home. But this time, the words had been anything but off the cuff. He wanted the umpires, if not on his side, then certainly having no cause to be upset by the behaviour of his players. There will be no dissent, he told them all, show them respect and try to keep on the right side of them. Little did he know how spectacularly successful his strategy would be. 'One of the umpires in the first Test gave JK [Lever] three lbws on the trot!' chortled Roger Tolchard. 'Mind you, we never saw him again all tour.'

Immediately the serious business started. John Lever, a surprise call-up, noticed a significant difference in the preparation for matches to what he had been accustomed on the county circuit. 'Practice was in the Dark Ages,' he reminded me, 'for example, tail-enders never got a look-in during nets. But Greigy had a plan. He made the non-batters have proper net practice and furthermore, there were plenty of matches before and in between the Tests, so we could get out there in the middle. Altogether, there was a lot more professionalism in our preparation.' *Incidentally, John, were you ever mistaken for the other Lever?* Peter Lever played for Lancashire and had been on the past two Ashes tours Down Under. John, known universally as JK, laughed. 'I'd had a pretty good season the year before and it did cross my mind that I might get the call. In the event, they selected Peter. I got a lot of stick from my Essex team-mates, who reckoned the selectors didn't know which one was which and had got the name wrong.' *Well, stick was the stock-in-trade of that Essex team, wasn't it?* 'Who, *us?*' he remonstrated.

Mike Selvey, another seamer, had not expected to tour. 'Everybody knew that India was spin-friendly. But as their spinners were better than ours, Greigy decided to attack them with bowling against which they had shown vulnerability in the past. So he decided to go into the Tests with three seamers and a spinner – Underwood – backed up by him bowling his off-spinners.' *Off-spinners? Weren't they more like off-cutters?* 'No. He bowled genuine offies. He'd get offended if you called them off-cutters.' Selvey then recounted an anecdote when they were sharing commentary duties later in life. 'Graeme Swann had just taken ten wickets in the match against India. People were saying it was the first time an England spinner had taken ten wickets in a Test since Jim Laker. Greigy was upset. "Suppose my ten in Trinidad doesn't count then," he said.' *Back to this tour. There were four of you therefore – you, Willis, Old, Lever – vying for three places. How did it work out?* 'There were four warm-up games before the first Test. In the first game, I pulled a muscle in my backside and couldn't move. I missed the next one, then played in two more. I thought I bowled well but JK did too and he got the nod. He bowled so well in that first Test that I couldn't get back in the side until the fifth. And that was only because Chris Old had declared himself unfit minutes before the toss.'

These warm-up games – first-class, don't forget – were something and nothing for the tourists. Those who were assured of a Test place tended to regard them as practice matches, useful for shaking off the cobwebs and ensuring that all working parts were in racing order. Those on the fringes of the side had a point to prove and therefore took them much more seriously. So, with half the team straining muscle and sinew and the other half protecting muscle and sinew, these matches often had a lopsided look about them. Take the third encounter of the tour, against the Board President's XI. Graham Barlow, having a go as an opener, scored 102. Greig, as captain the safest bet for the Test team, scored 5 and 1. Against the Combined Universities, Geoff Cope, who was unlikely to play much part in the series, and indeed did not play in a single Test, took 6-41 and a further three wickets in the second innings. Incidentally, Bob Willis, who was going to lead the attack in the Tests, had his feet up during both games. The first match against West Zone has a scorecard that needs a second look. MCC scored 585/5 declared; Brearley 202, Fletcher 118 and Greig 162 not out. Why didn't he get out a bit earlier, say, when he'd got his hundred, to give the others a chance of a bat? Roger Tolchard was so convulsed with laughter when he told me the background story that it was a job to make sense of what he was saying. 'We were using it as practice for the Test and it was agreed amongst ourselves that we would get out when we reached 50, so as to give the other guys a bat. Greigy got to 50 and then tried to get out. Well, he couldn't. The more he slogged, the further it went. In no time, he got to 100. By now he was trying to hit every ball for six. And still the ball was sailing out of the ground. All of a sudden he was on 150. I think he scored a hundred, that is 50 to 150, in about 30 balls. The crowd was going bonkers. People were saying it was the greatest innings they'd ever seen.' *Were you cross with him?* 'No, we were all falling about laughing in the dressing room. That was Greigy. He just loved playing cricket. He enjoyed every minute of that tour, on and off the field. He was just a great bloke. One of the lads. Anything went with him. And it usually did. That was how he played his cricket.'

Who knows why one team can emerge from the traps quicker than the other? Plans are laid, preparation is rigorous, practice is fruitful yet everything can go wrong … or right. To everybody's surprise, England outplayed their hosts in the first Test and won a convincing victory by an innings and 25 runs. Their strategy of playing three pace bowlers and one spinner, augmented by the captain's off spin, worked perfectly and, as a team, they looked a unified and effective force. The Indians, by contrast appeared uninspired, giving every impression of being exhausted after their recent series against New Zealand. All will be different by the time the second Test comes round was the feeling; the Indians will have regrouped and will put up a far better show. Tony Greig, who had been in this position before in India – 1-0 up – had no doubt this was true. In the meantime, he could take a look at his tired but happy team with satisfaction and no little pride.

Perhaps he wouldn't have felt in such high spirits on the first morning of the match walking out to bat with his team at 65/4 but he had become accustomed to crises. Together with Dennis Amiss, who went on to compile a monumental 179 in eight and a half hours, he steadied the ship to enable Knott and the debutant Lever to run amok later on in the innings. In response to England's 381, the Indian openers proceeded without alarm until the match, and arguably the series, was turned on its head. John Lever had the ball in his hand, nothing was happening and he was beginning to realise why he had made 53 so comfortably batting at No 9. He told me what happened next. 'At 40/0 they were going well. The ball was useless and doing nothing. But those balls did go out of shape so Greigy got the umpires to change it. The replacement went round corners.' This can happen. No two balls that are hand-stitched are ever quite the same. 'This one swung from the very first ball,' Selvey said, 'JK bowled them out and that was curtains for me until Old got injured before the fifth Test.' India were dismissed for 122, Lever taking 7-46. This Test match cricket is a doddle, he must have thought, especially once Underwood and Greig had bowled them out in the second innings and England had secured their victory.

In the immediate aftermath, both Tony and Lever were required to give a press conference. It seemed the whole world wanted a word from the pair. 'Greigy told the rest of the team to go back to the hotel in the bus while we stayed behind to talk to the press,' Lever said, 'After we had finished the press conference, we had the problem of no transport. So there we stood in the middle of the road in our whites. Greigy stopped the first motorbike to go past and then another, climbed on the back of one, told me to do the same on the other and instructed the riders to take us back to the hotel.' *And did they?* 'They thought they'd died and gone to heaven. My driver kept on looking back at me, a wide grin splitting his face. "Don't look at me," I shouted to him, "Keep your eyes on the road!" I've never been so frightened in my life.'

Christmas was now upon them and they could relax. Lunch was provided at the home of the British High Commissioner and he had not stinted with his hospitality in an attempt to make the team feel festive with turkey and trimmings, Christmas pudding, the lot. All was cheerful jollification. There was one cloud on the horizon, however. Keith Fletcher had slipped on the polished marble floor in the hotel and turned his ankle. He had chipped a bone and it seemed likely a key cog in the batting unit would be missing for the second Test. In fact, he struggled for fitness for the rest of the tour. Despite his outward bonhomie during Christmas lunch, Tony Greig was brooding. He looked around at his team, relaxed and enjoying the fun, and wondered whether they were losing their edge, whether they had become a little too pleased with themselves and complacent. What was required, he decided there and then, was a rocket. Once he had lit the blue touch paper, there was no stopping him. On his own admission, it was a 'verbal assault' in which his 'language was appalling'. But he felt it had to be done. This was not the time to take the foot off the gas. That is what happened on the last tour four years previously and he was damned if it was going to happen again. At length, he stormed out of the room, confident that his message had got through.

When I quizzed Roger Tolchard about this outburst, he couldn't remember a thing about it. This has less to do with fading memory than familiarity and repetition. Professional sportsmen are used to being upbraided in dressing rooms by captains and managers, often in the most vitriolic tones. It goes with the territory and is rarely personal or resented. Usually it is deserved, it needs to be said and if the response may be silent, even sullen, the point is taken and performance during the next session improves. Tony was prone from time to time to fly off the handle. It was soon forgotten and nobody minded. He had the team's interests at heart and everybody knew that. This side had no intention of taking its foot off the gas. Tony was pleased to note the following day that the intensity had not dropped off in the pre-match practice and nets.

Whenever a 'great' innings is played and then analysed, I am always reminded of Barry Richards's criteria when he runs the rule over what he has just seen. 'You have to take into careful consideration three things,' he always says. 'State of the game, quality of the bowling and the condition of the pitch. In other words, how much pressure is the batsman under?'

The pitch for the second Test in Calcutta was a shocker. It hadn't looked too bad the day before during practice but the England team were horrified to observe half a dozen groundsmen getting down on their hands and knees before the toss to scrub it with iron brushes. 'Normal practice,' an angry England captain was told as he accompanied Bishan Bedi out to the middle for the toss. Bedi jumping into the air once the coin had been picked up and examined told the players back in the dressing room all they feared to know. Whoever was going to have to bat last on that wicket was going to be the loser; that much was obvious. 'Well, we shall just have to bowl 'em out cheaply, hey,' was Tony's message to his team.

Thanks to some inspired bowling from Bob Willis, ruthlessly exposing India's weakness against fast bowling, bowl them out is precisely what they did. India folded for 155 (Willis 5-27). England's plan was obvious; bat for as long as it takes. It did not seem likely to be very long at all. Yet again the captain came in to face a crisis. He joined Tolchard, who was making his debut, with four down and only 90 on the board. Together, they put on 142 priceless runs in a stand that lasted four and a half hours. *Torturous going, Rog. Tell me about it.* 'We'd bowled them out cheaply. All we had to do was build a big lead. There was no time pressure on us at all. The wicket was turning and of course they had a phalanx of great spinners. But it turned *slowly* so you could play it. Except for Chandra, of course. He would bowl it quickly and for an hour or so I couldn't lay a bat on him. We both knew that if either of us got out, he could easily have run through the lot of us, as he did on several occasions subsequently. It was a great spell but somehow we survived.' *Greigy was ill, wasn't he?* 'A little bit under the weather, you could say.' In fact, Tony was really ill. He had a fever with a temperature of 104 and how he managed to stay out there, in the dust and the heat, was a marvel to his team-mates.

The contrast in style and technique with his partner Tolchard could not have been more marked. The Leicestershire man had been picked for the tour as the reserve wicketkeeper to Alan Knott but more specifically, Tony Greig had wanted him on board as a skilful player of spin. It was because of this that he was playing as a specialist batsman and as such he was repaying in spades his captain's belief in him. If Greig's strategy was to play predominantly off the back foot, relying on cuts and pulls for scoring shots, Tolchard would run down the wicket and attempt to nullify the spin by hitting it on the half-volley, or full if he was quick enough. He was renowned for the speed of his footwork and it was no surprise to me, though it might have been to his contemporaries, that he was a skilled ballroom dancer. Nobody was quicker between the wickets than he (though Asif Iqbal of Kent and Pakistan might have given him a run for his money) but he had to curb his instincts for the quick single given his partner's fatigue and debility. What both he and Tony shared was a taste for battle and a relish for the big occasion. There is no bigger occasion than a Test match at Eden Gardens in front of 80,000 noisy, excitable Indians. Tony described the din as Bedi came on to bowl as something akin to the roar of a football crowd. Tolchard told me, 'The crowd would jump out of their seats as every ball was bowled. It was all so exciting and I felt privileged to be a part of it.'

At last Tolchard's vigil was ended, bowled by Bedi for 67. He had faced 238 balls. Greig wrote of him: 'I felt a sense of pride for him. He had justified all my hopes and statements with his handling of the spinners, which at times was outrageously bold.' Roger's memory of his dismissal still makes him wince. 'Aaargh – played on! The ball squirmed off my front foot and rolled back on to the stumps, dislodging a bail. If I'd been quicker in my reactions, I could have kicked it away.' Fortunately, this was the era when a rest day was traditionally inserted into the middle of a Test match so Tony was able to spend it in bed to stabilise his fever and to re-gather his strength.

As the England captain recuperates, I thought I would depart on a little tangent and enquire about the standard of hotels in India at the time. I had been on a schoolboy tour of the subcontinent about ten years before and we had found the accommodation basic, and that is being kind. Much had changed, it seemed. 'Wonderful tour,' said Chris Old, 'hotels were top-class.' John Lever agreed. 'The hotels were fantastic. We were royally looked after, everything was clean and sickness was kept to a minimum.' The general impression was that things had improved markedly in recent years. They were put up in the best hotels and the 'bearers' (staff) were indefatigable in their attentiveness and service. India being India, however, there were occasions of unconscious comedy. Selvey recalls one such incident: 'It was Christmas. We were served the standard mutton curry. "Haven't you got anything more festive?" we asked. The waiter took our food away and reappeared with the same dishes but with a sprig of holly on the top.' Water was a problem, a hidden source of infection. They took their own bottled water with them wherever they went. On an internal flight, the authorities refused to allow the container into the hold. The captain (of the team, not the aircraft) put his foot down. The water comes with us or we refuse to fly. The airline relented and the team's water travelled with them. 'One thing about Greigy I never understood,' Tolchard told me, 'he would order a Coke to drink but wouldn't touch it until it had gone flat.' *Did you notice his smoking?* Tolchard laughed. 'When there was a drinks break, the 12th man would bring him out a fag hidden under a towel.'

Rested and rejuvenated, Tony Greig and his team set about the task of consigning their opponents to defeat when hostilities resumed. 'Basically, all we had to do was silence the crowd and grind the Indians into the dust.' Tolchard said, 'We didn't want to have to make any sort of total batting last on that wicket.' In fact, India did manage to make England bat again. The total set was 16, which the openers achieved without being parted. That England had been able to win at a gentle canter owed much to an all-round team effort, the wickets in India's second innings of 181 being shared around the bowling attack. The wisdom of Tony's tactic of attrition was underlined by Underwood's bowling. His figures of 3-50 off 32 overs do not tell the whole story. He was managing to make the ball turn and bounce sharply and heaven only knows what havoc the Indian spinners would have wreaked had England been forced to chase a total of anything in excess of 100. No, 16 was just about manageable they felt.

It was an emotional moment for Tony. He led the team out on a lap of honour in front of the massive, and surprisingly generous, crowd, dressed in their tour blazers of course. I wondered why they had become so popular in India when they were 2-0 up against the home favourites. Much of the affection in which they were held by Indian crowds had to do with the personality of the captain. He engaged with them at every opportunity, waving, blowing kisses, pretending to be shot every time a firecracker went off, generally acting like a pantomime figure in front of the crowded stands. Mike Brearley, his vice-captain, put it so memorably: 'Greig understood pageantry.' For example, according to Brearley, he made the team sprint out on to the field of play at the start of each session rather than making their way to the middle in stately procession, which had traditionally been a team's entrance. Nowadays, all teams do it. It makes a team look more 'purposeful'. Selvey said this of his captain. 'He was imperious in India, a huge figurehead on this tour. He was an extraordinary captain. I would have walked through fire for him.' Bob Willis said to me, 'Greigy was at his charming best in India. He had this knack of endearing himself to those huge crowds. He was an outstanding leader.' Roger Tolchard reminded me that Tony as figurehead had a faithful and resourceful sidekick in Derek Randall. 'Rags used to do cartwheels and throw his cap in the air to catch it behind his back. He was a natural comedian and the crowd loved him. On these laps of honour the crowd would go mad, clapping, shouting, laughing. Greigy would stop us in front of the ladies'4 stand and tell us to do our stretching exercises in front of them. They were giggling and laughing and Greigy was lapping it all up. Ah, happy days!'

Mike Brearley, in his book *The Art of Captaincy*, makes two interesting comments about Greig's leadership style. The first concerned his implacable competitive instinct. 'He was good at making his bowlers bowl aggressively at 9, 10, Jack,' he wrote. There had been an unwritten rule in cricket since God knows when – not always complied with, it has to be said – that it was considered bad form to bowl bouncers at tail-enders. They couldn't bat, so the feeling went, and they would soon give up the ghost and depart the stage without a fuss. Greig would have no truck with such niceties. If they were out there in the middle wielding a bat in a Test match, they were batsmen and as such were to be got rid of as soon as possible. No wasting time waiting for them to decide when to get out; they must be sent on their way, pronto. These days, with the advances in the ability and technique of lower order batsmen (nobody is a tail-ender anymore), the argument has largely become redundant. The second point Brearley made concerned what the press would call the team's refuelling habits. This would include the thorny issue of curfews. Cricket is a social game and cricketers, by and large, are a sociable lot. The post-match drink is as much a part of the game as tea and jam sponge. Some players on tour are 'early-nighters'. Others prefer creeping past the captain's hotel room after the midnight hour has chimed. One of Greig's great strengths as a captain, he believed, was that he understood the late-nighters. 'As poacher turned gamekeeper, he was in a strong position to mix firmness with freedom.'

Showmanship alone does not win Test matches. How was Tony Greig managing to outfox an experienced Indian side – in their own backyard – as well as charm their public? Like all good generals, he knew what his strengths were, and played to them, and crucially relied on others around for advice and support when they were required. As Selvey wryly pointed out to me, 'He had Brearley, Knott and Fletcher alongside him, so he couldn't go far wrong tactically.' That was undoubtedly true but the fact is that he listened to them. He might not always have followed their advice but he made it clear that he valued their opinion. They felt included in the decision-making process, a skill not always displayed by some England captains. 'He understood personalities,' Alan Knott told me, 'and he managed to get the best out of people. Derek Underwood always said he was the best captain he ever played under.' *Would you agree, Alan?* He gave the matter some thought. 'Probably the best for me was Illy. Close behind would be Greigy and Brearley. They had this knack of getting the best out of their players.'

Of course, Greigy being Greigy, there were times when the senior players believed he needed to rein things in. 'He could be a loose cannon,' admitted Tolchard. 'Fletch, Knott and Underwood were more conservative, solid, experienced professionals who knew what was what. Take Deadly, for example. He loved bowling maidens. He would do it all day if he could.' *I expect therefore that Greig felt the need to attack sometimes.* 'Exactly. He'd bring himself on at the other end and bowl a few long-hops and full tosses, which would get the treatment. Meanwhile, Deadly was going mad because runs were being leaked and his strategy was to build pressure by not giving away runs. And then Greigy would go and take a wicket!' Such bowlers in the trade were known as 'golden arms'. It seemed Tony Greig had the knack of taking wickets when least expected. 'God, he was so lucky,' said Tolchard, the affection clear in his chuckle. 'I know he's a good general but is he lucky?' was a question asked by Napoleon of his General Staff. As far as his team were concerned, Tony Greig could keep on being lucky; they were not going to complain. 'The thing is,' continued Tolchard, 'Greigy just loved playing and if things were getting a bit boring, he'd always try something to liven it up.'

For a final word on Tony Greig's captaincy on this tour, which more than any other defined his career as a leader, I sought the opinion of Keith Fletcher, one whose praise, not often easily bestowed, comes carefully and judiciously out of the side of his mouth. 'Look, he was a good bloke, an excellent tourist. He knew how to get the best out of his team. He was a motivator rather than a tactician. He got all of us going in the right direction.' *It was suggested, Keith, that he made all the big decisions while you and Knotty set the field.* He laughed. 'You could say something like that. But it worked! Bit like Close and Illingworth at Yorkshire. One did all the talking and the other quietly moved the pieces around the chess board. Tactically, Greigy was better than Denness because in essence he was a leader. He was never Mastermind, like, say, Brearley, but he consulted and crucially he got people behind him.' Above all, everybody agreed, it was a happy tour. And not many tours of India had been half as harmonious.

England were 2-0 up and in a wonderful position but the series was not yet in the bag. Win the third Test in Madras and a historic triumph was theirs; lose it and India would probably come back heartened and full of confidence and victory could well be snatched from England's grasp. Madras was hot when the teams arrived, very hot. In addition, the high humidity made conditions very uncomfortable for the Englishmen. 'As soon as you stepped out on to the playing area,' Tolchard said to me, 'you were drenched in sweat.' The suggestion how best to combat this problem caused a stir, which developed into a *cause celebre*, which in turn was whipped up by the press into something approaching a scandal, and threatened to derail the whole tour. Memories of the Vaseline Affair still rankle to this day.

First things first. The groundsman, obviously taking hospitality to its extreme, had prepared a greentop. The England team could not believe their eyes when they saw it. Greentops in India are about as rare as disciplined driving on the roads. Tony was delighted to win the toss though he did not emulate Bedi's leap of joy of the previous Test. Batting first, England found the going anything but straightforward and once more, Tony found himself at the crease at a time of crisis. There was nothing for it but to knuckle down and this he did; his 54 held the innings together. A total of 262 had been hard going but it proved to be the biggest score of the match. A look at the scorecard puzzled me. My old friend Roger Tolchard, batting at No 5, is carded as having scored 8 not out. *How come, Rog?* 'Amarnath got one to take off and it hit me on the back of my bottom hand. It was bloody painful, I can tell you. It had missed all the padding and hit me on the finger. I thought I'd broken it. I had to retire.' So the score when Greig came to the wicket was not 33/3 but in effect 33/4. Furthermore, not only was the wicket unusually quick, the odd ball was taking off. *But the scorecard says Tolchard not out 8, not retired hurt?* 'I came back in at No 11 to try and squeeze a few more runs. I couldn't hit the ball so I just ran down the wicket and kicked it away. The crowd were going mad as I was doing this.'

I bet they were. You always were an irritating fellow to bowl at, moving around at the crease and using your feet like the ballet dancer you were. 'Ballroom dancer,' he corrected me.

As expected, the England pace bowlers found the pitch very much to their liking, bowling India out for 164, with Lever continuing his good form taking 5-59. It was at lunch on the third day, when India were 126/7, that trouble bubbled up. Bob Willis and John Lever were complaining that the sweat pouring off their brows when bowling had been getting in their eyes and causing reddening and irritation. 'I'd played a lot of football,' said Lever, 'and I knew that the guys smeared Vaseline on their foreheads to prevent sweat dripping down into their eyes. "Got any Vaseline?" I asked Bernie.' Bernie Thomas was the team's physiotherapist. Much loved on successive MCC tours, he was in reality more than a physio; he fulfilled a variety of roles and performed a myriad of tasks for the players, who found him ever helpful and ever resourceful. 'He didn't have any Vaseline in his box of tricks,' continued Lever, 'but he did have some strips of gauze. So he put one strip over each eye and one longer one over Bob's. He looked like an Indian chief. God knows what I looked like.' Mike Selvey, who wasn't playing, remembers the scene well. 'I was sitting alongside Bob and JK and their eyes were red with the soreness. Bernie said he had no Vaseline but he did have something better – strips of gauze daubed in Vaseline that were meant for burns. So he attached them to their foreheads and out they went when the bell went. Didn't last long. They kept on falling off. I remember Bob tearing his off and throwing them away.' Not only did they keep falling off, Lever found that the grease, mixed with the sweat of his own brow, made the ball difficult to grip. So he discarded his.

How and where the strips of gauze were disposed of is a matter of some confusion. I don't think there is anything necessarily sinister in the fact that the players have different accounts of what happened to the strips. After all, it is over 40 years since the incident. Memories tend to get a bit fuzzy. Tolchard said that Lever handed his to the umpire. Selvey says he kicked it into the dirt. Lever says he threw his down at the base of the stumps at the end from which he was bowling. What is indisputable is that the umpire took a long hard look at the offending piece of gauze and spoke about it to Bedi, the Indian captain who happened to be at the non-striker's end.

All hell then broke loose. Bedi accused the Englishmen of cheating, adding for good measure that he had suspected that they had been interfering with the state of the ball ever since the first Test in Delhi when Lever had managed to get it to swing prodigiously. The furore soon escalated. The Indian Board seized the offending strips to send them away for analysis. The result came back, surprise surprise, with the assessment that they were indeed impregnated with Vaseline, something the England management had never denied. The next day was a rest day, ideal time for the press to go to town. The MCC back in London were dragged into the uproar and asked for an explanation from the England captain, Tony Greig, and manager, Ken Barrington. Both were adamant that nobody had cheated; the whole affair was an unfortunate and unforeseen accident. Their defence was measured, logical and consistent:

1. The ball wasn't swinging, either before or after the introduction of the strips of gauze.
2. If the team had wanted to apply a banned substance to the ball, they would surely have been more subtle about it than plastering it all over their brows for everybody to see.
3. The gauze strips had only been applied when the Indian innings had more or less collapsed. Why do such a thing when England already had the upper hand?
4. Far from aiding the bowlers, the Vaseline had actually been a hindrance as the ball became greasy and difficult to hold.

Lever might well have added two more reasons for the absurdity of the charges. 'Bedi, a Sikh, don't forget was under enormous pressure both with the public and the selectors. His side were about to go 0-3 down and lose the series. So he reacted hysterically and accused us of cheating. Furthermore, Vaseline doesn't help the ball to swing!' The frustration and anger in Lever's voice were obvious. The affair still rankled. He was known on the county circuit as an honest and affable fellow who bore no grudges but his quarrel with Bedi lasted a long time. 'I eventually made it up with him,' he said. 'Life's too short, eh?'

Many years later, not long before he died, Tony Greig gave an interview recalling the Vaseline Affair, in which he freely admitted it shouldn't have happened. He reaffirmed that it had been an honest mistake by Bernie Thomas and there had been absolutely no intention of deliberately interfering with the state of the ball. He too reckoned that Bedi overplayed his point, 'grasping at straws', he called it. However it *was* a mistake but one that they could do nothing about. All they could do was concentrate on winning the match.

All to whom I spoke were in agreement that both Greig and Barrington dealt with the fall-out from the affair with charm, tact and firmness. The MCC accepted their explanation; it had been a mistake with unfair advantage neither sought nor gained. So did the Indian Board, however reluctantly, and the match continued. There was ill-feeling in the stands when the game resumed after the rest day; Lever was booed and a banner **Cheater Lever Go Home Tony Greig Down Down** was unfurled but a few Randall cartwheels put them in a better mood. Tony did his best to console the unhappy target of the crowd's ire, telling him that the matter would be 'sorted' and that he had to concentrate on his bowling. 'Which to be fair, he did,' said Lever, 'he was brilliant.' The ball was now bouncing erratically – still not swinging, Vaseline or no Vaseline – England built up a substantial lead and India folded for 83, to give the visitors victory in the match by 200 runs and the series 3-0. It was fitting, to his team-mates at any rate, that it was Lever who took the final wicket, sending Chandrasekhar's off stump cartwheeling through the air.

The picture of Lever and Old chairing their victorious skipper off the field is symbolically eloquent and in no way excessive. It had been a truly momentous achievement. England had beaten India in India for the first time in five attempts since the war. No other side had ever clinched a series in India over the first three Tests. And the margin of victory in these matches, by an innings and 25 runs, by ten wickets and by 200 runs, had been overwhelming. Pleased though he was by his team's efforts and relaxed as he was as they celebrated (he with coffee and a cigarette, others with Champagne), he knew that the job was not yet done. There were two more Tests to play and it was not in his nature to let up now. He wanted a clean sweep.

However, on trips like this in those days, teams did not fly in and fly out, playing just Test matches with merely a couple of warm-up games beforehand (sometimes not even that!). Between the third and fourth Tests, MCC played two games up country and several of the party who had been heavily engaged up to that point were excused duty. Lever was one of those. 'Greigy approached me and asked me whether I needed a rest. When I said yes, he said that he and Underwood were going to Goa and would I like to accompany them. So we spent three days on the beach.' *How lovely. Did you have a good time?* 'Well, ye-es …' He seemed unwilling to continue but the amusement in his voice encouraged me to press him further. 'We suddenly found ourselves on a nudist beach. Deadly and I dived for cover. But Greigy was quite unabashed. "Hey, guys, this is great. Let's join them," he said, stripping off.' That was as far as Lever was prepared to go. I have to say it was probably far enough. I leave you with the image of the Blond Beanpole strutting his stuff on that beach.

All along Tony had been warning that at some stage India would get their act together and come back strongly. He was right about that, though the home supporters were of the opinion that it was a case of too little too late. That they won the fourth Test in Bangalore by 140 runs was actually no bad thing for the sake of the series and it probably gave credence to the assessment of how well England had played up until this point. India were still a good side and if conditions suited their spinners, which they did at this venue, they could, and should, beat anyone. For once they did not fritter away their advantage of winning the toss by capitulating to England's seamers, heroically though Willis bowled, taking 6-53. Chandrasekhar had threatened all series but never actually breached the defences of the England batsmen. Now, he ran amok, his 6-76 being the main contributing factor in England's below-par total of 195. Up against it for the first time, the England bowlers, particularly Underwood, toiled manfully but India were able to pile on the pressure, eventually declaring at 259/9, setting their opponents an unlikely target of 318. When England's fourth wicket fell with only eight runs on the board, the writing was on the wall. This time it was Bedi who was England's tormentor, taking 6-71 as England slid to defeat and were bowled out for 177.

Tony and his team, even though they had the series in the bag, were determined that the fifth and final Test in Bombay would be approached as if all hinged on the result. It was symptomatic of the positive cricket they had been playing all tour. On comfortably the best wicket of the series, India made their highest score of 338, underpinned by a century from Gavaskar – the Little Master, as the West Indians had named him. Greig with three wickets and Underwood with four were the pick of the England bowlers. With the bat, they achieved near parity, 317, the middle order held together by 76 from the captain, playing as fluently as he had ever done. India struggled in their second innings against the spin of Underwood, who was now confirming himself as a master of all conditions and in all countries. He secured another five-wicket haul, for 84 runs, but still, the target of 214, batting last on a wearing pitch, was daunting. At tea on the final day, England had lost three wickets in the chase but to score 122 in 90 minutes was not out of the question. However, the loss of Greig and Knott in swift succession gave them other ideas and sensibly they retreated. Thus an intriguing game was drawn, the only one of the series.

It would be hard to pick anyone in world cricket at this time whose stock was higher than Tony Greig's. It always helps a captain if his own game is in good order and that he feels confident that he is making significant contributions to the team over and above his captaincy. There was no trouble for England's captain on this score; he was batting as well as ever. His aggregate for the series of 342 runs was second only to Amiss's, as was his average of 42.75. He could be regarded as a front-line batsman alone. His bowling, mainly of the off spin variety, had not been as effective as it had been in the West Indies but he still took ten wickets, often at useful times. But it was as a leader that he was proving indispensable to England's cause. *Wisden* was fulsome in its praise of him on this tour. The team 'were inspired by their flamboyant and articulate captain ... Greig's charisma enabled him to extract maximum effort from his players.' Their correspondent used the phrase 'band of brotherhood' to describe the MCC team as it made its way across India, forging friendships and gaining respect wherever they played. Alan Knott, I think, spoke for everyone. 'He could have captained England for years. But then came Packer.'

A ticker-tape reception was not planned for the triumphant tourists when their stay in India came to an end; a rather awkward and not wholly welcome adjunct to the itinerary was a fortnight's trip to Sri Lanka. The point was two-fold: to fly the flag (the MCC one) and to gauge the progress the island was making in its cricket development. The memory of the players was one of stifling heat and bemusement at what on earth their administrative masters back home were thinking of when they organised the visit. Because what was on everybody's mind was not a few games against a non-Test-playing country but the eagerly anticipated Centenary Test in Australia – the glittering climax to their tour – and as any cricket lover knew, the wickets in Sri Lanka were nothing like, and no preparation for, the bouncy surfaces Down Under.

The very first official Test match was played in Melbourne in March 1877. There had of course been several unofficial tours of the country before then but they had been by private invitation only. The team assembled under the captaincy of James Lillywhite comprised professionals only. Lillywhite had been on a tour previously and it had not been a notable success. The amateurs and the professionals did not get on particularly well, underlining the class differences of that era and Lillywhite was determined the same mistake would not be repeated. Accordingly, all the amateurs were left at home. The trouble was that most of the best batsmen in the country at the time were amateurs. Traditionally, the amateurs were batsmen and the professionals were bowlers. As a result, the tourists were well stocked with bowlers but their batting was weak. However, it was felt that the team could cope. After all, the 'colonials' were not nearly as adept at the game as the English. To set off on a cricket tour with only 12 players would seem to be imprudent if you were merely contemplating a few friendlies on the South Downs; to set off on an arduous tour of New Zealand and Australia so under-equipped was madness. The folly of the lack of planning was underlined when the team departed New Zealand with only 11 players. They had to leave one behind who had been slapped in gaol.

By the time they arrived in Melbourne for the first official Test, the English were exhausted with the constant travelling and playing with no rest. The Australians were not without their problems too. Fred Spofforth, their best bowler, declared himself unavailable because he disapproved of the choice of wicketkeeper. Inter-state squabbling was a feature of the early days of Australian cricket. Spofforth it was who made a name for himself the following year on a tour of England. After bowling Grace for a duck, he allegedly exclaimed to his team-mates back in the dressing room, 'Ain't I a demon?' giving rise to his nickname 'The Demon'. Spofforth features large in the story of Anglo-Australian cricket. In 1882, he practically single-handedly secured victory for his side by the narrowest of margins – seven runs – by taking 14-90 at the Oval. This defeat for the home side gave birth to the famous obituary in *The Sporting Times*: 'The body of English cricket has died … it will be cremated and the ashes taken to Australia.' Thus a legendary sporting contest was born.

This was five years in the future. The Ashes were not at stake in Melbourne in 1877 but national pride most certainly was. It was a timeless match. Well, why not? What would be the point of going all that way only for the colonials to play for a draw seemed to be the prevailing view. As a result, it made for slow, some might say turgid, cricket. Australia were indebted to Charles Bannerman who made 165 (retired hurt) out of a total of 245. They took 170 overs to do it. England batted little quicker. Their reply of 196 occupied 136 overs. Australia collapsed in their second innings for 104, leaving the visitors to score only 154 to win. They fell, inexplicably, short by 45 runs. Turgid? It had been nail-bitingly tense. Australia were jubilant in victory. They had shown to all the doubters, not least themselves, that they could compete at the same level as their colonial masters. The fact that England squared the series in the second Test is largely forgotten.

One hundred years later, Tony Greig and his MCC team – all present and correct; nobody was left behind languishing in a Sri Lankan gaol – landed in Perth, not knowing quite what to expect. This was no conventional tour of Australia. The Ashes were not at stake. The Centenary Test was a one-off. It had no relevance other than its symbolic status. It had no narrative other than its history.

241

Was it an exhibition match in all but name or was it a full-blooded encounter between two traditional enemies? A warm-up game against Western Australia had been scheduled and, hello, who was playing against them? None other than Dennis Lillee. An announcement that Lillee would not be touring England the following summer because of ongoing problems with an old stress fracture in his back but that he would be playing against the tourists in the match and in the forthcoming Centenary Test served only to deepen the visitors' confusion. Nothing much wrong with his back if he's playing this week was the thought that went through the captain's mind and one or two others. The sophistry of this curious press release about Lillee's fitness would be exposed soon enough. To add further puzzlement, Tony met up with his old friend, fellow South African Barry Richards, and detected something odd, evasive even, during their get-together. 'I had a secret,' Barry told me, 'one that I was sworn not to divulge, even to Greigy. I nearly blurted it out but I didn't. Was he in the know, I asked myself. But I couldn't take the chance.'

In fact Tony was *not* in the know but he had more important things to worry about than an odd press release and some evasive comments from a respected compatriot.

If there were any uncertainties about the nature and the size of the event that had been organised, they were dispelled the moment the team set foot on the tarmac of Melbourne Airport. The assembled press corps was huge and media coverage intense as the party was transported from airport to hotel in a motorcade with a TV helicopter above flashing images of the journey around the land. The Hilton Hotel was rapidly filling with the 220 out of the 244 remaining Test players from the two countries who had accepted the invitation to attend, some of whom were instantly recognisable and others to whom Father Time had not been so kind. From Australia: Bradman, Hassett, Miller, Lindwall, Harvey, McKenzie, Benaud, Lawry .... From England: Larwood, Bedser, Hutton, May, Cowdrey, Laker, Lock, Trueman, Statham, Evans, Compton, Edrich .... Merely recounting the names evoked so many memories of great deeds and famous matches. The eldest from Australia was Jack Ryder, 87. From England, it was Percy Fender, 84. So eminent was the guest list and so poignant the atmosphere that Lillee memorably remarked, 'You almost expected the big bearded fellow to walk into the room.' Billy Griffith, the secretary of the MCC went on record as saying, 'This must be the most magnificent effort ever made by a cricket authority.' Don Bradman weighed in with this comment: 'I've never known a match where there was so much emotion in the air.' There were cocktail parties, Champagne receptions, gala dinners, speeches, pomp and ceremony, with the wine flowing as copiously as the reminiscences. Before the toss, there was a parade of 18 past captains in front of the pavilion.

Tony Greig above anybody else would have understood – and lapped up – the ceremony and hoopla surrounding the event and instantly recognised the important role he had to play in the festivities. He had to shield his team from all the noise and distraction so that they could concentrate on the matter in hand, to make sure that they played their part in putting on a show worthy of the occasion. To get rolled over, to perform at anything less than their best, to freeze on such a stage as had been provided, was unthinkable. They had a match to win. All other matters were peripheral. 'For goodness sake, guys,' he said, 'the Queen is coming on the final day. We need to be out there, still fighting.'

They were! In fact both sides were at it hammer and tongs as Her Majesty made her appearance at tea on the last day. The entire Australian team, plus the two England batsmen, had to forgo their cuppa to don their blazers with the rest of them in a line to be introduced by their captains. Dennis Lillee was in the middle of a marathon spell (whatever happened to his bad back?) but he still had the presence of mind – or the cheek – to flourish a pen and autograph book in front of Her Majesty, requesting her signature. Of course, custom and protocol would not permit such an act of *lese majeste* but he did receive a signed card from her later on via one of her equerries. With only one session to go, the match still hung in the balance. Clearly it had lived up to its billing and Tony had made good on his promise that his side would play its full part.

I was intrigued to know what was the feeling inside the dressing room about this extraordinary encounter. I asked Alan Knott. *Was it the greatest Test you have ever been involved in?* 'It was a great occasion but I hesitate to call it a great Test. You see, I believe that each match in an Ashes series – or any series for that matter – should have a context. That is, a battle over five matches to see which side comes out on top. This game was a one-off. It had no real meaning. So it didn't feel to me like a proper Test. Besides, it was more difficult for us because we had just come from a gruelling tour of India and didn't have proper time to acclimatise.' *How did Greigy approach the game?* 'We must play for a win, come what may, he told us. In a normal series, we would not have chased down, or attempted to chase down, that total because in the context of a series a draw might have been more valuable. So I doubt we would have lost.' *But what a game, eh?* He did not disagree on that point. Neither did anyone, playing or watching, who was present at the MCG over the five-day course of the Centenary Test.

On the morning of 12 March 1977, Greg Chappell spun the specially minted gold coin into the air, Tony Greig called correctly and elected to field. Bob Willis was not alone in disagreeing with the decision: Geoffrey Boycott, commentating on television, thought the choice would come back to bite the England captain. In fact, Tony had read the pitch right. His opposite number also believed that the groundsman had either misjudged, or not been able to effect, its preparation by a day or two but he would still probably have batted had the coin fallen differently. It took Willis only an over or two to realise that the pitch was still moist and had something in it. His nostrils flared. He scented blood. Sadly for Rick McCosker, the opening bat, it was real blood. He misjudged a short ball, it hit him on the jaw, breaking it in two places, and he was forced to retire, hurt *and* out, because the ball had dropped on to his wicket and dislodged a bail.

The England attack of Willis, Lever, Old and Underwood that had served Tony so well in India hunted down the Australian batsmen in a pack, remorselessly and effectively, and dismissed them for 138. Greg Chappell top-scored with 40 and reckoned he 'never had to work harder for runs in Australia'. First round to England. Not for long. They had bowled Australia out too quickly (44 overs); the pitch had not dried out. Lillee's dander was soon up – it never took much to raise it when a blue England cap was in his sights – and none was better suited to exploit the conditions than he, now at the peak of his pace, his form and his confidence. England were in turn humiliated, 95 all out. He did not get Greig. He received the ball of the day from Max Walker, who believed it was the best ball he ever bowled, nipping through Greig's gate and knocking out middle and leg. This time round the innings had lasted a mere 34 overs, Lillee taking 6-26.

By now, the pitch had dried out and flattened and it was the batsmen's time. The centrepiece of their innings – I could have said centrefold, so fetching had the young, golden boy of Australian cricket been marketed – was an explosive 56 from David Hookes. With confidence and temerity that bordered on the dismissive, he struck the England captain for five successive fours in one over, an act so insouciant that Bradman was moved to remark, 'For five balls, I thought Frank Woolley had been reborn.' Sadly, Woolley was one of the two-dozen or so former Test cricketers who had not managed to make it to Melbourne. He was living in Canada, was too ill to travel and died the following year.

This remarkable game continued to offer up drama. Australia had built up a lead but by no means a commanding one when Lillee joined Marsh with the score at 277/7. The pair, better known for a partnership separated by about 50 yards when Lillee was bowling, now joined forces with the bat, putting on 76 for the eighth wicket. By now, on his own admission, Willis was shot. He had nothing more in the tank, despite his captain's wish, command even, to blow away the Australian tail. He told me all about it. 'I was gone. I'd completely run out of steam. After the match, Greigy and I were at a barbecue in Sydney and he gave me a fearful bollocking as I sipped my beer. He told me I had let him down in that second innings of Australia's. He reminded me that he had carefully nursed me through the tour of India, never over-bowling me, always consulting with me over needed rest, so that I could do the business when required. Well, it was certainly required of me that day in Melbourne and I had been unable to repay his faith and his backing.' *Did you agree with him?* 'It had a profound effect on me. There and then, I decided to get *properly* fit. I devised a regime of slow, long-distance runs, which I kept up until I retired, to improve my stamina. Hitherto, I had always been subject to a variety of injuries but after that, I stayed pretty well injury-free and was able to extend my career by several years.' *So you didn't resent his harsh words?* 'Not at all. I owed Greigy a lot. I never forgot it. Actually, it was at the same barbecue that he mentioned to me that if I stayed fit, there would soon be an opportunity to earn a lot of money ...' *Hang on, Bob, we have a match to finish first.*

When Lillee was eventually out, Australia were 353/8, effectively 9, with McCosker *hors de combat*. A sufficient lead for Chappell to declare? Evidently not. A strange figure then emerged from the dressing room. His head swathed in bandages, his jaw wired and his baggy green cap perched comically on top of it all, Rick McCosker walked slowly to the middle. Once the crowd recognised who he was, not immediately obvious for he more resembled Baldrick from *Blackadder* excusing himself from sentry duty in the trenches than a Test cricketer, the crowd rose to him as one and serenaded him with 'Waltzing McCosker'. Marsh was astonished to see him out there but apparently McCosker had been insistent. He had convinced his captain he could do it and his team needed him. Tony Greig advised Chris Old to bowl him a gentle half-volley first up, which he admitted was 'hard to do'. However, this was a genuine contest and it was not long before McCosker's nerve was tested by a bouncer, which he hooked for four. His heroics allowed Marsh to complete his maiden Test century against England and when he was finally dismissed for 25, the pair had put on 54 for the ninth wicket. Chappell had seen enough. He declared his innings closed at 419/9, leaving England the notional target of 463 to win.

Had there been the narrative of a five-match series, as Knott reminded me, England would probably have tried to battle their way to a draw in order to fight another day. Tony was insistent that a boring draw was not what the occasion demanded. They would chase down that target, come hell or high water. It probably would have been hell had it not been for a truly remarkable innings from Derek Randall, one that would seal his everlasting fame, even if, truth to tell, his Test match career did not live up to its early promise. He came into this match with a mere four Test caps to his name and a highest score of 37. He came into this innings when England were 28/1. Ian

Greig recounted to me the story of the background to this innings of Randall's. 'After the India tour, Tony took Randall aside and told him he wasn't being selected and paid to get attractive 30s. He had been picked to score big hundreds and it was damn well time he made one.'

His captain's words evidently struck home. When Randall finally departed England were only 116 runs short of their target with five wickets left. It was an extraordinary spectacle. Lillee was at his snarling, fearsome best, eager to nail the Englishman, either by hitting his person or his stumps. The trouble was that Randall had an odd style, a sort of jack-in-the-box technique, fidgety at the crease, constantly on the move when playing his shots, many of which were improvised and unorthodox. In other words, a menace to bowl at. Lillee later admitted that he had found it 'difficult to hit a moving target'. Furthermore, Randall's temperament burned bright; he was a bundle of nervous energy, no better illustrated than in his speed and exuberance as an electrifying presence as a cover fielder. He used to sing *God Save The Queen* to himself when batting. Once Lillee put him on his backside with a rapid bouncer. Quickly he sprang to his feet and theatrically doffed his cap to the bowler. Another bouncer caught him on the back of the head. Everybody held their breath as he fell backwards only to do a back somersault, stand up, grin and tell Lillee, 'No good hitting me there, mate. Nothing to damage.'

The improbable run chase could not continue, surely. If so, nobody told Randall. In between his antics with Lillee and the short ball, he played some tremendous strokes of which any purist would have been proud. The score grew. 279 when the third wicket fell – Amiss. 290 when the fourth went down – Fletcher. In between, Randall reached his hundred, then his hundred and fifty. Tony was batting with him and was constant in his encouragement, never stifling his urge to attack but urging caution when his impetuosity threatened to run away with itself. When Randall had reached 161, he nicked a little outswinger from Chappell to Marsh, was given out and off he trudged. But in an act of sportsmanship befitting the occasion, Marsh called him back. He hadn't been sure that he had taken the catch cleanly. People at the time and subsequently were surprised by this unwonted act of chivalry from the hard-bitten Aussie but I have always felt that Rodney Marsh was never the aggressive oik he was made out to be.

Eventually Randall pushed forward at a googly from Kerry O'Keeffe and was caught by a tumbling Gary Cosier at short leg. He had scored 174 and batted for 446 minutes. He received a standing ovation from the Melbourne crowd, who recognised a great innings when they saw one. Randall acknowledged the cheers by shyly doffing his cap, then grinned broadly as he waved to the crowd before making his way up the wrong steps of the pavilion.

What now, as Tony was joined at the crease by Alan Knott? They could still do this, he urged his old friend. After all, both had played match-winning innings in Test matches before. However, Tony too perished to the leg spin of O'Keeffe, for 41, and Knott was left to marshal the tail and win the match on his own. That proved to be a bridge too far, even for this redoubtable and remarkable cricketer, and Lillee trapped him lbw for 42 to bring to an end a match that would linger long in the memory. Lillee was exhausted as his triumphant colleagues chaired him off the field. The pain and weariness on his face laid bare a man who had given his all for his country, perhaps for the last time – a thought that crossed his mind as he hung on to their shoulders. He had bowled 48 eight-ball overs in the game, never at any stage fully fit, and had taken 11-165. Greg Chappell later reckoned, 'That ball to Knott was the last he had in him.'

As handshakes were exchanged and the players slowly made their way off the field, the penny dropped in the scorebox. Australia's winning margin of 45 runs was exactly the same as that margin of victory 100 years ago. Uncanny, but somehow it seemed fitting. The England team lined up for the speeches and presentations in their tour blazers – you would expect nothing less with Tony Greig at the helm – while the Australians remained in their whites. Derek Randall was announced as the Man of the Match and came up to receive his gold medallion. 'I'd just like to thank Dennis for the boomp on the 'ead,' he said and fled back to the welcoming and amused arms of his team-mates. 'Randall won Man of the Match,' observed Chappell, 'but Lillee won the match.' Few disagreed.

The whole occasion had been a resounding triumph. For sheer extravagance, panoply and historic significance, there cannot have been a cricket match to rival the Centenary Test. Sir Donald Bradman was exultant. In a speech at the banquet after the game, he said, 'This will go down in history as one of the greatest sporting events of all time.' Here's to the past one hundred years, went the toasts. And here's to the next hundred, they might have added. The air was heavy with celebration, nostalgia and pride. But a certain heaviness in the air can betoken a coming storm and clouds were gathering over the horizon and out of sight the self-satisfied administrators and committee men who ran the game at Lord's and in the offices of the Australian Cricket Board were in for the shock of their lives. In retrospect, it is easy to heap scorn on their short-sightedness but they were not alone in their ignorance. None of us who were outside the tiny circle of people who were in the know had any idea either and we had been playing cheek by jowl with the 'rebels', as they were branded, all season.

Janus was the Roman god of beginnings, gates, doorways, passages and endings. He was traditionally depicted as having two faces in one head, since he looked to the future and back to the past, hence the month January. There can have been no more apt metaphor for the Centenary Test, looking back as it did over one hundred years of cricket and forward to the revolution that was about to convulse the game. While most of the MCC team returned to England immediately after the match, Tony remained in Australia, intending to spend a few days in Sydney, to look up friends and to explore a business opportunity that had presented itself. More of that anon. He made a return to these shores at the end of March to prepare for the 1977 season and was immediately surprised outside Victoria Station by Eamonn Andrews brandishing his famous red book. 'Tony Greig,' he intoned in front of the TV camera, 'This Is Your Life.' The stupefaction of any guest so confronted can only be imagined. For Tony, much as he loved the limelight, the honour could not have come at a worse moment. For he was harbouring a secret, one that he was sworn to keep, even from family and close friends, one that he knew would tarnish the eulogies that assuredly lay in that red book, one that would rip to shreds his gilded reputation in the eyes of the adoring cricket public and one that would more than likely tear asunder the game he had come to represent in this country. How he managed to maintain his *sang-froid* as family, friends, colleagues and cricketers from far and wide paid homage to him that night was a marvel as he smiled, shook hands and shared reminiscences in front of a television audience numbering millions. Ever the showman, he knew that the show must go on. It was an effort of will and concentration to match his innings in Calcutta. Nobody knew. Nobody suspected.

Chapter 9

Kerry Packer's Revolution and the High Court 1977

'A professional cricketer needs to make his living as much as any other professional man.'

Mr Justice Slade in his summing-up
speech in the High Court

I T is difficult, looking back after 40 years, to grasp the magnitude of the upheaval that convulsed the game when Kerry Packer's plans for a breakaway organisation, named World Series Cricket, were unveiled, or rather, unearthed, in the summer of 1977. It was an unconscious irony that the governing bodies of cricket in Australia and England in organising their huge jamboree celebrating one hundred years of the traditional form of the game had gathered all the best players from both countries, and plenty from elsewhere who were not directly involved, under one roof, so to speak, thus saving the rebel organisation the bother and expense of numerous air miles to recruit. It was always my belief, my assumption, that secret negotiations and headhunting for WSC were taking place during the Centenary Test. Surreptitious conversations in corridors and corners had been going on in the Australian dressing room but *not* in the England camp, it transpires. Tony Greig was adamant that he had nothing to do with Packer's plans until after the Centenary Test had finished. Only then did he avail himself of the opportunity to visit Packer in Sydney where the media tycoon's plans were first presented to him. With respect, I believe Tony was being a little disingenuous here. It is true he had signed up to nothing and was therefore in no position to recruit anybody at that time but he did know that something was afoot, a scheme which might benefit him and Test cricketers generally. He had met Packer before and had been intrigued by the man's charisma, influence and ambition.

Before we untangle Tony's association with Kerry Packer, I ought to set the scene. Kerry Packer inherited the media empire of Channel 9 and Australian Consolidated Press from his father on his death in 1974. He built up the company's interests and when he died in 2005 he was considered to be one of the richest and most powerful media magnates in Australia. Here I must confess to another misconception. Owing mainly to the unfavourable reception Packer had received at the hands of the British press, the popular picture painted was one of a venal, avaricious, aggressive, opportunistic businessman with a pugnacious and quarrelsome nature, someone who liked getting his own way and whom you crossed at your peril. Like many others in this country who had never met him, I was content to accept the caricature of the hard-nosed, ruthless philistine he was supposed to be – the archetypal Australian vulgarian. It did not take me long, once I had talked to people who actually worked with him and knew him, to realise how much lazy thinking had been informing my opinion. In the cut-throat world of commercial activity, Kerry Packer was clearly no pushover; he could be as ruthless, probably more so, as the next man. You do not get that rich and influential without stepping on toes. No doubt he behaved at times with scant regard for other people's finer feelings and he certainly didn't mince his words. He was ambitious and he did have big plans and he took no prisoners in his scramble for power and hegemony. But these characteristics did not fully define the man. How was it that so many people who worked for him, Tony included, thought the world of him? You do not inspire that loyalty if you have the heart of a villain. This is the enigma of Kerry Packer, a man, I would suggest, that the British never really 'got'.

Tony resolutely defended his mentor and friend. As a similar straight-talking sort of fellow, he was not abashed by Packer's brash manner. Furthermore, he believed he was utterly trustworthy. 'Kerry's word was his bond,' he always said. And nobody can deny that Packer fulfilled every jot and tittle of any contract he drew up for his players. Barry Richards said this of him, 'Kerry honoured every contract to the last letter.' Packer also had a nice line in witty one-liners and rapier-like rejoinders that spring muscularly off the page whenever he was quoted. 'He did not suffer fools gladly and rounded fiercely on anyone who lied to him or made excuses for poor performances,' Bruce Francis informed me.

In the same way that the English Civil War was not about religion, though differences about religion were at the very heart of the conflict, and that the American Civil War was not started because of slavery, though slavery ran through the fighting like Brighton through a stick of rock, the Packer Revolution was not about cricket though cricketers were the shock troops of the rebellion. The *casus belli* was not poor pay and conditions for cricketers but television rights. It was well known that Packer was a sports enthusiast, particularly boxing, rugby, cricket and polo. 'He loved his cricket,' Barry Richards told me, 'but his passion was television.' Packer had become transfixed by the spectacle of the World Cup in England in 1975. Colour television had just been introduced in Australia (it had been in use in Britain since 1968) and Packer inwardly mused what effect this would have on broadcasting in his own country, especially sporting coverage. Here was a business opportunity, his instincts told him. Millions were watching the action unfold on television and it was relatively cheap to broadcast. Crucially, it took all day. Filling airtime, particularly during the day, was an expensive business. Producing drama, entertainment shows, soap operas, news broadcasts, documentaries and the like were labour-intensive and cost a lot of money. Sport, especially cricket, was cheap. The road ahead was clear. This is Bruce Francis's take on the Packer project. 'Kerry had been tasked by his father in the early 1970s with finding the best ways to maximise the benefits of colour television. Channel 9 was to become the number one station for broadcasting sport.

To that end, he bought the rights to F1 motor racing, major tennis tournaments, major golf tournaments and of course cricket.'

But not yet. Packer was blocked in his desire to obtain television rights for cricket in Australia because the Australian Broadcasting Corporation had a monopoly on them. The Australian Cricket Board were more than happy with their cosy relationship with the national broadcaster and at every turn rebuffed Packer's advances. It did not go unnoticed that the acronyms ABC and ACB were practically interchangeable. 'It would be easier getting an audience with the Pope,' Packer famously quipped, 'and I'm not a Catholic.' After tendering several unsuccessful bids, the turning point came for him when he made his final offer to the ACB in March 1976. This too was turned down. It later emerged that the ACB had accepted the bid from the ABC, which was considerably less than what Packer was offering. He felt he had been well and truly shafted and Packer scorned was a dangerous animal. 'Fine,' he said, 'I want cricket, the public want to watch it, so I'll show my own.' And, as all who knew him say, Kerry Packer was as good as his word. It was a watershed moment. Cricket would never be the same again.

Now, where does Tony Greig fit into this jigsaw? During the winter of 1975/76, much to his chagrin, there was no overseas tour scheduled for the England team so he set off to Australia to play for Waverley CC in Sydney (very successfully his son Mark tells me – they won the league for the first time in 30 years). What transpired during those months is crucial to the story. Bruce Francis explained the chronology of events. 'The comedian Paul Hogan and one of Packer's associates, John Cornell, were opening a nightclub in Woolloomooloo on the wharfside of Sydney Harbour. This was in February 1976. It was called Pips. A former Miss World was there. Tony and I were invited.' *Of course he was, Bruce. Tony was just the sort of guy to end up in the same room as Miss World!* 'As it happened, Kerry Packer was there too and he was introduced to Tony.' Aha, now we're getting somewhere. I consulted Mark Greig for further details of his father's association with Packer. He was only a couple of years old at this time but he has faithfully reconstructed the timeline with the help of Francis. 'When Kerry was introduced to Dad, he told him how impressed he was by the adverts he had done on TV for Kellogg's. During the course of their conversation, he confided in Dad his plans to make Channel 9 the number one sports television network and his determination to get involved in cricket. He told Dad to get in touch when he came back to Australia in September. Dad returned to England to resume his cricket career.' Packer recognised a face for television when he saw one and instinctively realised that Tony, as England captain, was pure commercial gold. Tony was intrigued. Nothing concrete had been proposed but he could not help but be taken with the energy and vision of the man. Besides, he was as aware as anybody of the precarious nature of professional cricket. As England captain, he was relatively well off but he was acutely concerned that he was only one serious injury away from the junkyard and that his position as captain lay in the hands of a capricious board of selectors. He needed to think ahead.

The opportunity to meet up again with Packer was not long in coming. There was a gap between the end of the West Indies series in England (1976) and the tour to India (1976/77) so he availed himself of this brief respite from cricket to travel to Sydney (with his family) to film three more television commercials for Kellogg's. He arranged to catch up with Packer at his home. This was a seminal moment, son Mark believes, as Packer outlined his plans for a breakaway cricket organisation, thus convincing Tony of the huge potential of his plans. Mark's words: 'Dad had been seduced, and admitted in hindsight he probably subconsciously committed to joining Kerry's cricket venture at that moment.' So he *did* know what was in the offing when he went to see Packer after the Centenary Test (in March 1977) because he had spoken about it with Packer at this earlier meeting (in September 1976). Was his deception a deliberate falsehood or was it an understandable fib, a 'white lie', in order not to rock the boat just before a crucial MCC tour to India? Mark used the word 'subconsciously'. It is perfectly feasible that his father realised that big change was afoot but he was in no position then to tell anybody and explain what was going on.

'Tony knew everything,' Bruce Francis insisted. 'We discussed his thoughts about it all during that evening in the nightclub.' *Miss World was there and you discussed **business!** He ignored me. 'In late September and early October of 1976, Kerry gave Tony and me firmer plans. I spent many nights in Kerry's study discussing his plans and reported back to Tony during our three or four telephone conversations every week between then and March 1977.' So that would have been during the MCC tour of India up until they arrived on Australian soil for the Centenary Test. While Tony and his band of brothers were making their triumphant way around the subcontinent, Kerry Packer was putting in place the building blocks of his revolution. I recall now a long conversation I had with John Snow over a pint in a West Sussex pub. The subject of our discourse was World Series Cricket – he was one of the original English recruits – but he was anxious to put the whole affair into its proper historical perspective. The game was ripe for plucking, he maintained. The conditions, the opportunities and the will for change were already there. Like all social upheavals in history, he was saying, there was a progression, which eventually reached a tipping point and once that point had been passed, the momentum became unstoppable. 'If it hadn't been Packer, it would have been somebody else,' he said. The trouble was that the world was changing and the governing bodies were not willing or able to adapt to the change. 'Twas ever thus in the history of revolutions. *Plus ca change, plus c'est la meme chose.* The causes of the French Revolution of 1789 and the Russian Revolution of 1917, to take but two, were many and complex but at their heart was an inflexible method of government for which both absolute rulers, King Louis XVI of France and Czar Nicholas II of Russia, paid with their lives. The principles driving change in cricket were the same.

The word 'revolution' comes from the Latin, *revolutio*, a turn around. The change of ruler, government or policy is fundamental and usually quite rapid. What was it about the state of the game in Australia that provided Packer with such fertile ground for radical change? 'It was the easiest sport in the world to take over,' Packer observed. 'Nobody bothered to pay the players what they were worth.' Dissatisfaction among Australian cricketers about pay and conditions had been rife for years. Furthermore, it appeared to them that their governing body, the ACB, was acting towards them with disrespect bordering on arrogance whenever representations were made to them about financial fair play. 'If you don't like the pay and conditions,' the secretary of the ACB, Alan Barnes, was famously quoted as saying, 'there are thousands of others waiting to take your place.'

Let us go back half a dozen years to Illingworth's tour of Australia in 1970/71, the one that Tony was not picked for, to his intense chagrin. The third Test of that series was washed out without a ball being bowled. An extra Test was added to the itinerary, to everybody's enthusiastic endorsement – except the players. They had not been consulted. Nor were they paid. An extra $70,000 of revenue from the match went into the ACB coffers. Not one cent ended up in the players' pockets. Following the sacking of Bill Lawry as captain of Australia towards the end of that series, Ian Chappell took over as leader, heralding an era of world dominance for his team. His players respected him and responded to him because they trusted him to protect their interests, something he tirelessly sought to do, making himself unpopular along the way in the corridors of power. He moulded a team of talented individuals who caught the public imagination. They flocked in their droves to watch them take apart first England in 1974/75 and then West Indies in 1975/76. Bumper crowds were recorded at all venues. Cricket commanded big bucks. Where was all this extra revenue going? Certainly not in the direction of Ian and Greg Chappell, Dennis Lillee, Jeff Thomson, Rodney Marsh et al, who were the star performers. Less than 2% of the revenue from the Test matches found its way to the players. Rodney Marsh ruefully pondered the fact that, as one of Australia's most recognised sportsmen, he was earning one tenth of the sum his brother, Graham, a golfer ranked 16 in the world, was getting. Dennis Lillee, who had just broken his back – almost literally so – bowling Australia to victory in the Centenary Test in Melbourne (250,000 spectators went through the turnstiles over the five days) was paid peanuts for his efforts. Kerry Packer was uncharacteristically rendered speechless when Bruce Francis showed him the contract that he had with the ACB when selected for Australia in 1972. Greg Chappell told me this: 'When we defeated the Poms in 1974/75, the ACB grossed over $1 million in revenue. Yet it had only cost them $2,400 to hire the performers – us. That worked out at $200 per player.'

If John Snow thought the game was ripe for plucking, the truth was that the fruit was practically groaning on the branches. All that was needed was to give the tree a gentle nudge and the whole lot would come tumbling down. Kerry Packer, however, did not do gentle nudges. What he had in mind was nothing less than a complete *coup d'etat*; not content with scrumping the windfall, he intended to clear out the whole orchard. He was aware that his actions would no doubt benefit the players – and for this he was more than happy – but like the true businessman he was, he never let sentiment cloud his judgement and get in the way of his primary objective – exclusive TV rights for Channel 9. In answer to the question whether he could consider his actions to be half-philanthropic, he said, 'Half-philanthropic? That makes me sound more generous than I am.'

First of all, he had to get Greg Chappell on board. His signature was non-negotiable. This made perfect sense. Chappell was arguably the best batsman in the game at that time, he was the captain of the Australian team and his influence over his team-mates would be crucial. I asked Greg if Packer's offer of a contact was a done deal. 'Aw look, I was the Australian captain. I was fully aware of my responsibilities to the post and to the team. And I wanted to see how many others he was signing. Once I realised he was being serious, it became a no-brainer. I knew it was something I had to do, for me personally and for Australian cricket in general.' His brother Ian had by now retired from first-class cricket but he was only 32 and many believed he had plenty of runs still left in him. In addition to that, he was a talisman in Australian cricket and his signature was as crucial as that of his brother's. The conversation between him and Packer when he was recruited is as famous as it is illuminating. The story goes that Packer wanted him to lead the Australian side that he was assembling. Ian replied that he would have to ask his brother first, because he was currently the captain of Australia. 'What do you think this is, son?' retorted Packer. 'This isn't a f***ing democracy. You're the f***ing captain!' I wondered what Greg thought of this. *Were you happy to play under your brother?* 'Perfectly happy,' he smiled.

Having got the Chappell brothers on board, Packer understood that the signature of the England captain was now pivotal to the success of his venture. There were two reasons. In the first instance, Packer had envisaged three teams taking each other on in a still undecided notion of a triangular series: Australia, England and Rest of the World. Tony was therefore best placed to recruit players from England. Furthermore, with his telegenic looks and his natural instinct for PR, he was a perfect fit to head up the public face of the operation. Packer had already seen Tony at work advertising this and that on national television and had been impressed. As if to underline his credentials (though there is no evidence that he did it for anything other than altruistic reasons), Tony had written an open letter to the people of Melbourne, printed in the city's major newspaper, *The Age*, thanking them for their generous hospitality during the Centenary Test. Genius, thought Packer, I must have this guy working for me. The fateful meeting in Sydney between him and Tony, which had been arranged months before, now took place on the Sunday after the Test had finished.

Before we examine what transpired at that meeting, we need to take stock of the general mood among English cricketers at that time. Although there was common ground with their Australian counterparts over dissatisfaction with the way the game was being run, there were also significant differences. As a South African, and therefore coming from a different background from the English professional (he was, if you like, more akin to the Australian model), Tony was also the Sussex and England captain and thus well aware of current feeling on the county circuit. In this sense, he was uniquely placed to see the pros and cons on both sides. He had many friends in Australia and he knew some of the Australian players well. He was fully conscious of their disgruntlement and frustration with their board and had heard all the horror stories. He also knew only too well the insecure nature of the job of a professional cricketer in England and he, along with many others, worried about poor pay, no retirement provision, short-term contracts, excessive control by the authorities on newspaper articles, book rights and content, second-rate hotel accommodation, no wives on tour .... The list was a long one.

England was the only country where cricket was fully professional. The contracts were solely for the six months of the playing season.

The rest of the year, players were free and able to take up whatever employment they liked (or could find). Thus what they did, and whom they played for, in the winter months was their own affair. They would not be breaking any contracts if they signed for Packer because his matches would only take place during the English off-season. What possible reason would they have for *not* signing?

Of course it was not quite as simple as that and Tony knew it. He loved playing for England and the job of captain was one he relished and honoured. To give it all up – for that is what he would surely be forced to do – would be a huge wrench. After the triumphant series in India and the success of the Centenary Test, his stock in world cricket could not have been higher. And how would his public, to say nothing of colleagues and friends, react to his betrayal? He might well find himself echoing the despairing words of Othello:

> Reputation, reputation, reputation, oh, I have lost my reputation!
>
> I have lost the immortal part of myself and what remains is bestial.

Tony was on the horns of a dilemma and he was not at all certain he would agree to sign up, as he walked with his friend and advisor, Bruce Francis, up the driveway of Packer's house on Sunday 20 March, 1977. He had heard more of Packer's plans from Francis since their last meeting the previous September but wanted to know more detail. Accordingly, Bruce had him round to his parents' house where he and Tony chewed the cud. Also there was Bruce's father, Cass, who urged Tony to be under no obligation to anyone or anything other than the interests of him and his family and what would secure for them all a long-term future. If that could be done, Tony concluded, then he would sign. He then, together with Bruce, moved on to Packer's house. What he heard that morning took his breath away. The scale and audacity of Packer's sales pitch convinced him that surely cricket would never be the same again.

Packer reeled off the list of names whose agreement he had already secured, and by agreement he meant that he had their signatures on the dotted line of a watertight contract. Unbeknown to Tony – and I believe this to be true; he had more things to worry about than what was going on in the Australian dressing room – recruitment had been going on during the Centenary Test and Packer already had most of the Australian team under his belt, including all the superstars: the Chappells, Lillee, Thomson, Walters. Marsh signed not long after. They had all been sworn to secrecy and not a word had passed anybody's lips. Which would explain the cryptic comment that Rodney Marsh made to Dennis Lillee as they stepped on to the grass at the Melbourne Cricket Club for the Centenary Test: 'I guess this is the last time, eh, mate?' Lillee gave him a strange look. 'Surely you've signed too,' Marsh cried. Of course he had. But the two mates, though they went back a long way, had not uttered a word to each other.

Tony was therefore left in no doubt that this venture was going to take off, come hell or high water. Then Packer made his offer, $30,000 a year for three years. Those were mouth-watering figures, the sort of money that no English professional cricketer would ever earn. At that time, England players were being paid £210 per Test, less than the price of the tickets that he, the England captain, had to pay for so that his family could attend the Centenary Test. Yet still he hesitated. The money was attractive but not a great deal more than what he could currently earn, taking into consideration his commercial work. More than that, was this the right thing to do? He was the England captain. What responsibility did he owe to his country, to his employers, to his public, to his team-mates? What would his father, Sandy, think? He asked for time to think it over and a further meeting was scheduled for two days later.

After the meeting with Packer, Tony and Bruce Francis were guests at a barbecue. The social occasion took place at the home of Arthur Jackson, a hypnotherapist who was a close friend of Bob Willis. Among several England players in attendance were Willis, Mike Brearley, John Lever and Roger Tolchard. This was the occasion that Willis started telling me, before I interrupted him, about his captain berating him for blowing up during Australia's second innings in the Centenary Test. *Go on, Bob, you were saying* ... 'Look. You're a fast bowler, Greigy was saying, and if you get yourself fit – seriously fit – there will be opportunities for bowlers like you to earn a lot of money. I took the hint, in that I did set about getting myself properly fit for fast bowling. The other hint, about World Series Cricket, well, I didn't cotton on about that.' He was not alone. Brearley failed to pick up the significance of what Tony was saying. Both Lever and Tolchard expressed total ignorance of the hints. Francis was hopping from foot to foot. 'Armed with Kerry's plans,' he told me, 'Tony had a "wow" story to tell …. Tony thrived on "wow" stories and the response he would get from audiences …. Somehow he managed to tease them without mentioning Kerry's name.' Then he added this humorous rejoinder: 'I can understand two fast bowlers and a wicketkeeper not being bright enough to put two and two together but I am still nonplussed that Brearley couldn't add up.' Francis believes that his friend's natural indiscretion nearly cost everybody dear. The success or failure of Packer's plans lay squarely on the confidential nature of his recruitment process. 'In my view,' Francis said, 'that was Tony's luckiest moment because if the penny had dropped with Brearley and co, WSC could have been stopped.'

You can be sure that the two friends spent hours mulling over the details of Packer's contract before Tony was to give Packer the answer he had promised. He was logical and judicious in his thinking. In brief, he recognised the prized and privileged position he was holding as captain of England and if he signed, he would almost certainly be sacked. The cricket authorities would be severely jolted by the news; did he not owe them a debt of gratitude by warning them and staying loyal? Furthermore, his Test career would be put in the gravest jeopardy: was that what he really wanted after 50 consecutive caps and considerable personal success? If he signed, his name would be mud and the notable public image that he had so assiduously built up would be instantly shattered. As one who courted popularity, was he ready and willing to suffer character assassination? On the other hand, he was now 31, at an age when all professional sportsmen begin to contemplate life away from the footlights. What profession was he trained for? The answer – none. The England captaincy was never a secure appointment. The defenestration of his immediate predecessor, Mike Denness, provided evidence enough of that. Was the daily grind of seven days a week in county cricket in front of sparse crowds really what he wanted to do? As a devotee of the big stage, quitting the West End to see out his days in provincial rep held little appeal. He loved Australia, felt at home there and crucially he knew his family would flourish living in Sydney. He was convincing himself more and more as he chewed the cud with Bruce Francis that Packer's radical blueprint for the game would eventually be to the benefit of cricketers worldwide, whatever the personal advantages that would accrue.

He said that his mind was not fully made up when he met Packer for their second meeting on Tuesday 22 March, though Mark Greig and Bruce Francis felt that in his heart, he knew which way he was going to jump. However, there were one or two niggling points that he needed clarifying. For the following account of the conversation between Kerry Packer and Tony Greig, I am indebted to the verbatim record of Bruce Francis. The point that Tony was anxious to put across to Packer was his need, not for money, but *security*. Packer repeated his offer of $90,000 spread over three years. Tony agreed that was a lot of money for any cricketer in the world but for him it did not represent what he felt he was worth and what potentially he might be giving up. He explained the breakdown in his earnings over the past year, including salaries from Sussex, England appearance money, payment from Waverley CC, sponsorship and endorsement contracts from a variety of sources and the prospect of a benefit from Sussex in the near future, which a figure of £1 million had not been idly hinted at. Furthermore, the possibility of being banned by the Test and County Cricket Board in England was not something he could blithely ignore. 'Listen,' said Packer, 'I know you are important to the success of the project and I know the Germans, the South Africans and the Chappell brothers think they are the superior race and I know this will come as a huge surprise to you but you are not the best player in the world and consequently I can't pay you a lot more than the rest of your World XI team-mates, or the Australian superstars for that matter. I'll tell you what I'll do. I'll give you an extra $10,000 a season for being captain.' It would be hard not to imagine Tony playing down an amused smile at this. It would have been a form of address that appealed to him; he too believed in straight talking. However, he was not to be deflected from his original point – money was not altogether at the heart of his concerns.

'I'm nearly 31 years old. I'm probably two or three Test failures from being dropped from the England team. Ian Botham is going to be a great player and there won't be room in the England side for both of us.' In this he was remarkably prescient. Botham was still relatively unknown outside the county circuit but to those of us who had already played against him, it was clear he was destined for stardom. Tony went on, 'I don't want to finish up in a mundane job when they drop me .... I'm at the stage in my life where my family's future is more important than anything else. If you guarantee me a job for life working for your organisation, I will sign.'

'No problem,' Packer responded. 'You can have a job for life, starting on $25,000 a year. Do we have a deal?' One or two other details, such as a low interest loan to buy a house in Sydney, were agreed, 'Or do you still want more licks of the lolly?' Francis asked how and when the contract would be presented. Packer took mild offence. 'I'll give you my personal guarantee that you'll get every penny.' Still Tony prevaricated. Packer encouraged him 'to stop playing silly games and sign the flaming thing'. Tony did and Kerry Packer was as good as his word. Tony had a job with Packer up until the day he died.

So there it was. The die was cast. Even though Packer had as yet no teams, no format, no organisation, no itinerary, no grounds, no back-up staff, not even any umpires, he did have a number of the world's best players in his pocket and soon he would have more. The South Africans – Barry Richards, Eddie Barlow, Graeme Pollock, Mike Procter, Denys Hobson, Clive Rice – had already put pen to paper (as Test outcasts because of apartheid, they had little to lose). In addition he had in his pocket a dozen of the top Australians. What was now needed was an England team and this was Tony's job. Shortly, Packer made what many regarded to be his shrewdest signing of all, Richie Benaud, universally regarded as the *eminence grise* of cricket and its moral conscience. Arguably, nobody was better known and more widely respected than Benaud, with the possible exception of Sir Donald Bradman who as a prominent member of the Australian Cricket Board was unlikely to fall prey to any of Packer's blandishments. So it proved:

Bradman became an implacable adversary of the enterprise and never wavered in his opposition to what he felt was a betrayal of the game he loved. Benaud, however, always a man willing to embrace change, sniffed at the breeze and smelt the gathering storm. He proved to be a wise, experienced and knowledgeable guide to Packer as he negotiated his way through the precarious PR minefields in the coming months. Greig, too, soon became a constant sounding board for Packer. When he heard that several of Packer's legal and business associates were bound for the Caribbean in order to sound out the West Indies and Pakistan players about to embark on a series, he persuaded his boss that he, as a player and well known to the majority of the teams, would be better placed to bend their ears than suited strangers waving legal documents. Packer agreed.

First, Tony had to return to England. The start of the 1977 season was upon him and he had to report back to Sussex. Packer had wanted him to fly straight out to the West Indies but there was a problem. An agreeable problem but it necessitated his immediate presence in England. His agent informed him reluctantly that he was going to be 'surprised' by Eamonn Andrews carrying his famous red book to be whisked off as the guest for *This Is Your Life*. In addition there was an Ashes series coming up (though God knows – Tony certainly didn't – whether that tour would ever take place once the news broke) and he was still the England captain. Eamonn Andrews duly buttonholed him as he emerged from Victoria Station and he was driven to Thames Television studios to do the programme. I feel for Tony Greig at this moment in his life. This was meant to be a crowning acclamation of a momentous and successful career. Public recognition was what he had craved and here it was to be granted in front of family, friends and colleagues and an audience of millions. In addition, it should have been an emotional and poignant celebration of a life well lived, owing much to the dedicated love and support of his family, something that was dear to his heart and important to his sense of self. But nobody knew of the secret he was harbouring, one that would soon blow all the plaudits and eulogies out of the water. For Tony personally, the timing could not have been worse. He put on his thousand watt smile, took guard, looked up at the familiar faces gathered round … and played a blinder.

'It was a very emotional evening,' Ian Greig told me. 'Even Tackies was flown over from South Africa.' Tackies, you will remember, was the garden boy back in Queenstown who became Tony's 'net' bowler, the one with the distinctly dodgy action. After the show, the family repaired back to their hotel and returned to Hove the following day. *Tell me about the family meeting you had that evening.* 'I remember it as vividly as if it happened yesterday,' said Ian. 'We were all sitting around after dinner and one or two made as if to turn in for the night. "Hold it!" said Tony, "Ian, go and put the kettle on. I've got something to tell you." Anyway, after the coffee had been made and distributed around the family, he sat us all down. I was on his right. Dad was on his left. He then outlined Kerry's plans and what part he was asked to play in the venture. "What do you all think?" he wanted to know. One by one, we had our say.' *What was your contribution?* 'Can't remember! Of course, what he wanted to know, whose opinion he craved, was what Dad thought of it all.' *And what was Sandy's response?* 'Our dad was not one to shoot his mouth off. He carefully considered matters before offering an opinion. At length he said that he believed Tony owed everything to Sussex and to England. He wouldn't be where he was had it not been for the England selectors. He was captain of England, a unique and privileged position, and he owed Bedser and the others, to say nothing of his team-mates, a debt of allegiance. Don't sign, was his message.' *Oh dear. What happened then?* 'Tony thanked everyone for their advice but told them that he had already signed. He was off to the West Indies to sign up more players.' *What was Sandy's reaction to that?* 'He was mortified. He fell apart, basically. What hurt him was that Tony had asked him, his father, for advice, but he had already made up his mind. So Dad felt he had been let down, conned really, discounted. It really hurt him. Next day, he called me aside and told me to take him to Heathrow. "I'm going home," he said, "I don't want to stay here a day longer." And that's what he did, even though he wasn't scheduled to go back for another fortnight.'

We both fell silent for a moment, contemplating the family fall-out from such a scene. *I guess bridges, having been burnt, took some time to rebuild.* 'They were, eventually.' *Looking back now, can you remember what you thought of it all?* 'I think I was quite excited. After all, it was new and interesting and obviously a page was being turned in the history of the game. To be honest, the hardest thing for me when I went back to Cambridge was keeping my mouth shut!' Ian was in his second year at university. It is as well to point out that Tony had been instrumental in getting his younger brother into Cambridge and had helped to pay the fees.

Under the guise of a short holiday – although a holiday was no more than he deserved after the past few months – Tony and Donna then set off for the Caribbean on Packer's recruiting mission. It was ironic that their port of call was Port-of-Spain in Trinidad, the scene of the Kallicharran run-out incident on a previous MCC tour. This time there were no flamboyant gestures or playing up to the crowd. Tony went about his business quietly and efficiently. He was surprised how easy it was, a sad reflection on how international players from all around the world felt about their treatment at the hands of their respective boards of control. In short order, he had Imran Khan, Majid Khan, Mushtaq Mohammad and Asif Iqbal on board. From the West Indies team, Clive Lloyd, Viv Richards and Andy Roberts took little persuading, though Michael Holding only provisionally agreed. The reason was political. His country, Jamaica, espoused a hard-line policy of no sporting contacts with South Africa; if he signed up, he would be playing with and against the likes of Richards, Barlow, Pollock and Procter. How could he square this with his conscience and with his prime minister? It was one of many seemingly intractable problems that Packer found himself wading through in these early weeks and months. How this one was resolved can wait for a little later.

Soon the Greigs were back in England, having thoroughly enjoyed their 'second honeymoon', as they told their friends. You see, secrecy was still paramount. The Australians were due in the country shortly and if word had got out what was being planned, the tour would have been put in peril. Tony had to bite his normally garrulous tongue; he did not want to make things difficult for his friend and the Australian captain, Greg Chappell. In the meantime, he set about clandestinely trying to recruit an England team. This proved more difficult than was first imagined. John Snow, Alan Knott and Derek Underwood were willing signatories; others were less receptive. I asked Bob Willis why he had turned down the offer. 'I was invited by Tony to meet him and Richie Benaud at Benaud's flat in Chelsea. Derek Randall was with me too. They outlined the offer. The money was eye-watering, I have to say – 15 grand for three years. But above all, I wanted to continue playing for England and I felt sure that the Packer players would be banned. I think Randall turned it down for the same reason. Also, I had the prospect of a benefit coming up on the horizon at Warwickshire and I didn't want to jeopardise that. As it happened, an improved contract at Warwickshire helped to soften the blow.' *And you never regretted the decision?* 'No, I didn't. Though I have to say the whole business split dressing rooms around the country right down the middle. It was an uncomfortable time for everyone.' Indeed it was. I can vouch for that. The Hampshire dressing room had three Packer signatories – Richards, Roberts and Greenidge – and it was a standing joke, which wore a bit thin with those three, that we would pointedly ask every morning whether anybody had had a call from Australia overnight.

In early May, the cricket season cranked into life as it had been doing for generations and still no word had leaked out. One by one, the big names were putting pen to Packer's paper to sign on the dotted line: Wayne Daniel, Colin Croft, Joel Garner, Lawrence Rowe, Roy Fredericks, Javed Miandad, Zaheer Abbas. It would be more difficult to work out who was not on the list. Ah, but no Indians. It was Barry Richards who cleared that one up for me. 'Gavaskar was an obvious target but he was their captain and put under tremendous pressure by their board to stay loyal. Indian cricketers, don't forget, are treated like demigods in their own country and I think they were much more closely tied down by their contracts in playing for India. Also,' – this was added with a wry grin – 'I don't think the fast bouncy wickets in Australia would have been much to their liking! Their strength was in their spinners and spinners did not feature much in Australia.' It was a well-known fact that the intriguing tussle of cat and mouse between spinner and batsman did not greatly enthuse Kerry Packer; he preferred the violent clash between the fast men and their hunted prey. The Indians were scheduled to tour Australia that winter. That was another hurdle Packer had to overcome, not so much that he would be in direct competition with an established series (the Indians were hugely popular tourists in Australia) but that all the regular venues had already been booked. Where would he be able to play his WSC matches?

The Australians arrived for the Ashes series, something that traditionally stirs the blood of any cricket lover. Thirteen of the 17 tourists had signed for Packer. The secrecy demanded was a burden for all. Just imagine sharing a 24-hour flight with your Australian team-mates, not sure who had signed and who hadn't, pondering when the news broke, as it was bound to do sooner or later, how would those who had not signed feel about those who had? It would not, one imagines, make for a harmonious party (as was proved to be the case). Loyalties, allegiances, friendships, trust would all be put under enormous strain and jealousies inevitably fomented. All in the know held their breath and waited for the storm to break. Cricketers by nature are a collegiate bunch; nothing much can stay hidden in a dressing room. It was quite extraordinary that news had remained under wraps for so long.

It was a wet start to their tour. Rain seemed to follow them around wherever they went. Journalists with little to write about are a dangerous breed, especially when there's a story to sniff out. Rumours of an unofficial international series had emanated first in South Africa, which had been picked up by the Australian travelling press corps. They started to dig. As usual, Bruce Francis was able to fill me in on some of the detail here, most of which I, together with most professional cricketers at the time, was blissfully unaware. Tony had been devastated by his father's anger and quick return to South Africa. He persuaded Bruce to fly out there to see if he could do anything to pacify the man whom he worshipped. 'I landed in SA on Saturday 16 April. I was met at the airport by Joe Pamensky of the South African Cricket Board and taken to a dinner in honour of Lee Irvine, the former Springbok. During his speech, Irvine mentioned that an Australian TV magnate was setting up a rebel cricket organisation. The story duly appeared in the next day's South African *Sunday Times*. I phoned Kerry and told him what had happened.' According to Francis, it was Ian Wooldridge who got wind of the story and wrote about it in the *Daily Mail* here in England.

At this very moment, the Australian team arrived in Hove to play Sussex. It rained. There was no play. On the Saturday evening (7 May), Tony had organised a barbecue at his house for all the players from both sides and accompanying media. It was a typical gesture; he felt that if this was to be the end of his official career, he would like to thank all at Sussex who had been so generous with their hospitality towards him since he arrived on the south coast ten years before. This would be one way to repay that kindness. Sensibly, in view of the weather, he had ordered a marquee. As the tinnies were cracked open and the meat on the *braai* sizzled, the Australian and English journalists mingled and swapped stories about this international series. Together they pitched into the players, probing for information. Not a lot was forthcoming but neither were the denials wholly credible. John Snow, when approached, was asked whether he was involved so he quietly informed his captain that if the cat wasn't quite out of the bag, its claws were making short work of the laces. Tony immediately phoned Packer to tell him that news was bound to break the next day. Copy had already been filed in the Australian newspapers, followed hard on their heels by the Sunday papers in England. The dam had burst at last.

Of the many less than complimentary pieces written in English newspapers in the following days, one stands out in its straightforward comment. Under a report entitled '**World's Top Cricketers Turn Pirate**', Ian Wooldridge had written about 'the new dogs of cricket including England captain Tony Greig and 13 of the Australian touring party'. He judged that this would be seen by Lord's as a 'defection' and correctly predicted that Tony would be relieved of the captaincy. He finished with these words: 'Overnight, the whole balance of world cricket has shifted.'

The general impression in those early days – which did not, in truth, greatly change for several years – was that Tony Greig and his cohorts were a bunch of greedy mercenaries holding the game to ransom. John Arlott called the whole affair a 'circus' and the name stuck. Most of the terms used to describe the new venture were pejorative: pyjama cricket, pirates, Packerball, opportunists, traitors, money-grubbing etc. Sussex's next game against Lancashire was rained off, just what Tony didn't need. He felt obliged to call a press conference. For once, he did not manage to get his listeners to eat out of his hand. 'This summer is in the hands of Lord's,' he said. I had to re-read that quotation. No, he did not say that it would be in the Lord's hands, but he might just as well. His touch for simple truths uttered with charm and conviction had seemingly deserted him. 'In the winter, it will be in the hands of a possible compromise between Lord's and Packer. I will do anything possible to get them talking.' He had the strange sensation that nobody was listening. When he averred that all cricketers would benefit in the long run from what was happening, he knew that his words were going in one ear of the assembled journalists and out the other. Ian Greig remembered the occasion well. 'Tony told me, and later he made it plain to them at that press conference, that every county cricketer would benefit from what he was doing. But they didn't want to hear.'

The news, when it came, was no shock but deeply upsetting. On Friday 13th (would you believe!), Tony took a telephone call from Donald Carr, the secretary of the TCCB, informing him that he had been stripped of the England captaincy. Freddie Brown, the chairman, issued a press statement in which he said of the decision: 'His action has inevitably impaired the trust which existed between the cricket authorities and the captain of the England side.' Tony's response was to issue a statement of his own, dignified and measured in its tone but the regret was palpable. 'Obviously I am disappointed. The only redeeming factor is that I have sacrificed cricket's most coveted job for a cause which I believe could be in the best interests of cricket the world over.' What he didn't say but felt most acutely, Ian told me, was that 'he had set his heart on regaining the Ashes that summer as captain of a side that he had carefully built'.

Who was to take over the side he had 'carefully built'? With the benefit of hindsight, the answer was blindingly obvious. Mike Brearley had been Tony's vice-captain in India and had slowly but surely gained everybody's confidence and was enthusiastically endorsed by his predecessor. However, another candidate hove into view. Geoff Boycott had been in self-imposed exile since 1974; now he made himself available to play for England again. To everybody's relief, Brearley was duly appointed but Boycott did return to the side for the third Test at Trent Bridge (running out the local hero, Derek Randall, in the process of compiling a comeback hundred). He replaced Dennis Amiss (another Packer recruit) who never played for England again. It was as if Boycott had never been away. In fact, he was hardly away from the crease that summer; he finished the series with an average of 147.33. As ever, he divided opinion. Tony was not alone in his annoyance at his having abandoned the side, particularly during the Centenary Test, but neither could he nor his team-mates, including his new captain, gainsay his value to the side as a batsman. The abiding memory of a largely colourless series, which England won 3-0, was Boycott's achievement of scoring his 100th hundred in first-class cricket in the fourth Test in front of his adoring home crowd at Headingley, the first player ever to do so in a Test match. Those of a certain age can shut their eyes and still see the perfectly balanced and beautifully timed on drive off Greg Chappell to reach that milestone, then raising both arms aloft in triumph as he was mobbed by his worshippers.

And what of Tony and his form? First, it has to be said that it was to the surprise of a substantial minority of England supporters that he was in the side at all. But Brearley promised that he would remain loyal to him. The team would be picked on form and talent alone, irrespective of Packer affiliations. As Tony came out to bat at Lord's in the first Test, he was booed. It could not have been a comfortable experience. A month or two ago, he was being lauded to the heavens. But Tony was nothing if not a fighter; he made 91. For good measure, he made 76 in the second Test but thereafter his form fell away and apart from 43 in the fourth and the odd wicket here and there, he was clearly being supplanted as England's premier all-rounder by Ian Botham. The Oval is traditionally the venue for saying goodbye to familiar faces. Greg Chappell, who had announced his retirement from international cricket, was afforded a generous farewell. Tony Greig, who made 0, was granted no such acclaim on his final appearance as an England player. For the English public, the wounds were still too raw.

It was not an easy time for the Packer signatories that summer. The Australian camp was split in two and their lacklustre performances in the surrender of the Ashes must in part have been ascribed to the strains under which they were playing. On the county circuit, away from the intense glare of the Test matches, Greig, Knott, Underwood and Snow were subjected to various levels of public disapproval. At Chesterfield, Alan Knott was manhandled by a supporter. 'How come you're worth that amount of money?' was demanded of him. The answer was obvious but Knotty forbore.

Kerry Packer flew to England to stiffen a few sinews, soothe some fevered brows and attempt a rapprochement with the TCCB. One or two cracks had appeared in the ranks of the breakaway signatories, which the establishment hoped would deepen and widen into a significant fissure. Packer was anxious to reassure his players and prevent this from happening. First to break ranks was Jeff Thomson. Belatedly he had discovered that he had signed two contracts, one with his home state, Queensland, and the other with Packer (well, he was a fast bowler!). Clearly something had to give. His lawyer extricated him from his Packer commitments and he received a standing ovation when he next appeared on a cricket ground, at Trent Bridge in the third Test. Alvin Kallicharran was another defector. He too discovered a clash of interests in signing two contracts and withdrew from WSC amidst intense media interest.

The problem with Michael Holding was more complex and involved a fair bit of political chicanery to resolve. Tony admitted he had experienced more difficulties in getting Holding's signature than anybody else's. The Jamaican was on the horns of a dilemma, whether to join his West Indian team-mates to play WSC or to adhere to the strict policy espoused by his government of total non-contact with South African sportsmen and women. To go against the edict of his prime minister, Michael Manley, would risk social alienation at home; to spurn Packer would be to lose the financial security that all professional cricketers at that time craved. I am indebted to Bruce Francis, who was alongside Tony Greig and Kerry Packer every step of the way, for his recollection of the shenanigans involved as business and politics shadow-boxed.

'WSC had signed a number of South Africans and the Jamaican prime minister, Michael Manley, rang his counterpart in Australia, Malcolm Fraser, and told him that under the Gleneagles Agreement, Fraser had a non-negotiable obligation to stop the South Africans from entering Australia to play for WSC. Kerry was very angry when he heard this.' According to Francis, Tony Greig was instrumental in suggesting a compromise. The South Africans who had already been playing with and against West Indians in county cricket, namely Richards, Procter, Barlow and Rice, should be allowed to play and the others, Pollock and Hobson, banned. 'Amazingly,' said Francis, 'Mr Fraser bought the charade.' Later, he was chatting with Packer in his study and was asked whether the visas for the South Africans had arrived. 'A quick phone call established they hadn't. In my presence, Kerry rang Mr Fraser but he was unavailable so he got hold of the foreign affairs minister, Andrew Peacock. The conversation was very short,' Francis wryly recalled, 'Kerry told him, "I've tried to get Fraser, now I'm stuck with you. The f****** visas for my South Africans are f****** overdue. If they aren't on my desk by Friday, I'll take my team to South Africa and then we'll see what Manley thinks of you and Fraser." The visas for the South Africans were issued immediately.' Such are the devious ways of powerful men since time immemorial. Bruce Francis put it differently. 'The winner for the biggest hypocrite award is Prime Minister Malcolm Fraser!' Barry Richards had another phrase for it. 'We were cleansed!' he remarked wryly of the political expediency of the decision.

There is an interesting little postscript to the South African business. Like everybody who dealt with Packer, Graeme Pollock has nothing but praise for him because he honoured the contract that had been signed and paid every cent of the $25,000 per annum he had promised even though Pollock did not play. Lee Irvine, South African wicketkeeper-batsman, was another who had been approached. 'I needed time to consult with my employers about taking unpaid leave,' he told me, 'but while I hesitated, the decision was made and the offer withdrawn. Had I been quicker off the mark, like Graeme Pollock, I would have been $90,000 better off without having to lift a bat!' Garth le Roux, having been swiftly parachuted into the Sussex dressing room by Tony, was yet another South African signed up under the flexible rules of morality that governed his countrymen's participation in WSC.

Meanwhile, Kerry Packer had arrived in England. At this stage, he had 35 cricketers under his wing but with barely six months to go until the start of the Australian season, he still had no itinerary, no managers and no grounds. He wasn't even sure of his teams. It had been impossible to recruit a full England side, which had been his original intention, so the idea of having a third XI started to take root. Barry Richards remembers a phone call from Packer while he was playing at Southampton. 'I thought it was a joke at first. He asked me what I thought of this chap Greenidge. Needless to say, the next day I was driving Gordy up to London for Packer to sign him on. We walked into the Dorchester Hotel and there was John Snow. Packer came in and told Snowy he was over the hill but he'd sign him anyway. Snowy went puce – he had steam coming out of his ears. But Kerry was like that, brash and forthright.' We have a phrase in English: to be a Marmite figure indicates the extremes of love or hate. Packer was undoubtedly one. Tony was smitten by him, though he, having lived most of his life in Australia, would probably refer to him as a Vegemite figure. Packer was 'a big, brash Australian and the cartoonists had a ball with his belligerent profile'. Tony believed, however, that the public persona was a false impression. 'To meet him was to be impressed,' he said, 'he was an exciting man with huge influence.' Tony openly admitted he liked and admired the man because he was 'thoroughly human'.

The English public, seduced by the caricature image painted of Packer by the press, found themselves paradoxically and grudgingly nodding their heads in appreciation when he appeared on *The Frost Programme* on ITV. I don't remember the broadcast but Greg Chappell certainly does. He laughed at the memory as he told me, 'There we had in opposition an uneducated roughneck from the colonies, Packer, taking on the face of the establishment, Robin Marlar, Harrow and Cambridge, experienced and outspoken cricket correspondent for *The Sunday Times*. Packer wiped the floor with him!' Marlar's attack on Packer as a rich mercenary, with Greig as his South African lackey, did not go down well. Marlar was incandescent with rage; Packer, by contrast, was calm, measured, articulate … and funny. Chappell went on to tell me that Packer was brilliant at reassuring the younger members of the Australian touring party who had signed up for him. 'They were being put under intolerable pressure by the management and were beginning to waver. Kerry geed them up.'

Kerry Packer in his attempt to gee up the English cricket establishment failed abjectly. He met representatives of the ICC and the TCCB at Lord's in order to try and thrash out a compromise. The meeting lasted barely 90 minutes. Packer, exasperated by the refusal of the ICC to grant Channel 9 exclusive broadcasting rights – to be fair to the world's governing body, they said they had neither the right nor the wherewithal to grant this request – Packer stormed out and delivered his own declaration of war. 'I will now take no steps to help anyone,' he told the assembled press. 'It's every man for himself and the devil take the hindmost.'

Reaction from the establishment and its cohorts among the British journalists – most of them, in other words – was predictable and unequivocal. E.W. Swanton responded, 'And the devil take Kerry Packer.' Swanton had been Tony's staunch supporter throughout his career, don't forget. The respected *Times* cricket correspondent, John Woodcock, wrote in an article about Tony and WSC, 'What has to be remembered of course is that he is an Englishman not by birth or upbringing but only by adoption. It is not the same thing as being an Englishman through and through.' That did hurt. Tony was not one to bear grudges but to the end of his days, he regretted he had not challenged Woodcock – a man he knew well and liked – over this comment. It was as if Woodcock and others had completely discounted the brave, dangerous and selfless service of his father, Sandy, during the war. What more had the Greig family to do to prove their loyalty to the Mother Country? But he stuck to his guns. What he was doing, he repeated, would be to the benefit of cricketers and cricket – just mark his words.

If war was what Packer wanted, he got it. On 22 July, just before the Trent Bridge Test, the ICC announced that all Packer players would be banned from first-class and Test match cricket from 1 October 1977. The reaction in the Australian dressing room was one of dismay. The reaction in county dressing rooms was mixed. Some players were relieved that the authorities had put their foot down. At least everybody now knew where he stood. You can't have a civil war if both armies are changing in the same dressing room. The battle lines were now drawn. Others were deeply upset. Lifelong friendships, loyal team spirit, bonds that tied were now put in jeopardy and the dressing room, formerly a place of comfort, security and fellowship, was now riven with suspicion and dark mutterings. I shall never forget Barry Richards coming into the Hampshire dressing room once the banning order had been announced practically skipping with joy. 'We've been banned! We've been banned!' Though we knew and understood his disaffection with the daily grind of county cricket and his resentment at having his great gifts denied the grand stage they deserved, we felt that he could perhaps have expressed himself more delicately. Some of us *did* want to play county cricket. It was more acrimonious in the Warwickshire dressing room. There was Dennis Amiss who had signed, Alvin Kallicharran who had signed but had turned, or been turned, and there was Bob Willis who had not signed. There were times when you could have cut the atmosphere with a knife, Willis told me. No, it was not a comfortable time in English county dressing rooms.

Oddly, Sussex was not one of them. For confirmation, I probed the memories of former friends and opponents of mine who were there at the time. 'No good asking me.' said Peter Graves, 'I broke my finger early on in the season and that was it for me until the following year.' I had forgotten. It also provided an uncomfortable reminder that all professional sportsmen and women operate with the threat of injury; one mishap can ruin everything. John Barclay remembers no animosity towards Tony Greig from his team-mates that summer. 'As a traditionalist, I suppose I probably supported the establishment. But I was just keen to get on with the business of playing.' John Spencer said that nobody was surprised when the news leaked out. 'We knew that Greigy was a pioneer for decent pay for cricketers at all levels; he saw the large amounts of money being accumulated by the TCCB with little being passed on to the people who counted – the players.'

Spencer then took me completely by surprise. 'In fact I knew about it all before Greigy!' *Spence, you bowled me many balls in our time that I never got anywhere near but that one has just knocked out my middle pole.* 'Let me go back to the beginning,' he explained. It was a detour but I was happy for him to take it because it tells us a lot about Kerry Packer and the way he operated. In the winter of 1976/77, Spencer was employed by Cranbrook School in Sydney as cricket coach and geography teacher. 'Out of the blue, I was contacted by a chap called Kerry Packer. I didn't have a clue who he was but he wanted me to coach his son, Jamie.' *I have heard that James Packer was not over-endowed with talent.* 'Well, that's the thing. At the time he was batting No11 in his prep school's under-10 "B" side. But he improved, so much so that was soon opening the batting in the '"A" side and scoring 50s.' *I'm surprised Packer didn't sign you up on the spot with a three-year contract at $25,000 per annum.* 'Not quite. But listen ….' It soon became clear to Spencer that Packer was nuts on cricket and they would chat about the game over breakfast following the Sunday morning net session (6–8am!). 'He gave me the keys to his Jag and told me to take my wife out for the day – and I wasn't allowed to pay for, or replace, any fuel used.' During these long and enjoyable chats, Packer mused aloud about the possibility of unearthing 'the next Dougie Walters from the outback' if the proper coaching – such as his son was enjoying – were put into place. Spencer sensed some plan was afoot.

Later – it must have been sometime in February 1977 – Packer all of a sudden asked Spencer to name his top 14 Australian cricketers and his top 14 from the rest of the world. This time, Spencer was sure he was up to something. Under questioning, Packer admitted that he was planning his own breakaway outfit but that it had to be kept 'under wraps'. This was before the Centenary Test, before Tony Greig had been apprised of the big plan. 'When I got back to Sussex at the beginning of the English county season, Greigy, who by now *did* know all that was going on, took me aside and explained it all. The cricket world is about to be hit with a sledgehammer, he told me, but I was of course sworn to secrecy. He dropped a few hints – typical of him – but nobody had a clue what he was on about. Except me. And John Snow, who had already signed.'

This indiscreet trait of Tony's, which many of his friends found amusing, prompted Bruce Francis to say this about his great buddy: 'I can't recall anyone who not only loved being recognised in public as much as Tony but who also enjoyed sharing his stories with strangers.' I had heard this from many others. Tony was an African and felt at home recounting tales of spending time in the bush. He could spin a yarn for sure. Francis remembers a time when Tony went out to buy fish and chips in Vaucluse in Sydney and came home with four strangers. 'The only thing that was missing that night as Tony waxed lyrical to his captive audience were the camp fire and the African stars. Tony just thrived on the "wow" response from his audiences.' But he added this with a wry grin: 'He did often tread a very fine line between telling stories and revealing important secrets.'

That was the open and honest nature of the man. Spencer again on his captain: 'Greigy was always out there. That was what he was like. Say it how it is, face to face … no side to him at all, no devious dealings … just say what you mean and act on your beliefs.' That is what he did with his Sussex team-mates. There was no resentment, no recrimination, no jealousy. He had made no secret of the fact that he wanted to be the first millionaire cricketer and he never passed by an opportunity to boost his image and maximise his earnings but who could blame him for that? Certainly none in that dressing room. Good luck to him seemed to be the prevailing attitude. Mind you, it might have helped that a number of Sussex players were recruited to join Packer's organisation to assist in his larger plan to spread the gospel with coaching clinics in the remoter areas of Australia. 'Me, Paul Phillipson, John Barclay, Peter Graves, Jerry Morley, Alan Mansell, Chris Waller, Clive Radley, with Phil Slocombe and Peter Roebuck joining later.' *And did you unearth the new Dougie Walters?* 'The Waugh brothers!' he laughed, 'who were only 13 at the time.' He added, 'It was very interesting being out there and involved when it all happened.'

Paul Phillipson added some interesting comments on these coaching clinics, which were consigned to the outer margins of the 'Packer Effect' amidst the furore over WSC and are now largely forgotten. 'Tony Greig and John Spencer selected and recruited all the coaches. Greigy was quick to remind us all that we would have to put in some hard graft while earning very decent cash.' *Not at all like Easter coaching of local kids back home before the season started?* He snorted. 'Listen to this …. One of the main coaching features was the bank of video recorders erected at the end of each of the eight nets so every player could get to see himself bat and bowl.' I whistled in disbelief. Video cameras had never been heard of in England nets, let alone on the county circuit. 'Thanks to the technicians from Channel 9, the coaches could view and analyse every player in the group.' *And this was all for kids! We're not even talking about professional players.* He reminded me that two boys in particular – the Waugh twins – benefitted from the use of new technology. 'It raised coaching to another level. Despite the intense heat and the long days, I thoroughly enjoyed my time there.'

Was Greigy much in evidence? 'The clinics were in the December/ January holidays and featured many of the WSC players; it was part of their contract to make these appearances. Greigy popped in from time to time, just checking on how his young Sussex players were getting on.' *And Packer? Did he ever make an appearance?* 'One day, Greigy rocked up with Uncle Kerry, who cast an eye over proceedings before quickly disappearing, probably in the direction of the blackjack tables!'

But I run ahead of myself. In early August, 1977, Tony Greig went up to London to discuss the ICC bans with Packer. He had got wind of the fact that several of the Packer players were beginning to waver in the face of almost intolerable pressure from all sorts of directions. Take Kent for example, he told his boss. Underwood, Knott, Asif, now Woolmer and Denness as manager, had all been told to report to the County Ground in Canterbury following the announcement of the ban. I got the story from Derek Underwood. 'We were informed that our contracts at the county were not going to be renewed at the end of the season. And, to add insult to injury, we were told if we wanted to leave immediately, no one would stand in our way. Poor Knotty was practically in tears.' All were dyed-in-the-wool men of Kent and felt they were being shabbily treated by their employers. For my own amusement, I did a quick bit of arithmetic, intrigued as I was by the number of years of loyal service these five players had given to Kent; 53 is the answer. Joining Packer would probably have brought their

Test careers to an end – that they knew and accepted – but as these matches were to take place in the English winter, when they were out of contract with their county, what possible reason could be put forward to prevent them playing for Kent in the summer? It was their job, their means of employment. What were they supposed to do in the meantime – cut the grass, paint the kids' bedrooms, sort out the loft, clean their boots and oil their bats?

Such were the concerns of Tony as he outlined them to Packer in his Dorchester Hotel suite. If Packer was worried by developments, he wasn't showing it. Famously, he once said of the British, 'They reckon everything can be solved by compromise and diplomacy. We Australians fight to the very last ditch.' No doubt, he exuded the same pugnacity with Tony. If the ICC wanted a fight, they would get one. Restraint of trade was what the bans amounted to, they both agreed, and plans were laid to take the matter further, to court if needed. They were needed. Despite clandestine efforts at some sort of *rapprochement* between the two sides, which Packer by now felt were doomed to fail, the ICC would not budge. His cricketers – and by now, having got them to sign for him, Packer took an almost avuncular interest in their well-being – needed support and protection. He hired the six best and most expensive lawyers in the land and prepared for the inevitable court case. In the event, he only used two. Tony was intrigued by this tactic. To Packer, the reasoning was simple. 'If I'm trying to back the winner at Wimbledon,' he said, 'I'd rather have my money on the first six seeds than on the seventh. The TCCB will have to hire the seventh-best QC in England.' Tony's eyes widened, as they seemed to do every time he came across this extraordinary man. His admiration was growing almost daily and he felt confident that in Packer's hands all would be well. 'Kerry's enthusiasm was infectious,' he said. 'I had come to know the man extremely well and marvelled at his all-round expertise ... Kerry was not just the key, he was the whole house.'

Amidst all this to-ing and fro-ing, there was still an Ashes series going on. During the fourth Test at Headingley – which England won by an innings and 85 runs but is better remembered for Boycott's 100th hundred – Mike Brearley took his former captain on to the balcony and asked him whether he was available for the forthcoming tour of Pakistan and New Zealand. Tony suppressed a laugh. Of course he wasn't; he was committed to Packer and his 'circus', as it was now popularly called. But he appreciated being asked the question. He and Brearley had always got on well and he understood that Brearley and the selectors would be making their plans, a process that Tony as captain would have been doing himself had not Packer intervened. He did ask Brearley whether he would be playing in the fifth and final Test at the Oval, something that he did not feel sure would happen. Now he had publicly made himself unavailable for the winter tours by nailing his colours firmly to the Packer mast, there were no guarantees that the selectors would not drop him. No, Brearley assured him, he would stick with the same winning team. Another unselfish act by Brearley that Tony never forgot. There was talk of excluding the Packer players from an equal sharing of win money in the Tests. Brearley would hear none of it; bonuses were shared out equally among the team. While he and others of the touring party went through the usual and familiar routine of meeting at Lord's to get measured for tour blazers and kit, Tony felt wistful. This had been a part of his life for so long and now it was no longer. At his farewell at the Oval, he was booed.

Instead of preparing to tour Pakistan at the head of an MCC team, Tony found himself preparing for a totally different challenge. Under the auspices of Kerry Packer's lawyers, the decision was made to challenge the ICC ruling in the High Court and an injunction to overturn the ban was issued under the names of Tony Greig, Mike Procter and John Snow. But before the case was heard, another court was brought to order, this time at Edgbaston, home of Warwickshire CCC. But this court had no legal authority though it did have moral weight, if the brotherhood of professional cricketers can ever be accused of morality. The Professional Cricketers' Association was holding its annual conference and the hall was packed that morning of 5 September. This in itself was unusual; cricketers never were the most militant unionists. However, 1977 was different. Packer, WSC, the ban, pay and conditions were on everybody's lips. Some county players were vehemently anti-Packer and supported the ban, some were more conciliatory but most of us were confused and didn't know what to think. I say 'us' because I was there. At Hampshire, we were encouraged to attend *en bloc* and I noticed looking around and recognising many familiar faces, that most other counties had obviously followed suit. 'Well, why not?' commented a friend. 'A day off from nets!'

It was a fascinating experience. To refresh my memory – or at least to confirm my impressions – I contacted my old friend and Hampshire wicketkeeper, Bob Stephenson, who was at the time our PCA representative. 'The trouble was,' he said, 'that we were all worried about our futures and what this would all mean for the average county player. There were all these superstars getting shedloads of money – well, we didn't know exact figures, of course, but obviously it was a lot of money – and what was in it for us? All we could see was that the fabric, the bedrock, of the game was being threatened and that was us – the ordinary foot soldiers, the workers, if you like.' *So you were for the ban?* 'Yes, I suppose so.' *In retrospect, have you changed your mind?* 'Look, clearly the game, or the running of the game, needed a kick up the backside, which it got. And better pay and conditions did trickle down gradually.' *Too late for you, eh?* 'Too late for me,' he smiled, 'but it is much, much better now. And good luck to them.'

In point of fact, I remember little of the detail of the day's proceedings but I do remember Ray Illingworth speaking persuasively about his worries that county cricket would become a nursery for Packer's 'circus' which would cream off all the best young players – 'Does he mean me?' whispered my friend excitedly – and leave the first-class game in this country denuded of its stars. Tony Greig pleaded for a year's grace, a sort of moratorium, in which no more recruiting would go on, in order to allow the two sides to talk, negotiate and hopefully come to a mutually acceptable agreement. As I remember, his call was rejected. But sparks did not fly, boos and heckles were not heard, there were no discourteous interruptions and nobody invaded the platform with a placard. It was all very thoughtful, reasonable and civil, affirming my resolute belief that at heart cricketers are decent people who 'play the game', to borrow Henry Newbolt's phrase from the most famous of all poems about cricket, *Vitae Lampada*. Once again plumbing the depths of my shaky memory, I think a motion encouraging Packer and the TCCB to reopen negotiations was carried pretty well unanimously (how about that for sitting on the fence, or setting an 'in-out field' as we used to say?) but the motion to support the ban of Packer players was passed narrowly. 'So what was the use of all that?' grumbled my friend at the close of play. Not much, I had to agree, a view shared by Tony Greig, who claimed, logically enough, that the two motions were contradictory. No such prevarication was expected in the High Court, whose proceedings started three weeks later.

On 26 September, the bailiff of the court in the Royal Courts of Justice in London called everybody to order with the familiar cry, 'All rise! The court is now in session, the Honourable Mr Justice Slade presiding.' There were two actions before him: *Greig and others v Insole and others* and *World Series Cricket Pty Ltd and others v Insole and others*. The naming of Tony Greig, and that of Doug Insole, chairman of the TCCB, for that matter, was the quaint but customary legal method of heading a case but it ensured that Greig's name was at the forefront of all press reporting of the proceedings. That was considerable because this legal battle had excited huge public interest. In hiring Sir (later Lord) Robert Alexander QC as his lead barrister, Packer had made good his promise to engage the best in the land. The irony of ironies was that Robert Alexander, representing three 'rebels' against the establishment, later became a president of the MCC. In his preamble, Alexander set out the reasons for the injunction sought by Greig, Procter and Snow within the context of what had been happening the past extraordinary six months. He accused the TCCB in their attempt to ban the players of setting up 'a 19th-century lock-out', calling it 'illogical, dictatorial and penal' and 'a naked restraint of trade'. He pointed out that from cricket alone, discounting money made from sponsorship, endorsements and other outlets, Greig only earned £10,000 per annum – and he was one of the most recognisable sportsmen in the land. The absence of stars, such as Greig and co, from the English first-class game would greatly reduce the attractiveness of county cricket to the public and he ended his opening address with the assertion that the events leading up to this case had become 'a controversy which has passionately divided cricket in this country'. That much was true. The stakes could not have been higher and his words resonated far wider than in England.

There is a famous photograph, which made the front page of all the dailies, of Tony Greig and Kerry Packer strolling towards the High Court deep in conversation. Packer is smartly suited, quite unlike any caricature previously drawn of him by cartoonists in this country as an oik from the Australian outback; he looks exactly as he was, a prosperous, confident businessman. One hand is placed negligently, confidently in his trouser pocket and his suit jacket is tidily buttoned around a powerful-looking frame. Tony resembles a successful lawyer himself, nattily attired in a pinstripe suit, tie neatly knotted, hair carefully combed, tall, blond, good-looking, in the prime of life. In one arm is clutched a folder of documents and swinging in his left hand is an impressive leather briefcase. The image made me laugh out loud when I first saw it and it still does. Here was Greigy, we all thought, playing the game, and playing it to perfection. He always grasped the value of appearances – he 'understood pageantry', as Brearley put it – and it was important, he believed, to look the part.

Looked the part he may have but underneath, as he later admitted, he was as skittish as a cat on a hot tin roof. 'As my turn in the witness box approached,' he wrote, 'I found it more frightening than waiting to bat in a Test match.' At least in the sanctuary of the dressing room as he waited his turn in the middle, he could smoke. Many did back in those days, astonishing though it might sound to the modern reader. When it was time for him to take the stand, his nerves knew no bounds. He said he felt like the criminal, even though this being a civil case, there was no 'criminal' in the dock. Anyone who has had a police car on his tail while driving will know exactly how he felt. He was called on day three of the hearing. Under questioning, he said that the cricket authorities 'needed a jolly good shake-up' and that he had expected some sort of negative reaction from them when news came out of his involvement in Packer's enterprise 'but I did not expect they would blackball us altogether'. He agreed that he had always been dissatisfied with the restrictions placed on wives while the England team was on tour. A maximum of 21 nights with your husband over what was sometimes six months away from home was unfair, he claimed. He cited the example of Alan Knott, a recognised home bird, who had nearly withdrawn from their recent tour of India for this very reason. He reiterated his claim that what was happening with World Series Cricket would inevitably benefit players the world over. Already, he said, the fee for an England player per Test match had jumped from £200 to £1,000. 'That would have taken 100 years!' He admitted that Packer had offered him a job in TV commentating and helped to buy his house in Sydney.

His time in the witness box had been 'a gruelling exercise'. It was not yet over. He was called on the next day. The strain was unrelenting. He was asked, and he answered, what was the exact remuneration he was getting for signing for Packer. Converted into sterling, the amount was £18,750 per annum plus £6,250 for captaining the Rest of the World side. He furthermore accepted that there might be a potential clash of interests between Packer fixtures, in which he would be contracted to play, and the 1978/79 Ashes series in Australia. And so it went on, the cut and thrust of courtroom drama, one to which he was not accustomed and one he thoroughly disliked. 'It became a battle,' he wrote, 'with the opposition trying to pull me apart and Alexander protecting me.'

He was relieved when it was over and he was stood down. When you depart the crease, you can always look up at the scoreboard (if you need reminding) to see how well you have batted. There was no scoreboard in court; the expression on the faces of onlookers was neutral. Later, his counsel assured him that everything had gone well but the result was not going to stand or fall on his evidence alone. John Snow's testimony was of interest. Most of what John Snow says is of interest. He told the court that he had nightmares about having to become an umpire after his career came to an end. If he had nightmares, consider what night terrors would have been in store for county batsmen with John Snow in a white coat standing 22 yards away. The implication was clear to everyone; he needed financial security once he had retired and under the current system, he was unlikely to get that. What reward was that for one of England's finest fast bowlers in modern times? He had repeatedly made representation to his employers at Sussex and at the TCCB for greater remuneration for players but without success. Typically, he had a colourful image for those who sought to ban him. Their actions came as no surprise to him because, 'When a donkey kicks, you know which way he kicks!'

Then it was Kerry Packer's turn to take the stand. The England captain, lately deposed, may well have had the hacks in the press box sharpening their pencils but it was the appearance of the Big Beast that was always going to provide the feeding frenzy. He was the heart of the affair; without his drive for TV rights in Australia this peculiarly British drama would never have taken place. First, he wanted the court to know that his great desire was to make a contribution to his nation's sport, being an enthusiast himself. His generous sponsorship of a number of sporting ventures gave credence to this. He explained the success John Spencer had had in coaching his son, James. As a result, he had been convinced of the importance of coaching in the development of young players, which explained why he had already invested $200,000 in setting up a national coaching scheme back home. When he was questioned about the negotiating details for exclusive television rights of cricket in Australia, he made the point that he had offered the Australian Cricket Board $500,000 a year over five years but that they had accepted ABC's offer of only $85,000 over three years. 'At that point, I got the message they were playing ducks and drakes with us.' The refusal to grant him TV rights was 'a deliberate attempt by the ICC to break down negotiations'. When asked how much he stood to lose if WSC did not go ahead, his reply was blunt. '$8 million.' Furthermore, 'his goodwill, prestige and believability would be destroyed'. His firm belief was that the ICC was 'self-centred and only interested in perpetuating their own power'. When asked to comment on the way in which he had signed up so many of the world's leading players, he made this damning comment: 'The alacrity with which the players had signed was frightening.' Frightening to whom? The implication was lost on no one. He went on to suggest that the TCCB and the ICC were being used to fight the battles of the ACB, 'to your detriment and their benefit'. 'Who's paying for this court case and who will carry the can if they lose?' he asked. It wasn't the Australian Board. Finally, he made this confident forecast: 'Supertests will be good for the public, for television and for the players.'

Packer had no need to glance up at any scoreboard at the end of his marathon innings in the witness box, spread over three days. By all accounts, his performance had been impressive. Anybody hoping for a theatrical show of bravado and boardroom bullying was in for a disappointment. He was calm, measured, eloquent and reasonable, with a sure grasp of his facts and always respectful of the court. He had not self-destructed as some hoped; in point of fact he had loosed off some dangerous depth charges of his own. Dispassionate observers were now beginning to understand what Tony Greig had grasped early on. You made him your enemy at your peril. But if you remained loyal to him, you had a friend for life. And a very generous one too.

Even the great dramatists in literary history felt constrained to release some of the pressure that was inexorably building up to the tragic conclusion by inserting a scene of low comedy. Remember the gravediggers' scene in *Hamlet*, a spot of knockabout humour before Hamlet met his inevitable quietus at the point of a poisoned épée during a duel. The comic play-actor in the drama, *Greig v Insole*, was in the form of Geoffrey Boycott. He was, and remains, a divisive figure; you either like or loathe him. I do not profess to know him well but we did once engage in conversation during a county match when it was raining and of course I have listened to him as a commentator and pundit on radio and television. I have always thought he had a talent for humour, unconscious though it may be. He knows the game inside out and his views on cricket are invariably pertinent. As for the rest, I believe people make the mistake of taking him too seriously. In court, he certainly made his mark.

It is important in this story of Tony Greig to go back a few months. Tony had begged Boycott to tour with him in India but he had remained in his tent, like Achilles, licking his ego. Tony would much rather have had him alongside him when facing Lillee and Thomson in the Centenary Test instead of his making critical comments from the safety of the press box. At the beginning of the recruitment process, Packer had briefly considered Boycott, as one of the leading players and best-known faces outside Australia, as a crucial cog of the English contingent. The pair had met and a brief discussion had taken place but nothing came of it. According to Tony, Packer did not take to Boycott.

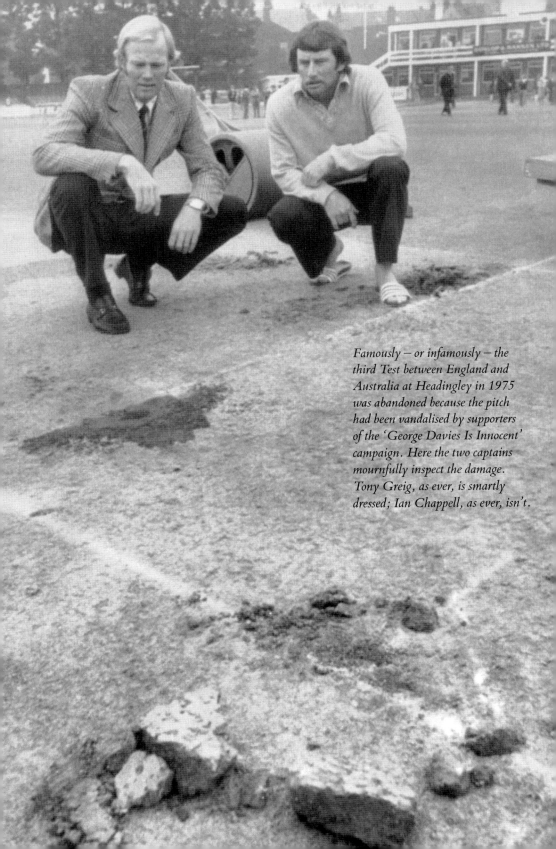

Famously – or infamously – the third Test between England and Australia at Headingley in 1975 was abandoned because the pitch had been vandalised by supporters of the 'George Davies Is Innocent' campaign. Here the two captains mournfully inspect the damage. Tony Greig, as ever, is smartly dressed; Ian Chappell, as ever, isn't.

Tony Greig and Kerry Packer relax at the Dorchester Hotel during the trial at the High Court in September 1977 the result of which changed the face of cricket forever.

Tony and Donna Greig outside their Hove home.

Greig stands tall, all 6'7" of him (or 6' 8", depending on who you speak to) and whips a delivery high over midwicket. The venue is Lord's, the match is the 2nd Test against Australia in 1975 and the wicketkeeper is Rodney Marsh.

In typically determined mode, Greig purveys his alternative off-cutters in the second Test against India at Calcutta in 1977. Derek Randall prowls the covers in the background.

Just made it! Greig dives for his crease during the 1st Test in Delhi on the 1976/77 tour of India

All I can say is that Jeff Thompson did well to get the ball up to chin height given Greig's great height. The two do battle in the second Test between England and Australia at Old Trafford in 1977.

First Test (Jubilee Test) England v Australia at Lord's in 1977. St Peter — I beg your pardon — Tony Greig batting. He had recently been sponsored by the sports company St Peter (note the famous SP logo on the bat and the iconic boxing gloves) which gave rise to his nickname The Messiah. Rodney Marsh is behind the stumps and Rick McCosker is at slip.

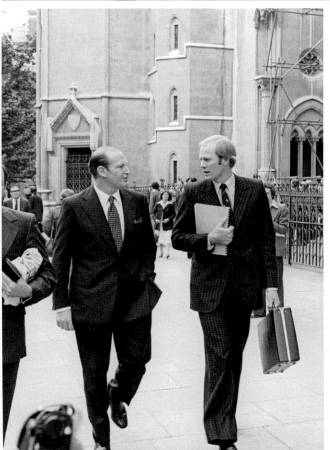

Looking every inch like the lawyer he was not, Tony Greig accompanies Kerry Packer to the High Court in September 1977.

Australia v England Centenary Test at Melbourne 1977. Back row l to rt: Dennis Amiss, Bob Woolmer, John Lever, Bob Willis, Chris Old, Graham Barlow, Derek Randall. Front row l to rt: Keith Fletcher, Alan Knott, Tony Greig (c), Mike Brearley, Derek Underwood. Oh, for those iconic MCC blazers, alas no longer worn by England teams overseas.

OK guys, who's next? Captain Greig looks to see who's in next during the Grand Final of the Supertests between Australia and Rest of the World at Sydney in February 1979. Garth le Roux isn't bothered; he is already rolling up his sleeves in anticipation of another scalp. Looking on, l to rt, Barry Richards, Clive Rice, Asif Iqbal, Eddie Barlow, Mike Procter and Zaheer Abbas.

Bruce Francis lbw bowled Greig 10. Australia v Rest of the World at Brisbane in November 1971. 'The worst decision in the history of the game!' Francis told me. Alas too late to get Tony's steer on the decision but judging from the position of Farokh Engineer the wicketkeeper, it's hard not to see that Francis has a point. The two of them, batsman and bowler, became lifelong friends.

Shot, sir! That looks like four. Note the extra large pads he wore.

The Greig clan gather to celebrate Joyce's 80th birthday. L to rt: Tony, Molly Joy, Sally Ann, Ian.

A delightful shot of Tony enjoying a meal at Doyles in Sydney with his parents.

A painting of Tony Greig. Reproduced with the kind permission of the artist, Ruel Hudson.

The Dream Team. Channel Nine's line-up of commentators for the Ashes series in Australia 2010/11. Tony Greig, Mark Taylor, Richie Benaud, Ian Chappell, Bill Lawry.

A poignant tribute. Tony Greig's trademark Panama hat placed on the stumps before day one of the third Test between Australia and Sri Lanka at Sydney on 3 January 2013. He had died five days earlier.

According to Boycott, Boycott did not take to Packer. In all respects, would anybody have been surprised at the mutual antagonism? Sooner or later, one of them would have been pushed out of the nest.

As we are in the middle of a legal case, I thought I would invoke the law of unintended consequences. Since Boycott's return to the national colours, his 100th first-class hundred in the Test match at Headingley and his final series average of 147.33, he had resumed what he considered to be his rightful place at the head table of English cricket. Now, Tony discovered, he was going to appear as a witness for the defence in the High Court. In other words, he was supporting the establishment, a body with which he had frequently been at loggerheads in the past. The delicious irony of Boycott pouring mud on the most recent captain of England in support of the TCCB who had appointed a number of England captains over Boycott's head in the past did not pass Tony unnoticed. As it happened, on a separate matter (a mutual interest in St Peter cricket equipment), Tony phoned Boycott and asked him to bring down a few of their bats for him to London. As a parting shot, the way cricketers do, Tony remarked that his legal counsel (Sir Robert Alexander) was looking forward to 'throwing some mud at you when you give evidence'. It was meant as a joke, in much the same way a fast bowler might inform you to look out for a bouncer or two on the morrow. Boycott did not see it that way. He reported the matter to his solicitor, who brought it up with the judge. Mr Justice Slade's initial response was to remain silent, believing the remark to be nothing other than what it seemed – a piece of innocent jocularity – but later he thought better of it. He instructed Alexander, 'If there were any attempt to influence witnesses on either side, I would be bound to take a very serious view. I am sure you will speak to Mr Greig about this.' Alexander assured the judge that he would and Tony was suitably chastised. Not impressed, Tony felt he had been well and truly 'dobbed in it', to use a phrase beloved of schoolboys of the time.

Boycott settled himself in the witness box, rather like he took guard, ready for the long haul. When asked of his opinion of those who had signed for Packer, he made his now famous remark, 'A man cannot serve two masters.' He agreed that players had for some time been asking for better pay but he felt that the Packer players 'wanted the penny and the bun'. The idiom refers back to the old English nursery rhyme, *Hot Cross Buns*, but I am told that it is frequently used in management consultancy. I can imagine our Geoffrey feeling pleased at both allusions. He admitted that he had met Packer, who wanted his opinion on his son as a cricketer. 'I expressed my opinion, which his father didn't like.' The reasons for his refusing to sign the contract offered were two-fold – he felt uncomfortable with the 'body and soul' conditions and he was unhappy that there might be inherent conflicts with his commitment to Yorkshire. He had asked for a new contract to be drawn up, dealing with these concerns, but that was the last he heard of it. The ban might be a good thing for English cricket, he averred, because it would open avenues for younger players whose paths were blocked by the more experienced Packer players. He denied that the motivation for his presence in the witness box supporting the TCCB owed everything to his very public desire to captain England. It is worth pointing out at this juncture, though Alexander did not, that Boycott had just been passed over again for the England captaincy. It was Mike Brearley who was about to lead the MCC tourists to Pakistan and New Zealand. As it transpired, he did get his wish to captain his country that winter; Brearley broke his arm on tour and Boycott took over for two Tests, to mixed reviews. Brearley took hold of the reins again on his return and that was the extent of Boycott's tenure as captain.

He then made what he believed was a telling point about the proposed WSC Supertests; they would inevitably cut across the official Test series between Australia and India and adversely affect gate receipts. He was asked therefore was it his belief that the presence of local heroes in a Test match significantly increased the gate. For example, what about Derek Randall, a Nottinghamshire player, appearing for England at his home ground of Trent Bridge? 'Randall at Trent Bridge?' spluttered an indignant Boycott, 'I thought they were 10,000 Yorkshiremen come to see me!'

I have a witness to the court proceedings that day and he says, 'The whole place erupted into laughter.' Mike Vockins, as secretary of Worcestershire, would later appear as a witness for the defence and his memories of both his evidence and his impressions of what was going on are of great interest. More of that in a while. In the meantime, he was struck by the unself-conscious honesty of Boycott, which occasionally led him into making unguarded, controversial statements but which every so often resulted in pure comedy. 'He didn't want to go, you know.' *What do you mean? Go where?* 'When he was asked to stand down, he looked bewildered and disappointed. He was muttering something like he hadn't finished what he wanted to say.' Just as well the Decision Review System was not in operation at that time in court. You can just see Geoffrey making the now familiar sign for a review and then blinking in disbelief at the board, which has just flashed up the verdict 'Out!' and dragging himself reluctantly from his crease, sorry, the witness stand.

Court cases can have their *longueurs*, just like five-day Test matches. It is not all theatrical cut and thrust, as in *Perry Mason, Rumpole of the Bailey* or *Silk*. From time to time, arcane legal argument can intrude and attention starts to wander. Even Tony Greig found that he became bored with the occasionally tedious but necessary debate over legal niceties. For example, I would imagine that disputations over judicial points of order, such as here described in the court notes, would fail to grab the notice of the ordinary onlooker: 'The defence ask for – and are granted – an amendment to their defence under the Trade Union Labour Relations Act of 1974: that they are employers' associations within the meaning of the act and as such are entitled to immunity if found to be in restraint of trade.' Far more interesting were the human touches, as remembered by those who were there. One such was John Barclay. 'I went along to the court case,' he said. 'I wasn't called as a witness or anything but I was fascinated by the whole thing. Christopher Slade, the judge, was my younger sister's godfather.' *Aha, John – friends in high places. I always suspected the secret of your success.* He smiled benignly. In point of fact, it has been Barclay's affability, not his connections, that has been at the heart of his success in life. 'One thing I noticed about him, the judge, was that he wrote and wrote and wrote all the time when people were giving evidence. And then, just occasionally, when the moment was ripe, he would interject with a pertinent comment or question. His summing up was a masterpiece—' *One moment, John, we haven't reached the climax yet.* 'I remember when Doug Insole was talking. He was a bit nervous and started stammering. "Mr Insole," the judge said, 'I think this question requires a simple yes or no.' Brilliant!'

Insole was in the witness stand defending his position as chairman of the TCCB and the ban they sought to impose. He reiterated the fact that talks with Packer broke down because he wanted exclusive television rights which the ICC could not give. If Packer did come to town, he said, every effort would be made to deny his circus suitable grounds to play on. The ban, he claimed, was not to put pressure on the players to change their mind but to protect the game.

Mike Vockins, meanwhile, had been kicking his heels outside the courtroom waiting to be called. 'I was there for two weeks,' he said, 'but I was only in the box for a couple of hours. One thing I remember clearly was the matter of contracts. Very few players back then had updated their contracts with their clubs; sometimes nothing had actually been written down. The judge told everyone that a verbal contract was as strong as a written one. I was asked about the likely effect on the first-class game by the loss of key players to Packer. I said it would cost a county about £50,000 over five years to produce a county player, who might then be snaffled by Packer. The ordinary players would feel that their talents were subsidising the Packer players by providing a vehicle for them to parade their gifts during our summer months, which would be the off-season in Australia. That wouldn't go down well in the English county dressing rooms. There would inevitably be friction. Some counties might select their Packer players; some might not. It wasn't an ideal situation.' We both agreed that this is exactly what happened when Pakistan and West Indies picked their Packer players for Tests whereas England and Australia did not. It wasn't a fair and level playing field. Mr Justice Slade's eventual judgement might have sorted out the problem in England but, as we have seen, the affair stretched far beyond these shores.

Where was Tony Greig as the case played out? In Australia was the answer. The wheels of English justice grind slowly; he had work to do and he could not afford the time to sit around and observe proceedings with interest, as John Barclay. His role as Packer's right-hand man in the setting-up and organisation of WSC – one that he embraced with typical wholeheartedness – required his presence in Sydney. So he quit the country, no doubt a little relieved after all the criticism he had been enduring in the British press, in mid-October, long before the legal wrangling in London had been brought to a close. Not for the first time, he had mislaid his passport and it took a personal intervention from the Australian prime minister, Malcolm Fraser, to enable him to enter the country without one. As we know, Mr Fraser usually jumped when Kerry Packer put a call through to his office.

Back in England, the case finally came to a close after seven weeks of legal deliberation. Mike Vockins describes the scene as Mr Justice Slade gathered his notes, adjusted his glasses and began to speak. 'We, in the defendants' corner, felt we had a good case. Our optimism was in no way punctured as the judge time and again complimented the cricket authorities on their actions and palpable desire to do right by the game. 1-0, we thought. Then another goal went in. 2-0. When the third goal was scored, making it 3-0 to us, we thought we were home and dry. Lunch changed everything. Swiftly goals for the opposition started to hit the back of the net. The score became 1-3, 2-3, 3-3 in quick succession and before we knew it, we were staring at a rout, 13-3 to them. How on earth did that happen? We were left shaking our heads in shock and bafflement.'

John Barclay had an insider's glimpse into the rationale behind Mr Justice Slade's judgement. 'In private, he told my dad that there was no case to answer. It was a clear restraint of trade from the outset and he wondered why so much time, money and emotion had been wasted.' To put more flesh on the bones of Mr Justice Slade's decision to find for the plaintiffs, I consulted notes of the court proceedings. As Barclay said, or was about to say before I interrupted him, Slade's ruling was a masterpiece of clear and incisive English, leaving no room for confusion or misunderstanding. First, he made the point that all the evidence that had been put before him relating to pay and conditions in English county cricket 'could fill a book' and would undoubtedly provide rich pickings for future historians. He made the point that he could perfectly understand the nature and the force of the criticism levelled at Mr Greig because when he was captain of the England team, he had signed for WSC and recruited others to do so. There was 'an obvious case for saying his responsibilities to the TCCB were of a special nature'. That must have been when the first goal went in, according to onlooker Mike Vockins. Furthermore, the defendants – the ICC and the TCCB – were acting in good faith and in what they considered to be in the best interests of the game of cricket. 2-0.

The judge continued …. Was the monopoly of the ICC with regards to promoting the game good for it? Undoubtedly yes over the years. 3-0. But that was not the question put before the court. Was this the moment when the first seeds of doubt in the defence team were sown? The question posed was whether the steps taken by the ICC and the TCCB to combat the threat from WSC were legally justified. His Lordship had come to the conclusion that the introduction of the bans being of benefit to the game at large was 'speculative at best'. The disadvantages of the bans were by contrast 'many and obvious'. The plaintiffs – Greig, Snow and Procter – had signed no contract with the TCCB, which precluded Mr Greig and others from playing cricket for a private promoter. Obviously. Snow was at the tail-end of his career and unlikely to be called up by England again. Procter was a South African and banned from playing Test cricket anyway. Greig as a current England player might have *assumed* he would be picked for England again but there was no contract signed with the TCCB tying him to further employment. Contracts for winter tours were drawn up and signed once the team had been picked.

Then His Lordship made this telling observation. '*The very size of profits made from cricket matches involving star players must for some years have carried the risk that a private promoter would appear on the scene and seek to make money by promoting cricket matches involving world-class cricketers.*' To put it bluntly, the cricket authorities had fallen asleep at the wheel.

There was no justification in law for the course the ICC and TCCB had taken however great had been their desire to protect the game. Thus the changes to the rules of the ICC banning the plaintiffs from playing Test cricket were *ultra vires* and void as being an unreasonable restraint of trade. As were the TCCB's changes to the rules governing the qualification and registration of cricketers playing Test cricket and county cricket in this country. '*A professional cricketer needs to make his living as much as any other professional man,*' he concluded.

After a five and a half hour summary of his findings, Mr Justice Slade decreed that judgement was given for the plaintiffs in both actions, with costs. He removed his glasses, gathered his papers and as the court rose, he quit the scene amidst a stunned silence. It was an epochal moment, everybody felt, but no one was quite sure in what way things would change. The loss of prestige and influence of the cricket establishment was immediate and obvious. Tony was in bed in his home in Sydney when Kerry Packer, immediately apprised of the result of the court case, roused him from his slumbers with a telephone call late at night. 'I thought you'd like to know we've just stuffed 'em,' he told him. Although elated at the decision, Tony was not quite so gung-ho in his attitude to his former employers. Yes, he would be allowed back into the Sussex dressing room the following season in England but he had lost the England captaincy, he was no longer an England player and it was unlikely he would soon, if ever, be recalled to the colours. In addition, old associations had been fractured, trust eroded and friendships broken. He recalled with immense regret an incident that occurred outside the High Court as he was making his way to give evidence. He spied Alec Bedser on the other side of the road. He, as England captain, and Bedser, as chairman of selectors, had enjoyed an effective and mutually respectful partnership; indeed Tony would have gone so far as to call it a close friendship. Under normal circumstances, wild buffalo would not have stopped him crossing the road for a chat. But the incident earlier with Boycott had made him wary. He thought perhaps that, under the current circumstances, he had better hurry along without speaking. Bedser was now batting for the opposition. That hurt him. No matter what had happened on the field of play, as was always the way with South Africans, a friendly chat with opponents over a beer at the close of play was *de rigueur*. He never really made it up with Bedser, and felt sad about that. Bedser for his part felt let down by somebody he had trusted and supported through thick and thin. 'Why didn't you tell your boss?' Sandy Greig had demanded of his son. 'Because I couldn't, Dad,' had been his response, 'I was sworn to secrecy. Had anything got out it would have been curtains for everybody.'

In the immediate aftermath of Mr Justice Slade's ruling, the ICC and the TCCB had to digest what the costs of the case, for which they were liable, would be. Conservative estimates were in the region of £200,000; others believed they would be closer to £250,000. As Packer remarked in that acerbic way of his, they would have been better advised spending that money on their players. They were given leave to appeal but after further consultation and some shilly-shallying, they announced in February of the following year, 1978, they would not. The £250,000 cost of the case had put a considerable hole in the coffers – to say nothing of further costs should they lose an appeal – but both organisations were not exactly on their beam-ends. It was felt that the umpire had made his decision and that was that. There was little to be gained from pursuing the matter further. The landscape had changed forever; the question now was how were they going to adapt to unfamiliar surroundings?

For an answer, I sought the opinion of Mike Vockins, who was unashamedly (his role as secretary of Worcestershire CCC would have demanded no less) on the side of the authorities in this case. He is however a reasonable man, capable of rational reflection; one could never accuse him of being a die-hard traditionalist. Change for change's sake would not have been his mantra but if change is good for the game – bring it on! First, he had felt a certain amount of sympathy for Tony Greig. 'The whole affair had caused deep ructions within the game and in dressing rooms up and down the country. Greig caught it full on the chin.' He had a lot of respect for Tony Greig, found him affable and amenable whenever Worcestershire played Sussex and admired the way in which he extracted every last ounce of talent out of himself as a cricketer. 'As a captain, he was hard-nosed, nothing wrong with that. The only run-in I had with him was later, when he was commentating for Sky. I felt that TV should serve the game, not the other way round, as Sky seemed to be behaving in the early days.' The tension that played out between televised sport and the demands of the broadcasting companies is something that will concern us later.

What of the repercussions of the whole business, Mike? What lessons were learned? 'World Series Cricket made English cricket think seriously about how the players were paid. I had always thought that the system was feudal in its outlook. Take us at Worcester. Don Kenyon, our captain and a huge figure in the county game, was paid not much more than an uncapped player. There was a ceiling on wages and it was pretty low. We knew things had to change and we had already been re-visiting our pay structure. As far as we were concerned, the money *had* to be found.' Sponsorship was growing, he claimed, and clubs such as his did not have their heads so deep in the sand as some claimed. Such ideas as sponsorship for players' lunches, advertising boards around the boundary edge and other initiatives were already being kicked around. The John Player League, the Gillette Cup and the Benson and Hedges Cup were set up in response to market demand resulting in huge gates. The Schweppes County Championship and Lord's Taverners' Trophy had swiftly followed. According to Mike, things were moving. But were they moving fast enough?

I wondered aloud what would have happened if the TCCB had won their case. 'The game would have lost some appeal,' Vockins admitted, 'but where gaps appeared, other players would have filled them. Look at Bob Taylor, one of the finest glovemen in the game. When Knotty went off to play for WSC, Taylor got his chance to play for England. And what a fine Test career he had.' He agreed that attempts had been made to try to get England players to withdraw from their WSC contracts, arguing that their commitments for a short period of time (three years) could be a threat to their long-term prospects as a professional cricketer. If that were so, it was probably a futile gesture. Packer's contracts were famously watertight. As far as Packer was concerned, his players, for the length of their contract, belonged to him body and soul. As he made clear in another of his trenchant comments to the press, 'I make no apologies for the fact that the contract is tough. I told every player that the only way he could get out of it was to get pregnant.' It is worth recording that not one of his WSC players did get pregnant.

Finally, Mike, looking back on the whole affair, what are your lasting memories? 'World Series Cricket brought the counties into the modern world. It introduced new and novel ways of covering the game. It brought home to us that in order to pay the players more – which was desperately needed – we needed to become much more energetic in raising funds. Sponsorship needed to be taken seriously. It was a kick up the backside and it caused huge convulsion and a lot of bitterness but it had to happen.'

Ian Greig put it all into perspective with this poignant story. 'After I had finished at Cambridge, Sussex offered me a full-time contract. This must have been sometime between September and December 1980. I sought Tony's advice. Should I sign or not? "How much?" he demanded to know. In fact the salary was £3,500 a year. He smiled, shook his head and said sadly, "If only they'd believed me." You see, I was being offered more as an uncapped player than he was getting as captain only three years before.' *Was he bitter?* 'Not at all. "Delighted for you, buddy." Eighteen months later, I was picked for England. We were paid £1,250 per Test. Tony had only been paid £210. And he was captain!'

Chapter 10

World Series Cricket 1977–79

'This is it.' Tony Greig

'I think you're right.' Kerry Packer

Both were standing on the top tier of the Noble Stand watching thousands of fans lining the streets and queueing up at the turnstiles of the SCG.

THE scene now shifts to Australia. It was in Australia that the rift had first opened and although the affair had repercussions in this country, the story was essentially an Australian one and it was in Australia that Packer's revolution was going to succeed or fail. The omens were not propitious. There seemed so much to do and the start of WSC was only weeks away. Currently, the assembled players were busy practising on net surfaces that were variable. All the best facilities had of course been snaffled for the official tourists from India in a concerted effort by the Australian Cricket Board to deny Packer anywhere decent to play. Tony Greig's role, though not clearly defined, constituted much more than captaining the World XI. Packer had invested a great deal in the figure who was going to be the public face of the enterprise so Tony was here, there and everywhere, setting up this, organising that and checking up on something else. So busy was he that his absence at practice was noted, and frowned at, by members of his team. A man cannot serve two masters, opined Geoff Boycott. Tony was finding that a man in the service of one master, and a very demanding one at that, cannot be in two places at once.

What were those practice sessions like, Barry? I mean it must have been odd having a net with players who were formerly in opposition. 'It was a little odd at first,' Barry Richards replied. 'I remember walking across to the nets and the Australians were there. Many of them I knew well. At first I was going to ask if some of them would bowl to me but Eddie Barlow put a restraining hand on my arm, saying he didn't feel that would look right. They were now our opponents. He was right of course.' *As I remember, you weren't the greatest netter in the world. Did you take these sessions seriously?* He rolled his eyes. 'I've never known sessions more intense. Packer wanted it taken seriously. He told us in words of one syllable that if he unearthed any evidence of collusion between the teams, we would be on our bikes. And that included any talk of sharing out the winnings between the teams.' Shrewd businessman as he was, Packer had worked out that money talks, even among sportsmen. The winning cheque was for the team that won the series; there was no money for winning a match. The losers got nothing. 'He wanted it to be competitive,' said Richards, 'and believe me, it was.'

As in any new venture or initiative, there were teething problems. Packer was prepared to pull out all the stops to sort things out and Tony, as his right-hand man in cricket affairs, took it upon himself to check and double check the detail. He knew the importance of getting it right. The scope of his responsibility was mind-blowing and he did not stint in his tasks. Inevitably, this took him away from his team and he was not happy with that. When England captain, he saw his role as being solely responsible for his team; there were other people who dealt with the administrative side of things. The MCC had been organising overseas tours for 100 years. There was no such blueprint for WSC. They had to make it up as they went along. Tony recognised that he was short-changing his World XI but he accepted there was nothing he could do about it. If there was nowhere for them to play, his role as captain and their role as a World XI would be redundant anyway. I imagine that the dilemma on whose horns he uncomfortably sat would have been familiar to any captain of a club side in the recreational game.

Take the wickets they were going to play on. All major cricketing venues having been denied him, Packer was forced to use stadiums that were large enough but of course had no pitches. Anybody who knows anything about the preparation and treatment of that sacred strip of turf 22 yards long understands it takes time and patience, years even. WSC had to prepare wickets in a matter of months. And not any old wickets. These were the best batsmen in the world and they did not want to face the fastest bowlers in the world (a whole stable full of them) on an unreliable surface. Somebody could get killed. And if anybody was, that was money down the drain.

Necessity is the mother of invention. Drop-in wickets and the wearing of helmets – now commonplace – were just two of the many innovations spawned by WSC. The science, to say nothing of the technology and engineering, of the operation was unproven and met with scepticism across the board. Melbourne was one of the first guinea pigs. Not the MCG where a mere six or seven months previously, England and Australia had fought out the epic Centenary Test but the Victoria Football League Park, an Aussie Rules football stadium, with a capacity of 100,000 spectators. Tony Greig's job was to visit it and report on the progress of the drop-in wicket that would be used for WSC matches. Tony's dismay as he first clapped eyes on the building site soon to host a game of cricket was profound. There was no way it could possibly be ready in time. 'To my disbelief and dismay, there was a huge hole in the centre of the playing area, with great piles of sand on the surrounds … The whole scheme for an awful few minutes seemed to be doomed to failure.'

I can only recall one other incident in his career when doubt seriously entered Tony's soul. That was following the mauling by the West Indies fast bowlers on a sub-standard pitch at Old Trafford in 1976, when he contemplated resigning from the England captaincy and Alan Knott had managed to dissuade him. On both occasions, then and now, his panic was wholly understandable. A lesser man would have thrown in the towel, but the Greigs were not built like that. Tony was not going to buckle now. He was impressed by the ingenuity and resourcefulness of the engineers and his natural optimism was soon restored. He considered the whole operation 'an incredible feat' and left the contractors to apply the finishing touches greatly buoyed by what he had seen. 'After that success, anything was possible.'

If Tony's assurance had taken a knock, albeit a fleeting one, it appeared that Kerry Packer's faith in the project was impregnable. 'Kerry's enthusiasm was infectious,' Tony wrote, 'his finger was on the pulse of everything.' The British public's judgement of him as a brash multi-millionaire who had inherited a fortune and who simply got what he wanted by chucking money at it was wide of the mark. Tony got closer to him than any of his players but to all I've spoken, there is nothing but respect for their boss. He clearly had great leadership qualities. He inspired affection and loyalty, as well as a little fear, in his employees who were prepared – always – to go the extra mile for him. These were attributes that Tony, an inspirational leader of men himself, would have recognised and valued. Packer was everywhere that year, organising, delegating, encouraging, berating, issuing writs, appearing on TV shows, flaying opponents, converting disbelievers and stiffening backbones. Like any great general, his attention to detail was legendary but he never lost sight of the big picture and he inspired others with his vision. At the same time he had the common touch. Tony was astonished early one morning to arrive at the ground in Perth to find his boss sitting on the roller, helping out in the preparation of the wicket. Nothing was beneath him. If he demanded the best bottle of Champagne in the house, well ... he deserved it. That was the justification for his *modus operandi*.

He also demanded the best groundsman in Australia (or 'curator' as they are known over there). Some of these drop-in pitches, according to Barry Richards, were good, some were dreadful. So Packer enlisted the services of John Maley, curator at the WACA in Perth, renowned for its pacey, bouncy tracks, and things immediately began to improve.

Very early on, Tony grasped the simple fact – which others did not – that WSC was first and foremost a commercial undertaking and as such the product had to be sold. Tony knew all about self-promotion;

in a sense he had been doing it all his life. Packer had seen something in him in those advertising commercials on television and had staked much on making him the figurehead of his campaign. Tony was intent on not letting him down. His life in these weeks was a whirligig of plans, meetings, visits, telephone calls, interviews, site inspections and … oh yes, net practice. He was indefatigable, his energy inexhaustible. He said later that he put into the endeavour 'blood, sweat and tears'. Mind you, was there anything in his life that he did not approach with all guns trained on the target?

At last, on 2 December, the phoney war ended and WSC Australia took on WSC West Indies at the VFL Park, Melbourne. They had been banned by a court order in Australia from naming their sides 'Australia' and 'West Indies' in order not to be confused with the official national teams so they came up with this compromise. It is interesting that so many West Indian players had been signed up – what did this say about the players' opinion of the West Indies Board of Control? There were now enough of them to form their own team. Sometimes some of them played for the World XI, sometimes they played under their own banner. Confusing? Never mind. This is showbiz. Lights … Camera … Action!

I use that well-worn phrase from the studio floor advisedly. Lights, cameras and action were what WSC was all about. The very idea of playing a game of cricket under floodlights had been met with the utmost scepticism. Floodlit cricket will never work, grumbled the naysayers but Packer was convinced the effect would electrify the game, if you will excuse the pun. Being a television man through and through, he was more interested in the experience of the viewer than the spectator. One thing about the traditional TV coverage of cricket that he could never understand was the positioning of only one camera at one end. Why not have cameras at both ends? He said he was sick of watching a batsman's backside every other over. And, while we're on the subject, why not have cameras positioned at particular points all around the ground? Today, there are in the region of 30 cameras covering a televised match.

Tony was fascinated by the whole process and immersed himself in the business of broadcasting, maybe sensing that this was where his future lay. He spoke with wonder of Packer's ubiquitous 'red phone', the direct line to the producer of the game, one that he would pick up at any time wanting to know what the hell was going on with camera 4. It was an exciting time, the dawn of a new era in broadcasting and Tony had made sure he was at the epicentre of the revolution. Barry Richards believed that Tony was already thinking ahead to life after cricket, hence his close association with Packer and his frequent absences from his World XI as they were preparing for matches.

For the matches themselves he was ever present. *How did you find him as captain, Barry?* 'Fine. Only he could have gelled those disparate talents and personalities from different countries together. As for tactics and decisions ... well, to be truthful, a robot could have captained a team of that much ability. He was a good figurehead, though.' And a combative one, it seemed. In the first match under lights, the two captains, Greig and Ian Chappell, mindful of concerns about visibility, agreed on a mutual self-denying ordinance on bouncers. Notwithstanding the agreement, Tony could not resist slipping one in against his opposite number, exacerbating an increasingly fractious relationship between the two, which worsened as WSC went on.

As Packer had predicted, the spectacle of night-time cricket under lights was compelling. The white ball was easy to see against the backdrop of a dark sky but not so easy to pick up against the white clothing of the players. One or two contentious lbw decisions had gone against the bowlers because the white ball was difficult to distinguish from the white pads. Coloured clothing was the obvious answer, adding to the razzmatazz of the occasion. Richards laughed when I reminded him of pictures of the gaily-attired Packer cricketers. 'It was the 1970s,' he reminded me, 'not an era noted for its fashion sense. All the shirts were tight-fitting with huge collars and the trousers were flared. We played in light blue. That was all right. The Aussies were in canary yellow, a bit bright but just about okay. But whoever put the West Indians in bright pink should have got his marching orders. Let's just say that the colour suggested they were batting for the other side, if you take my meaning. And those guys were not impressed.' The following season, the bright pink had been toned down. A little. For not much was toned down about WSC.

The advent of helmets, which many, Barry Richards included, believe revolutionised the way the game was played more than any other of the Packer innovations, was a reaction rather than a pro-action. It came about because of an accident, a nasty one too. At Hampshire, we all marvelled at the number of batsmen Andy Roberts hit in his career, not with glee on our part but amazement and consternation, allied to a sense of relief that he was on our side and we didn't have to face him ourselves. It wasn't just county players he nailed; he did it in Test matches too. In mid-December, as WSC Australia took on WSC West Indies at the Sydney Showground (not the SCG), he felled the golden boy of Australian cricket, David Hookes, the same Hookes who had creamed Tony for five successive fours in one over during the Centenary Test. Hookes was escorted off the field, his jaw broken. Packer, impatient at the time it took for an ambulance to arrive, bundled the player into his own car and broke every speed limit in the city as he drove him to hospital. When Hookes's jaw had been wired up and he returned to the ground, Packer was insistent that he went out to bat again. 'He's 81 not out,' he exclaimed. Of course, that was impossible and wiser counsel prevailed but Packer wouldn't let the matter go. 'Look, if I put you in a crash helmet, will you go out?' Hookes did not, thankfully, but the concept of the helmet was born and the game changed forever.

Dennis Amiss was the first to wear the prototype and Tony soon followed. The memory of the battering by the same West Indian fast bowlers on an unpredictable Old Trafford pitch not so long ago was too raw in his mind for him not to. Barry Richards pointed out that the original design was soon scrapped. 'We couldn't hear each other! We abandoned them when there were four run-outs on the trot. But they soon got better.' He put it plainly and simply why he feels that the arrival of the helmet revolutionised how the game was played. 'Batsmen go after it much more now because they know if they miss it, the worst they will get is a headache. Before helmets, if we missed it, we'd end up in hospital.' Bigger bats, stronger physiques and shorter boundaries have all contributed to the increase in scoring rates and the proliferation of sixes but by far the most significant contribution to that change, Richards asserts, was the birth of the helmet. Would that have happened if Packer's WSC had never got off the ground? Probably. Eventually. But once again, Kerry Packer was ahead of the game.

Christmas came, a welcome respite from the hectic schedule. Wives and families were invited by Packer to the teams' hotels to celebrate the occasion, with reduced airfares and concessionary rates for rooms on offer. Everybody was made to feel welcome and Tony really appreciated that. It was hard for him not to draw unfavourable comparisons with the way that wives and families had been treated on tours with the MCC. The holiday gave him and others in the Packer inner circle time to reflect on how things had gone so far. Nobody could pretend that WSC had been a rip-roaring success. Tony was aware of this as much as anybody and fretted about it. Crowds had been poor, the weather inclement and the pitches sometimes not up to scratch. Then the sun had come out and the traditional Boxing Day Test in Melbourne between the 'official' Australian side and the Indians had drawn a crowd of 82,000. The matches involving WSC had been attracting paltry crowds by comparison. On the other hand, the standard of cricket in the Supertests had been extraordinarily high and viewing figures on television had been encouraging.

Back in England, the apparent struggles of WSC to attract the crowds were met with a certain amount of *Schadenfreude* within the corridors of power. In the press, the mood was more one of glee. As an example of the scepticism of the new brand of cricket and the fear of the damage it was doing to the game, I quote from one of Michael Parkinson's scathing articles in *The Sunday Times*:

'Kerry's problems with crowds – I have seen bigger attendances at the quarter-finals of the Barnsley Shin-kicking Competition – is easily solved. All we have to do is look to history for the answer. Then we discover that once upon a time we dealt with a similar problem by deporting our criminals to Australia. Thus, at one masterstroke, we can rid ourselves of one problem and solve another for our dear Aussie friends. I would suggest that if we shipped over there a boatload or two of hooligans who make up soccer crowds, Kerry's problems would be at an end.'

I always enjoyed Parky's acerbic articles, usually delivered with wit and humour, even if I did not wholly agree with all the sentiments expressed. He certainly had a point about soccer hooliganism in the 1970s, which culminated in the Heysel tragedy of 1985, when 39 fans died in a riot before the start of the European Cup Final between Liverpool and Juventus. With regard to this particular article, I shall only make two points. First, it was unusual to find Parky on the side of the establishment. The second point was emphasised by Tony's son, Mark. According to him, Parky and his father made up in later years and became good friends, remaining so until the day of Tony's death. Parky told Mark that everybody is entitled to his opinion and everybody is entitled to change it. Later, he came to understand the good that WSC had done for cricketers and said as much. He also pointed out that it was a mark of Tony Greig's good nature and his maturity as a man that he never held grudges and was content to let bygones be bygones. There was another quip by Sir Michael Parkinson, as he now is, that made me smile. With Tony's South African accent firmly in mind, he coined a new phrase – '*to grigg*', meaning 'to fall from a great height'.

The poor attendances at the WSC matches left everybody scratching their heads. Several reasons were advanced. The 'official' Australian side were engaged in an enthralling series with India, played in all the traditional cricket venues, something denied WSC. This was a new venture and it would take time for the Australian public to warm to the cricket on offer. Furthermore, this was a battle fought in the media over the media. The matches got full coverage in the newspapers belonging to the Packer empire but his rivals were not giving him an easy ride. Greg Chappell explained to me how vicious this war was turning out. 'Channel 7 were televising the Australian Open tennis at the time. They took out a full-page ad in all the newspapers – except those owned by Packer of course – with a photo of six lonely people in an empty stand when we were playing at Waverley AFC ground with the caption: "These are some of the people not watching the tennis on Channel 7'!" *Were you at all discouraged?* 'No, we knew it would take time. Packer was not one to give up easily.' This was a view shared by Barry Richards. 'Packer poured money and resources into marketing the show, giving it the full works, advertising, the lot. His masterstroke was to get Richie Benaud on board. Once he was part of the team, WSC could not fail.'

Slowly, the tide turned. Clearly, day-night games were the real deal and people began to switch on to the idea and crowds started to increase. The culmination of the season was Greig's World XI taking on Ian Chappell's Australian XI in a three-match series. The first Supertest had been won by WSC World XI by four wickets, rather more comfortably than the final score suggested, with the two West Indians, Viv Richards and Andy Roberts to the fore as match winners. Tony Greig scored 38 and 8 and went wicketless, rather indicative of his meagre form throughout the season. The second Supertest in Perth proved to be the climax; there was a huge amount of money resting on the outcome, not on the match, remember, but on the series. It was a memorable game for so many reasons.

First, just look at the stars on show. The World XI had been dubbed the Team of all the Talents and if you remember that a 'talent' was a unit of currency in Ancient Rome, it would be hard to disagree with that tag. Richards (Barry), Greenidge, Richards (Viv), Lloyd, Asif, Greig (c), Imran, Knott, Daniel, Roberts, Underwood. Has such a team with so many great players ever taken the field in the history of the game? And Australia had brought along pretty well their A team, including the two Chappells, Marsh, Gilmour, Lillee and Walker, missing only the double-booked Jeff Thomson. The game took place at Gloucester Park, the harness racing oval in Perth. The drop-in pitch was a beauty. Barry Richards takes up the story as he opened the batting with his Hampshire team-mate, Gordon Greenidge. They both raced to their respective hundreds. 'By now, Gordy was starting to limp,' he said. I started to laugh and he grinned. Gordon limping was not an uncommon occurrence back at Hampshire. 'He said he'd pulled a muscle.' *Well, to be fair, he had more than his fair share of muscles to pull.* 'The Aussies had no respite. Out sauntered Viv.' Oh, how I wish I had been there. How I wish it had been televised back home in England. How I wish any word on the match could be found in British newspapers. Sadly only 3,500 were there in person to witness an unforgettable exhibition of batsmanship, the two Richardses in tandem, arguably the best batsmen of their generation, flaying the bowling to all parts. Barry eventually holed out for 207, Viv scored 177 and Greenidge returned, muscle mended, to finish up with 140.

Tony kept the screw turned as tight as he could. There was no thought of declaring. The World XI finished up on 625. To give credit to the Australians, they did not throw in the towel. Greg Chappell played a monumental innings of 174 in a desperate rearguard action but it was all to no avail. The World XI won by an innings and 73 runs and eagerly pocketed the winner-takes-all cheque for $100,000.

At the close of the match, during the customary handshakes and expressions of congratulation between the two teams, a quarrel that had been simmering between the two captains broke out into open hostility. Though never the best of buddies, Tony Greig and Ian Chappell, two opposing captains in an Ashes series, don't forget, had a reasonably amicable and respectful relationship earlier in their careers. Tony recognised a fellow competitive spirit when he saw one and admired Chappell's no-nonsense style and ability to get the best out of the players under his command. Chappell too saw something of Greig in himself, one who never took a backward step and had grudging respect for his combative style, which always seemed to rise to the occasion. He also nodded appreciatively when Tony quickly agreed to abandon the Headingley Test when it became clear that to proceed on the sabotaged pitch would be unfair. However, personal relations had deteriorated during the course of this season to the extent that Tony took grave offence when Chappell shook everybody's hand in the World XI except Tony's at the conclusion of the match with these words, 'Well done guys. You're the best bunch of cricketers I've seen – with one exception.' Quickly, it was made clear to Chappell that his presence was no longer welcome in the World XI dressing room.

What was at the bottom of this unseemly spat? Both offered differing reasons. Chappell believed that Tony's personal performances did not warrant his place in the World XI and that his business commitments and marketing duties were distracting him from his priorities as captain of his team. Tony found Chappell continually argumentative and uncooperative, even over niggly little things. For example, Tony believed that each of the teams should be smartly dressed in blazers and ties when 'on duty' but he knew from bitter experience that Chappell would 'wear what the hell he liked', as he put it. Blazers and ties were not in Chappell's wardrobe and nothing would shift him. It wasn't just a case, Tony maintained, of a difference in sartorial style or fashion. They were trying to sell the Packer brand and he thought certain standards should be set.

If Tony had found the pressure was getting to him, it would hardly have been surprising. Despite their success on the field, the World XI were not in any sense of the word a conventional team. 'It wasn't like we were representing our country,' said Barry Richards, 'with all the attendant history, shared goals and public expectation. We were a gathering of very talented players who were thrown together by circumstances. We got on fine and Greigy did well to mould us as well as he did but the pale blue was not the same as the Springbok green.' Or the West Indian maroon or even the egg-and-bacon colours of the MCC, he might have added. As an example of the political minefield Tony had to negotiate, take pre-match training, something everybody, or nearly everybody, had come to realise was now the *sine qua non* of the brave new world of highly paid professional cricketers. A quick limber up followed by a fag and a cup of coffee in the dressing room was no longer considered acceptable preparation before going out on to the field of play. However, old habits and cultural differences still reared up from time to time. It seemed the Pakistanis were not so keen on the training regime. Asif Iqbal baulked at any suggestion of shuttle runs. 'When anybody can beat me in a sprint,' he remarked, 'then I shall do it.' He had a point. Asif's reputation as the fastest runner between the wickets in the game was largely undisputed. So a certain amount of flexibility was required. Tony found this hard. All for one and one for all had always been his maxim.

Furthermore, he had just had an unwelcome telephone call from home, if Hove could still truly be called 'home'. The story needs unpicking. While the Packer 'pirates' had been busy raiding and plundering and Australia and India had been engaged in an absorbing Test series, England had been heavily involved in Pakistan. An unfortunate injury to their captain, Mike Brearley, breaking his arm, meant that Geoff Boycott, as vice-captain, took over the reins to fulfil his lifetime's ambition to captain his country. Whether his elevation went to his head and he felt secure enough now in his position to vent his pent-up resentment over what he saw as the pernicious effect of

WSC on the game he loved, we shall never know. In any event, he secured a spot for himself writing a newspaper article. He lambasted the players who had turned their backs on their country in order to line their pockets, labelling them 'disloyal' and 'traitors' and coining the memorable phrase, 'Have bat, will travel.'

Stung by this implied criticism, Tony responded in the only way he knew. Getting firmly on the front foot, he took out a newspaper article of his own in which he wrote that equally memorable phrase, 'Boycott has the uncanny knack of being where fast bowlers aren't.' Both should have counted to ten before going into print. Both subsequently regretted the intemperance of their utterances. Both at heart had a high regard for the other and had got on well as England colleagues. Both buried the hatchet, made up and later shared commentary boxes in perfect amity. However, for Tony the article was to have distressing repercussions. The TCCB took a dim view of the article and as Tony had not cleared it with them before it went into print, they deemed him in breach of his responsibilities as a county cricketer and slapped a two-month ban on him, effective from the start of the 1978 season. Tony had been sacked as England captain and been dropped from the Test side but he was still a Sussex player and fully intended to take up his position as Sussex captain for the English county season. Alas, even this shred of comfort was to be denied him. The telephone call from England was from the chairman at Sussex regretfully informing him that he had been relieved of the Sussex captaincy into the bargain. Tony felt hard done by, as well he might. Had Boycott got permission to print his article? He suspected not. Yet he had not been punished. England must have seemed an unfriendly place when he returned at the conclusion of his Packer commitments in April 1978.

Back in England for the 1978 season, he kicked his heels for eight weeks playing club cricket. Any county player who has been forced for one reason or another to drop down a peg or two, a whole rung in Tony's case, will know what a dispiriting experience it is. He did his best to keep up his spirits but his rare forays into the Sussex dressing room confirmed all his worst fears about how his legacy as captain was being slowly dismantled. In a way, this was inevitable. You would expect a new captain – in this case, Arnold Long (known affectionately as 'Ob', one of the better cricketer nicknames) – would want to stamp his authority and style on his new team. Sadly, it bore no resemblance to the one Tony had been at pains to develop. When he had served his suspension and returned to action, the poor form that had dogged him in Australia proved difficult to shake off. Theories abounded. He was short of practice. He was tired and in need of a rest after his winter's exertions in Australia. He was tired and in need of a complete rest after a succession of seasons, playing winter and summer, with no respite. He had lost his appetite for English cricket following his sacking from the England and Sussex captaincies. We at Hampshire had another opinion. Shortly after Tony was reinstated, Sussex played Hampshire at Hove in mid-June. Out of a sorry Sussex total of 77 in their first innings, one line in the scorecard stands out. A.W. Greig c Greenidge b Roberts 0. Hampshire went on to win the match by an innings and 141 runs but that is not my point. The contrast in fortunes between Tony on one side and two other Packer players on our side is startling. Greig 0, Roberts 5-20 and Greenidge 211. Roberts did for Tony in the second innings too. The feeling in the Hampshire dressing room was that Tony Greig was no longer the player he was. Quite why did not concern us then but it concerns me now. Clearly Tony was not happy and frankly he looked a little lost. This wasn't his Sussex team and he felt out of place.

This wasn't his home either, or so it increasingly felt as if criticism of him, far from abating, if anything seemed to intensify. Some of it was uncomfortably personal. News of his epilepsy was leaked which distressed him enormously. Up until this point, though it was known on the county circuit, it had been considered a personal matter and therefore not for public consumption. Now it was being splashed across the newspapers and he felt a line had been crossed. He was the bogeyman of English cricket and personal attacks were coming from all quarters. For some reason, one that he could not readily fathom, the other Packer players in English cricket – Knott, Underwood, Snow, Woolmer, Amiss – did not appear to suffer the same personal abuse as he did. There were awkward moments experienced by all that summer but the vitriol was reserved for the former England captain alone. The running sore of his not being a 'true' Englishman was difficult to ignore. This intensely irritated him but his shoulders were broad; he could put up with it if the attacks were aimed at him. The straw that broke his back was when his family was dragged into it.

Samantha, Tony's daughter who was four at the time, had a particular friend in her year group and the two had often been in and out of each other's homes. The tradition was that the whole class would be invited around for tea when it was someone's birthday. Samantha had had hers and invitations issued to everybody as usual. Today was the birthday of her friend but no invitation was given to Samantha. Thinking it had been nothing more than an oversight, Tony approached the girl's mother only to be told abruptly that Samantha wasn't invited. 'I have never been so hurt in my life,' he wrote. 'I took three strides towards Samantha, who jumped into my arms, tears streaming down her face.' For confirmation, I asked Ian Greig if it happened exactly as his brother described. 'Absolutely. An attack on him was fair game, even if it was ill-informed and personal. But on his children ... well, that was beyond the pale.'

That was it. The die was cast. 'From that moment,' he said, 'my life in England was finished.' A short discussion with Donna ensued. Both were agreed that the time had come to leave. He secured an immediate release from his Sussex contract and within days, the family was on the plane bound for Sydney. Kerry Packer was typically supportive of the decision. The airline tickets were waiting for them at the airport. Never one to look back, Tony made this assessment of his situation, 'We were leaving England for good. I was now a Packer player and Packer employee through and through.'

Reaction to his sudden departure was mixed. For some, it only confirmed what they had always thought; Greig's true colours were now firmly nailed to the mast. Traitor to the England cause he had been and now he was fleeing the country. Others were more sympathetic. What else could he have done? As Mr Justice Slade had said in his summing up, 'A professional cricketer needs to make his living as much as any other professional man.' Australia was now his workplace; why should people expect him to remain in England? His team-mates at Sussex had no problem with his decision. Cricket is a short-lived career. Everybody has to shift for himself when the final innings is played out. 'We wished him well because it was obviously his future,' Peter Graves said, a view shared by all the Sussex players to whom I spoke. History will be kinder to me, Tony reasoned with himself and in that he was right. In the meantime, there was work, much work, to be done.

Not that he had been exactly idle in Packer's cause during his shortened season in England. He signed up three more players, all South African and all, in their different ways, set to become significant figures in the world game: Clive Rice, Garth le Roux and Kepler Wessels. Kepler I particularly remember. He had scored a double hundred at the age of 18 while he was on trial for Sussex. He was a seriously good player even then and later went on to play for Australia. I was always intrigued as to how he ended up wearing the baggy green. I found out in a roundabout way during a conversation with Barry Richards. Tony Greig was at the forefront of the story. After Barry had scored that memorable 200 for the World XI, he was approached by one of Packer's henchmen, who informed him that the boss wanted to see him. Tony Greig and Ian Chappell were in attendance when Barry entered the room. 'Once the pleasantries had been dispensed with,' he said, 'Kerry announced I was now going to play for Australia!'

It took a second or two for the ramifications of what Packer had said to sink in. 'When he asked me what I thought, I said it was a terrible idea. I knew that the Australian team had had a bit of a hard time of it up against the might of the World XI but really … me in the green of Australia!' *Don't you mean canary yellow?* 'Quite. I didn't think it was in the spirit of the whole thing, for people to chop and change sides like that. Greigy was hopping mad, shouting, "No, no, he's one of us!" Chappell was furious too. "He's not a fair dinkum Aussie!" Packer just shrugged and said, "He soon will be. Get him a passport!" And for my trouble, I was to get an interest-free loan over ten years of $30,000. We shook hands on it.' For once though, Packer changed his mind. Or rather, had it changed. Tony argued long and hard against parachuting Richards into the Australian team and much as Chappell liked Richards as a man and respected him as a cricketer, he too wanted only Australian-born players in his team. Eventually, Packer capitulated and the idea was permanently shelved. 'But he paid me the money,' Richards was keen to point out, 'once Kerry had shaken on an agreement, he always kept his word.'

All of which begs the question; how come Kepler Wessels, a South African, ended up in Australian colours, playing 24 Tests for his adopted country before retiring from international cricket? Why and how he switched horses again and then played for South Africa when they made their return to Test cricket in 1991 is another story. 'It was Greigy who sorted it out,' said Richards. 'Obviously he knew him from Sussex and understood well enough his potential. So he recommended him to Kerry, even though Kepler was a relative unknown at that stage. As he was unknown, Greigy argued, it would create far less of a fuss in getting him a passport than if it had been me with my face plastered across the front pages of all the newspapers.'

The reason for Kerry Packer's eagerness to get Richards to swap sides was obvious enough. Australia on their own were no real match for the World XI. Above all he wanted his cricket to be exciting and competitive. Hence the formation of a third team, the West Indies, which created more interest and more evenly contested games. He was tireless in his efforts to improve his product. 'We were amateurs this year,' he said at the conclusion of the first season, 'next year we're going to do it properly.'

The turning point, pretty well everybody agrees, came in November of 1978. Packer's masterstroke had been the securing of proper cricket venues for his matches. The Gabba in Brisbane, the Adelaide Oval and the Sydney Cricket Ground all agreed to host WSC matches. The jewel in the crown was the SCG, resplendently lit up by its newly installed floodlights, and it was here that players and administrators, with some relief in one or two quarters, finally realised that they had cracked it.

Tuesday, 28 November was a balmy night in Sydney and as Tony and Kerry Packer stood on the balcony high up in the Noble Stand in the SCG watching the thousands of fans lining the streets and queueing up at the turnstiles, Tony admitted to having a tear in his eye. 'This is it,' he said to his companion. 'Yes, I think you're right,' was the simple reply. 'Deep down', Tony wrote, 'I think he may have felt quite triumphant that night but he didn't show it. It was almost as if he knew it would happen.' When the ground capacity of 44,000 had been reached, the gates were closed. Seeing the queues still snaking around the stadium, Packer ordered them open again, this time with no payment required. Conservative estimates were that over 50,000 watched the game that night.

The previous season, WSC had been hampered by the opposition – the engrossing official series between Australia and India. This year, England were in the country, the Ashes were at stake and nothing took precedence over that historic rivalry in the public imagination of both countries. You would have expected therefore that anything competing against the Ashes that summer would struggle for attention. Strangely, this did not happen. The first Test at the Gabba yielded only 43,000 spectators over the whole game, comparing unfavourably, as Packer's newspapers reminded everybody, with the 50,000 for one evening at the SCG. How come? The reason is not hard to fathom. A hugely depleted and disheartened Australian team lost the series 1-5 – and it might well have been a whitewash had it not been for winning the toss in the sole victory at Melbourne – and their public clearly tired of supporting a losing team. In the space of 20 months, Greig's successor as captain, Mike Brearley (dubbed the Ayatollah because of the full beard he now sported) had beaten Australia eight times in 11 Tests – and this was before the miracle of 1981, 'Botham's Ashes'. Visiting English journalists noted the well-oiled and professional publicity machine of WSC and compared it critically with the marketing by the Australian Cricket Board. *Wisden* gave the Ashes series a haunting image: 'A lone trumpeter on the sparsely filled Hill at Sydney symbolised Australia's embarrassing defeats.'

While Brearley was being lauded to the heavens as a tactical genius with 'a degree in people', as Rodney Hogg memorably described him, Greig was coming under increasing pressure as captain of the World XI. In one sense, the criticism was understandable; in another, especially if the comparison with Brearley is advanced, it makes no sense at all. Both were captains of successful sides (though obviously Brearley did not have at his disposal the same firepower as did Greig) and both were in the team, not because their performances justified inclusion, but on account of their undoubted leadership qualities. Which is a polite and slightly disingenuous way of avoiding the unpleasant fact of their wretched current form. In 12 innings during the Ashes series, Brearley averaged 16.72. In 14 innings in Supertests, Greig was averaging 8.00. The Australian tradition in selecting national sides was always to pick the 11 best players and then appoint the most suitable captain. The English tradition has not always been so cut and dried. The chosen captain, especially on overseas tours, has not always been a shoo-in for the Test team on ability alone; his character and leadership qualities would overrule his deficiencies as a player. That is why Brearley's poor performances with the bat were overlooked because he was leading a winning side. Had he been captain of an Australian team, no such slack would have been afforded him. Greig was no longer leading England. He was leading a World XI in Australia in a thoroughly Australian competition. He wasn't worth his place in the side and Ian Chappell made sure that he did not forget it. Questions were being asked both publicly and privately about his position.

To Tony, a competitive animal down to his bootlaces, this must have been an excruciating time. Not so long ago, he was the leading all-rounder in world cricket. Now he couldn't buy a wicket or a run. All cricketers lose 'form' from time to time but this prolonged period of drought was worrying and quite frankly embarrassing. He decided to drop himself from the team. He was encouraged by his supporters not to but on this occasion he would not be dissuaded. While the game progressed, Tony was seen in his light blue helmet practising in the nets under the watchful eye of Garry Sobers. Had his brother Ian not been bent over his books at Cambridge University he would no doubt have been flown out to Australia to bowl from 18 yards. Tony was determined to prove to himself that this barren spell was no more than a blip in his career. He was not finished yet, the four-hour net session proclaimed.

However, Old Father Time waits for no man. There was a final flourish in store for Tony Greig but in truth his cricketing days were drawing to a close. Why? He was of no great age (32). He was still fit and had remained relatively injury-free throughout his career. This prolonged net session with Sobers gave credence to the impression that here was a man determined to find his way back to form. What had gone wrong? Several theories did the rounds at the time. First, he was never that good a player in the first place. In other words, his figures had flattered him. Nonsense, I say. He may not have had the same natural talent and flair as one or two of his contemporaries or other gifted all-rounders about to burst on the scene (Imran, Kapil Dev, Hadlee, Botham) but all those who played with him are adamant that he made the very best of his abilities and at his peak was fit to rank with the best. Another assumption was that Tony played better in front of a large audience and WSC crowds, for the most part, were meagre. There is some truth in this; he was a showman after all. Furthermore, he was hardly ever called to the bridge, his natural station, to steer a sinking ship to safety. The World XI was rarely holed below the water line. For further elucidation, I put the question to Bruce Francis, by now a close colleague and firm friend of Tony's, and he put forward a variety of explanations.

'He was at Kerry's beck and call 24/7,' was Francis's blunt summation. He went on to elaborate, 'He was a WSC administrator, first and foremost. He was the media front man, as well as fulfilling his commitments to individual sponsors, doing TV commercials and personal appearances.' This was confirmed by Derek Underwood. 'Out there, he was an administrator as well as a cricketer,' he said. 'If there was a problem, he had the job of sorting it out.' Furthermore, Tony had a contract with a radio station, reporting on cricket across the board, including WSC matches, the Ashes series and Sheffield Shield games. This went on air every morning at 7.30 and was 'an onerous task', Francis said. He describes exactly how: 'I wrote the report. I then picked up Tony's PA and drove her to the studio. She would telex it to Tony's hotel room wherever he was staying. Tony then phoned the radio station and recorded the report. I had to stay to check it was acceptable. Sometimes we did three or four takes.' The first year of WSC wasn't too bad, he maintained, but the second year 'was a nightmare because play under lights didn't finish until 10.30. I then had to write the report, pick up his PA to go to the radio station for her to create the telex and send it to Tony. On such occasions, he never received the telex until after midnight.' Midnight – the witching hour for professional cricketers. The fabled captain of Hampshire,

Colin Ingleby-Mackenzie, once gave this explanation of his curfew rules: 'I want my boys in bed by midnight. If they're not, I insist they come home.' Tony wasn't gallivanting at midnight; he was still working.

By any yardstick, that was a heavy workload. 'He had too many things on his plate,' was Francis's perspective, 'and he wasn't able to concentrate enough on his cricket.' Much as Tony tried to explain this to his team-mates, that he was working hard on their behalf, there were still those who thought his priorities were skewed. His attention on the job in hand, captaining his team and contributing on the field, was being distracted by his off-field commitments. He should recalibrate his loyalties – no wonder he isn't getting any runs, they said, he's never here at nets. Francis would have none of this. 'Tony was the nanny to every overseas player who had a whinge,' he snorted, 'he had to deal with a lot of organisation, the pitches, the grounds, the small crowds, trying to keep everybody happy.'

There may have been another reason for his lack of form. He was no longer playing for England. He was no longer captain of England. The team he had built and led so successfully were carrying all before them in the same country at the same time. They even crossed paths on occasions. In Perth, as the MCC team arrived, WSC players were also present in the airport lounge. Tony wondered how he would be greeted by his erstwhile team-mates. He should have had no fears. Friendships forged on tours and in dressing rooms are not easily broken. He had a long chat over coffee with Mike Brearley and even Geoffrey Boycott came over with a smile and a handshake. Tony had thrown in his lot with Kerry Packer and never regretted his decision but he would have had a heart of stone not to feel a pang of nostalgia in such circumstances.

At last Tony managed a score in a one-day match against the West Indians at the SCG. Coming in with his side in deep trouble at 49/7, he pulled things around with a brave and resourceful score of 62. 'It was the first time I've ever been cheered by an Australian crowd,' he wryly commented later. Such an innings only underlined Bruce Francis's point about Tony, his special abilities and his struggles in WSC. 'He was a back-to-the-wall sort of cricketer and that was rarely needed playing for the World XI.' This innings was to prove to be his highest score in WSC. He was not to know it of course, that this really was the end, but it did restore confidence enough for him to feel able to retake his place in the side for the remaining Supertests.

The climax of the season was played out in early February 1979. The preliminary rounds of the triangular tournament had brought together a final between Australia and the World XI to be played at the SCG. It turned out to be a low-scoring game on an unpredictable pitch, ingredients that often produce fascinating cricket in a two-innings match. Australia were bowled out for 172, with le Roux taking 5-57 and Procter 3-33. The World XI fared no better, being dismissed for 168. Dennis Lillee was tormentor-in-chief, taking 5-51. At one stage, it looked as if Australia would seize a critical initiative but a last-wicket stand of 64 between le Roux and Underwood spared the blushes of Tony's team. In their second innings, Australia could only muster 219 in the face of hostile fast bowling from Imran Khan (3-60) and le Roux (4-44). The target for victory and the $100,000 cheque was 224, if attained, the highest score of the match.

That they achieved it was wholly owing to Barry Richards. He told me about the innings that he regards as one of his best. It was nothing like the swashbuckling double hundred at Perth the previous season; this was one born of extreme pressure and the toughest of circumstances. 'If I got out, the Aussies would win,' he said simply, 'if I stayed in, we would win. It was as simple as that.' Simply expressed but not easily done. It was a searching test of skill and temperament, the sort of challenge that Barry relished. 'It was no blitzkrieg, I can tell you. It was bloody hard work.' Chewing his fingernails and smoking countless cigarettes, Tony was wracked with nerves yet full of admiration as he sat in the players' enclosure, padded up, desperately hoping Richards would not get out. He did not. His undefeated 101 ushered his team home by five wickets.

Barry recounted to me an incident while he was out there in the middle, one that made his eyes crinkle with amusement but which informed me about what was to happen later in the award ceremony. 'Ian Chappell was giving me a lot of stick while I was grinding it out,' Barry said, 'telling me it was the worst innings he'd ever seen. "Worth $100,000," I replied. That shut him up!' In fact he and Barry got on well. Chappell respected Barry as one of the greats of the game, not something he was prepared to bestow on Tony Greig. With two runs needed for victory, with Richards and Imran at the crease and Tony next in, Chappell put himself on to bowl and delivered the widest of wides that has ever been seen in a cricket match, the ball hitting the boundary board without anybody moving a muscle. Why? Apparently, he and Lillee had been desperate to get Tony to the wicket in order to rough him up a bit, even though the chance of victory had long disappeared. It was all part of the ongoing feud between Tony and his opposite number and it was about to boil over once more. *But why the four wides, Barry?* 'I guess he was just hacked off at losing and wanted to deny me the honour of hitting the winning runs,' he philosophically replied.

At the conclusion of the match, Chappell walked down the line of World XI players shaking their hands and congratulating them on their success. Tony Greig he cut dead with these words, 'Great contribution from you – again!'

Before the match, Tony had promised everyone he would score a hundred. He made 0. Chappell lounged about during the presentations, all the while smoking a cigar, a cantankerous demagogue to the end. Tony's disappointment at his own contributions to the triumph of his team was in part recompensed by the winnings and the self-evident success of the venture for which he had laboured hard and long. It was a deeply satisfying moment.

The spat with Chappell had left a nasty taste in the mouth. The quarrel lasted well into their time as co-commentators long after WSC. What lay at the heart of it? Who better to ask than Bruce Francis, who knew both well? The rivalry had spilled over into mutual dislike, he reckoned, when he, Francis, had made a request to Kerry Packer before the game for 30 tickets to entertain sponsors of the match. Packer agreed so long as he could write Tony's column, ghosted by Francis, in *The Sunday Herald* for him. Francis acquiesced. It was, surprise, surprise, a provocative piece, intended 'to wind up the Australian public so that they would come to the game'. Ian Chappell, believing that Tony had written it or at least been behind it, took offence. Hence the snub over the handshake and Tony's response in ejecting him from the dressing room. 'When questioned later about the snub to Tony by a journalist,' Francis told me, 'Ian said that Tony should not have been in the team.' And so it rumbled on.

That total victory for WSC was just over the horizon, Tony did not let on. In the meantime, Brearley's England team had retained the Ashes by defeating Australia in the fourth Test and the Australian Cricket Board now had two dead Tests to sell to the public. The ACB were losing money, the contract for television rights with ABC was up for renewal and the first cracks in the façade of the establishment were beginning to appear. With hindsight, it was just as well. The WSC players were knackered. It had been a long and gruelling two years and most of them were now in their 30s and were starting to feel the strain. Although their contracts were for three years, it is not inconceivable that some of them might have called it a day, resigned and retired from the game. It only took a quick glance around the respective dressing rooms for the more discerning of them to ask themselves what plans were in place for Packer to replenish his teams with fresh talent. Apparently none. Packer was gambling that the endgame would come sooner than later and, as usual, he was right.

On Wednesday 19 April, Tony was giving a speech in Adelaide at a lunch in aid of the Epilepsy Association. He had some news and as always he was finding it difficult to keep it to himself. 'A compromise is imminent,' he said. 'I will only be happy when it is all resolved.' He didn't have long to wait. On 30 May, a news report stated that Channel 9 had been awarded exclusive rights to broadcast cricket in Australia and that Kerry Packer had gained a ten-year contract to promote and market the game solely through his company. Game, set and match to Packer. He had got what he wanted. Contrary to what some feared, he had no desire to take over the running of the game. His sights were trained on exclusive TV rights and on nothing else. There was nothing left to do but to wind down the operation, pay off the remaining year of the players' contracts and concentrate on dragging the broadcasting of cricket kicking and screaming into the new technological era.

'Believe me, nothing except a battle lost can be half so melancholy as a battle won.' So announced the Duke of Wellington as he cast his eye over the battlefield the day following his victory at Waterloo. I doubt

Kerry Packer surveyed the scene with quite the same melancholy – nor Tony Greig, whose feelings of justification can only be imagined – but in every conflict there are casualties. Revolutions are rarely bloodless. Who were the winners and losers?

At first, not much seemed to change. Everybody breathed a huge sigh of relief. Test cricket resumed and the 'rebels' were reintegrated back into their home dressing rooms. But it was not long before the repercussions of the Packer schism began to be felt. One-day cricket proliferated, more and more grounds installed floodlighting for day-night games, pitch technology advanced, helmets and protective equipment improved, coloured clothing, white balls, pink stumps, jingles, cheerleaders, fireworks, all the razzmatazz of the circus – the game today is unrecognisable from the sepia-tinted pictures of yesteryear. The Packer Revolution did not bring all this about on its own, it is true to say. Its importance lay in what it made possible. For the first time the players had an expectation of what they were worth and the insatiable marketing of the game has fuelled and financed those expectations. 'All along,' Greg Chappell told me, 'we were not seeking to take over the game ourselves. We just wanted how it was run to be changed. We wanted respect.' There is little doubt that the drive by both Chappells and Tony Greig to legitimise and raise the profile of professional cricketers everywhere was a success.

Most of the Packer players were of an age to benefit from the better salaries, bigger prize money and larger appearance fees almost straightaway. As Tony pointed out, the fee for a Test match immediately went up from £210 to £1,000, soon to be raised to £1,500. Today, England players are not paid on a Test-by-Test basis; they are all centrally contracted which can be worth in excess of £1 million per annum. Would this have happened anyway, had not Packer stuck his oar in? 'Probably,' Tony agreed, 'but it would have taken them a hundred years.' Even allowing for his penchant for hyperbole, was Tony right? Was his firm belief that what he was doing would, *inter alia*, be for the benefit of all professional cricketers? One person who is in no doubt about the Packer effect is Barry Richards. 'Greigy could see this as plainly as anyone,' he declared unequivocally. 'He was a trailblazer, though he got little thanks for it at the time.' John Snow is in agreement. 'Look, the conditions were ripe for change,' he said, 'it would have come sooner or later. The door was ajar but Greigy kicked it open.' Almost all the former colleagues of Tony's to whom I spoke are puzzled, and even a little sad, that he got so little praise for what he did, especially in this country. It is true that recognition did eventually come his way but it was late in the day. The charge of betrayal, bolstered by his abandonment of his Hove home to take up permanent residency in Sydney, took a long time to live down. The press took no prisoners. There was a headline in *The Times* on the occasion of Kerry Packer's death in 2005: 'The man who took a bulldozer to the sacred temple of sport.' In the public's mind, there was no doubt who was driving the bulldozer. Tony's friends in the game, of which there were many, were less censorious.

The winding up of WSC had another sombre outcome. For Tony, that was it. His race was run. He never played again. That entry on the scorecard of the final of the triangular Supertest series, A.W. Greig c Marsh, b Lillee 0, was his last hurrah. Others returned with success to the international arena. Some went from strength to strength. A few, the South Africans, had no Test career to return to. Tony's fall from grace must have been a hard thing to bear. His decline was overshadowed by the meteoric rise of Ian Botham. When idle talk turns to the great English all-rounders, Greig's name rarely comes up. If it does, it is usually at the tail-end of a list starting with Grace, with a mention of Hammond, through to the modern titans, Botham, Flintoff and Stokes. This is a travesty. 'People forget what a great player Greigy was,' says Bob Willis wistfully, a view wholeheartedly endorsed by Alan Knott. 'The best batting all-rounder England have ever had,' he said. 'You can look at averages – and his stand to rank with anybody's – but in the end they don't tell the full story. Those who are great thrive under the greatest pressure. And he played against the very best.'

'There are three kinds of lies: lies, damned lies and statistics.' Wrongly attributed to Mark Twain, this sardonic comment on the persuasive power of numbers was coined by Benjamin Disraeli. Bruce Francis's assessment was that Tony was essentially a back-to-the-wall player, at his best when the pressure was at its most intense and not too worried about his figures. 'Level of difficulty', as Barry Richards said. Barry told me that he always had the utmost contempt for county batsmen who would fill their boots playing against the weaker sides – the universities, festival teams, MCC matches – in order to boost their averages for better end-of-season inspection. Yet averages, especially Test averages, are not wholly untrustworthy. Let us have a look at them in an attempt to place Tony Greig in his rightful place in the pantheon of great English all-rounders. WG Grace, Wilfred Rhodes and George Hirst belong to a different world altogether so I shall set them aside. Wally Hammond was undoubtedly one of history's greatest batsmen (58.45), who took useful wickets (83 in 85 Tests), but a true all-rounder? Trevor Bailey, Raymond Illingworth and Fred Titmus were essentially bowlers who made useful runs. Comparing like-for-like, we have Ian Botham, Andrew Flintoff and Ben Stokes. Stokes is still playing so he must be discounted. Flintoff had a batting average of 31.77 and a bowling average of 32.78. A doughty warrior in England's cause undoubtedly, but if we count the accepted gold standard of true class as an all-rounder being that the batting average should always exceed the bowling average then Flintoff falls just short. Which leaves us with two contenders for the crown. Botham's batting average was 33.54 and his bowling average 28.40. Greig's was respectively 40.43 and 32.20. Conclusive? I think not. In most people's eyes, Botham attained the heights of greatness more often than Greig. He would be the people's choice. But if you factor in Greig's inspirational captaincy (Botham's tenure as England's captain was less than harmonious), the balance starts to reassert itself. Let me just leave it that Tony Greig stood fit to rank with the best and it is a crying shame that fact is not more widely appreciated.

Before we put WSC to bed, there is another unpardonable oversight in history's assessment of the Packer Revolution. Tony was not alone among the players who considered the cricket to be the most challenging, intense and competitive they have ever played; 30 or 40 of the world's best players going at it hammer and tongs, no quarter asked and most certainly none given, provided some of the most riveting passages of play ever seen. The tragedy was that not many people were watching. The travesty is that it features as no more than a footnote in the statistical history of the game. WSC matches were not considered to be first-class, a status that has not even been bestowed retrospectively 40 years later. Viv Richards considered WSC to be the hardest he's ever played. Barry Richards told me, 'It was brutal combat out there.' Barry averaged 79.14 in the Supertests; Viv was second in the averages at 55.69. You would have thought that the world's two premier batsmen at the time might have known a thing or two about standards. Not to give WSC official first-class status is in effect to treat it as if it never happened which is, quite frankly, ludicrous.

That summer of 1979, cricket in England returned to normal with the Prudential World Cup and a four-Test series against India. Cricketers from WSC for the most part returned to their counties, their countries and their homes. For Tony Greig a completely new life beckoned. He always maintained he had no regrets. He spoke of having 'found contentment … at peace with myself and never been happier'. Methinks he doth protest too much. Very few top performers quit the stage without regret. He was 33 and restless for a new challenge. He was never one to look back, always ready to embrace new ideas, to set new goals. But nothing can replace the smell of the greasepaint and the roar of the crowd and he would not have been the man I think he was if he had not shed a quiet tear for a life signalling his own fours. Henceforth, he was going to signal other players' fours from the commentary box.

Chapter 11

The Commentary Box
1980–2012

*'Clearly the West Indies are going to play
their normal game, which is what they
normally do.'* (Tony Greig)

*'He's blazed that one through the off-side field. Go
and fetch that!'* (Tony Greig)

*'The cor pork's full and there's going to be plenty of
cornage here today.'* (Tony Greig ... or was it?)

I HAVE a very good friend who loves his cricket. He is a regular
visitor Down Under at times of the year which, odd to relate,
exactly coincide with Ashes series. One year, on his return, he
came round to my house in a state of considerable excitement. His
mood could not have been born of pleasure at England's performance
in the series – they had been well and truly hammered.

'Have you heard the 12th Man?'

'Don't talk to me about 12th man. It was a position in the
Hampshire side that I filled more times than I care to remember.'

'Yes, what was it like, Murt, running the bath for Gordon
Greenidge and posting letters for Barry Richards?'

'Huh.'

'Anyway, the 12th Man ....'

'What do you know about being 12th man, Jamie? You've told me that at your club you're lucky to get 11 players at the ground, let alone 12.'

'No, listen. I mean, listen to this.'

He handed me a CD. It was indeed titled '*12th Man*', roughly, in pencil, clearly a pirated copy. I confess I put it away without further thought, not wishing to be reminded of drawing baths and running errands. It was only when my two sons started humouring me with their impressions of cricket commentators that I sat up and took notice. 'Bruce Reid! Oh my Gord, 'e's snapped in orf!' one of them exclaimed. The references were obvious to me. The bowler, Bruce Reid, was indeed of spectacularly thin physique. And the voice was undoubtedly Tony Greig's. 'How did you learn to take off him?' I asked. '*12th Man*, Dad, you've got to listen to it.'

So I did. I rescued the CD from a dusty drawer and played it. By the end of the recording, I had a stitch in my side through helpless laughter. I subsequently discovered that *The Twelfth Man* was a series of comic sketches by a well-known Australian satirist, Billy Birmingham. He was a skilled impersonator and his favourite subjects were the denizens of Channel 9's commentary box, in particular Richie Benaud, Bill Lawry and Tony Greig, presumably because they had such distinctive accents and speaking styles. Birmingham's recordings were hugely successful in Australia but took a little longer to impact on the British public. His skits were indeed humorous, often scatological and frequently profane but his impersonations of cricket personalities of note were spot on. His mimicry of Tony was uncanny. What struck me forcibly wasn't so much the Sorf Efrican accent, which he had down to a T, but the sheer, unbridled enthusiasm of the personality behind the voice. Tony never did reserve, reticence, restraint, and Birmingham captured this characteristic perfectly. Tony was already a well-known personality in Australia; *The Twelfth Man* sent his profile into the stratosphere.

Cricket lovers of my generation had grown up listening to a breed of commentators whose *modus operandi* was by and large one of understatement. Rex Alston, John Arlott, Jim Laker, Jim Swanton,

Peter West and broadcasters of their ilk tended not to get excited and gild the lily. Brian Johnston might get a fit of the giggles from time to time but for the most part they assiduously played their role as a calm and dispassionate analyser of the action. 'If you have nothing to add to the picture on the screen, don't say it,' was the maxim of the doyen of the commentary box, Richie Benaud, whose career incidentally spanned both this earlier era and the later, more conversational style. When did Peter West metamorphose into 'Bumble' (David Lloyd)?

In England it took a while. There had been no internecine strife in the broadcasting world – with cricket, at any rate – as there had been in Australia. The Test and County Cricket Board had no quarrel with the BBC – there was no opposition – and cricket continued to be televised by the national broadcaster. It was not until Sky (originally BSkyB) thrust its foot in the door in the 1990s that BBC's hegemony was at last challenged. Eventually, Sky took over the broadcasting of cricket in England in 1994 and the BBC was left with nothing after 60 years of uninterrupted domination. It is true to say that the new kid on the block swiftly took its lead straight from Channel 9, which had been ploughing its merry furrow since WSC. It is ironic that Channel 9 has recently lost its rights for excusive coverage of cricket in Australia to Channel 7, those rights so fiercely striven for 40 years ago. Tony Greig and Richie Benaud had died, Bill Lawry had retired and the replacements, former players and captains, lacked the sparkle and charisma of their predecessors. It was felt that Channel 9's coverage had become stale; the same names, the same faces, the same gags no longer generated excitement. Everything, including the commentators (no women, for example, nobody of colour, nobody who had not been a former Test player), had become middle-aged and past its sell-by date. In short, it had failed to reinvent itself. Rather like the ACB and the BBC, it had to cede to a new generation eager to move things along – a salutary lesson for all broadcasters. Nothing lasts forever.

Back in 1979, it was all so different. Tony Greig was as excited by the challenges that lay ahead as anyone. He took his lead from his boss. Cricket was a game to be marketed aggressively and sold on television. The days when the game was run by well-meaning amateurs were finished. Cricket was now a business and had to be run by businessmen. Tony's defection to Packer had nothing to do with any attempt to take over the game; he just wanted the players to have more of a say in what was going on and more of a share in the profits that were being made. He also believed that the marketing, of which television was a large part, should be modernised. Working for Channel 9, he was fascinated by the way broadcasting was changing, with the introduction of many innovations and inventions. It wasn't just commentating on the action in the middle that intrigued him; he became interested in the production of the programmes, what went on behind, as much as what happened in front of, the camera. Such things as creative style, camera angles, interview spots, use of video recording, calling which cameras to go live, instructions from the producer in his earpiece – he had a hand in everything and was always searching for improvement. It all boiled down to teamwork, he concluded, which wasn't a lot different to captaining a cricket team and he loved that. He believed, correctly, that viewers only watch if the product is good and Channel 9 was the best in the business in his opinion. He wrote at the time he was involved in WSC, 'Without the players, there is no game; without the spectators there is no game.' By now, he might just as well have added, without the viewers there is no game and he did his best to ensure that the viewers were kept happy.

Far from shying away from the new technology, Tony embraced it. There is an irony here because he was no 'techie', according to his family. Like everybody of his generation, computers arrived late on his screen but though not particularly expert at finding his way around a computer, he fully endorsed any new gimmick or concept it threw up. He approved the spate of cameras situated around the ground and enjoyed playing with all the fancy gizmos at his disposal. Not always did it all go to plan, much to the amusement of his fellow commentators. It was the early days of animation (remember the dreaded duck quack-quacking its way across the screen when a batsman was out for 0?) and Tony was trying to explain to his viewers why he believed the slip cordon was standing too deep. With the aid of cartoon-sized mannequins on-screen, he tried to reset the field. Except the fielders simply would not go where they were told. As the mirth backstage bubbled over, he wrestled with the uncooperative little fellows until finally, he lost control of his team and chaos ensued. 'No, we don't wornt him to go there, that's for sure,' cried the exasperated puppet master, 'that wouldn't help at orl.'

Despite the odd mishap, he opened his mind to the many different ways the technicians sought to improve the viewer experience. Multi-angle replays, file footage, speed guns, super slo-mo, pitch maps, graphic overlays, leading on to hot spot, snickometer, Hawk Eye and Decision Review System, were all innovations which helped him to do what he loved doing most – talking about cricket. Channel 9 did not of course bring about all these novelties but it certainly paved the way for the huge advances made in the way cricket was televised. Just take a look on YouTube at any recording of Tony's innings. The strokeplay is fine and dandy, as flamboyant as you would expect, but the recordings seem so dull, stale and unimaginative compared with the pictures that we have become accustomed to these days. Channel 9, with Tony at the helm, was quicker than most to appreciate that cricket broadcasting needed a shot in the arm and he was determined it got it.

An integral part of the new, viewer experience was the role of the commentator. Tony was aware from the outset that he was in the entertainment business and his job as a conduit between picture and viewer was more than just an interpreter of the action and a mouthpiece for facts and figures. The world had changed since the days of carefully enunciated vowels and restrained delivery and Tony led the charge. As an example of different ways, different mores, let me take you back to newsreel footage of Jim Laker's historic performance in the Old Trafford Test of 1956. He strides off the pitch having just taken all ten Australian wickets in the second innings, to go with the nine he took in the first, thus recording the finest bowling figures of all time, 19-90. He takes his sweater from the umpire and slings it over his shoulder as he walks towards the pavilion. A few team-mates offer hearty handshakes; others pat him on the back. It is a scene almost surreal in its inhibition of emotion. Today he would have been lost at the bottom of a mass pile-on by ten hysterical colleagues. As a commentator, Laker was – unsurprisingly – similarly understated, very knowledgeable, very perceptive and very professional but excitement rarely entered his voice. Tony was of a different breed.

Back here in England, we had largely lost sight of Tony Greig once he quit Sussex to make his home in Sydney. We were vaguely aware that he had become a commentator on Australian television but his voice was muted, distant, 10,000 miles away. Reports filtered back from those who had visited Australia and occasionally highlights would be broadcast from that country during Ashes series. He seemed a bit excitable to conservative English ears but we concluded that histrionic delivery was simply the Australian way. It took a while before British reserve started to fall away. And then came Billy Birmingham and *The Twelfth Man* and suddenly Tony Greig and his style of commentating, together with those of the rest of the Channel 9 team, became instantly recognisable. *The Twelfth Man* was a series of satirical sketches, employing humour, irony and exaggeration and the reason for its success – it is the same for all satire that hits the spot – was that the characters were believable. The Tony Greig in *The Twelfth Man* is undeniably Tony Greig. That is not to say that it is a faithful portrayal of the man, an eerily accurate impersonation of him – Birmingham is not an actor playing Tony Greig in a drama. We are sucked into the humour by the fact that Tony Greig *might* have said this, *might* have reacted like that, *might* have knocked the microphone over in his excitement. If he had not been a character, if he had been insipid and dull, he would not have been worthy of mimicry. Imitation is the sincerest form of flattery.

That may be so but it takes a big man – and on this occasion I am not talking about Tony's height – to shrug off satire that is personal. Remember *Spitting Image?* Mrs Thatcher tried to put on a brave face whenever she was confronted by the unnervingly accurate puppet used in the show to mock her; the rictus smile was always a little forced. She clearly *hated* the lampooning of her image but calculated it would do no good to her reputation if she took offence. She had to grin and bear it and Mrs Thatcher wasn't very good at that. Tony Greig got the joke, was unflustered by the unrestrained leg-pulling it generated and broadly speaking went along with it. How do we know this? Because no less an informed observer than Billy Birmingham said so himself. 'He saw the positive side of the whole *Twelfth Man* thing instantly, that Channel 9's cricket coverage had become an iconic broadcast and both the commentary team and the coverage were benefitting from this series of recordings this idiot was doing.' Not all in the Channel 9 commentary box saw it in quite the same way. Richie Benaud, perhaps because he came from an earlier generation, did not approve of its profanities and did not take kindly to having his wife mentioned in the sketches. But it was unobjectionable for Tony. He'd heard worse in the dressing room.

By now, as a cricket commentator, he was a well-known front man, a considerable national figurehead. We in England sat up and took notice.

In search of empirical evidence, I decided to go and see for myself. In truth, the reason for my visit to Australia in the New Year holiday of 2004 was not solely to catch Tony Greig commentating on Channel 9 but to visit my son, who was on his gap year working at Geelong Grammar School. Australia were playing India that winter and we went to watch day one of the Sydney Test. Tendulkar had been short of runs earlier in the series (it happens to even the best) and it had been mooted in the press and media, Tony included, that the Aussie pacemen might at long last have got the measure of the Indian maestro. Tendulkar had already featured in some of the most memorable quotations of Tony Greig's commentary career back in 1998, during a one-day series in Sharjah. Tendulkar had launched a mighty blow off the 6ft 6in Australian off-spinner, Tom Moody: 'The little man has hit the big fella for six. He's horf his size!' The remark had caused no little amusement amongst his fellow commentators, as had a later observation when India had won: 'They're dorncing in the aisles in Sharjah!' But on this tour, Tendulkar was struggling.

Sometime after lunch, Tendulkar came to the crease. Brett Lee, who had been bowling well, was unleashed at him. What followed was one of the most fascinating passages of play in a Test match I have ever witnessed first hand. Tendulkar, easing himself back into form, totally eschewed any cross-bat shot; he chose to hit the ball – those that he did not leave alone – solely in the V between mid-on and mid-off. Frequently the ball went straight to the fielder but that did not faze him. It wasn't runs he was after but occupation. It was slow, not a lot was happening, the crowd got bored and restless (most lost interest and indulged in herculean drinking competitions) but I couldn't take my eyes off the physical and mental battle taking place out in the middle. At the close of play, Tendulkar walked off undefeated on 73, a tired man but still there, ready to fight another day. On day two, he scored an unforgettable 241 not out and I watched most of it on Channel 9.

First, I noticed that the 'team' had not changed since the original quartet of Tony Greig, Richie Benaud, Bill Lawry and Ian Chappell had strapped on their pads some 20 years previously. It had been added to but the core of the programme remained the same. There was jovial banter, nostalgic reminiscing and much use of catchphrases and in-jokes. The camaraderie within the commentary box was obvious and tangible. Whatever you thought about the relentless hyperbole and the naked bias — oh, all right, the lack of criticism of the home players — there was unmistakeably excellent camerawork and high production values on view as well as all the bells and whistles with which the viewer had now become familiar. Rarely was the picture on the screen allowed to speak for itself. If the Trappist monks are required to take a vow of silence, the Channel 9 team had taken clamour as their order's prescription. At first, it grated on English ears, but if you relaxed into it, as I grudgingly did, the energy and enthusiasm of the commentators started to grow on you. The synergy, the relationship, the teamwork between the pair at the microphone was key. Benaud was always the supreme professional, known universally as the voice of cricket and would grace any commentary box. The partnership, characterised by genuine friendship, between Tony Greig and Bill Lawry was legendary, one the solid opener, the other the mercurial all-rounder. They played off each other expertly, disagreeing about all and sundry which often made for entertaining listening. But what about Tony Greig and Ian Chappell and their enduring feud?

Mark Greig touched upon the controversy, bringing a wry smile to my face in view of my previous occupation as a schoolmaster when he described them as 'behaving like petulant schoolchildren'. Bruce Francis recounted for me a telling anecdote about the pair's mutual loathing. It was in the early 1980s when he and Tony were flying to Hobart. The flight stopped off in Melbourne and Ian Chappell came on board. 'He didn't see us because we were in first-class and he took his seat in cattle class. We stopped again in Launceston and we saw Chappell stand up, retrieve his hand luggage from the overhead locker and disembark. "He thinks we're in Hobart," I said. "We ought to tell him." Tony said, "Shut up," so I said nothing as Chappell got off the plane. Not sure exactly what happened but I can imagine the look on the taxi driver's face if Ian had summoned one and asked to be taken to his hotel in Hobart. Mighty long fare from Launceston. Anyway, he made it back to the plane just in time before the gates were shut. He was the last to board and he looked hot and bothered.' *So how did the two of them manage to work together?* 'Aw look, they buried the hatchet a couple of years later and actually became close friends.' Mark said that the penny dropped when they realised that they would be spending many hours side by side in the commentary box. Chappell realised that the ongoing quarrel would have a detrimental effect on the quality of their work. In a generous tribute after Tony's death, he said this about their working relationship, 'Because I had been the main offender over the years, I thought it was up to me to get back on good terms with him. Nothing was ever spoken but we just got on with our job. It was sort of a case of that was then and this is now.' At the end of his piece, he wrote, 'We will miss him greatly.' For his part, Tony shrugged his shoulders and said, 'Life's too short.'

I have yet to meet a cricketer who has not missed playing the game once Old Father Time has sent him on his way back to the pavilion for the last time. Tom Graveney told me that he was eternally grateful to the BBC when he was invited on to the commentary team after his retirement. 'They had given back to me the game I loved,' he said. My guess is that the current team of Sky commentators (almost exclusively ex-England captains, you will notice) feel the same. Certainly Tony Greig would have been in full sympathy with Graveney's comment. His abiding passion for the game never dulled and his new role behind the microphone kept him in touch with the players, the trends, the developments, the politics, the crises and the human stories behind the action on the field of play. He embraced his job with all the boyish enthusiasm he displayed as a player. Ever since a young lad, he had energetically pursued adventure and drama. He was a man of action and hated apathy, boredom, lethargy. If nothing's happening, let's try something, *anything.* That was his philosophy as a captain and that was the philosophy he carried forward into the commentary box. The game of cricket is played out over long periods of time, days even. There are bound to be stretches of time during play, its inevitable *longueurs,* when neither side is in the ascendancy and each is striving to get on top without ceding the initiative to the other. Tony was not a patient man. He would prefer to seize, or attempt to seize, the initiative than to play a waiting game. He was easily bored and as such probably sympathised with the viewer who was equally unexcited by the game of chess being played out in the middle.

Ever mindful of the business he was in, he saw his role primarily as that of an entertainer. Not the resident clown, you understand, but an intelligent and informed interpreter who had a sense of humour, a predilection for a bit of fun and one who was prepared to liven up proceedings when they got a little dull. This he did not find difficult. It came naturally. Tony Greig never knowingly undersold himself nor the enthusiasm he had for cricket. In the commentary box, it was a rare occasion when he tamely pushed back six balls for a maiden. If six balls were delivered, he could make it sound as exciting as a hat-trick. Talking of hat-tricks, I am reminded of Shane Warne taking three in three against England at the MCG in 1994. Tony was lucky enough – it always seemed to be so – to be at the microphone for the historic moment. Excitement built, reflected in Tony's voice. 'Yes, he's goddim. Lbw. That's the end of DeFreitas!' Next ball. 'Out! Cort behind. Goddim out first ball!' The tension was almost unbearable as Warne prepared to bowl his third ball. Ian Chappell, Tony's co-commentator, was calmly setting the field he reckoned Warne should have and encouraging him to bowl the top-spinner to England's rabbit, Devon Malcolm, to bring lbw and bowled into the equation. 'For if Warnie bowls a leg break,' he drily observed, 'there's no way he's going to get an edge on it.' Tony felt constrained by no such temperateness. His voice was already an octave higher as Warne shuffled in to bowl. 'Here we go .... Yes! Aaaargh! Goddim! He's gone, he's gone, yes, he's gone! That's a hat-trick for Shane Warne and a great moment in his career! And what a catch by David Boon! You won't see many better catches at short leg than that!'

Hat-tricks, like lions on a safari, are covert beasts and rarely seen. As far as my research can uncover, there have only been 43 in over 2,000 Test matches. I never took one in my career (not even in the back garden) and I was never involved in a match when one took place. Tony Greig was indeed fortunate that he was on air when that one occurred. When I heard that he had actually been at the microphone for another Test hat-trick, I first rolled my eyes in disbelief, then laughed. That's Greigy! The occasion was India versus Australia, the venue Eden Gardens in Calcutta and the date 11 March 2001. Coincidentally, Shane Warne was again involved, only this time as a victim, not victor. Australia were cruising along nicely, well set at 252/4. Harbhajan Singh, the off-spinner, ambled up to the crease. I leave the commentary to Tony Greig. 'Ponting's on strike … big appeal! Yes, goddim! Lbw! Is he out? Ricky Ponting out lbw! Harbhajan Singh is making his comeback here.' Next ball. 'Goddim! Yes, he's goddim! Yes, he's goddim! Adam Gilchrist out first ball! The crowd here are on their feet!' Next ball. 'Right now …. Imagine the roar if he got Shane Warne …. No Indian bowler has ever taken a Test hat-trick.' Here let us pause for a second. How did he know that fact? Why should he have that statistical information at his fingertips? The man did his homework. Back to the action. 'Here we go …. Can he do it? Ohhhh – has he goddim? Has he goddim? He's going over to square leg for celebration.' Clearly the Indians thought it was a fair catch, a jolly good one in fact. Warne was unmoved. By this time replays were in use as umpire assistance. The viewers were shown the replay. The pictures were inconclusive. 'We need another angle. We need another angle here,' announced Tony. Another angle was shown. Then the red light went on and Shane Warne was on his way. 'Yes, he's given him! He's given him!' Gosh, the drama. In fact, it was not at all clear from any angle that the ball had come full toss off the face of the bat (out) or whether it had been jammed into the ground before the catch was taken (not out) but no matter. Tony Greig – and Harbhajan Singh – had his moment of glory. As an English teacher, I always discouraged the use of the exclamation mark. It can be overdone. On these occasions, you will forgive their superabundance. Tony Greig commentated in exclamation marks.

Although not entirely comfortable with this new style of commentary, I accepted it as the new fashion, much as what was happening on our television screens back home during football matches. The era of understatement was clearly over. However, Tony's impassioned descriptions of events did not immediately sit comfortably with all Australian viewers. He was criticised for his histrionic delivery from time to time but he refused to moderate his tone. He knew he had his boss's full backing. Excitement was what Kerry Packer wanted and he thoroughly approved of his protégé's skill in building the drama that was unfolding on the pitch. Viewing figures bore out his confidence and that was all he wanted. People wouldn't watch if they were bored.

Tony was rarely lost for words; in fact, they tumbled from his mouth like a box of practice balls emptied on to the grass. He knew exactly what he was talking about, he hardly missed a trick, he called it as he saw it and never let the game drift, no matter how uneventful was the play in the middle. The viewer was left with the unshakeable impression that here was a man who had played at the highest level but one who had never lost that profound enthusiasm for the game that he had as a boy. Commentating was not a day job, not an employment, not a chore but a passion. Dickie Bird, the umpire, always said, 'I 'ad best seat in 'ouse out there in t' middle.' In that case, Tony had the second best seat in the house and he loved it.

It is hard not to warm to somebody who is excited as a thrilling catch is taken or a big six is hit or a sharply-turning googly bamboozles a batsman. It takes us back to our own childhood and the unalloyed glee with which we used to get one over our brother in the Test match taking place in the back garden. Sometimes, Tony Greig reminded me of an overgrown schoolboy and I mean this in no way unkindly. 'It's miles in the air – it's a wonderful catch! The greatest catch! Unbelievable!' I bet it was too. You know it's genuine, it's exciting and it's *live*. 'Straight up in the air …. Waugh won't drop this. Oh, he's dropped it! I corn't believe it. What's going on here?' He saved the highest pitch of his voice for the highest sixes. 'That's a great shot … what a little beauty! That's gorn miles over the torp of midwicket!'

However, on one occasion his exuberance landed him in hot water. There was the occasion when the camera lingered on a young woman in the crowd. 'Oh boy, doesn't she look gorgeous!' remarked an appreciative Tony Greig. Silence ensued. The camera maintained the close-up. 'Well, go on, say something,' he encouraged his colleague. Further silence. The young lady remained engrossed in the cricket. 'He won't say anything,' Tony said about his co-commentator, Bill Lawry, 'it's got to be a pigeon before he says anything.' At length, Lawry replied, 'You dig a hole, you fill it up, mate.' All the while, there is muffled laughter off-stage.

More serious was the time when the camera panned across the ground and lighted upon a wedding party. It zoomed in on the bride, who was Asian, and the groom, who was white. 'Do you think she's been flown in?' mused our unreconstructed, definitely un-PC commentator, with a clear reference to mail order brides. Oh dear. In the considerable press criticism that flowed Tony's way, one pertinent point was frequently omitted. He never intended to share his aside with the viewers; he had fallen foul of the technical bugbear that haunts anybody who has ever put a microphone to his mouth. He believed it had been turned off and he was sharing his comment with his mates in the commentary box, not the whole country. We can all think of similar 'off air gaffes'. Prince Charles was heard to remark about Nicholas Witchell, the BBC royal correspondent, 'I can't stand the man. I mean he's so awful, he really is.' Richard Keys and Andy Gray lost their jobs as football pundits at Sky for making unfavourable remarks about female referees. Neither thought he was on air. All suffered fall-out for their unguarded comments. Frankly I found the subsequent media frenzies rather distasteful, smacking as they do of sententious hypocrisy. Once apologies have been made, why cannot people accept that slips of the tongue are occupational hazards of anybody in the public eye? Tony immediately apologised to the bride. Some viewers took offence. Some saw it as no more than a humorous aside. The majority, including his boss, just gave a shrug. That's Greigy!

The producers, and not least the boss, Kerry Packer, recognised that the double act Tony formed with Bill Lawry was gilt-edged in broadcasting terms. Lawry was a former Australian opening batsman renowned for his stubborn defence at the crease, so much so that he was once referred to by the British press as 'a corpse with pads on'. He captained his country in 25 Tests and retired in 1972 having been dropped as player and captain. Thereafter he forged a career in commentating on radio and television, joining Channel 9 when WSC started. The partnership that he formed with Tony was to endure for 35 years, up until Tony's death and was characterised by long-running but good-natured arguments and leg-pulling. Perhaps it would be more accurately described as nose-tweaking. The size of Lawry's prominent proboscis was the source of much banter between the two. For example, during a lull in play when Australia were playing South Africa, this exchange took place. They were discussing the former South African fast bowler, Peter Pollock. 'You think of Pollock,' said Tony, 'and you think of those 15 stitches on your head, just above your eye.' Short pause. 'Thank goodness he didn't get my nose,' admitted a rueful Lawry. Dot ball. Tony couldn't resist it. 'By the way, before we get back to the cricket, that's a minor miracle he didn't get your nose, there's no doubt about that.' The producer cut to the camera on the other side of the ground peering in through the window of the commentary box. Both men were grinning hugely.

Anybody who makes public speaking his stock-in-trade will understand the risk of making verbal blunders. For the commentator with no fixed script to follow and at the mercy of events as they unfold, the pitfalls are ever present. Name me a single reporter, commentator, interviewer or pundit who has never got it wrong, mangled his words or mixed his metaphors. They cause amusement at the time – notwithstanding the blushes of the perpetrator – and often add to the popularity, if not sometimes to the mystique, of the culprit. Tony was no exception. How about this for an example of unconscious malapropism: 'In the back of Hughes's mind must be the thought that he will dornce down the piss and mitch one.' This amusing bit of tautology of Tony's we can all recognise and understand: 'Clearly the West Indies are going to play their normal game, which is what they normally do.' Anybody who scoffs at these mistakes has never been behind a microphone. The wonder is that there is not a compendium of Tony's verbal infelicities, given the amount of time he was on air but in truth they were few. He may have regarded himself primarily as an entertainer but he was professional to his fingertips. 'He worked hard at his job,' said Mark Greig, 'and did his homework.'

Tony loved commentating and never took his position for granted. In the same way he drove himself to make the most of his abilities on the field of play, he strove to be the very best behind the microphone. He researched personal details of the players before a match, perhaps not rivalling the English football commentator, John Motson (Motty in the Sheepskin Coat) for an encyclopaedic knowledge of sporting trivia but he had enough facts and figures to hand to fill in any awkward gaps. I particularly enjoyed this exchange on air with Michael Holding:

Greig (knowledgeably): 'Brian Lara called his daughter Sydney after he had scored that wonderful double hundred in Sydney.'

Pause

Holding (drily): 'Just as well he wasn't playing in Lahore.'

Another example of Tony's careful preparation was his assiduous practising of the pronunciation of the names of Sri Lankan players, many of which were real tongue twisters. This may or may not have contributed to his huge popularity in that country, a place he visited many times, but it was something the players appreciated. Unlike his alter ego in *The Twelfth Man* series, he didn't often get it wrong. In my research for this book, I discovered that he was appointed in 2010 official brand ambassador for tourism in Sri Lanka. That is one of the awards in his life of which I was completely unaware. How come? He first visited the island for a stopover on the journey from India to Australia for the Centenary Test in 1977 with the MCC but that was a brief sojourn. The love affair – it was entirely reciprocal – must have dated from the 1996 World Cup. The Sri Lankans, despite the presence of several talented players, were still new to the top table of international cricket and were considered rank outsiders. Tony didn't agree. In one of the earlier rounds, he had this to say about them: 'I just love the way these little Sri Lankans play. I really think they can win this World Cup if they play well.' Prophetic words. They demolished Australia in the final. One ball from Warne was deposited over the square-leg boundary by Ranatunga for a big six. Tony's enthusiasm knew no bounds. 'These Sri Lankans are giving the Aussies a real hiding' and at the conclusion of play during the presentation ceremony, he called their victory 'a little fairy tale'. His growing legion of Sri Lankan admirers for once disagreed with him; it had been a *huge* fairy tale. According to Mark, his father loved the place, wasting no opportunity on air to sing the praises of its mangoes and pineapples, its seafood, its beaches, its golf courses. When he was appointed brand ambassador, his friends wondered why the official recognition had come so late; he had been unofficially filling that role for years. Mark believed that his father found peace in the country and serenity amongst its people. 'Sri Lanka taught Dad calmness,' he said. When news of Tony's illness reached the island, prayers and blessings were offered up for his recovery and the outpouring of grief at his death, not just from former Sri Lankan players, but also from ordinary people in the cities and in the villages, was genuine and widespread.

Tony's mind may have got a rest on holiday in Sri Lanka but there was rarely much peace at work. He was always thinking about ways to improve broadcasting standards in order to benefit the viewer. Tony soon worked out that fielding restrictions would have to be introduced in one-day cricket, otherwise captains would place all their fielders on the boundary and what dull viewing that would be. He it was who first suggested the fielding circle with a radius of 30 yards from the stumps with a stipulation that a certain number of fielders would have to position themselves within it, thus encouraging the batsmen to go for their shots. More fours, more sixes, more excitement. Glaringly self-evident now.

He introduced the famous Weather Wall, not unknown in meteorological circles but a new idea for pre-match reports from a cricket ground. Equally popular was the Player Comfort Meter, something which players from previous eras tended to scoff at ('In my day, sonny, it were never comfortable,') but I was fascinated by it when I first saw it. The level of detail that Tony Greig and his colleagues at Channel 9 went to in order to keep the viewer informed was hugely impressive. The light, the humidity, the wind direction, the wind speed, the ambient temperature, the weather forecast and the player comfort gauge (though I was never quite sure whether a score of ten was perfect or unbearable) – it was all there. Scott of the Antarctic might not have set off on his ill-fated expedition to the South Pole had he but bothered to switch on to look at Tony Greig's chart.

When I casually remarked to Ian Greig about Geoffrey Boycott's little ruse of inserting his car key into the pitch during his pitch reports, he nearly brought down the communications satellite with his indignation. 'That was Anske's idea!' Indeed it was. Tony was the first to brandish his car key (always a Toyota, I believe – the Jag had long gone) and insert it into the pitch to discover what lay just beneath the surface. If it went in easily, there was underlying moisture, which ought to have the seamers licking their lips in anticipation. If it was dusty, with cracks opening up, the pitch was obviously breaking up and the spinners' eyes would light up. If the pitch was hard and true with few marks or indentations, it was going to be a long day in the field for the bowlers. Actually, reading a pitch is not that simple, not that cut and dried, I am tempted to say, but it made for good television and provided interesting discussion. Quite why the ground authorities have seen fit to ban the practice is beyond me. It seems harmless enough. The supporters of George Davis needed more than a car key to wreak damage on the Headingley pitch in 1975. Perhaps it had something to do with a mishap that befell Tony in 1981. In exploring the alarming cracks that had started to appear in the Perth pitch, he inserted his key … and lost it! As far as anybody knows, the key is still down there, somewhere. Possibly it will re-emerge at some later date, rather like a burial ground yielding up its bones, and be held responsible for a remarkable delivery. How Tony got home that night is not recorded. It can safely be assumed that his fellow commentators, as always amused by his antics, did not offer a lift.

One of his pitch-side reports immediately went viral, if that phrase was in common use in 1988. Richie Benaud in the studio handed over to Tony Greig and as soon as the Bald Beanpole (the mop of blond hair by now had disappeared and been replaced by his trademark panama) appeared on-screen, it was hard not to laugh. He looked for all the world like a modern Old Father Time, with a scythe slung over one shoulder. At first, he gave no inkling as to its purpose, concentrating on a problem area in the bowlers' run-up just in front of the bowling crease. He then moved on to the pitch itself. He informed everybody that he had previously criticised the ground authorities for 'not getting rid of some extra little bit of green grorss here' and had made the suggestion that it might be a good idea to use a scythe. Whereupon, the scythe was removed from his shoulder and waved across the troublesome area. He agreed that perhaps the scythe might not have been his greatest idea but 'they'll probably need to work with one of those Gillette G2 double-edged, swivel heads to get through the valleys they've got here'. I bet Gillette were delighted with the plug though I have no evidence Tony was working for them at the time.

'Change is inevitable. Change is constant,' said Benjamin Disraeli, a former British prime minister. Like Disraeli, Tony was at heart a conservative, in manners and conviction, but if a certain way of doing things had outlived its usefulness, he quickly and wholeheartedly embraced the new method, the new style. His conservatism no doubt stemmed from his background and upbringing. Nowhere was more traditional than Queenstown in the immediate post-war years where he was growing up and his family, particularly his father, was no loose-and-happy, permissive parent; Tony's upbringing was strictly conventional. If anybody had doubts about this, in view of the wide swathe Tony cut through social circles, listen to Bruce Francis, his long-standing and loyal friend: 'Tony was incredibly conservative. We all went to a John Denver concert in Sydney. Between songs, Denver remarked to the audience that he smoked pot. Tony was horrified!' *Nothing exceptional about that; pot was all around at that time of our lives. Being a sportsman, I suppose he might have had cause to avoid it more than a pop singer.* 'But he most definitely disapproved. When Donna arrived a few weeks later, Tony told her about this admission of Denver's, that he had smoked pot. He went on and on about it until in exasperation, she asked what was wrong with smoking pot. "Do you know anyone who's smoked pot?" he demanded. "Don't be ridiculous," she replied, "I smoked it when I was at finishing school in Switzerland." He didn't believe her. He thought she was joking. When he realised she wasn't, he was mortified.'

As a boy growing up in a strictly traditional environment, Tony's physical energy and restless pursuit of fun and games may well have led him to push against the boundaries but he was no rebel. He engaged in a bit of stealthy naughtiness but he would no more have kicked over the traces than go out to toss without his blazer. However, he had enormous reserves of self-confidence and once convinced of a course of action, he never looked back. His style of commentating was different and did not meet with everybody's approval but he really could not have done it any other way. Or wanted to. Mark Pougatch, the well-known sports front man on British television, when asked what advice he would give to putative commentators, replied, 'Be yourself'. Tony was himself behind the microphone. He had his detractors and he had his disciples but most importantly he had the unwavering support of his boss. His relationship with Kerry Packer – as intense and as resolute as that with his father – was obviously hugely significant in his post-cricket career and is one we shall examine shortly. For the time being, its importance lay in the self-assurance with which Tony felt able to perform both in front of and behind the camera.

Traditionally, in broadcasting cricket, or any other sport for that matter, the commentator describes what happens and the co-commentator, or pundit, or expert critic, offers opinion and informed judgement. Tony filled both roles, equally competently and equally enthusiastically. He offered assessment on everything under the sun, and the sun itself in his Weather Wall. In other words, as in his younger days, he was an all-rounder, a true all-rounder, not a journeyman who could turn his hand to many things, but a specialist in several fields. It might be said that he rewrote the handbook on cricket commentary but in fact he was reverting to a *modus operandi* that had been in vogue long before he ever imagined. The word 'commentator' comes from the Latin *commentor*, to deliberate, to discuss, to argue over, later, to interpret. That is precisely what Tony did. 'Look, if not a lot was happening,' said Jeff Thomson, 'Greigy would start an argument just to liven things up.' He saw this as his job, to act as an instigator, a provocateur, a wave maker, anything to get the discussion going. When he was young, he would play cricket until the cows came home; when he was older, he would talk about the game long after they had all been milked. He firmly believed that his business was not restricted to describing what was happening, finding the right words, identifying the players, calling it correctly (though this was important) but also imbuing the action with passion, giving it emotion and perspective. Good communicators get their message across effectively; great orators invest the message with something more elevated. It might even be called poetry.

There is an undeniable cadence in Tony's voice and his use of language evokes an emotive response, which are constituents of all poetry. Tony Greig a poet? His style was more that of a professional storyteller and that kind of storytelling has a long and noble tradition in popular culture. A storyteller would wend his itinerant way around the country, telling his tales, spinning his yarns, conveying events in words, images and sounds, which were often improvised and embellished. People *listened* to Tony in their sitting rooms, just as they listened rapt to the storyteller around the fireplace in the inn or in the town marketplace. Tony was compelling. A supreme craftsman too. Nobody would have survived so long at the top of his profession – even with his boss's support – had he not been so good at what he did.

All leaders – presidents, commanders, prime ministers, chief executives, headmasters – like to have an accompanying circle of acolytes about them. Usually it comprises faithful retainers and loyal servants who remain uncomplainingly at their master's beck and call, willing and anxious to take some of the weight off their boss's shoulders. Invariably they owe their position to grace and favour and as a result are not often willing to rock the boat. On the other hand, any leader worth his salt will want at his side an aide who does not owe his position to patronage and is therefore empowered to whisper things in his chief's ear that he does not always want to hear. When a Roman general in Ancient Rome was accorded a 'triumph' through the streets of the city, it was the custom to have a slave at his shoulder in the chariot whispering in his ear, '*Memores sumus vestri in mortale.*' (Remember thou art mortal.)

Where did Tony Greig belong in Kerry Packer's entourage? Was he one of the few prepared to stick his head above the parapet? In the trenches during the First World War, tall soldiers perforce suffered the highest mortality rate at the hands of snipers. I doubt the Blond Beanpole would have survived long in the killing fields of Flanders.

Nor can one imagine him hiding behind the sycophants in Packer's organisation, not willing to speak truth unto power. His whole life had been an exercise in telling it how it was. He made a few enemies with his directness but the overwhelming majority of his team-mates, friends and associates appreciated his honesty and forthrightness. You knew exactly where you stood with him. I cannot believe he was any different with Packer. He owed much to his patron – some might say everything – so his loyalty was unquestioning. But he was no pushover; he was not Packer's lapdog. The relationship was much more complex than that and worked both ways.

Both brother Ian and son Mark believe that Kerry Packer adored Tony from the outset. Undoubtedly he recognised in his protégé the potential as a front man for WSC and undoubtedly Tony worked hard to justify his boss's faith in him. And it is true that Packer had promised Tony a job for life and he was not one to go back on his word. But that could have extended only so far as his role as a commentator for Channel 9. Packer went further than that; he appointed him as managing director of Lion Insurance, one of his many commercial interests. Actually – Mark put me right here – the name of the firm was originally The Brokers; the impetus behind the change of name was Sandy Greig. He advised Tony from South Africa (they were now back on speaking terms) that his experience in the field of insurance suggested that any advertising feature put out by The Brokers would be gleefully seized upon by their competitors 'because they're all brokers!' Swiftly, Tony changed the name. Lion it was. Let's be honest; he wasn't going to turn his back on his African roots and call it something like Kangaroo.

At this juncture, Sandy Greig re-enters the narrative. For some time, Tony had become increasingly worried about the well-being and safety of his parents back in South Africa. Apartheid was still in the ascendancy but social upheaval was ever present and he was not at all sure that Sandy and Joyce, now getting on in years, were best placed to look after themselves if unrest broke out into violence. Furthermore, he realised that managing a firm of insurance brokers was not the same as captaining a cricket team. He needed help and advice. Who better to give it than his father, experienced in the field, capable of speaking directly to his son and totally dispassionate in his views? Get them over to Australia was his thinking, thus killing two birds with one stone. He approached Packer, who gave his blessing, and in 1984, his parents moved, lock stock and barrel, to Sydney. Sandy was soon installed as general manager of the newly named Lion Insurance with Joyce working on the front desk as a receptionist. By all accounts, they were happy in their new environment.

Tony's indebtedness to Kerry Packer was never in dispute and he repaid it with steadfast loyalty and tons of hard work. At the end of each working day, he would meet all the other senior managers of the various concerns in the Packer empire to chew the cud with their boss. He always fancied himself as a businessman and had immersed himself in countless money-making enterprises over the years but he was the first to admit that he had much to learn about work at the coal face of seriously large companies. He enjoyed the variety of challenges it threw up, immersing himself in politics and the business world. 'Every morning,' Bruce Francis told me, 'he read all three Sydney papers, cover to cover, before going to work.' When not commentating, he was away speaking here, advising there, banging the drum somewhere else, rarely letting up on his busy schedule as the visible face of Channel 9 and Packer Enterprises. Living out of a suitcase might not be everybody's cup of tea, or coffee in Tony's case, but it was no more than Tony had been doing all his life really, only he had swapped a cricket bag for a travel bag. Talking of coffee reminded me of something Bruce Francis had said. 'Tony drank 30 cups of coffee a day, with four spoonfuls of sugar.' I didn't ask how many cigarettes he got through daily.

I wondered what effect Tony's continual absences had on the family. 'Aw look,' said Mark, 'it certainly took its toll. My mother was stoical and long-suffering about it but she accepted that he was working for Packer, it was no conventional nine-to-five job, there were demands on his time and that was the price he had to pay for financial security for all of us, his family.' He then paused and added thoughtfully, 'I guess she did find it more and more difficult.' *Before we touch on the dark period of his life shortly to come, please tell me a bit more about your father and Kerry.* 'They were exciting times. I remember nothing but kindness and friendship that he extended to all of us in the family.' He spoke of happy memories of being invited to Kerry's holiday home on Palm Beach in the northern districts of Sydney and playing golf as his guest at the Australian Golf Club, which I am assured is the most exclusive in the country, let alone Sydney. He remembers the occasion when his father and Packer were on the phone and he picked up the extension, the way mischievous young lads do, and blew a raspberry down the line. He received a good hiding for that. Packer was a huge polo enthusiast and owned his own team, so horse riding was very much part of the scene. As were the quad bikes and ultralights (I had to look up that one; an ultralight is a single-seater lightweight aircraft). Tony crashed his on landing after his maiden flight. It left him with an injured ankle but an entertaining story, which he wheeled out at every opportunity. Magical times, wonderful memories. Clearly it was not all work and no play in the Packer orbit.

There is little doubt that Kerry Packer was hugely fond of Tony. For a start he never forgot the sacrifice Tony had made in forsaking the England captaincy for WSC. He knew what a wrench it had been and how upset Tony had felt – though he was the last to admit it – by the rough ride he had been given by the English press and the English public. WSC would never have got off the ground without him and Packer recognised this clearly and was grateful. 'Tony stood shoulder to shoulder with Dad when it was not always fashionable.' Those were the words of James Packer, Kerry's son, after Tony's death. But it cannot have been solely a matter of loyalty. It was more than that. Packer must have trusted Tony when he placed him in important and influential positions and Tony must have repaid this trust. Packer would never have got to where he was by supporting lame ducks.

Mark Greig wondered out loud whether Kerry Packer was a little star-struck. Packer respected Tony's cricket career and knew what he had to do to get such an influential and charismatic figure on board. It was true, as Mark has admitted, that Packer was drawn to all famous sportsmen and liked to charm them into his sphere of influence. But that does not fully explain the deep and enduring affection he held for Tony. History is littered with second-in-commands, number twos, right-hand-men who prove to be effective, vital foils to the leadership of their commanders. Captain Hardy was Nelson's preferred flag captain at the Battle of Trafalgar. He was a strong character, willing and able to risk his admiral's displeasure to do what he thought was right. Hardy was self-contained and imperturbable, quite different in personality to the mercurial Nelson but they worked well together and formed a close professional and personal bond. In the same way, Packer seemed to take criticism from Tony, which he would have disregarded from the lips of anyone else. He appreciated Tony's willingness to speak up, even though he may not have shown it at the time. Remember the hare-brained scheme to get Barry Richards to change sides (and nationality) halfway through WSC? Barry was sure an Australian passport was about to be thrust unceremoniously into his hands before Tony intervened. Barry also told me that some of the other contracted players, to say nothing of other employees of Packer's, rather resented Tony's close relationship with the boss and the fact that he had his ear when others close to the action did not. 'My father was one of the few who would dare to disagree with him,' said Mark. As an example, he remembered James Packer, Kerry's son, misbehaving on the golf course, something to do with the young boy messing about with the golf carts. Packer gave his son the most fearsome of public scoldings, after which Tony stepped in and suggested he had been too harsh on the lad. Packer exploded, telling Tony to mind his own business. Mark remembered his father telling him that he had to smile when 'he saw Kerry walking towards the practice fairway with his arm around James's shoulder'.

Mark suggested that their relationship was more equal than people gave credit. 'They looked out for each other and both had each other's backs,' he said. Packer owed Tony a debt of gratitude for keeping private stories out the press. There would have been much in the richly colourful life of a multi-millionaire press magnate that rival papers would have given anything to get their hands on but Tony – exceptional for one as garrulous as he – never dished the dirt. Put simply, they got on from the outset, they became friends, enjoyed the same pursuits and preferred each other's company to most others. They both had a wild streak in their personality and never forsook an activity just because there was a whiff of danger associated with it.

Both men were fiercely competitive to their fingertips, neither willing to take a backward step, Tony in sport and Packer in business. Tony had been a gambler on the pitch, believing that a risk-free environment got you nowhere. Packer was a true gambler; the amounts won and lost on the gaming tables were legendary. In short, they had a similar outlook on life. 'Life is not a dress rehearsal,' Packer was fond of saying.

The test of true friendship comes at times of personal crisis. 'When sorrows come, they come not single spies but in battalions,' cried Claudius in Shakespeare's *Hamlet*. Tony felt similarly overwhelmed during the most harrowing period of his life towards the end of the 1980s. First up came financial woe in the form of a bad business judgement. The details may only interest a lawyer or a financial advisor but the upshot reminds us that even a fine batsman can miss a straight one and an experienced businessman, for surely that was Tony by now, can be undone by a mistake. He agreed to invest in a financial venture with an old school friend from Queenstown. Even his son referred to his action with horror, saying, 'In a moment of madness, he stupidly signed a personal guarantee as part of the transaction.' The business hit turbulent water, the 'friend' fled the country and the bank called in the loan. There was nothing Tony could do but pay off his creditors as best he could and file for bankruptcy. Kerry Packer bailed him out. Though a very wealthy man, Packer contributed large sums of money to charity but he always insisted his generosity was bestowed in a low-key manner. The same with his act of kindness to his friend. Few knew of the means or the extent of his magnanimous gesture. Even more reason for Tony to feel loyal to his benefactor.

The strain, to which Mark had earlier been alluding, in the family life of the Greigs, caused by Tony's frequent and prolonged absences, was by now beginning to tell. By 1988, a crisis point had been reached. Tony and Donna separated and later that year they divorced. The reasons for the breakdown of any marriage are invariably complex, distressing and unfathomable to those on the outside. I doubt it was any different on this occasion. The point is whether the details surrounding this unhappy episode concern us, or add in any way to the narrative of Tony's life or have any part to play in the public interest. I think not. So I shall leave it there. The divorce had personal repercussions for their children – that much is obvious – but it says a great deal for all concerned that relations between father and son and daughter were eventually repaired and they were as close as they had ever been at the time of Tony's death. Later, Donna contracted cancer and died on 6 April 2002. Tony remarried in 1991. For reasons explained in my acknowledgements, Mrs Vivian Greig prefers not to feature in any way in this book and I shall thus respect her privacy.

In 1989, Sandy Greig suffered a heart attack. It happened while he and Joyce were on holiday in England. Desperate to get back home to Australia before there was another attack, which was on the cards, with typical force of will, he managed to cope with the long journey. The following year, he entered hospital again, this time for a routine eye operation to remove a cataract. While there, he contracted pneumonia, then his kidneys packed up. All attempts to pull him round failed and once the doctors put him on a life support machine, the end was inevitable. Together, Joyce and Tony made the grim decision to have the apparatus turned off. Squadron Leader Alexander Broom Greig DSO, DFC had flown his final mission and died on 30 November 1990. Poignantly, it was St Andrew's Day. To this day, the Greigs never forget their Scottish roots.

In the same year, Kerry Packer also suffered a serious heart attack. Apparently his heart stopped for seven or eight minutes before it was shocked back into life with a defibrillator used by the paramedics in the ambulance. He survived but it was a close-run thing. Whether this brush with mortality led to deep metaphysical discussion long into the night with his sidekick we shall never know but it would be odd if they never pondered what lay in store when the bails were removed. Packer was sure that life was to be lived to the full, a philosophy perfectly in tune with Tony's. 'Look, son, I've been on the other side and let me tell you, there's nothing there,' Packer famously said after his close shave. Tony's religious beliefs remain shadowy. It is Mark's contention that his father's deep immersion in the traditional Christian worship of his childhood probably left the vestiges of a vague faith but he was too busy, too determined to put behind him what he called 'the worst period of my life' to worry too much about the hereafter.

How much was one dependent on the other? What is in no doubt is Tony's regard for his boss and this story from Ian illustrates it clearly. In 1990, the newly formed Sky Sports broadcast for the first time live coverage of England in the West Indies. Recognising their lack of experience in just about everything to do with outside broadcasting of cricket matches, they employed Tony as their lead commentator and he proved to be a huge success. His relationship with Geoffrey Boycott, hitherto uneven, was the surprise combination behind the microphone. Tony recognised that his colleague was a controversial figure who divided opinion but believed that his combative tone and his contentious views were part of his appeal. The same might be said of Tony. On air, the pair hit it off and the viewer was the beneficiary. Tony also dispensed valuable advice to producers and cameramen; after all, there were few in the game more experienced by this time than he. Sky made a swift and sensible assessment of his worth and offered him the job of leading commentator full-time. Apparently the cheque flourished under his nose was blank. His response was that he was already under contract to another employer. But as everybody knows, contracts can be broken. Packer was aware of this more than anybody. When negotiating (unsuccessfully) with the Australian Cricket Board in 1976, he spread his arms wide and said, 'There is a little bit of the whore in all of us, gentlemen, don't you think?' Back home, Tony went to see Packer and explained that he had been made an offer by Sky, 'a huge deal' he admitted. Packer advised him to take it. Tony said no, and tore up the blank cheque. 'You have always been good to me,' he said.

By 2000, Packer's health was failing. He had now suffered several heart attacks and his kidneys were malfunctioning. He underwent a kidney transplant and survived a further five years, dying in December 2005, aged 68. Tony went on air soon after and paid this tribute to his friend: 'Cricket has lost one of its greatest friends and supporters. Australia has lost a truly great Australian. People will not know how different things could have been without Kerry Packer. He was a very generous man, a bloke with an incredible sense of fun and that charisma that was all around him.'

I have a friend who emigrated to Australia and never regretted it. I often wonder if he really means it when he says that nostalgic thoughts about the old country never intrude, trotting out as he does all the well-worn clichés about grey skies, crowded motorways, warm beer and burnt sausages on the barbecue. Did Tony Greig ever miss England? He had no regrets about his decision to up sticks and relocate in Sydney. After all, he had done it before when he left Queenstown. He was certainly happy in Australia, content with his life and fulfilled in his career. Even during this turbulent period, encompassing his divorce and the death of his father, the thought of fleeing elsewhere never entered his head. Sadly, old friendships from Sussex withered on the vine, as they do when not watered by frequent contact, and ex-team-mates and opponents slowly lost touch. There was no animosity on his part for having been ostracised by the establishment for his part in WSC. He did not avoid England because he felt he would not be welcome. It was simply that his job was all-encompassing and he had no professional reason to return. Anybody from the past who came to Australia and bothered to look him up was always welcomed warmly and chaperoned hospitably.

Of the many former players I have interviewed for this book, all who had caught up with him when visiting Sydney are fulsome in their praise for the way Tony looked after them and, with a laugh, end up by saying, 'The same old Greigy, minus the hair.' Alexander the Great famously never returned to Macedonia, his birthplace, as he was too busy conquering kingdoms, building cities and being great. Tony may once have been compared to a Greek god but he never turned his back on England, no matter how unfairly damaged he believed was his reputation. Anyone from home was welcomed with a huge smile, a bear-like embrace and a friendly chat. Bob Willis found him as engaging as ever when their paths crossed in commentary boxes. Peter Graves was on holiday in New Zealand and stopped off on the return journey in Sydney and found Tony 'a lovely host'. John Lever bumped into him when he was hosting cricket tours Down Under. 'Larger than life,' he said. 'Greigy hadn't changed a bit. We had a lovely chat. It was good to see him again.' Keith Fletcher came across Tony when he was the England coach and 'Tony was about with a microphone in his hand. Same old Greigy!' John Barclay managed to see him on the few occasions Tony was in England and though a little saddened to see this 6ft 7in colossus had put on weight and was now a little puffy around the cheeks, the charm and the energy were 'undimmed'. Tony Buss remembers with fondness and gratitude the way 'Greigy reacted when my son was in Sydney and rang him up on the off chance. He put him up for a week and gave him his car to drive. He was always a kind bloke like that.' This generosity of spirit is a theme Bruce Francis was anxious to emphasise. 'Tony was always a very generous man. I remember once – when he was playing for Waverley – he organised a cocktail party at his home for 30 people who had been good to him and then took them all to a Neil Diamond concert. All paid for.'

Here is another example – one of many – of Tony's hospitality. His brother Ian captained a combined Oxford and Cambridge University side on a tour of Australia towards the end of 1979. 'It was a pretty useful team,' Ian told me. 'We had Derek Pringle, Nigel Popplewell, Dave Surridge, Simon Clements, John Claughton, Peter Roebuck, Paul Parker .... Tony helped organise the tour, looked after us fabulously and gave us all a barbecue at his house when we were in Sydney.' All well and good but it could be said that this was for a brother and nothing out of the ordinary. Ah but wait .... 'He got hold of British Leyland who provided us with half a dozen Mini Mokes so we could all drive around Sydney and up to Newcastle in convoy.' I should point out that he is referring to Newcastle in New South Wales. The original Newcastle in mid-December would have blinked in disbelief at the sight of six Mini Mokes roaring through the centre of town manned by students in jeans, t-shirts and flip-flops. *What fun! You must have had a fabulous time.* 'Indeed! I got two job offers while we were there. One at the University of Perth and the other at the University of Brisbane. I asked Tony's opinion. "Go to Brisbane, not Perth." So I did. I met my wife in Brisbane and here I stayed.' That made sense. Perth to Sydney is 2,500 miles. Brisbane to Sydney is a mere snip at 500 miles. Thus could Ian maintain closer contact with his beloved brother.

It was during that temporary assignment with Sky in the West Indies during England's visit in 1990 that Tony Greig was slowly reintroduced to his British audience. Or rather, in view of his long absence from our screens in this country, to a completely new generation of viewers who were for the first time exposed to his flair and expertise. He was to them no *bête noir*, the man who had betrayed English cricket, but a refreshingly different, forthright and entertaining voice that obviously knew what it was talking about. His verbal sparring with Boycott and his excited outbursts started to become as familiar to viewers as Richie Benaud's cream jackets and Henry Blofeld's parked pigeons and passing buses. Both Boycott and Greig sported similar panama hats when on-screen out of doors. Skin cancer and the danger to cricketers playing outside in the sun for hours on end was beginning to take hold of the public consciousness, even in England. It was about this time that I became aware of boys in my cricket teams starting to mimic Tony's voice at strategic moments during play. 'What a biggie!' 'That's gorn into the trees!' 'He's gone! Goodnight Charlie!' Billy Birmingham had done his job. Tony Greig was now a well-known figure in English cricket. The Second Coming, you might say.

Privately, his visits back to the Mother Land had never been fraught with any stickiness with the everyday cricket lover and general public. He was never as unpopular as he first imagined when the furore over WSC had blown up so there was little resentment on either side whenever he was back here. Mark Greig remembers a particularly happy pilgrimage back to his father's home in Hove. It was 1989 and Tony was working in England during an Ashes series. 'I was 14 and Sam was 16,' he said, 'Dad was really missing his family and I recall seeing his big smile above all the other heads when we walked through the Arrivals gate at Heathrow. He showed us Brighton General Hospital where we were born and we also visited our family home in Dyke Close. He knocked on the door and when the owner answered, he recognised Dad instantly.' Of course. Tony Greig was not a figure easily forgotten and it illustrated to the two children that not so long ago, their father was the most feted sportsman in the land. The current owner of the house gladly showed them around their old home. 'Dad got a real kick out of that visit and told us countless stories as we walked around and the memories kept flooding back.' He reminded them of the time Imran Khan stayed with the family and spent his lime lounging on the floor playing his records. There was also the spot where Sam's pet tortoise used to hide and countless other family reminiscences. For Tony it was nostalgic; for his children it was illuminating and no doubt a touch melancholy at a time when their parents were getting divorced. 'Sam and I loved hearing about the fun times Mum and Dad enjoyed with us during those years in Hove.' Alas no longer, on any level.

Slowly Tony's reputation in this country was restored. In 1998, the MCC proffered an olive branch by making him a Life Member. The president at the time, who canvassed staunchly for this long-overdue honour, was Tony Lewis, captain of that arduous but enjoyable tour to India, Pakistan and Sri Lanka in 1972/73. It says a lot about Lewis that although he was not impressed with all of Tony's antics on that tour, he recognised that the club had been remiss in not earlier honouring a former England captain and made sure that the omission was put right. The MCC was changing (not before time, in some people's opinion) and Lewis was one of several reformers. Another of his changes was the abandonment of the men-only rule in the pavilion.

Tony was further bolstered by the fact that his television career was going from strength to strength. In 1999, Channel 4 wrested away the sole rights to broadcast England's home Tests from the BBC, which had been in possession of an exclusive partnership with English cricket since the dawn of time (1938, to be precise). The demise of the BBC was controversial and not to everybody's satisfaction. There was some bloodletting but nothing on the scale of the bitter war that erupted in Australia two decades earlier. There was unhappiness that the deal struck was all about money but relief that at least cricket would be available to all viewers, not just those who had paid for a subscription channel, such as Sky. By the time the much-anticipated Ashes series of 2005 hove into view, Channel 4 were on top of their game and had already won a BAFTA and several Royal Television Society awards for their cricket coverage. The game was in safe hands, it was felt. Shrewdly, they employed Tony for the series. The former England captain, now living in Australia, a national figure in that country with a reputation for panache and outspokenness .... Who would he support? Who would he root for? Who would come out on top in the verbal sparring matches with Geoffrey Boycott? It was a match made in heaven.

It was not long before press and pundits alike were trumpeting it as the greatest Ashes series of all time. The usually more sedate analysis by the 2005 edition of *Wisden* was equally fulsome: 'If there has been a more compelling series, history forgot to record it.' The five matches transfixed the imagination of the British public for a whole summer; no contest has ever been so tense for so long. The outcome was in doubt until the last afternoon of the final match. Interest did not build over a period of time to reach fever pitch. It started when the 'egg and bacon' brigade (MCC members sporting the club's yellow and red tie) started queueing outside the gates of Lord's at five o'clock on the morning of the first Test and ended with every rooftop surrounding the Oval occupied on the evening when the fifth Test came to a glorious (for England) finale. And Tony Greig was there!

Of course he was. That's Greigy. For once his critics – a steadily diminishing band as his British public grew used to, some might say fond of, him – had no cause to complain about the excitable commentary. There was more than enough excitement out there on the pitch for any amount of pigeons and passing buses to go unnoticed. Tony's partnership with Boycott behind the microphone contributed to the fascination of the series as much as the contest between Shane Warne and Kevin Pietersen in the middle. In point of fact, as Tony would have been the first to point out, successful commentary is all about teamwork and Channel 4 had what many nostalgic, misty-eyed viewers would regard as the dream team: Mark Nicholas as MC, Michael Atherton, Richie Benaud, Ian Botham, Geoffrey Boycott, Tony Greig, David Gower, Michael Holding, Nasser Hussain and David Lloyd, with Simon Hughes as the Analyst Man. Seven Test captains, note, and only two (Nicholas and Hughes) who had not played Test cricket. It did not take the production team long to work out that the pairing of Tony and Boycott was television gold dust and sure enough their lively exchanges on air became compulsive viewing. Sometimes it felt that the two of them were vying to replace Morecambe and Wise in the public consciousness as national treasures (Eric Morecambe had died the previous year). Here is one typical exchange I dug out from the archives. A waggon wheel, which is a graphic indicating where a batsman has scored his runs, was displayed on the screen. 'Can I just orsk you what's this here – Scotch mist?' said Tony, circling an area with his pen. As we know, he loved playing with the latest widgets thought up by the technical designers, not always with happy results. 'That's all off 'is legs,' retorted a scornful, Boycott, adding for good measure, "E's a left-'ander, you dozy twit!'

But it wasn't all knockabout stuff. Both had years of experience out there in the middle and years of experience commentating subsequently. Whatever one thought of their respective styles, their knowledge and understanding of the intricacies of a complex game were indisputable. That was why they became popular; they dared to explain without being pompous. Cricket is a game to be enjoyed, both seemed to intimate, and their enthusiasm was infectious. How many fours had Tony Greig seen in his life? Incalculable. But he greeted each one as if it was his first. And even Boycott would purr with delight as a beautifully timed cover drive was unfurled from Michael Vaughan: 'Even me grandmoother couldn't 'ave played it better.' Ah, that was because Vaughan is a fellow Yorkshireman, I hear you cry. True, but he had equal admiration for the brilliant maverick, Kevin Pietersen, who certainly did not come from Yorkshire.

What did Tony Greig think of Kevin Pietersen? That was a question to which everybody was anxious to hear the answer. Because of the similarities in their background – both being native-born South Africans who left their homeland to play for their adopted country, England – it was assumed that both were cut from the same cloth. Tony was anxious to put that one to bed, firmly. They were two quite different characters. Pietersen was a genius with a bat in his hand and we all know that geniuses do not make comfortable bedfellows. Tony was wonderfully gifted with both bat and ball but even his most ardent admirer would admit he fell just short of greatness. Pietersen seemed to make himself unpopular in just about every dressing room he frequented, a charge that could never be levelled at the gregarious Greig. Not that unpopularity should preclude a gifted player's presence in the team, argued Tony, and he used as an example the man with whom he once had a very public spat and who was now his new best friend, his fellow commentator, Geoffrey Boycott. 'Look, there are different characters in every dressing room. Nothing new under the sun there,' he said, 'but the first thing to be said is that I'm always in favour of picking the best side you have available.' That was why he wanted Boycott in every England side that he captained, putting it on record that he would contact him before every Test to check on his availability, alas unsuccessfully, even though Boycott wasn't always an easy person to captain. In such cases, somehow middle ground had to be found. That is why Tony was a good captain and Pietersen wasn't (as subsequent events proved). Pietersen was 'entitled to make the most of his talent,' Tony continued, 'and get the rewards for it, as I did. But I worry he's going the wrong way about it.' The difference between Tony's situation and Pietersen's, he maintained, was that he joined Packer, yes, for personal gain, but also in a much-needed attempt to better the lot of his team-mates. He could see no such altruism in Pietersen's later actions. Then he made this observation about his fellow countryman when Pietersen, three years later, was appointed England captain and how prophetic his words sound now. 'What will determine whether he is successful is how he gets on with the people around him. I was lucky. I had a great bloke in Alec Bedser as chairman of selectors. There was also Len Hutton. They told me they had made me captain and that all I had to do was to be flexible in selection but they understood I had to go out there and do the job.' Without doubt, both Greig and Pietersen were no strangers to controversy during their playing careers, as the press repeatedly reminded everybody, and both suffered from charges of being mercenaries. Be that as it may, Tony brought spirit and togetherness to his England dressing room. Kevin Pietersen rent his asunder.

The Greatest Ashes Series Ever – as it was popularly dubbed – had come to a close and Tony had thoroughly enjoyed the experience. At last, he believed that he had been welcomed back into the bosom of the English cricketing family. It was not quite a case of the return of the prodigal son because the British public had never turned against him with the same venom that the press, media and establishment would have had him believe. The hysterical taunts of 'traitor', 'mercenary', 'have bat will travel' had never sat comfortably with the ordinary cricket lover. It was true that folk did not much like his acting as Packer's recruiting sergeant while England's captain but in truth how many English players had he actually 'turned'? (Only two who had been regulars, Underwood and Knott.) Furthermore, it had become increasingly clear to most dispassionate observers that the game – or at least, the governance of the game – had needed a jolly good kick up the backside. Cricket lovers were certainly eager to let bygones be bygones and felt it was high time he got the full credit he deserved for improving the lot of professional cricketers. He sensed this as he travelled the country in his role as commentator. Gatekeepers, car park attendants, barmen, tea ladies, bystanders, autograph hunters, club officials, old friends, former foes, presidents and paper shufflers, big cheeses and small fry, all welcomed him warmly and he loved it.

The partnership with Geoffrey Boycott was unbroken at the end of the summer (something of a surprise if you consider Geoffrey's reputation for running his partner out) so the MCC made a surprising but gracious request, seeing that Tony was in the country, for him to take part in a question-and-answer forum at Lord's. The tradition – if tradition it could be called as it had only been going for five years – was that it would immediately follow the Spirit of Cricket lecture. To give it its full name – The MCC Spirit of Cricket Cowdrey Lecture – will give a clue to its provenance. The annual lecture was inaugurated in 2001 in memory of Colin Cowdrey and was delivered by eminent cricket figures from across the globe. Previous speakers had been Richie Benaud, Barry Richards, Sunil Gavaskar and Clive Lloyd. No 5 in the batting order was Geoffrey Boycott. 'Flippin' 'eck,' he said, 'I'm not used to being number five. I usually open!' Later, after speaking, he was joined on stage by Tony and Rodney Hogg, the Australian fast bowler, with the proceedings conducted by Mark Nicholas. The banter and the wit flowed as you would imagine and Geoffrey and Tony were on fine form. The subject of sledging cropped up. It is a subject that has interested me too. Ex-players of my generation claim that sledging was 'never around in our day'. The word might be new (allegedly, it originated in the mid-1970s in Australia) but seeking to gain advantage by verbally abusing an opponent has been around since the game was first played. It depends whether you regard it as friendly banter or intimidation. The controversy arises when a line is crossed and I think most reasonable people would have a pretty good idea where that line lies. Tony Greig was South African. He loved to stir things up but rarely did he stray into the territory of personal abuse. His opinions and those of Boycott would have been of significant interest. 'The Australians were always sledging me,' Tony announced. 'That's because they knew it got to you,' said Boycott with that wonky grin of his, 'they never bothered with me. They knew it didn't affect me.' Tony couldn't resist it. 'Now why was that, Geoffrey?' The answer came back with commendable swiftness. "Cos I were always a better batsman than you.' Tony laughed. As did the audience. No need, no cause, no justification for reminding everybody of Boycott's 'uncanny knack of being where fast bowlers aren't'. That hoary old chestnut had long since been buried. Tony did not bear grudges. And to be fair to Boycott, he too had put aside their spat and enjoyed their verbal sparring as much as anybody.

It is significant that this event took place at Lord's. It certainly wasn't lost on Tony. He felt it was all part of his rehabilitation in the eyes of the establishment. Packer and WSC was a long time ago and the MCC had by now changed out of all recognition. He had been appreciative of his reception over here and gratified that people wanted to hear him speak and express his opinions. One matter that he was more than qualified to comment on, both as a former Test player and current broadcaster, was the decision by the English Cricket Board to give exclusive rights to televise cricket in this country to Sky, a subscription channel. The axing of Channel 4 in favour of Sky was hugely controversial. In some ways, the strife it caused resembled Packer's battle with the ACB but of course in another way it was totally different. Channel 9 in Australia is not a subscription channel but terrestrial, as we call it here. At no stage during WSC did the viewer have to pay to watch the cricket. Richie Benaud, always a staunch defender of cricket being 'free-to-air', as Australians put it, and therefore available to all, would never have joined a subscription channel; he resolutely rebuffed any attempts by Sky to lure him away. The news that Channel 4 had lost the bidding war with Sky broke soon after the epic 2005 series. Tony was still in the country and his views were sought. His words make interesting reading.

Tony saw the implications immediately. He had this to say when questioned whether Sky's smash-and-grab would be bad for cricket's future: 'It will be years before we can measure the extent of the damage inflicted on English cricket by the decision to do an exclusive deal with Sky and wave goodbye to live free-to-air coverage of the game in this country. It may be that we will never be able to measure it but I am sure an injury has been sustained and it could be serious.' He absolved Sky of any blame in this. They had been covering England touring overseas, which no other broadcaster had been prepared to do, and being a business, they had made a bid and secured the deal – all legal and above board. The blame, he believed, lay squarely at the door of the ECB. Once the ECB managed to convince the government to remove Test cricket from the protected 'crown jewels' of sport, thus freeing them to barter for big bucks, the fall-out was inevitable. 'We should not forget' – and Tony knew of what he spoke here – 'that cricket is a business and the ECB was bound to be attracted by the size of Sky's offer.' The result of taking Sky on board was that '70% of the population would not be able to access its product'. Where was the compromise? Channel 4 was prepared to do a deal but the ECB all along were 'leaning' towards Sky. He finished with this trenchant prediction: 'I hope you enjoyed the Ashes. Next year, the 70% of kids without Sky will tune in to watch the World Cup instead of cricket. They won't see Andrew Flintoff taking wickets or Kevin Pietersen hitting sixes so they won't try and emulate them in the park later on. Perhaps they'll just kick a ball about.' I was interested whether Tony had got his figures right so I did a bit of ferreting around. During the Ashes series of 2005, Channel 4's viewing figures peaked at 8.2 million. During the Ashes series of 2009, Sky's viewing figures peaked at 1.92 million. 'Cricket will suffer,' was Tony's parting shot and who can say he was wrong?

He was not right on all things. Not everything he touched turned to gold. It was Mark Greig who reminded me of his father's role in the setting up of the first 20/20 competition in India. 'Don't forget the ICL,' he told me. *ICL? What's that?* 'The Indian Cricket League.' *Don't* *you mean the IPL, the Indian **Premier** League?* 'No, the Indian Cricket League.' I had to confess ignorance and set about rectifying it. Tony had seen with his own eyes how successful the T20 competition had been when introduced in England in 2003 and reckoned he could spot a market for something similar in India. So did a few other interested parties and in 2007, Zee Sports Ltd, a sports entertainment channel in India, took hold of the concept and announced its intentions to set up the Indian Cricket League. Tony was co-opted on to the board, with the specific task of recruiting players. Four teams – World XI, India, Pakistan and Bangladesh – took part, with John Emburey as coach of the World XI, Steve Nixon in charge of India, Moin Khan of Pakistan and Balwinder Sandhu of Bangladesh. In addition, there was a separate competition for nine domestic teams based around the subcontinent. The chairman of the enterprise announced, 'We believe in order to make ICL the pinnacle of cricket, the game should be run by people who have played it.' He was as good as his word. Kapil Dev, appointed as head of the board, said this when the news was announced: 'I will use my experience of guiding and motivating both as captain and coach.' He had been captain of the Indian side that had captured the World Cup in 1983, so this was a big coup. Tony was impressed. 'I am excited to team up with Zee Sports for the upcoming ICL 20/20 tournament and look forward to joining Kapil Dev with whom I have had a lot of on-field rivalry.'

From the outset, the new venture ran into controversy and opposition, despite its initial popularity. There was friction with the Board of Control of Cricket in India (BCCI), which ran the game in India and which saw the renegade competition as a threat to its power and influence. Kapil Dev was in the firing line for his role with ICL; a clear conflict of interests was cited, as he was currently the chairman of the National Cricket Academy, owned of course by BCCI. Kapil was immediately sacked and all the players involved in ICL were banned. Which way would the International Cricket Council jump? Support the rebels or ban them internationally? Predictably neither. They said it was a domestic dispute, the BCCI should sort it out themselves and whatever conclusion they came to, the ICC would support it.

Deja-vu all over again …. Tony Greig engaged to recruit players for a breakaway tournament, entrusted with the task of persuading them that this was good for their career, their bank balance and the game in their country. As 30 years previously, threats of legal action and court cases hung in the air. But the ICL did not have a Kerry Packer behind it. And that made all the difference. While the political and legal wrangling continued, the BCCI eyed up the lucrative pot of gold that ICL had opened and started their own 20/20 competition. For one reason or another – in many people's opinion, a failure to sign up all the big names in Indian cricket – the ICL failed to capture the public's imagination during its second year after its promising debut. Slowly, followed by a rush, the ICL players defected once a blanket amnesty from the banning order was brokered. Kapil Dev made peace with his board and the writing was on the wall. The Indian Premier League was launched and the rest is history.

Today, the ICL is no more than a fading memory. It is never discussed in the media, cricket pundits do not talk about it and records and scorecards of the matches are hard to find. Was it a total waste of time? Tony believed not. Its significance, he pointed out, lay in the fact that increased professionalism was introduced into the game in India. Its domestic structure underwent a long-overdue overhaul, players' wages and conditions of service were improved and a complacent national board of control had been given a short, sharp shock to its system. The BCCI had been pointedly reminded that they needed to get their act together and stay vigilant because free market economics makes it possible for any eager tycoon to stage a coup. Other national boards were forced to sit up and take notice. Now all countries have their own equivalent of the IPL. Not as rich, not as bloated, not as powerful as the IPL, as Tony later and unequivocally pointed out, and when one national board dominates the rest, the dangers are there for all to see. His warnings, as we shall see shortly, brought him into direct conflict with his Indian friends.

My story now comes round full circle. In the summer of 2012, Tony was in London for the unveiling by the Queen of the official memorial of those in Bomber Command who had lost their lives during the Second World War. President of MCC at that time was

Phillip Hodson, Tony's brother-in-law, a former Cambridge Blue, who had played for Yorkshire second XI, the CEO of a large firm of insurance brokers and a member of the Club since 1979. It was his task to identify and invite the speaker at the annual Cowdrey Spirit of Cricket Lecture. Hodson's job was not an easy one. He had to persuade someone he knew to follow in the footsteps of such notable figures as Barry Richards, Sunil Gavaskar, Clive Lloyd, Geoffrey Boycott, Imran Khan and others.

His choice was Michael Atherton. A former captain of England, respected journalist and an integral member of the Sky Sports commentating team, noted for his wry humour and straightforward opinions, he seemed the ideal choice. Furthermore, Hodson was able to employ their shared Cambridge University background to twist his arm. The trouble is that Atherton's arm was never for twisting. 'He told me that he wished me well in my capacity as president,' Hodson told me, 'but that he had to let me down and decline. He didn't like public speaking – even though everybody knew he was damned good at it – and besides he had his "own platform", as he described it, writing for *The Sunday Times*.' *Stumped then. How did it come about that you asked your brother-in-law?* 'This is strange but true – nobody at the Club knew that my wife, Sally Ann, was Tony's sister. And I have always been loathe to pull familial strings, but …. I went to Colin Maynard, the No 2 at Lord's—' *Why the No 2? As you were president, the door to the secretary's office would have been open, surely?* 'Keith Bradshaw was the No 1 but he had just resigned. Anyway, I chewed over the idea of asking Tony with Colin and he was very enthusiastic. What's gone has gone, was his attitude, the controversy over Packer and the England captaincy is history. Let's get on with it and let bygones be bygones. I asked Tony and he accepted with alacrity.'

By now, Tony felt much more comfortable when visiting England, reassured that old wounds had healed. Another event, when he was invited on to the speaking panel at a dinner for former England captains in 2009, added further encouragement. By all accounts, he had his audience in the palm of his hand. He was always a skilled and entertaining performer with a microphone in front of him, hardly surprising really, when you consider his years of experience. His listeners warmed to him not on account of his smooth delivery – that you would expect – but because he was honest, straightforward, knowledgeable, humorous and charming. I use the word 'charming' advisedly. It can have an undertone of insincerity, probably because it originates from the old meaning 'to cast a spell'. Tony had his audiences spellbound all right but there was no trickery involved. His charisma was not superficial; it was tangible.

Accordingly, he was gratified and excited to be asked … and not a little nervous. This was no after-dinner speech, delivered to a room full of cricket enthusiasts cheerfully oiled and expecting to be entertained. Nor was it a question-and-answer turn, with other panellists with whom he could spar and banter. Nor a dialogue with a sympathetic interviewer gently leading him down well-trodden paths. This was a *lecture*, with all the depth, gravitas and above all the message that such a speech traditionally demands. It was a daunting prospect. What could he say? What form should it take? What tone should he adopt? What issues should he address?

For help, he turned to his old friend Bruce Francis. What Francis had to say about the process of its construction was surprising and illuminating. 'Tony was an exceptional public speaker, a great story teller. Almost every time he got to his feet to speak, he did it off the cuff with the minimum of notes. Where he was not so good was when he had to read out a prepared speech. During his time co-hosting *Wide World of Sports* on Channel 9, which went out for three or four hours on Saturday and Sunday afternoons, he wasn't good when reading from his autocue.' *How come?* 'I have a feeling,' Francis continued, 'and I've never really put this out there, that Tony was in one way or another slightly dyslexic. The evidence I have is not explicit but observational. For example, I wrote some of his editorials and found I had to spell phonetically so he could get his tongue round the words.' If that were so, it was another obstacle that Tony had to cope with on his own. Dyslexia is now a familiar and recognised condition and ways and means of combatting the problem have been heavily researched and are on hand. Back in the 1950s in a small town in the Eastern Cape, I doubt anybody would have heard of it, let alone explain or even spell it. In those days a bad speller was a bad speller. 'Our dad used to go nuts over Tony's spelling,' Ian informed me. 'As a meticulous newspaper editor, he would pick up on all of Tony's spelling mistakes in his letters from England. One that springs to mind is "irly" for "early"! Amazing.' If Tony had dyslexia, mild or severe, he kept it to himself and battled on, as only he knew how.

'I advised him to do the speech off the cuff, with the minimum of notes,' Francis went on. 'I'm sure he would have felt more comfortable and given a better account of himself had he done so. But other counsel prevailed. I also told him to visit Lord's first and check out the lie of the land. He was a tall man and needed a tall lectern but this too he failed to do. When he got up to speak and stood at the lectern, it barely reached his waist. He had to bend down to read his script. I had the whole thing typed out in large font but he would lose his place every time he looked up at his audience then down again at the printed page. Despite hours of practice, the message – relevant then and still is – got lost in the delivery.' I wondered whether Phillip Hodson was equally disappointed by the performance. It was clear from the tone of his voice that he felt Tony was not on comfortable ground. 'It was okay but you could sense his audience were not fully engaged. What's that? Sorry, it's Sally Ann telling me something ... oh, she's saying she's heard better.' Well, there we have it. Three of Tony's most fervent supporters did not believe the 2012 MCC Cowdrey Spirit of Cricket Lecture was a resounding success.

'Never mind the quality, feel the width!' If I can use that well-known expression favoured by unscrupulous tailors trying to persuade gullible customers that quantity trumps quality and turn it on its head – never mind the delivery of Tony's lecture, what did he *say*? I am not sure that it is everybody's opinion but it is certainly mine that I would much rather listen to an expert on a subject who is not particularly eloquent than a smooth operator whose knowledge is limited. Once you get past the hesitations, the repetitions, the mixed metaphors, the mangled syntax and reach the essence of what is being explained, all the inarticulacy is forgiven and forgotten. What was Tony Greig's message going to be? Here again, opinion is divided. He sought the advice of Francis and Hodson but it appeared that he did not always follow what was offered. Several drafts were penned without mention of Packer and WSC. He was encouraged to tackle the controversy head-on. He had been dubbed by the British press a 'traitor'; now was the time when he could tell his side of the story. Thankfully, this message was taken on board, late on in the day, it was true, but he did open up with an account of his role in unfolding events. 'Look, make this personal,' Hodson said to his brother-in-law, 'people want to know about your cricket exploits, your background and how you got to where you are now. Remind everybody of your Scottish roots, the exploits of your father in the war, your schooling and how you came to England.' *Reading the transcript, Phillip, it would appear that he did not follow your advice.* There was a grimace. 'It was emasculated. A pity.'

If his audience was hoping for personal reminiscences or amusing anecdotes or entertaining waggishness (where was Bill Lawry when you needed him?), they were clearly in for a disappointment. But that is not to say that the content of Tony's speech was devoid of interest and topicality. He clearly viewed this as a serious assignment and was determined to make some political points about the governance of the game and its relationship with the concept of the lecture, the Spirit of Cricket. It may have lacked the personal touch, which was his stock-in-trade, but the opinions he espoused were thoughtful and relevant. Having disposed of the Packer affair and the launch of WSC, in which he defended his position and his role as recruitment officer (all of which I have spoken about in an earlier chapter), he set out the major problems which in his opinion confronted the game currently. Its image worldwide, the effectiveness of its governing body, the International Cricket Council, the international calendar, the different formats of the game and their competing interests, gambling and corruption, the inequality of resources among nations and India's disproportionate influence on how the world game is run – they all bore his close and forensic scrutiny.

He singled India out as the major player on the world's stage. Far from decrying the commercial muscle that the BCCI was now flexing, he said that we should 'praise India for embracing the spirit of cricket through the financial opportunities it provides', without which some countries' cricket boards would have gone to the wall. But with economic control goes ethical responsibility. Here, he believed,

India was falling down. Many ex-players from all countries with huge experience were sitting on various committees of the ICC, making sensible and enlightened recommendations only for them to be vetoed by India because they didn't sit easily with their commercial interests. He cited several instances of India's insularity and self-centredness: their indifference to Test cricket; the bloated schedule of the IPL; their supine response to charges of corruption; their refusal to adopt the DRS, now in operation everywhere else. Mention of the Decision Review System made my ears prick up. Tony always was at the vanguard of new technology being used to facilitate umpires in their decision-making. Quite why India did not embrace it was beyond him, as it was beyond most cricket lovers, and it was not until recently, 2018, that the BCCI put aside its reservations and accepted it.

The problem lay with the BCCI's preoccupation with their enormously successful and lucrative IPL at the expense of Test cricket. Why? He contended that commercial rights had been sold to private companies with board members having a foot in both camps, thus laying themselves open to charges of a conflict of interest. The BCCI weren't going to rein in the size and influence of the IPL; that would be like turkeys voting for Christmas. Instead of rushing headlong to generate billions of dollars, India should take heed of the spirit of cricket and do more to foster the game worldwide. Strong words indeed but with more than a kernel of truth therein contained. Once again, the Bald Beanpole was putting his head above the parapet – he had little choice really, considering the low position of the lectern – and proclaiming what others thought.

The reception from the 200 or so people in the room was warm and generous. If it had not been the *tour de force* he would have wanted, it had obviously been the product of a lot of work and had provided food for thought. The audience at Lord's would have been broadly in agreement with the sentiments; the brickbats from further afield would come later. As had become tradition, following the speech, Mark Nicholas hosted a question-and-answer session, with Tony being joined on stage by Derek Underwood and Stuart Broad. 'As president, I stood up to introduce the panellists,' Phillip Hodson said to me. 'I made a reference to the tall, blond, good-looking England all-rounder (Broad) and told the audience to take a look at him because his handsome looks won't last forever. This was a sly reference to my brother-in-law and the ravages of time. Well, it brought a laugh and Tony enjoyed it as much as anyone.' *How did the Q&A session go?* 'Tony was relaxed now and came into his own. Mark Nicholas is very good at coaxing stories out of his guests and Tony opened up and wowed them all, the way he always did in such an environment.' That was not the end of the occasion. 'Afterwards, we had dinner in the Long Room. All very relaxed and enjoyable. No speeches. All that had been done and dusted. Just cricketers and cricket lovers savouring good company and a pleasant environment.'

The backlash was not long in coming. Tony's comments – often quoted out of context – received widespread coverage in the Indian press and yet again in his life, it seemed that he had stirred up a hornets' nest. These are some of the furious responses in Indian newspapers over the following few weeks: 'Full of inaccurate history, nostalgia, clichés and wishful thinking'; 'His lecture consisted of things India should do'; 'Never misses an opportunity to take a pop at the BCCI'; 'IPL taking players away from their country – but didn't Packer do the same?'; 'BCCI. We want the money you bring into the game. But we do not want you to control the game'; 'The BCCI are responsible for all the evils in the game'.

Most of this Tony could shrug off. His shoulders were broad enough and it wasn't the first time he had angered the finer feelings of a country's press. He stood by what he had said. His concerns for the future of Test cricket were informed and heartfelt. He was sure that the genuine cricket lover was listening.

However, one arrow did wound him, mainly because it came, not from outside the palisade but from within, a fellow commentator and journalist, one whom he knew, if not well, then certainly on speaking terms in a professional capacity. Harsha Bhogle was – still is – widely acknowledged to be the voice of Indian cricket, as much as Christopher Martin-Jenkins was in England. He wrote a piece for ESPNcricinfo, the popular sports news website, taking Tony to task for his 'inflammatory' remarks. 'The interesting thing about Tony Greig's Colin Cowdrey Lecture was not that he took off on India – he

can be quite predictable that way – but that it took so long coming.'
He continued, 'It is all too easy to lay the blame for all the game's ills at
one door.' India is not the enemy and to call her so was merely a decoy
from deeper problems. 'If India is wrong,' he argued, 'the rest of the
world can come together and alienate India. But they don't. Because
they want Indian money but not an Indian point of view.' He pointed
out that England and Australia, and South Africa too, when they
dominated what was then called the Imperial Cricket Council, acted
in their own interests to the disadvantage of the smaller members. His
point was that people in glass houses should not throw stones. People
like Tony Greig, he thundered, 'waste their skills by taking the lazy
option of attacking someone they think is an opponent'.

Bhogle is on record as having watched when he was a young boy
Tony Greig play on both of his Indian tours and would have known
enough of Greig the cricketer to appreciate he was unlikely to allow a
long-hop easy access through to the wicketkeeper. Bruce Francis has a
copy of Tony's written response and I am grateful to him for allowing
me to quote from it. 'Dear Harsha,' he starts, 'I don't know how you
can rip me to pieces without quoting a word I said in my lecture .... It's
time you, and Indians like you, grew up and stopped being so sensitive.'
Game on. He pointed out that in his comments on India, the positive
far outweighed the negative. He had a grudge against India? Stuff
and nonsense! 'On what basis,' he asked, 'do you suggest I expressed
"glee" at India's shortcomings? Another attempt to denigrate me.'
He went on to take issue with his antagonist for claiming that anti-
doping measures and rejection of DRS were 'minor issues'. Bhogle had
'dismissed' Tony's concern for the future of Test cricket. 'You know
and I know that Test cricket was sacred in India [but] crowds have
declined far more in India than in England or Australia.' Furthermore,
he pointed out, it was evident for anyone who had eyes to see that
recent performances in Australia during Test matches showed that 'a
number of Indian players weren't as focussed as the Australians'. This
really would have made Tony's blood boil. To play a game of cricket,
especially when you are representing your country, and not be fully
focussed would have been as heretical to him as arriving at Lord's
in shorts and flip-flops. Returning to the main thrust of Bhogle's

criticism, Tony had this to say: 'I said Indian cricket has saved world cricket. I said India was the leader of world cricket. I expressed the hope that India would govern for world cricket, not just for India.' By now his eye was in and he decided to hit a few boundaries of his own. 'Name me one player in my era,' he fulminated, 'who embraced India more than me!' He dismissed Bhogle's googlies with a contemptuous flick of the wrists, calling them 'gutter journalism', reaching triple figures with this flurry of sixes: 'I suggest you read your article again and then read my lecture and then decide who is the better human being.' With that, he put his bat under his arm, marched off the field, up the pavilion steps and into the sanctuary of the dressing room.

This being the cut and thrust of Test cricket, Bhogle would have expected a second innings. Except there was no second innings. For several months now, Tony had been plagued by a persistent cough. He wasn't well at the Bomber Command commemoration service, as his sister Sally Ann had noted. He wasn't at his best at the MCC Cowdrey Spirit of Cricket Lecture, but he ploughed on regardless. According to Bruce Francis, he'd had this cough for some time before he had set out for England. 'I'd been telling him for three months to see a doctor. I'd had a similar cough and they eventually discovered it was a reaction to the medication I was taking. Once they sorted it out, the cough disappeared. I thought that perhaps something similar was happening to him. But he wouldn't take my advice.' Whether earlier intervention would have made any significant difference, no one can tell. 'When he arrived at Sydney Airport back from Sri Lanka in early October,' Francis continued, 'he told me that he had three months to live.' Initially assured that the cough was merely bronchitis, when Tony eventually did seek a medical examination in Sri Lanka, a small tumour was discovered in his right lung. Further tests revealed the full extent of the cancer. Prognosis was gloomy. Ian told me that his brother, not one to take anything lying down, was prepared to fight the disease all the way. Two major operations were performed, with a hefty course of chemotherapy scheduled to follow. It never took place. All there was time for was one light session a few days before he died.

An interview, poignantly the last time he was ever seen on television, with Mark Nicholas made sad viewing. It was during a lull in play at the first Test of the Australia v South Africa series, one that Tony had been looking forward to immensely and was distraught at missing. The mellifluous tones of Mark Nicholas came on air. 'Tony is not with us today at the Gabba but he is at home in Sydney watching every ball … and what's more, we're linked into him. Greigy, g'day!' There he was. As large as life, dressed in his trademark panama, looking not at all bad, if truth be told. With a wry smile, he reminded everybody that this was the first Test he had missed at the Gabba for 33 years and then launched into an account of an amusing prank that had been played on him by his erstwhile nemesis, now good friend, Ian Chappell. Tony had been rung at home in Sydney early that morning to be told by Chappell that he was late and his normal lift to the ground for work was awaiting him downstairs. Slowly, Tony came to his senses and realised he was not in Brisbane but sick at home in Sydney. Typically he laughed when it was obvious he had been 'had'.

'Good to see that big smile on your face, Big Fella,' said Nicholas, and then asked for an update on his illness. Tony met this head-on. 'Well, I mean it's not good, Mark. Truth is I've got lung cancer and it's just a question of what the doctors can do.' Following the operation, he said, he would be embarking on a course of chemotherapy. 'We'll start to fight back after that. The plan is to see if we can make a bit of a dent in the little setback I've had.' He then went on to explain his feelings – the regret in his voice was tangible – at missing the Test. 'You've no idea what one misses when not going to the cricket on a day like this.' As if to spare the two of them further anguish, Nicholas asked Tony his opinion of the day's play so far. Tony's analysis was as sharp and as insightful as if he were there in person. Eventually, Nicholas brought the interview to a gentle conclusion. He asked Tony when the viewers were likely to see him back in action. 'Mate, with setbacks like this, you've got to be positive and I certainly aim to be back in that chair sometime.' 'We wish you well,' Nicholas signed off, 'I don't mean those of us here, I mean a lot of people around the world …. Good luck with it.'

There was an imperceptible pause but, watching it again, it seems an eternity. With a sad smile and a little nod of the head, Tony said, 'Thank you very much.' And his face disappeared from the screen to be replaced by Kallis leaving one from Siddle outside off stump. The cricket continued. It always does.

For Tony, time was short. All too short. Ian came down from Brisbane regularly to be with his brother. 'There was nothing left unsaid between us,' he told me simply. Bruce Francis said, 'Tony spoke to his mum, Joyce, every evening and then it was my job to keep him talking on the phone until midnight when it was time to take his final medication for the day. We covered a lot of ground. No stone was left unturned.'

The end, when it came, was swift, brought on by a fatal heart attack following a couple of epileptic fits. Death, like birth, is an intensely private thing. Tony's families, both of them, and his close friends will have their own memories and emotions; it ill behoves us to intrude. Tony Greig died on 29 December 2012. He was 66.

Quickly, tributes flowed in from all four quarters of the globe. One in particular caught my attention. Mike Atherton had this to say in *The Sunday Times*: 'The recent OBE awarded to Mike Denness, Greig's predecessor as England captain, means that of all the men who have captained England with any longevity since then, only Greig had not received any official recognition, reflecting his outsider status …. It cannot be rectified now.'

Acknowledgements

ONE of the great pleasures of writing a book like this is that it puts me back in touch with former team-mates and opponents from a world which filled every waking moment but one that now seems long ago. Even if I did not know personally some of the people whom I interviewed, there were usually friends or acquaintances common to us both, providing easy and pleasant outlets for reminiscence. Cricket is a social activity, one in which you get to know those with whom you share a dressing room more intimately than most other games, for the one compelling reason that you spend so much time in each other's pocket. Matches take a long time and play takes all day; I can think of no other team game where days drift into weeks and weeks into months with such little respite. So there is a common bond among cricketers that is never shaken off, even in the long years of retirement.

For my purposes as a biographer, this is a boon, which I am able to exploit shamelessly. There is no need for my interviewee to explain what a 'bunsen' is, or a 'jaffa' or a 'split five-four field'. If he refers to 'leaving the gate wide open', he can be confident I know he is not referring to a forgetful farmer. We understand the lingo, the practice, the tradition, the history, the culture of this fascinating game. With this insider perspective, of course, goes a certain responsibility. What goes on tour stays on tour is a bit of a cliché but it is an accepted code between professionals in any sport. That trust cannot be betrayed. Thus certain things are best left unsaid, I judge. In this respect, I see my role slightly differently from that of an expositor or a reporter or a historian. I am no journalist in search of a 'story' or a 'line of enquiry'. I seek not to rattle skeletons long secreted in cupboards. Muck-raking doesn't interest me. What is already in the public eye is of relevance and not to be ignored. But by and large, what is private should remain private, other than that which my subject, or anybody speaking on his behalf, is willing to divulge.

What interests me is the cricket and the men who play the game. There is more than enough drama, crisis, artistry, heroism, adversity, humour and all that life can throw at you in a single Test match to worry whether I have sufficient human interest in my story. I might be accused – and sometimes have – of not delving deep enough into the darker areas of a man's psyche, concentrating on the good rather than the bad, painting a rosier picture than I might, writing a hagiography even. What I try to do in my books is to tell the story, as truthfully as I can, but in an entertaining manner that eschews sensationalism and avoids scandalmongering. In short, I have to 'like' my subject. He has to be of interest and with all his faults he must be a man whom I can admire, one whose company, even if vicariously, I enjoy.

Tony Greig ticked all these boxes, and more. He was a compelling and charismatic figure and for a time he bestrode the Test match scene like the Colossus to which he was often compared. He was also generous and a loyal friend whose good points hugely outweighed the bad. Furthermore, he was stimulating company with a streak of mischief and a sense of fun and adventure, who enjoyed life to the full. What was there *not* to like about the man? Invariably, with any anecdote or memory that was being recounted to me by friends, colleagues, team-mates, opponents, there would go the accompanying laugh, the roll of the eyes and ... 'That's Greigy!' There did not seem to be a malicious bone in his body. That is why, I am sure, St Peter opened the pearly gates for him with a welcoming smile, especially when Tony had explained to him that he used his bats and wore his clothing. The Epilogue which follows gives an account of what happened next, once he had gained access to HQ.

First, back in this world, I have to thank the man himself, whose towering presence fills the page as much as his personality filled a dressing room or a commentary box. Writing about Tony Greig was never dull. Secondly, I am indebted to his family (his first), without whose help and support I would not have been able – nor wanted – to write this book. Sister Sally Ann, with her husband Phillip Hodson, brother Ian and son Mark have guided me carefully and protectively along the path. Tony's second wife, Mrs Vivian Greig, made it plain to me early on in this venture that she did not want to contribute; in fact, she was insistent I did not publish. She has her reasons but if one of her concerns was that I would not do her husband justice or worse that I might do a hatchet job on him, I hope the evidence to be found in these pages allays that fear. Other than that I have refrained from mentioning her and her family at all, respecting her wish for privacy. I hope my readers understand. One source whose opinion and knowledge of Tony stand high above others is his manager and closest friend, Bruce Francis, and I cannot thank him enough for his assistance and guidance. Bruce says it as it is and I am in awe – and not a little jealous – of his fearless comment and trenchant prose.

The following in no order other than as they appear in the book also contributed to this narrative of Tony's life: Bruce Burnett, Air Commodore Graham Pitchfork MBE, Alexandra Broom, Paul Ensor, Kenny McEwan, Mike Selvey, Roy Taylor, Paul Phillipson, Geoff Dakin, John Barclay, Keith Fletcher OBE, Mike Buss, John Snow, Mike Taylor, Tony Buss, Peter Graves, Jim Parks, Mike Griffith, Antony Clark, Barry Richards, John Spencer, Roger Knight OBE, Mervyn Brown, Chris Old, Bob Cottam, Mike Brearley OBE, Alan Knott, Roger Tolchard, Geoff Arnold, John Lever, [the late and sorely missed] Bob Willis MBE, Greg Chappell, Lee Irvine, Derek Underwood MBE, Bob Stephenson, Rev Mike Vockins OBE, Di Charteris ....

The Eddystone Rocks lie hidden at the entrance to Plymouth Sound, which has been for centuries an important naval harbour in this country. The need for a lighthouse to warn shipping of its dangers is obvious and compelling. My lighthouse has been my wife, Lin. During the course of writing this book, her powerful beams of light have guided my way to calmer waters. She provided the perfect device to set up the narrative from the outset, described in the introduction, and the rest simply followed. Once the text had been completed, it had to pass through her hands and none is more alert to possible pitfalls than she. Mistakes, bloopers, oversights, repetitions, indiscretions and all the misjudgements that any writer is prone to were surgically removed. I have a tendency to meander, to go off on a tangent, to yield to self-indulgence, to play a few wafty drives; she would shine her beam mercilessly on the rocks I was steering towards and a swift change of course suggested. 'Don't patronise or underestimate your reader,' she always says, 'sometimes less is more.' It is advice that I am anxious to follow, not always successfully. Her proofreading skills are second-to-none. It is amazing how many times I typed 'Grieg' instead of 'Greig'. The finished work owes as much to her help, advice and encouragement as anyone's.

If any wreckage is found floating on the water, don't blame her. The mistake will have been mine alone.

Finally, I should like to pay tribute to Jane Camillin, Dean Rockett, Graham Hales, Duncan Olner and all at Pitch Publishing who continue to be such loyal and enthusiastic supporters of my writing career. I cannot thank them enough.

Andrew Murtagh
11 February 2019

Epilogue

The Scene: The Good Lord's Pavilion

Kerry Packer, dressed in a white suit and MCC tie, is sitting with his feet up on a long mahogany table, large cigar clenched between his teeth, reading the *Paradise Post*. Behind him, hanging on the wall, is the famous painting of the boy Jesus tossing for innings.

A tall, gangling figure appears in the doorway.

Greig: Kerry!

Packer looks up, drops his paper and eyes the stranger warily.

Packer: Tony, is that you?

Greig: Sure is, buddy. You look as if you've seen a ghost. Didn't think you could get rid of me that quickly, did you?

Packer: Well, stone the crows!

Greig: Yah, it's me, buddy.

Packer: Aw, look mate, am I glad to see you. But I thought ... given your reputation with the establishment, you'd be on your way to The Other Place.

Greig: Had a helluva job to get in, I can tell you. Those gatemen, they're worse than at the other Lord's. 'Tiny Grigg,' I said. Shook his head. 'England captain.' 'With that accent – are you having a lorf?' 'Channel 9,' I tried. 'Only one channel up 'ere, mate, an' that's ABC – that's Absolute Being Corporation to you.' I was getting nowhere. 'Get me the head honcho,' I told him. So up totters this old *bakkies*—

Packer: *Bakkies?*

380

Greig: Ach, sorry, Orfrikaans for 'bloke'.

Packer: Not a language much used up here, mate.

Greig: Anyway, this chap all puffed up with his own importance came over and orsked what was the problem. I looked at his name badge and it said St Peter. So I had a brainwave, rummaged around in my corffin and took out my old St Peter bat. I can tell you the old fella was wreathed in smiles. 'Welcome to Paradise, Tiny,' he said. 'Why, are we in Sorf Efrica?' I orsked. 'Better than that,' he said, and then told the gateman to take my corffin and escort me to the Long Room. And here I am.

Packer: Jumped the queue, as usual. You South Africans are all the same. Bet you parked your hearse right outside the gates. Aw look, it's good to see you, mate, however you got here. This calls for Champagne. Waiter!

A **Passing Angel** stops and gives a quizzical look.

Packer: A bottle of your best Champagne, mate.

Greig: Look, if you can manage it, a packet of fags as well. I'm dying— ,sorry, I'm desperate for a smoke.

Exit **Passing Angel** with a perfunctory nod.

Greig: Now I'm here, I've got to orsk you, Kerry. How come they let you in, seeing as you didn't believe this place even existed?

Packer: Tricky one, mate. Had to wait a long time. It was sheer bloody purgatory hanging around outside. Kept on demanding to see the president but he was always unavailable. Honestly, it would have been easier to get an audience with the Pope and, as you know, I'm not Catholic. Though it doesn't seem to matter what persuasion you are up here. Even the bloody Poms are about.

Greig: So, pal, how's business?

Packer: When I arrived, it was bloody moribund. Everybody sitting on their backsides as if it was a bloody holiday camp. The economy was crook. Since then, I've rattled a few cages, kicked a few arses, stirred things up a bit.

Greig: Any cricket going on?

Packer: Don't get me all worked up, Tony. Bad for the old ticker. I would've thought they'd've given me a new one by now but I'm assured I'm on the waiting list. Could be an eternity at this rate.

Greig: Tell me, The Don – is he up here? Or is he …?

Packer: He's around. Not had much to do with him. Look, mate, he's only gone and organised Test matches up here. By the time I arrived, he was CEO of the whole damn shooting match. And he plays in his own team.

Greig: Can he still cut the mustard? Is he as good as he's made out to be?

Packer: Well, the bastard's average has now gone up to 199.94.

Greig: Jeez! That's a helluva statistic. Wonder what Bill Lorwry would make of that?

Packer: It's boring, mate. Timeless Tests, he calls them. They go on forever. Now look, pal, I've got an idea. Can you keep your big trap shut for once in your afterlife?

Greig: When have I ever let you down, Kerry? I gave up the England captaincy for you. Without me—

Packer: All right, all right, keep your hair on, mate! Oh sorry, you haven't got any. What happened to the golden locks? No worries though. Easily sort you out with a halo. Two a penny up here.

Enter **Passing Angel**, carrying a silver salver with an ice bucket, Champagne and two cut-glass flutes.

Packer: The best Champagne? And two glasses, you little ripper. Put it on my account.

Passing Angel: Now that is something St Matthew would like to have a private word with about, Mr Packer – your account.

Packer: St Matthew! Which bloody fishing boat did he sail on?

Greig: Matthew. He was a tax inspector, Kerry. He wasn't a fisherman.

Packer (incandescent): I don't care if he's the bloody Pope's accountant. If he wants to meddle in my financial affairs, I'll see him in court.

Greig (conciliatory): Sorry about that, pal. He doesn't mean it. Anyway, cheers for the booze. Any fags?

Passing Angel: I've sent Gabriel to get some.

Greig: Gabriel?

Passing Angel: Yes. He's the messenger around here.

Greig: I see. Rather like a 12th man. Anyway, cheers, buddy.

Exit **Passing Angel**.

Packer: Now, listen up, Tony. This is my plan. Get rid of these boring timeless Tests they have up here. They're interminable, never ending, like watching paint dry. I'm going to organise three teams to play each other. Coloured clothing – not your boring all-white robes they wear.

Under lights, bright lights, heavenly lights. Fireworks, shooting stars, meteors, comets, lightning bolts, the whole damn shooting match. Music, jingles, heavenly choirs. Dancing fairies, sylphs and nymphs. We'll even get Santa Claus ... whatsisname ... St Nicholas, yes, that's right, St Nick. Met him. Fair dinkum bloke ... he can make an appearance for the kiddies. Crowds will be huge. Viewing figures will go through the roof. There's only one channel, ABC, and I've negotiated with St Peter sole rights. This is going to be bigger than World Series Cricket. Galaxy Stars Cricket: The Clash of Demigods and Demons. Paradise Lost, Paradise Regained.

Greig: It'll be a helluva spectacle. But listen, Kerry, if there's one thing I would change if we had our time again ...

Packer: (warily): Ye-es?

Greig: More Indians.

Packer: Too many chiefs last time? There's only one chief here, mate. And surprisingly, it's not me.

Greig: No, I mean from India. Their spinners are the best in the world.

Packer: It may have escaped your notice, Tony, we are no longer in the world. Time to think outside the box. Besides, spin bowling bores the pants off me. Loada cissies, if you ask me, mate. What I want is blood and thunder, fire and brimstone. Fast bowlers testing a batsman's technique and bravery.

Greig: This'll shake up the orthorities, that's for sure.

Packer: Here's my plan .... Three teams. Heaven XI, captained by you.

Greig: Jeez, what a team! Grace, Bradman, Macartney, Trumper, Hobbs, Holmes, Hendren, Hammond, Hutton, Hassett, Harvey ...

Packer: Whoa there, Tony! Not all have to be—

Greig: OK then ... some youngsters like Hookesey and poor Phillip Hughes—

Packer: No, I mean—

Greig: Oh, from other countries than England and Orstralia ... well, Hanif, Hazare, Heine, Hadlee, the father, of course ...

Packer: Bloody hell, Tony! Anyway, I'll leave selection to you. Now ... the second team will be Angels XI. The four archangels will obviously want to play ... as for the other seven ... well, they've got millions to choose from. All damned good players.

Greig: They corn't be.

Packer: Eh?

Greig: Damned. Otherwise they wouldn't be here. And the lorst team?

Packer (conspiratorially): Now look, this has got to stay between you and me .... You said it would be a helluva team ... well, you're damned right, it will be ... a Hell XI.

Greig: Ach no, man, Kerry, you corn't!

Packer: Watch me.

Greig (dubiously): Well, I suppose Satan would have to be captain. And they'll have Spofforth to open the bowling.

Packer: Spofforth?

Greig: Yes – the Demon Bowler. As for the other nine ... corn't think for sure who's down there. You'll need a recruiting sorgeant and—

Packer: Now, that'll be your job.

Greig: Nah, nah, nah! I corn't go down there. No way, Jose.

Packer: Look, mate, there'll be no worries. I'll get you a passport, visa, ecclesiastical dispensation, papal indulgence, saintly status, whatever paperwork is needed. St Peter on the gate – he's in my pocket.

Greig: Look, Kerry, you probably know more people down there than me.

Packer: Only in business. Cricket is your field. C'mon, mate. You must've known all the bad boys in the game during your time. Pick your team and I'll make 'em an offer they can't refuse. After all, everyone has his price, especially down there ...

Discussions, arguments, plans went on long into the night. And the early hours. Seemingly forever.